ARTISTS
AT HOME

ARTISTS AT HOME

Susie Hodge

FRANCES LINCOLN

CONTENTS

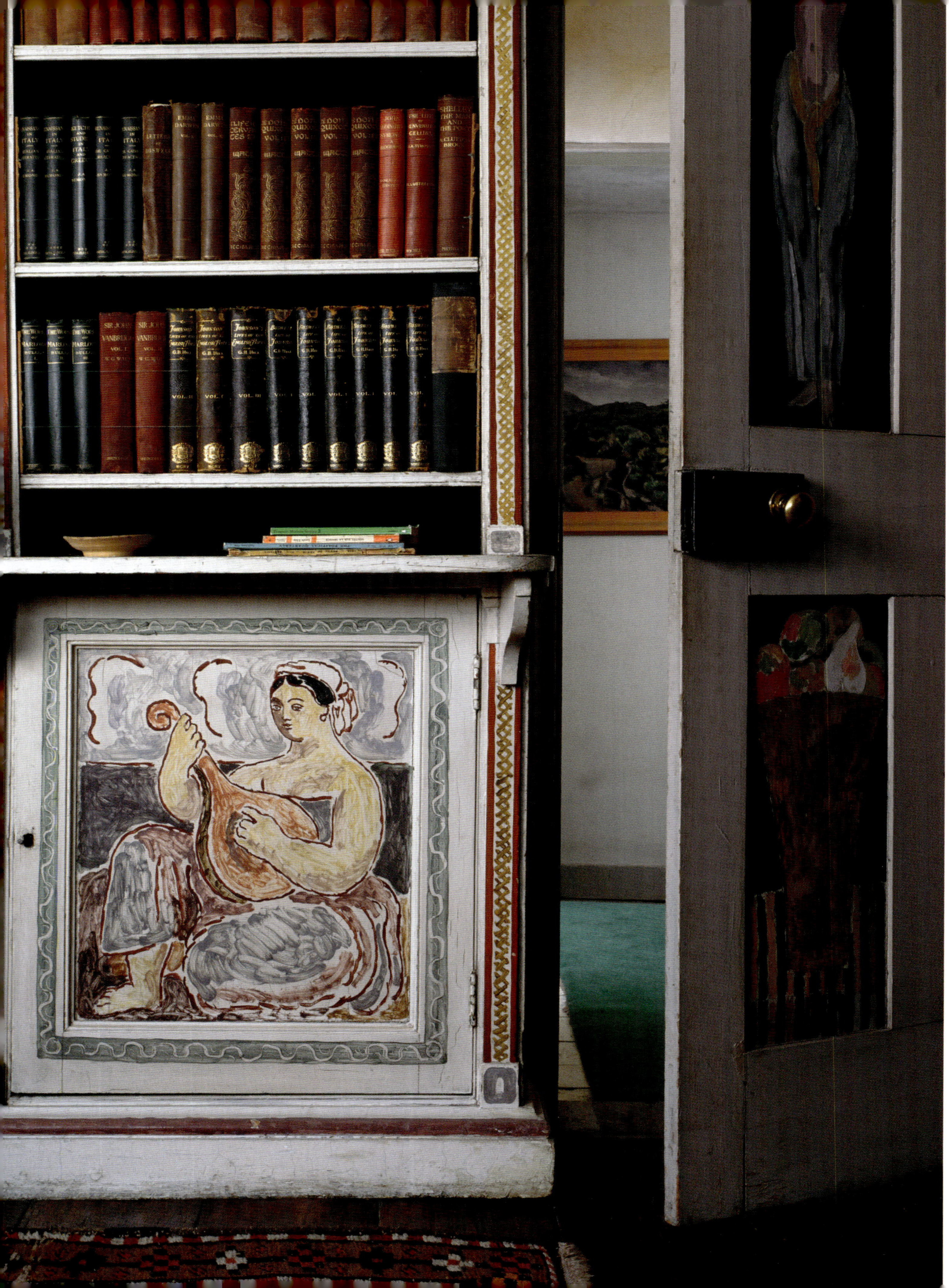

INTRODUCTION

Imagine if you could step inside an artist's home. You would see the actual place where sparks of inspiration have been stimulated, where great works of ingenuity have been executed, and where a fertile mind has both worked and relaxed. You would experience the environment where some incredible visions have been nurtured and nourished: the catalyst for creativity.

This book does just that. It takes you into the homes of thirty artists from all over the world. Some lived long ago, such as J. M. W. Turner, whereas others are living now, such as Yinka Shonibare. Some, such as Frida Kahlo in New Mexico, lived in hot climates, and some lived in cooler countries, such as René Magritte in Belgium. Some of the artists lived in their homes with their families, such as Pierre Auguste Renoir and Claude Monet, and others lived alone, such as Georgia O'Keeffe. Some, such as Vanessa Bell and Duncan Grant, lived with extended families, including children, friends and lovers. Some, such as Rosa Bonheur, shared their homes with beloved animals; others, such as Roland Penrose and Lee Miller, entertained in their homes almost constantly, sharing the space with friends. Like their art, the artists' homes are all different. Salvador Dalí's, for example, began as a hut, but became a mansion; others began as family homes and were turned into one huge studio.

For most artists, their homes are where they are comfortable and can be themselves, where their personalities and inner thoughts can be free and are visible, and where their inventiveness can thrive and flourish. So seeing their homes can help us to understand some of the ideas behind their art. If the artists have built or extensively renovated their homes, the buildings themselves reveal even more about the owners' personalities. Added to this are the locations of the homes, the furnishings and décor choices, and other elements such as colours, gardens or surrounding views. Equally significant is where the artists worked and the sizes of their studios, who was or was not allowed in them, the light there, the artefacts and tools. All these aspects augment our understanding of each artist's mind, including their relationships, preferences and interests.

Artists' homes are literally where art meets life. They can show us a great deal about the individuals who lived there and the reasons behind their creations. Some artists felt at peace and happy in their homes, whereas for others they were the places where they lived turbulent and difficult lives. Some lived in their homes briefly and others lived in theirs for many years. Artists such as Frida Kahlo and Paul Cézanne lived in the homes of their parents, while others, such as Otto Dix, were forced to flee from where they had wanted to be and settle elsewhere. Some lived in relative opulence – for example, Picasso's mansion in Aix-en-Provence and Frederic, Lord Leighton's house in London – while others lived more frugally, such as O'Keeffe in New Mexico and Barbara Hepworth in Cornwall. Some, such as William Morris, lived surrounded by personal art; his house was designed and furnished almost entirely by him and his friends.

In investigating such a wide variety of artists and their homes, this book explores many aspects of their lives, including where and when they lived, and why and where they took up art. There's some information about the work they produced, and then the actual homes are explored. Every place conveys the artist's individual character; for instance, Leighton's house began as a simple brick structure with a secret doorway that allowed his models to enter without being seen by strait-laced Victorian neighbours. After huge reconstructions inspired by Leighton's travels, the house ended up being a place where the public regularly visited to marvel at the surroundings. One of the most

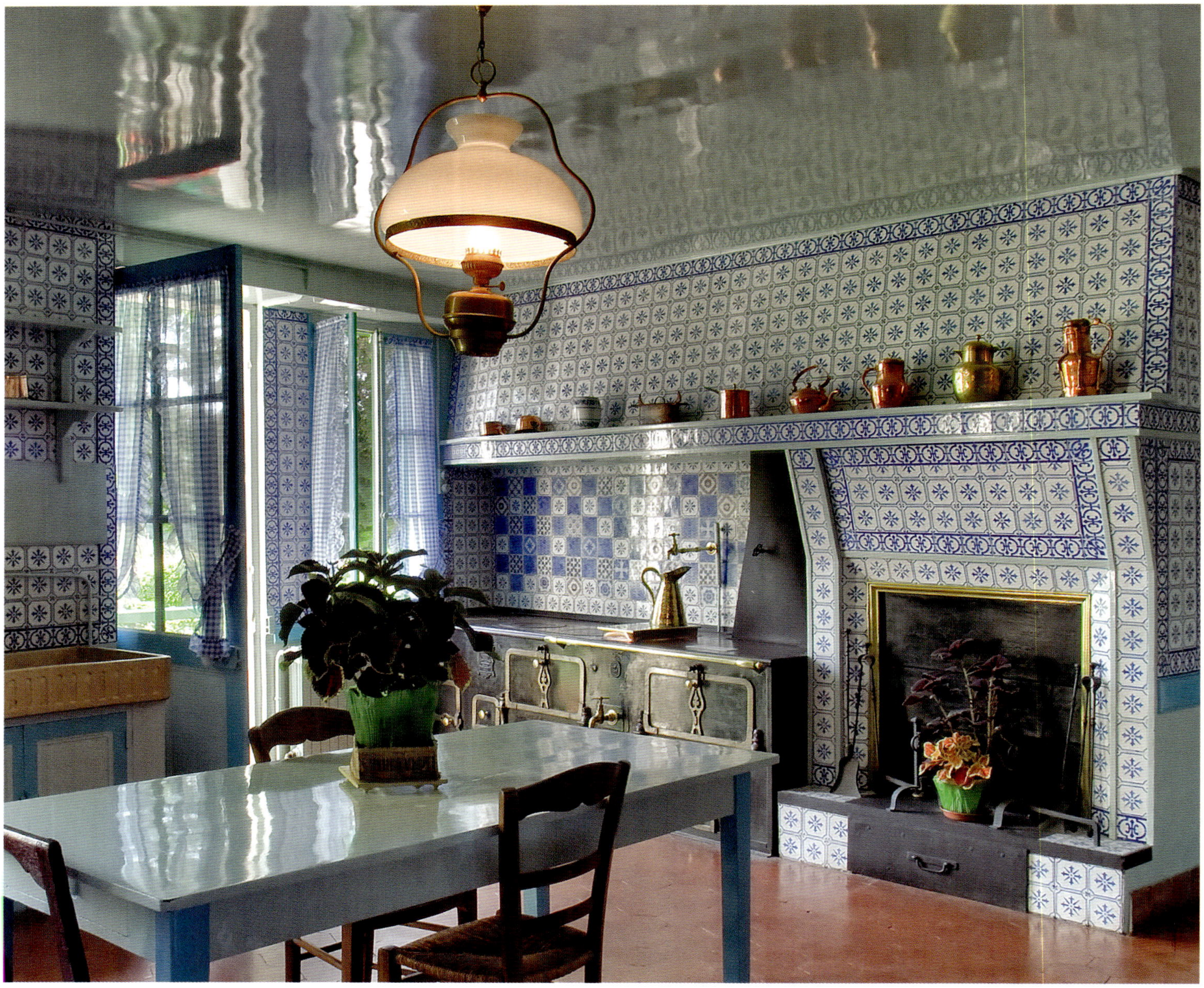

breathtaking areas was the Arab Hall, inspired by a twelfth-century palace in Sicily, with a mixture of Moorish tiles, fretwork, friezes, columns and a fountain.

Some of the artists were keen gardeners – for example, Vanessa Bell in Sussex and Claude Monet in Giverny. Some lived low to the ground, such as César Manrique with his subterranean house in Lanzarote, whereas others chose to live up high, such as Suzanne Valadon in her apartment at the top of Montmartre. Some of the studios within the homes doubled as playrooms for the artists' children, such as Renoir's; others were strictly solitary, such as Cézanne's. Lucian Freud's London studio became an important aspect of his work and featured prominently in his paintings from the 1980s onwards. Shonibare shares his studio, having created a separate exhibition space for emerging artists.

This book literally opens doors. Turn the pages and step inside some of the most personal places: the dwellings of artists who are often notoriously private about their working methods. In some ways, artists are rather like remote ancient alchemists, and the following chapters offer the keys to their homes where the magical chemistry happens.

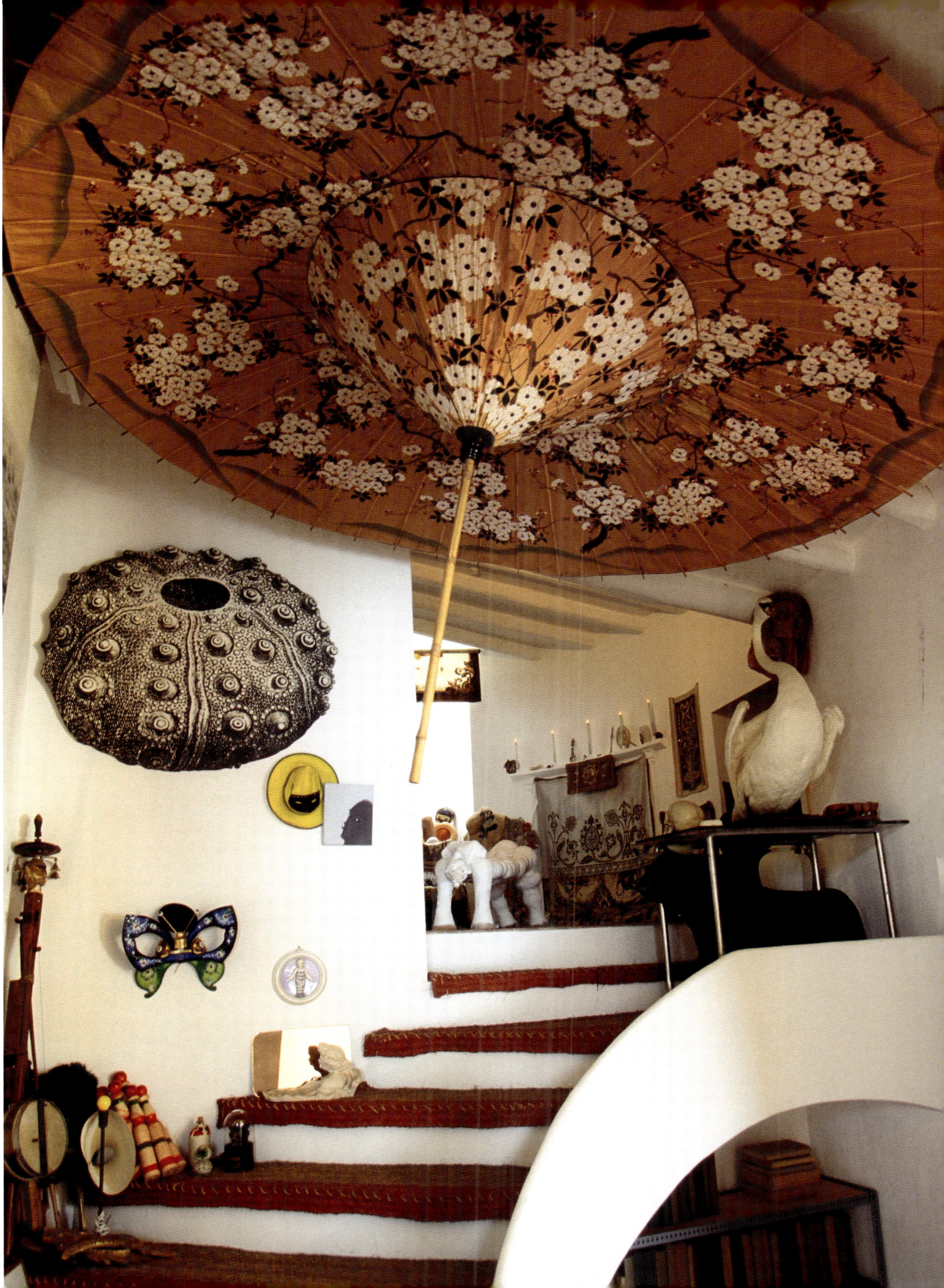

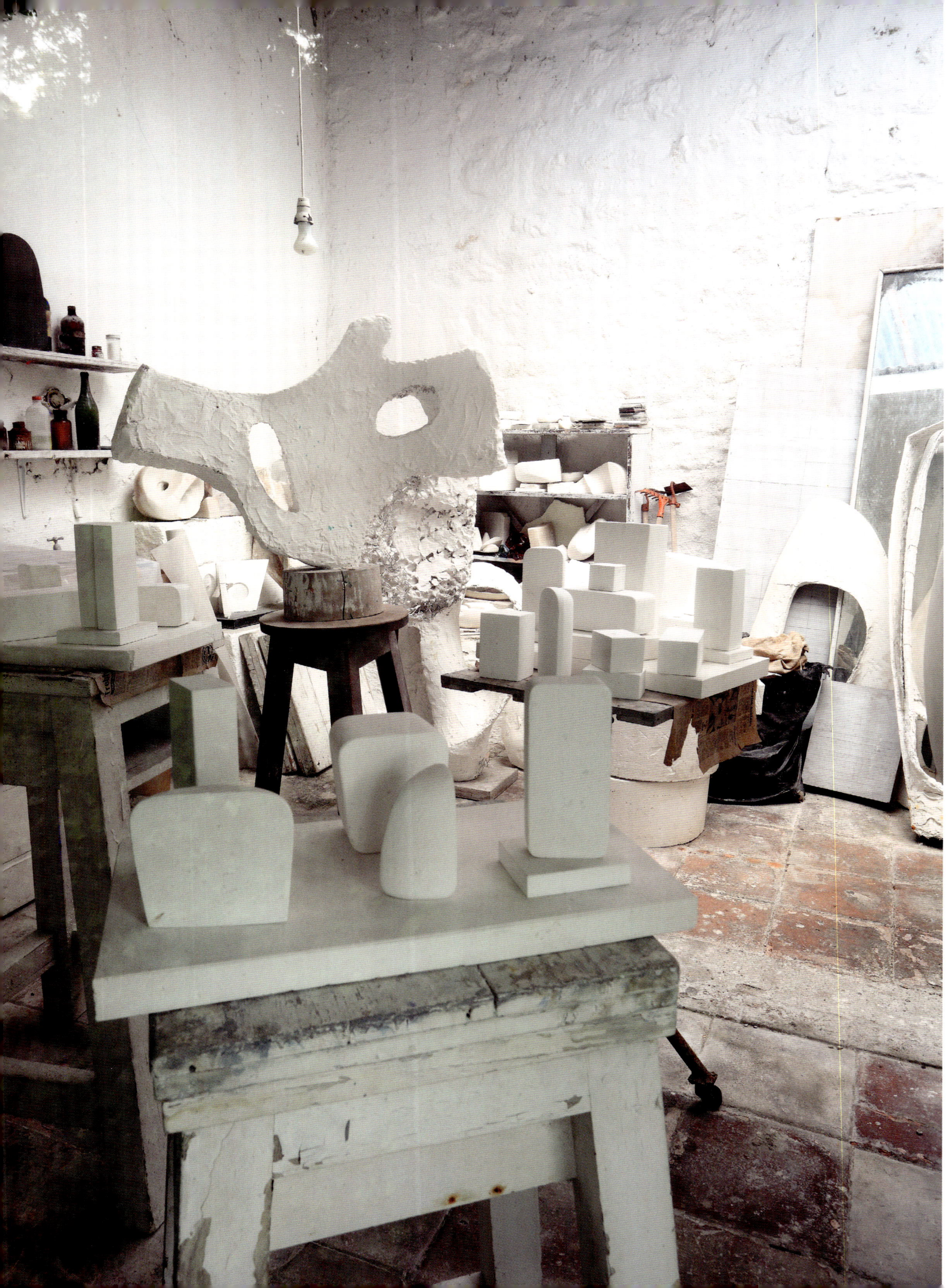

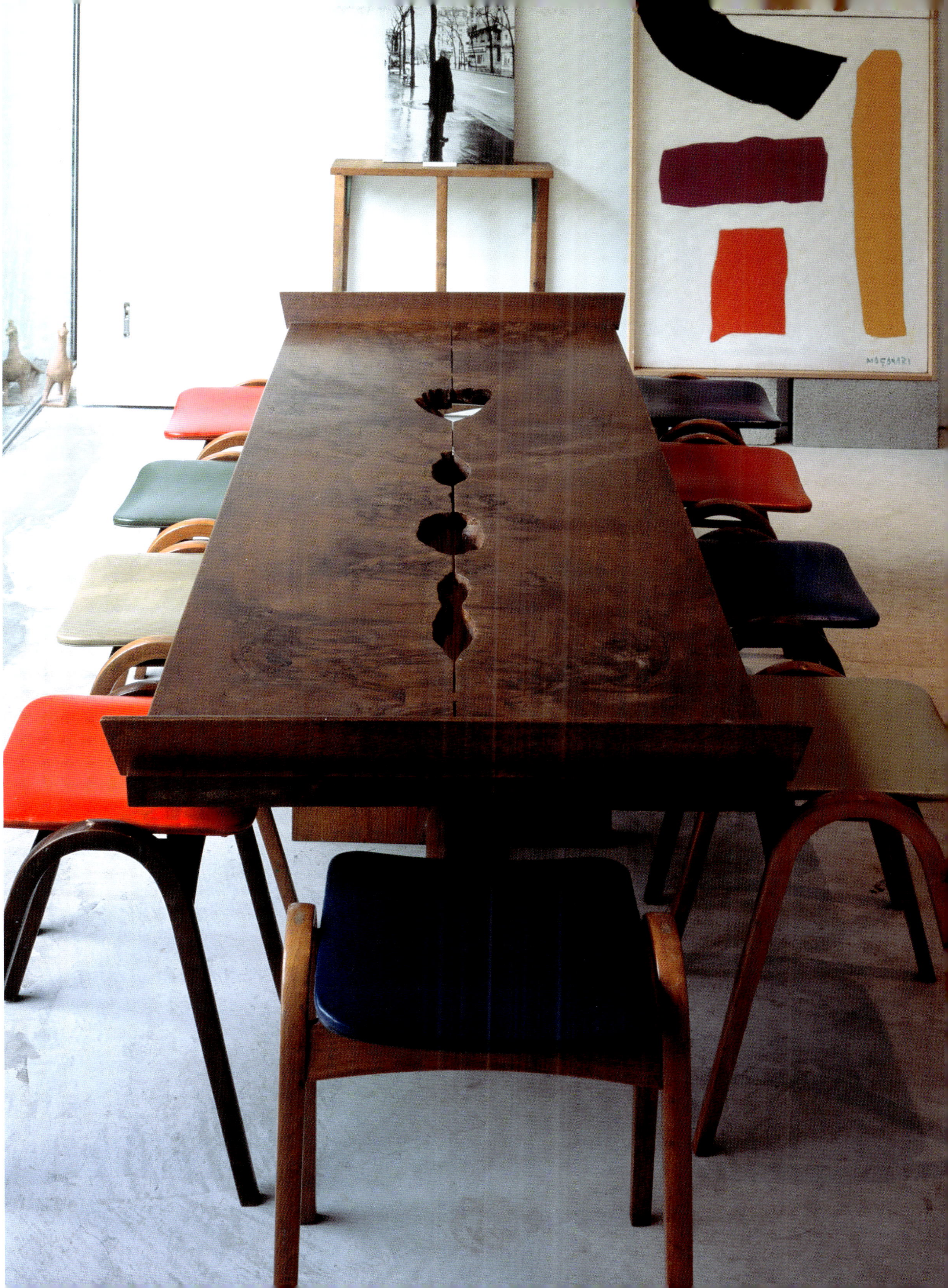

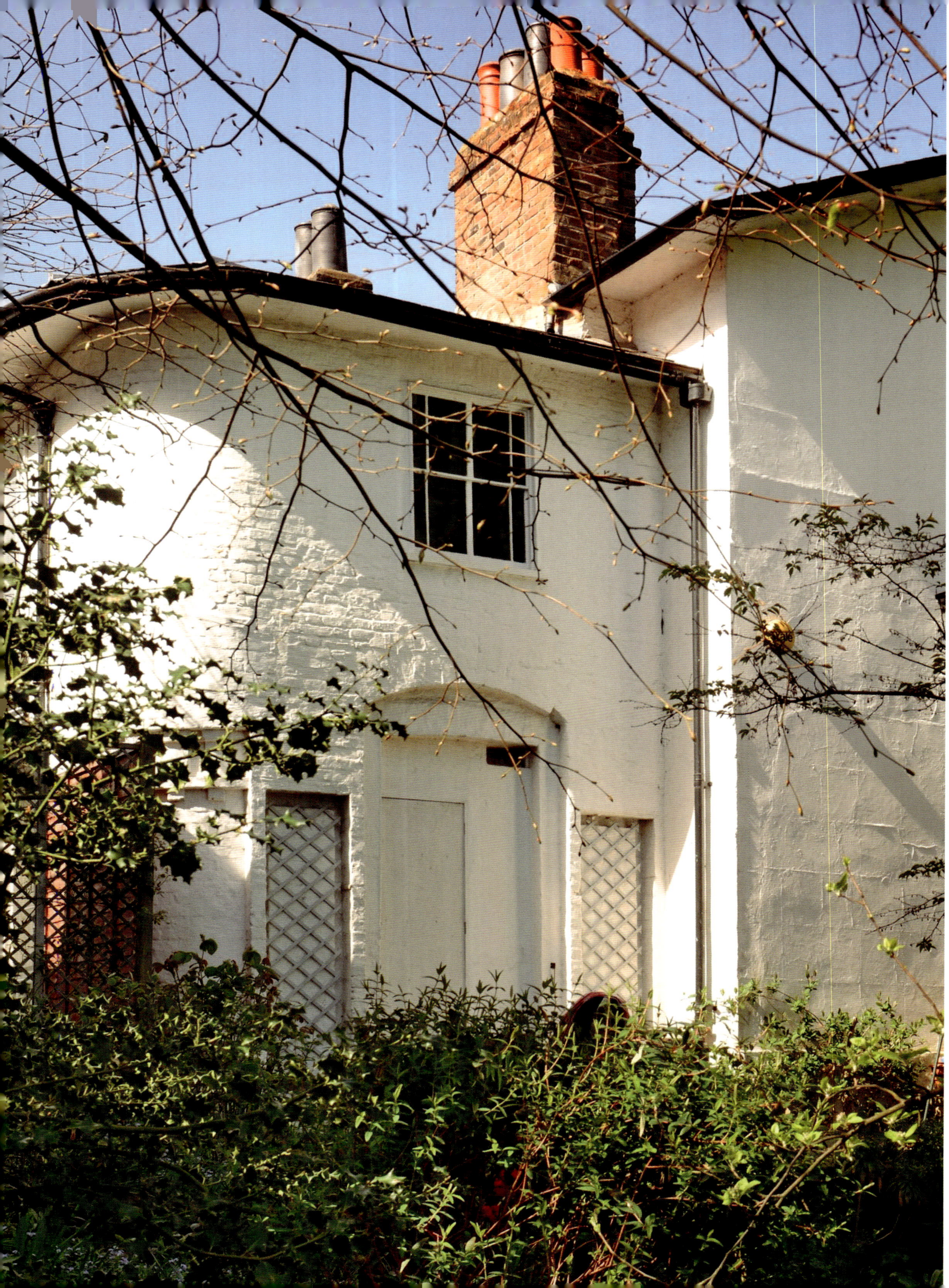

JOSEPH MALLORD WILLIAM TURNER

Twickenham, UK

In 1807, thirty-two-year-old artist Joseph Mallord William Turner (1775–1851) bought two plots of land near Marble Hill, between Twickenham and Richmond Bridge, which at that time was a rural area. He intended to build a home away from the bustle of London, where he could relax and sketch, and his father could live with him in his retirement from his trade as a barber and wigmaker in Covent Garden.

In the late eighteenth and early nineteenth centuries, Twickenham and Richmond to the west of London were popular places to live with many artists and writers, and Turner knew the area well. Although he was born in London's Covent Garden, when he was ten years old, his mother had started to show signs of mental instability, and he was sent to stay with an uncle in Brentford. He also later rented houses in Isleworth and Hammersmith. All three locations are fairly close to Marble Hill.

Turner had been a child prodigy. His father had exhibited his young son's drawings in his barbershop and even sold them for a few pence. At fourteen, Turner became a student at the Royal Academy of Arts, exhibiting his first work there the following year. His first commissions were architectural and topographical watercolours, but he soon also explored themes in history, literature and myth, and began painting expressive views of nature. He was elected an associate of the Royal Academy in 1799 and a full Academician in 1802. From this time, his paintings sold well; he became fairly prosperous and he moved with a friend into a flat in the highly respectable Harley Street, in London. He also travelled around Europe; something that had so long been impossible because of the Napoleonic Wars. Whether abroad or at home, he filled his sketchbooks with dramatic land- and seascapes. In 1804, he opened his own art gallery and, four years later, he was appointed Professor of Perspective at the Royal Academy, so could then add 'PP' to the 'RA' after his signature. He lectured at the Royal Academy until 1828, and while teaching, he produced a vast number of paintings, drawings and prints.

Overall, Turner broke with the conventions of painting, infusing a new dynamic into landscapes and seascapes. In some of his later works, especially, his painting style became particularly expressive and almost abstract, emphasising the power of nature in unprecedented ways. Additionally, he often included motifs from the modern industrial era into his paintings, such as steamships and railway trains that had generally been considered too vulgar and unattractive for art. He was hugely influential; many subsequent artists followed him, which in turn inspired new art movements.

SOLUS LODGE

The plots of land that Turner bought near Marble Hill amounted to two acres. One was wedge-shaped, with a pond, and the other was triangular. For nearly six years, from 1807 to 1812, Turner filled sketchbooks with his house designs, and even considered including a tower to make the most of the views along the nearby River Thames. He created approximately forty sketches of ideas for his house. The project helped to fulfil his long-held ambition to be an architect, and the house was built in 1813. The following year, Turner moved in with his father, William Turner, whom he called affectionately 'Old Dad'. William kept house for his son, minded the garden, and cooked and cleaned, while Turner walked and sketched along the Thames, or painted in the grounds, or entertained friends. The house had two storeys, with single-storey wings on either side and a basement. Inside, the ground floor contained a large central room with French windows and a fireplace. Small single rooms were in each wing, one probably used as a dining room. At first Turner called the house 'Solus Lodge' to emphasise his longing for peace and solitude there, but he later changed the name to Sandycombe Lodge.

Twenty years older than Turner, John Soane was one of his good friends and a fellow Royal Academician. The architect of many highly respected buildings, including the Bank of England and Dulwich Picture Gallery, Soane had a strong influence on Turner's house design, which is especially visible in the Neoclassical proportions, the series of arches in the small entrance hall and corridor, and the large, plain oval skylight above the stairs. When it was built, the slightly Italianate house was surrounded by farmland, with a dirt lane running past the front door and open, extended views of Marble Hill House and the River Thames from the windows, which are large and with full-length wooden shutters. A balcony projects over the front porch, with another small balcony at the back. The entrance porch opens up to a wide hall, which leads off to the parlour and sitting room. Spiral stairs go up to Turner's wallpapered bedroom and his father's smaller bedroom. The same spiral staircase also leads down to the kitchen where 'Old Dad' cooked.

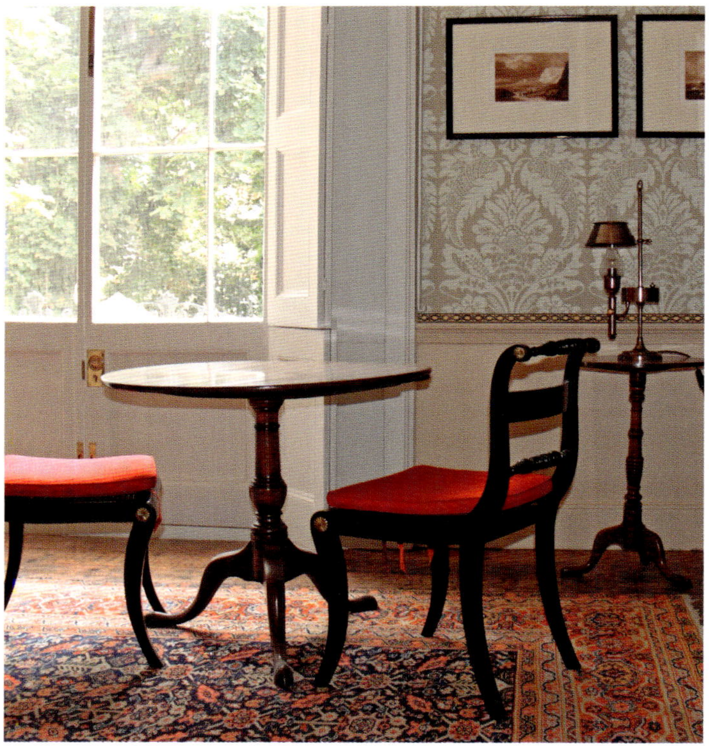

Previous page: The cream exterior of Sandycombe Lodge in Twickenham, designed and built by Turner in 1813 as his own country retreat and home for his father.
Above and opposite: The Neoclassical style house was peaceful, with views of the Thames, and plenty of nearby walks.
Following page: The bedroom at Sandycombe Lodge.

RESPONDING TO HIS SURROUNDINGS

Turner had a fresh way of conveying nature; he always carried sketchbooks, and made many drawings and paintings at Sandycombe. He walked around the area a lot, sketching the views, which he used in later paintings. He loved walking along the towpath by the river, but his favourite spot was on Richmond Hill, where he could take in the panoramic views. It took him about half an hour to walk to the top of the hill from his house, and there he would study the light, the weather and the landscape around him, especially the views of the Thames – and from these, he created pencil sketches, oils, watercolours and prints.

Although an important consideration for him was that he could see the River Thames from his bedroom window, unusually, Turner did not include a studio in his house design. For finishing work, he kept a house and study on Queen Anne Street in Marylebone, London, but used Sandycombe mainly as a peaceful residence. As well as the surrounding areas, Turner loved spending time in his large garden, with its huge pond where he often fished, either alone or with one or two close companions. One of these was often Soane.

In the years when Turner lived at Sandycombe, the Napoleonic Wars rumbled on, and at some points, England was under genuine threat of invasion. Throughout that time, Turner continued to draw, paint and print, responding to both the surroundings and topical events. When he managed to travel, he missed his home and wrote about it to his friends. However, in 1826, his father's health was declining and Turner had more opportunities to travel around the Continent once again. He sold Sandycombe Lodge to his nearest neighbour for £500, and moved back to London.

> 'Sandycombe sounds just now in my ears as an act of folly, when I reflect how little I have been able to be there this year.'
>
> *J. M. W. Turner*

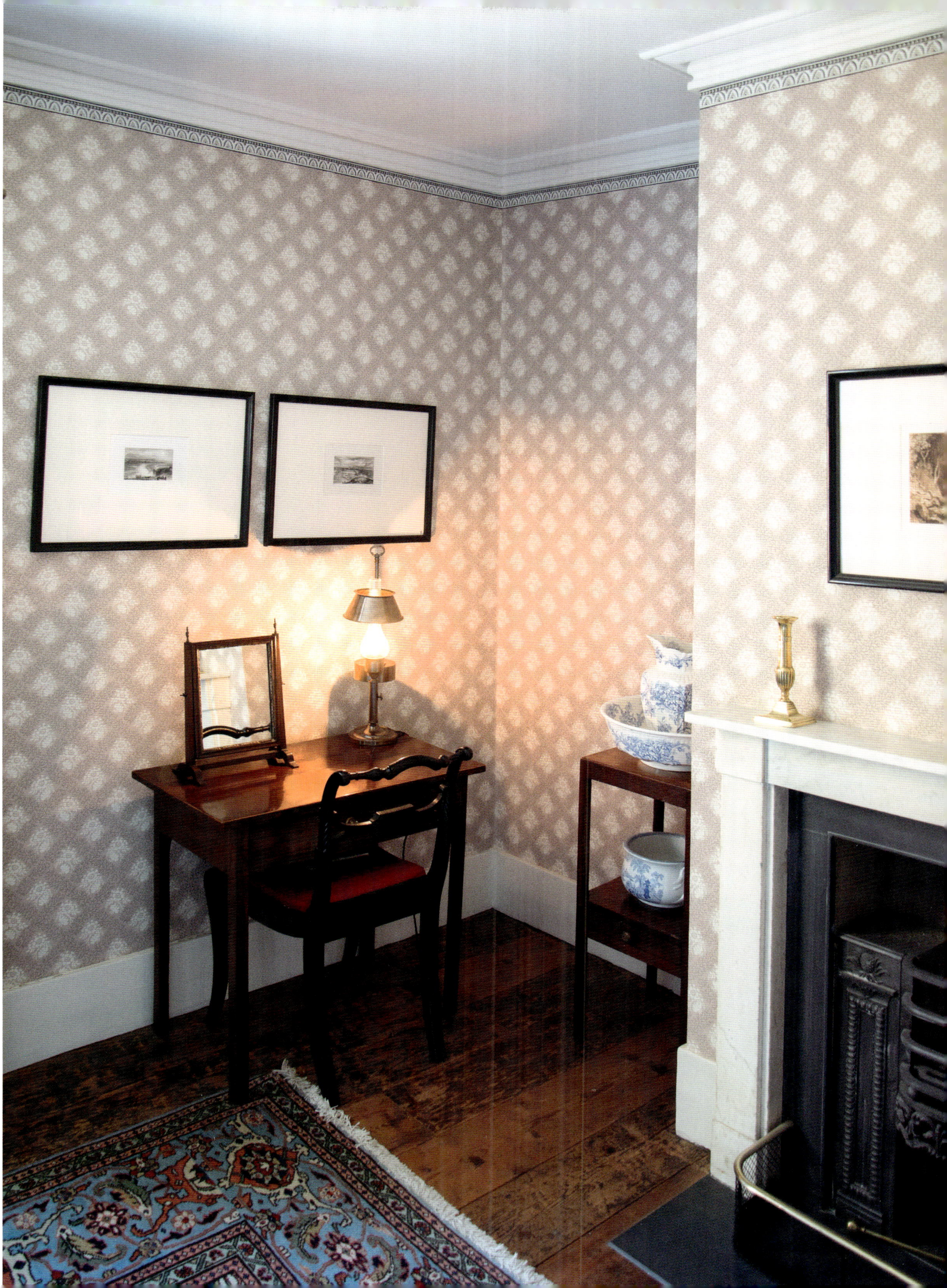

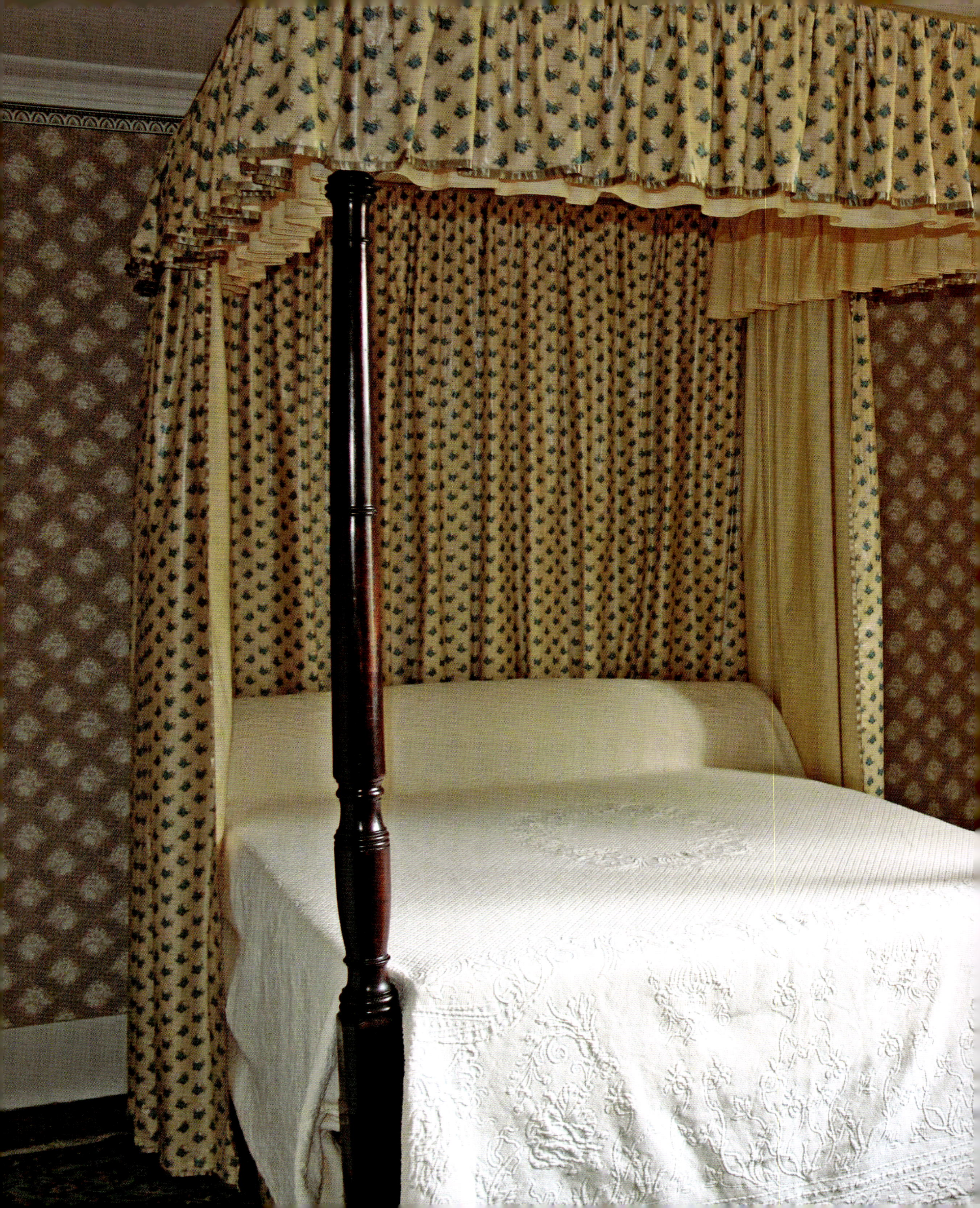

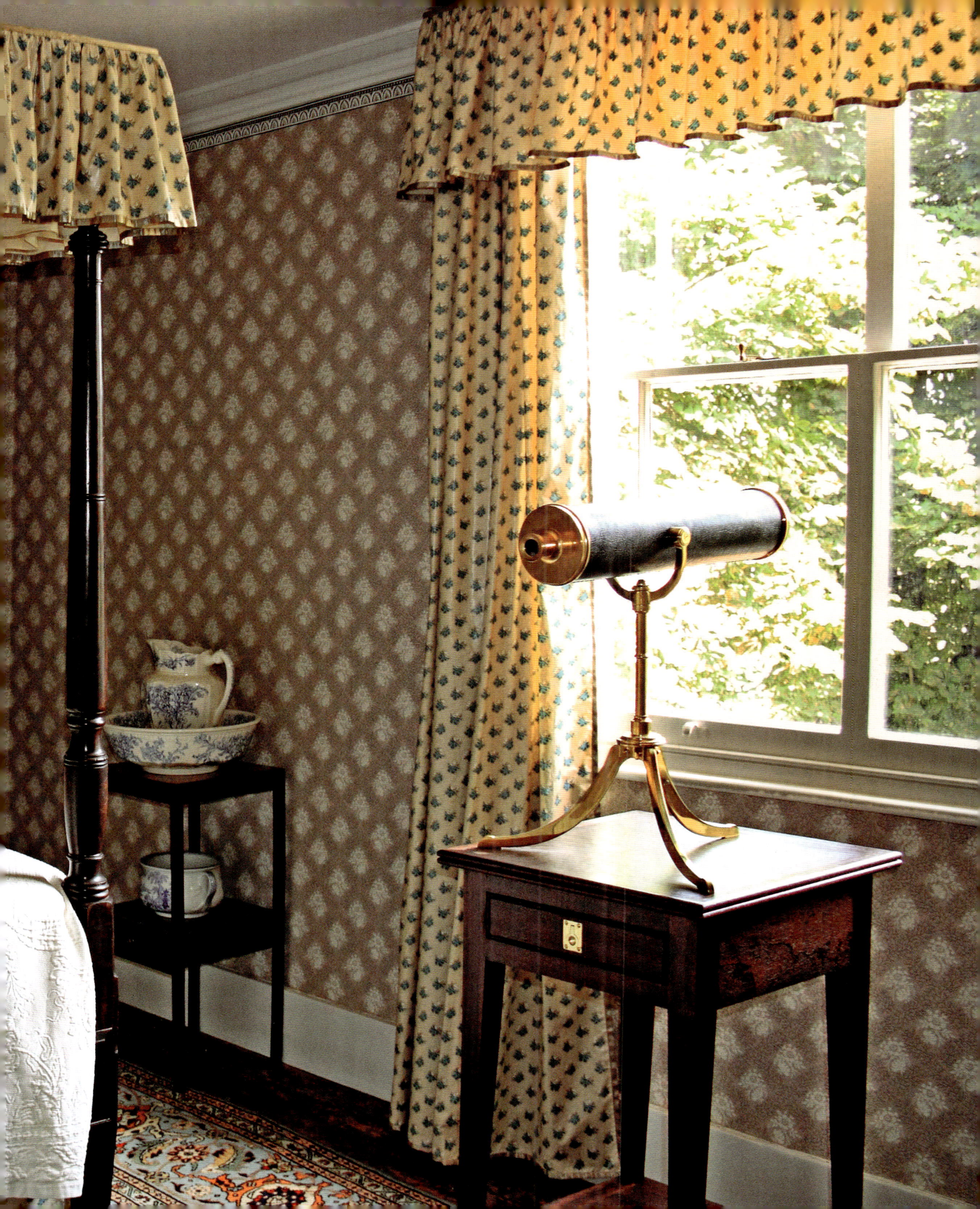

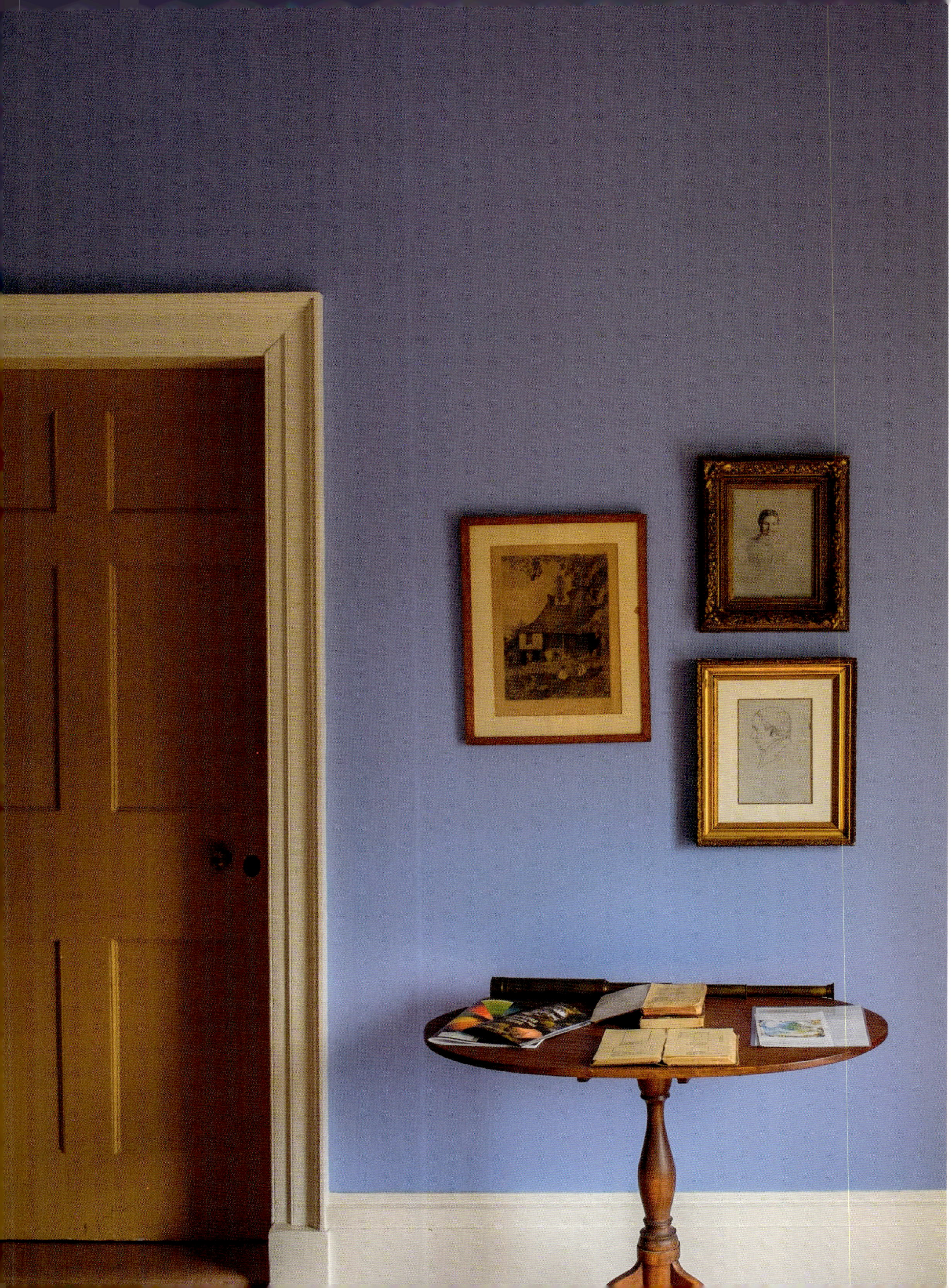

THOMAS COLE

Catskill, New York, US

Known for his exhilarating depictions of the vast American landscape, and his founding of the Hudson River School of painting, the artist and architect Thomas Cole (1801–48) lived and worked at Cedar Grove, Catskill, in New York, from 1833 until his death fifteen years later.

In 1818, when he was seventeen years old, Cole emigrated with his family to America, from Lancashire in the north of England. Initially, he settled with his parents and seven sisters in Ohio, but a few years later, he moved to Philadelphia independently to work as a wood engraver; he then returned to Ohio to join his father's newly established wallpaper manufacturing business. He continued to move around, living for short periods in Ohio, Philadelphia and Pittsburgh, and he studied for two years at the Pennsylvania Academy of the Fine Arts. Overall, however, he was mainly self-taught as an artist and initially, he received commissions for portraits and landscapes. He also wrote poetry, kept a detailed journal, contributed articles to *The Knickerbocker* – a popular periodical of the time – and, from the mid-1830s, he worked as an architect. Later in life, he travelled to Europe, and on his return, he applied the motifs and techniques of European Romantic landscape painting to the scenery of North America, which no other artist had done before.

CATSKILL

While on a sketching trip in 1825 along the Hudson River in New York, Cole discovered the eastern Catskill Mountains, and from his drawings of them, he produced five dramatic paintings. He managed to convince the owner of a bookshop in New York City to display three of these in his window, where three prominent figures of the New York art world saw and bought them. They were painters Colonel John Trumbull and Asher Brown Durand, and theatre producer William Dunlap. They subsequently promoted Cole's talent to others, introducing him to several wealthy patrons, and soon his arcadian landscapes became known within New York's artistic community. He remained in New York and became a founding member of the National Academy of Design there.

Cole's paintings of the sweeping scenery along the Hudson River expressed the idealism and religious sensibilities of many Americans at that time. Deeply religious, he used his art to warn of the destructive course that Americans were taking, as the natural world became erased through the continuous expansion of industry. He believed that the American people were disregarding God's will, and to convey this, he painted several allegorical paintings, implying that a time of judgement was imminent.

Four years after his first visit to Catskill, with his reputation firmly established, Cole embarked on one of his extended tours of Europe. While exhibiting in England, he met the landscape painters Turner and John Constable, and portraitist Thomas Lawrence. Before leaving for Europe, Cole had been maintaining a studio in New York City and, during the summer months, also renting a cottage on a farm called Cedar Grove on the west bank of the Hudson River, in the village of Catskill. Owned by local merchant John Alexander Thomson, Cedar Grove had astonishing views that Cole never tired of painting. He returned there in 1832 after his European trip. Three years later, he wrote what became an influential essay on the American landscape, and the year after that, he made Catskill his permanent home when he married Thomson's niece, Maria Bartow.

Once married, Cole and Maria moved into the main house to live with the extended Thomson family. Having been built in

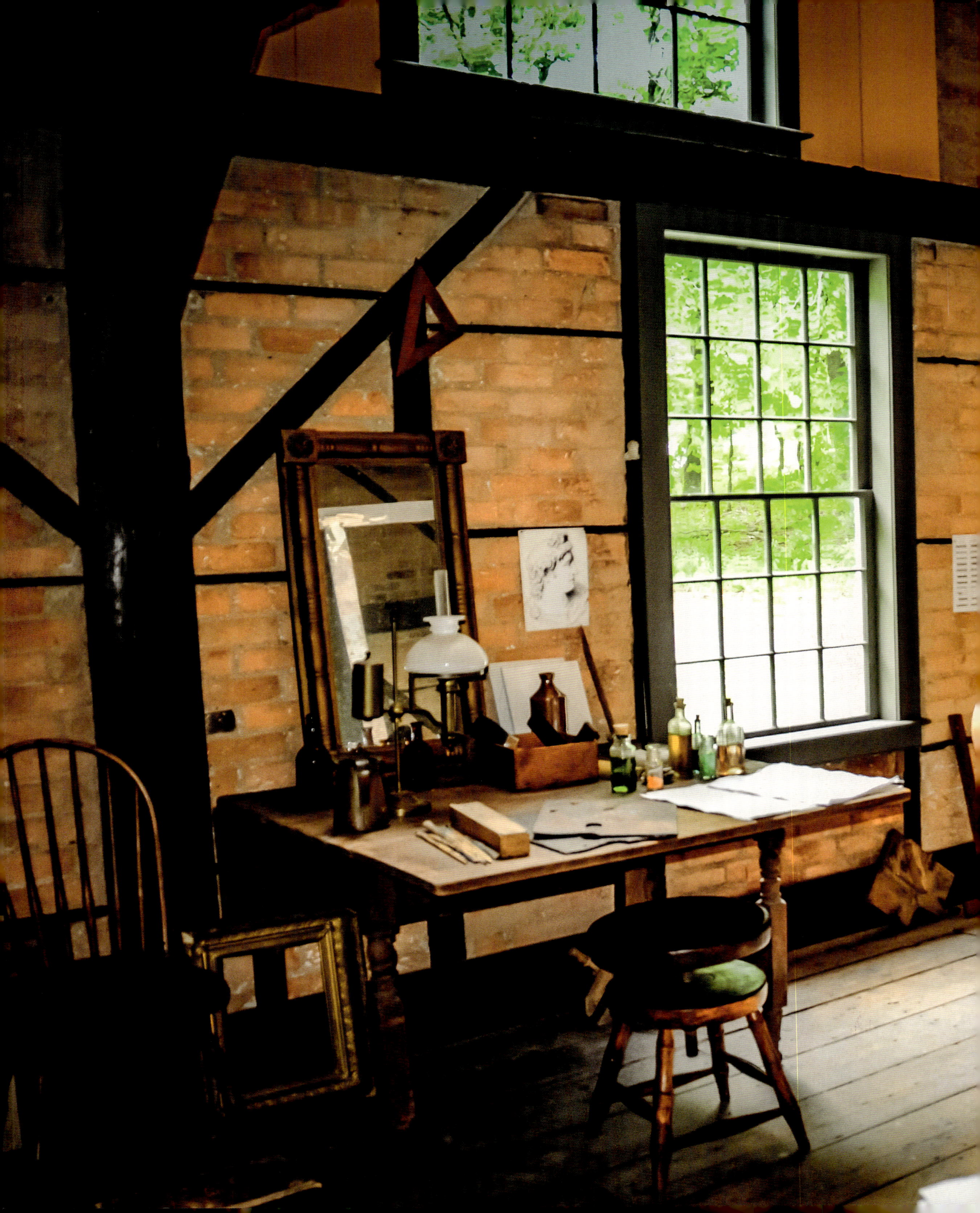

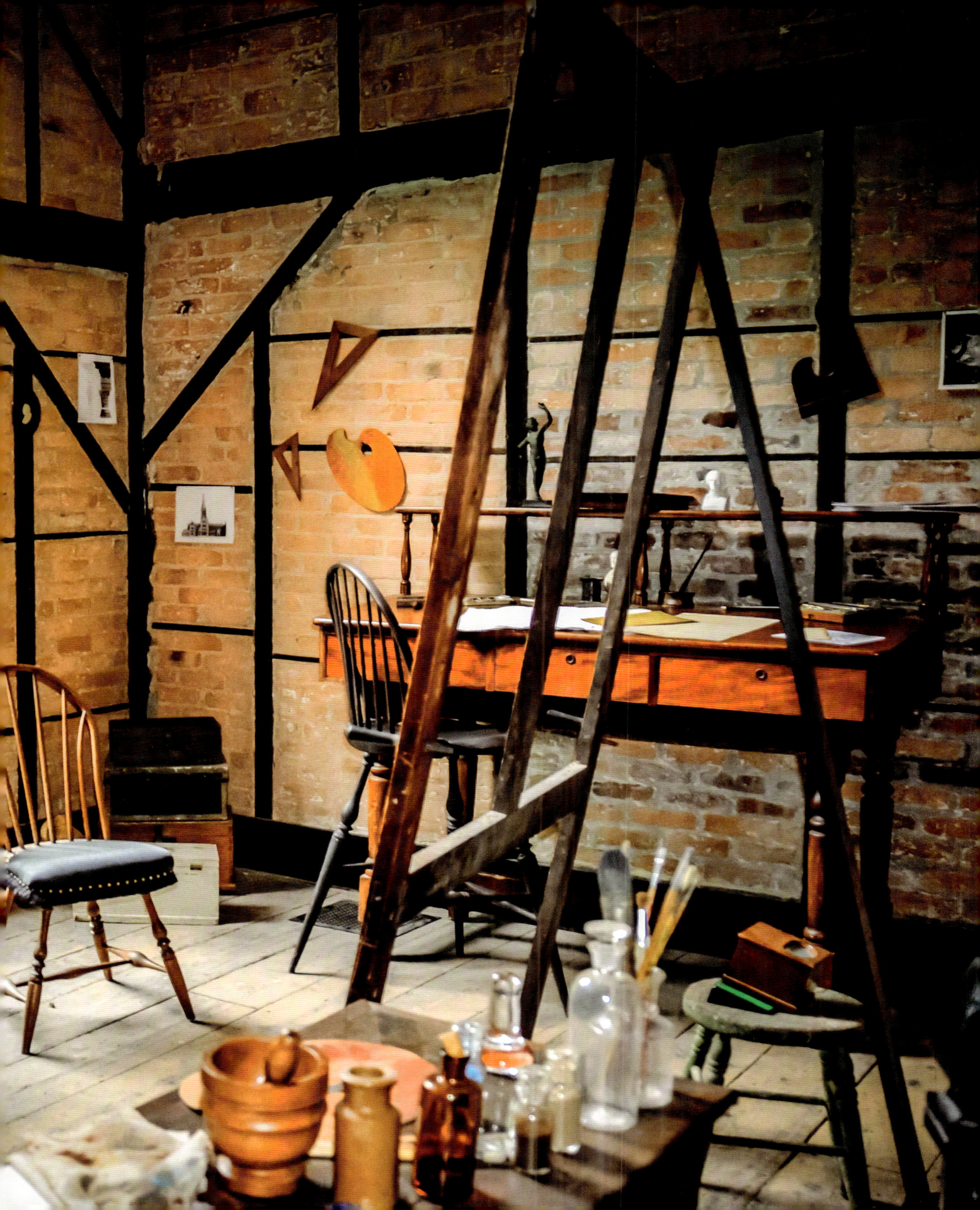

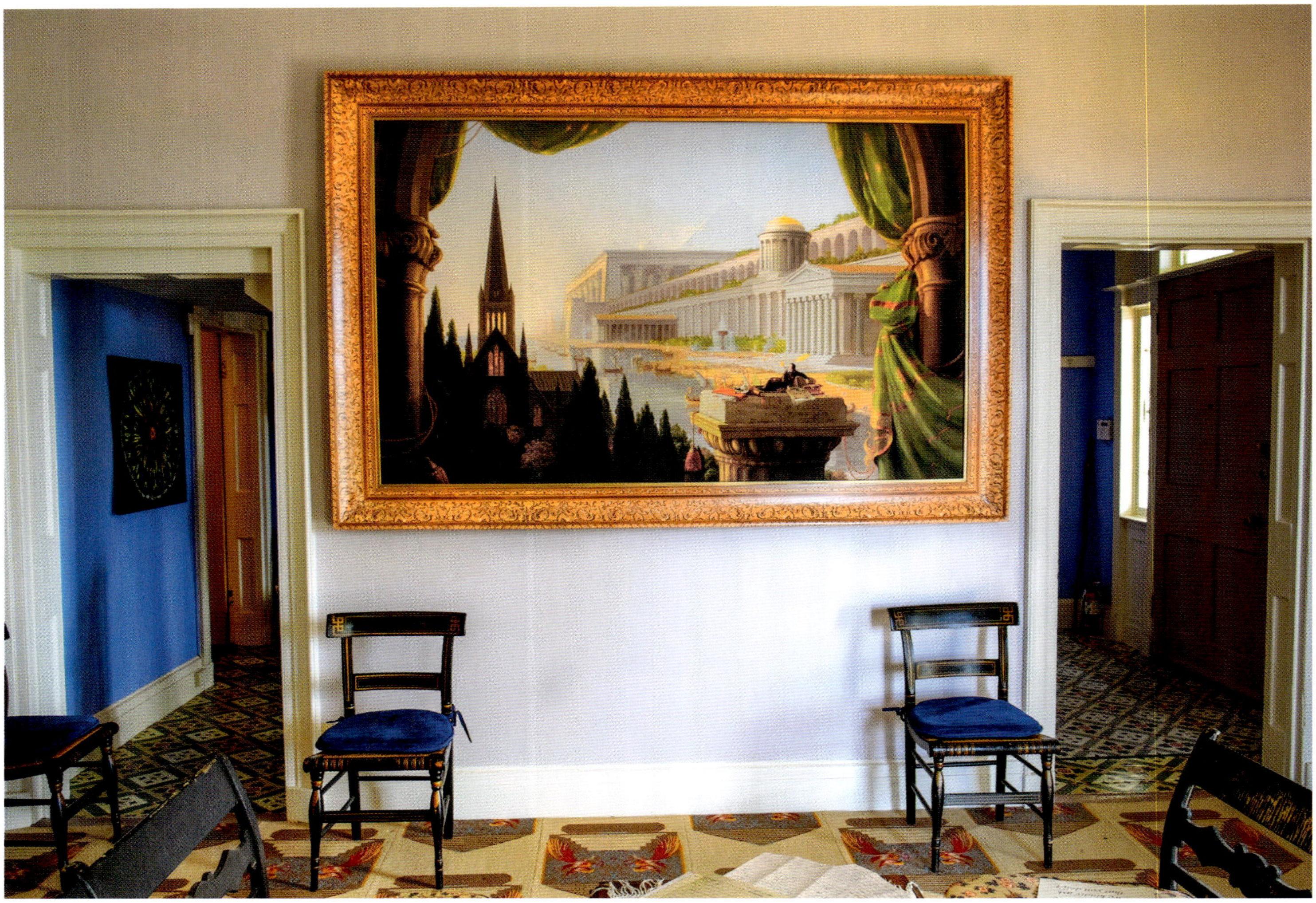

Above: Flanked by doors on to the hallway, Cole's living room also features floor-length windows and exudes airiness and light.
Opposite: The elegant, Italianate façade of Cole's Catskill home.

1815 by Thomson's brother, Thomas T. Thomson, the house had a calm sense of order, with symmetrical forms and tall ceilings. John Alexander, known as Uncle Sandy, had inherited the house, land and outbuildings on the death of his brother in 1821 and in 1839, Cole bought a 2.5-acre site on the edge of the plot to build a separate house for his family. This was something he had wanted to do for several years. Since he also worked as an architect, he made his own drawings and these were Italianate in style, following the latest fashions for luxury villas. The house was to be on three storeys, with wide front and side porches and a hipped roof. It would also feature a tower to provide panoramic views of the surrounding landscape, although not of the Hudson River itself, and a studio on a lower level. However, for financial reasons, the house was never built. Cole, Maria and their five children – Mary, Emily, Elizabeth, Thomas Junior and Theodore Alexander – plus Maria's sisters and other members of the extended family remained living in the main house together. Cole, Maria and their children occupied the second floor, which had a sitting room, a nursery and a master bedroom. For seven years from 1839, Cole used a storehouse on the site as his studio, but in 1846, he had his own studio built to his design. Grand and spacious, it was rectangular and twice the size of the storehouse. It featured a vine-covered porch, beige clapboards, green shutters and enormous windows – almost floor to ceiling in height, facing north, west and south. Tragically, just a little over a year after the studio was completed, Cole died of pleurisy at the age of just forty-seven.

HUDSON RIVER SCHOOL

Cole was the founder of the Hudson River School: a group of American artists who sought to depict the unspoiled magnificence of the American landscape, particularly around the Hudson River Valley in New York State. Cole was the first to paint this territory, taking steamboat trips up the valley. Inspired by Romanticism, he blended idealism and realism, and inspired several artists, including Frederic Edwin Church, Albert Bierstadt and Asher Brown Durand. Like Cole, most Hudson River School artists believed that the American landscape was being destroyed against God's will, and several of their paintings convey implications of retribution to come. They also depicted the scenery as unadulterated and dramatic, bathed in golden light with vast vistas of mountains, forests, vegetation and far-reaching skies.

'O Cedar Grove! When'er I think to part / From thine all peaceful shades my aching heart / Is like to his who leaves some blessed shore / A weeping exile ne'er to see it more.'

Thomas Cole

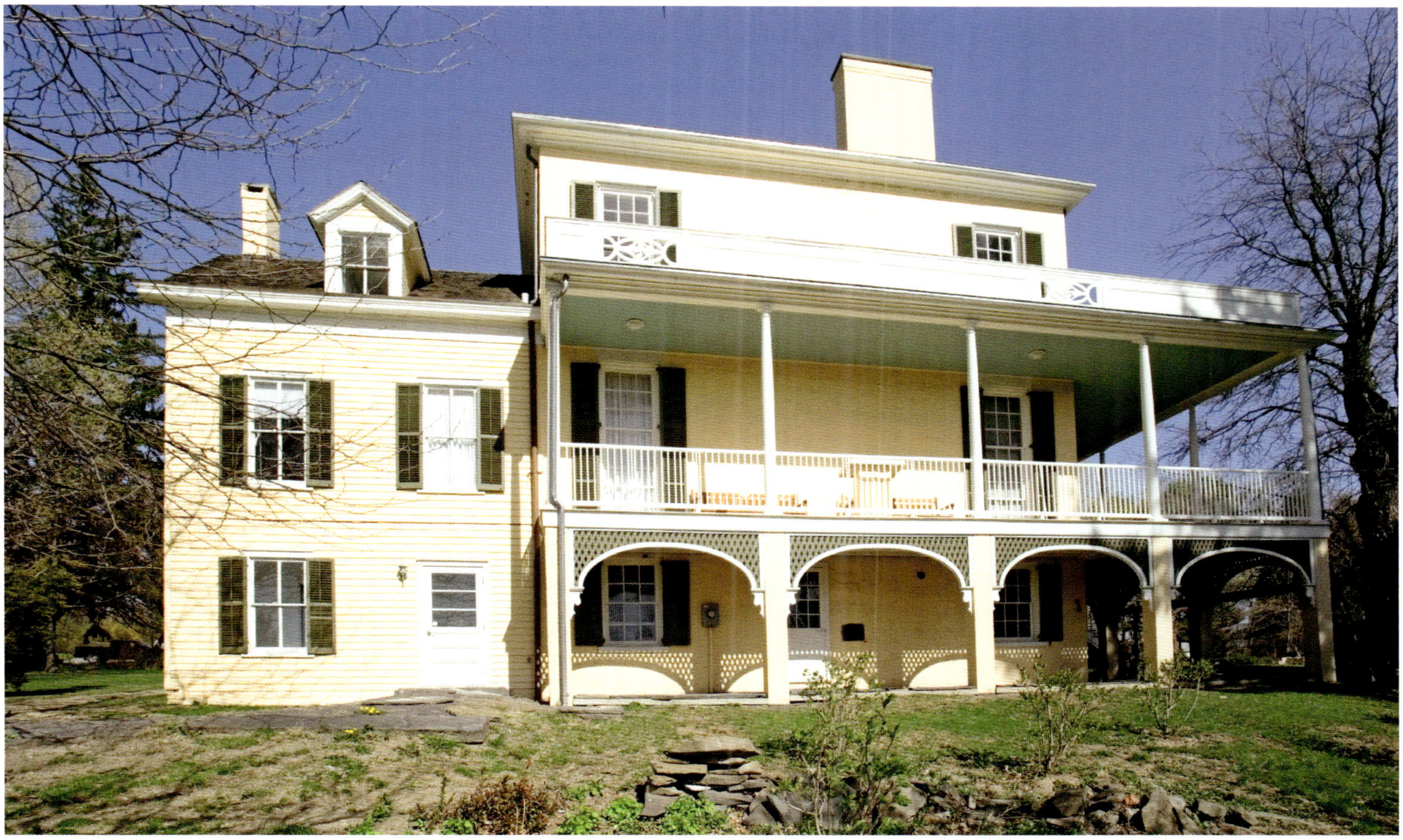

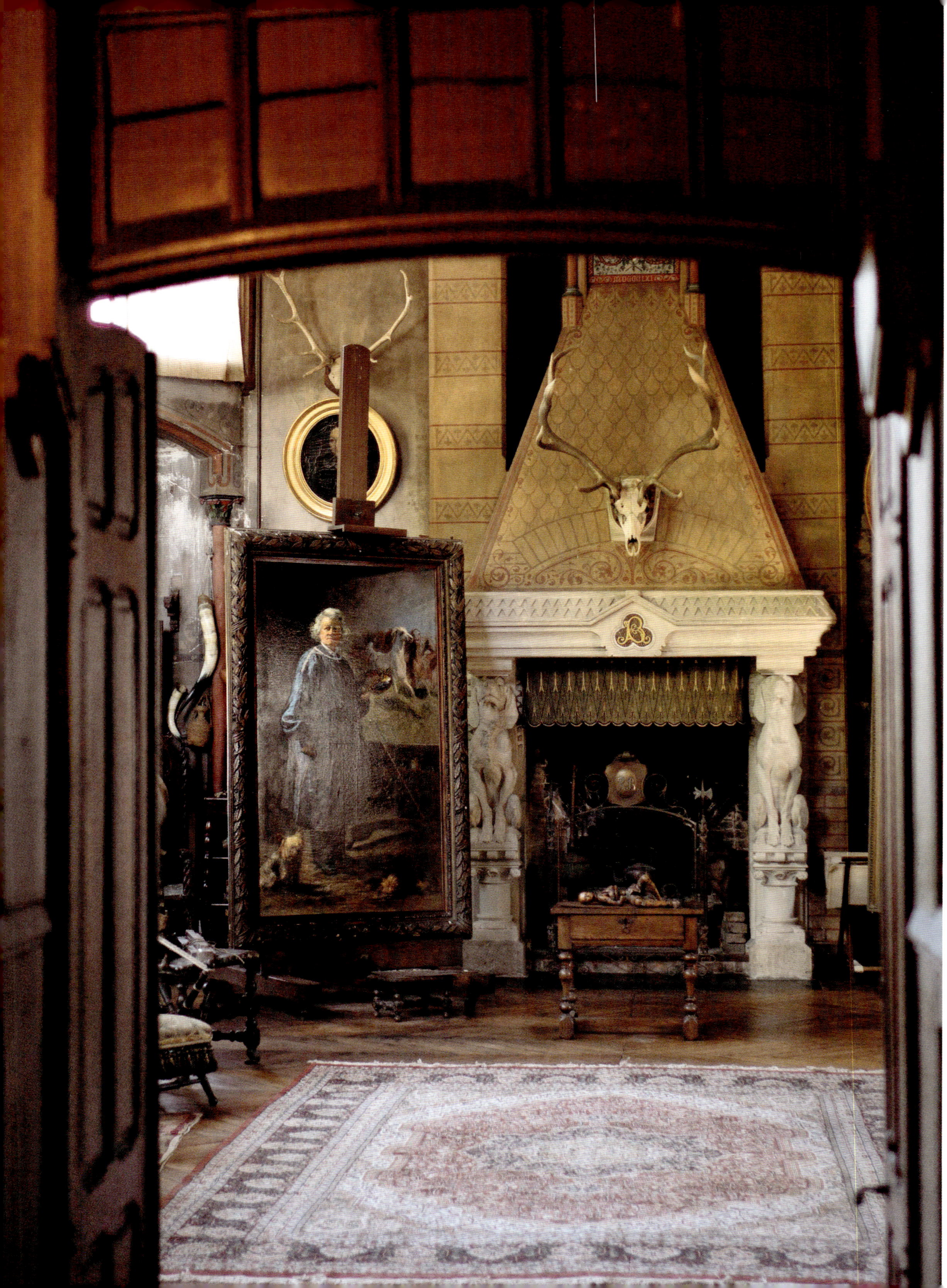

ROSA BONHEUR

Fontainebleau, France

One of the most celebrated artists of the nineteenth century, Rosa Bonheur (1822–99) became the first woman in France to buy a property with her own earnings. The Château de By (later renamed the Château de Rosa Bonheur) is on the edge of the Fontainebleau Forest, south of Paris and close to the River Seine.

Hugely admired for her precise and evocative depictions of animals, the diminutive artist Rosa Bonheur was so successful that not only was her work in demand across the world, but Queen Victoria of England invited her to visit, songs were composed about her, and dolls were even made in her likeness and sold widely.

Bonheur was born in Bordeaux, and when she was six years old – with her artist father, music teacher mother and three younger siblings – she moved to Paris. Her parents followed a Christian-socialist sect that advocated harmony in society and, in particular, decreed that women should be educated equally to and alongside men. As a result, all four Bonheur children were well-educated and confident, and did not recognise class or gender distinctions. They all also became artists.

As a young child, Bonheur learned the alphabet after her mother asked her to draw an animal for each letter. She maintained that this exercise inspired her lifelong love and understanding of animals. Her father taught her to draw, paint and sculpt, and often brought live animals into the studio for her to draw. She continued making studies of domesticated animals in the wild wherever possible; she studied animal anatomy in the abattoirs of Paris, and she dissected dead animals at the National Veterinary Institute, also in Paris.

EARLY SUCCESS

From her early teenage years, Bonheur painted prolifically and soon began receiving prestigious accolades. By the age of twenty-three, she had exhibited eighteen works at the Paris Salon and had been awarded medals for many of them. She was commissioned by the French government, and she became particularly popular among British and American buyers. However, the life she had chosen was not straightforward for a woman of the time. To visit slaughterhouses, livestock sales and farms, she obtained a *permission de travissement* – or a licence that allowed her to wear men's clothes, as the wearing of trousers was illegal for women. She also cut her hair and smoked cigars, and only wore dresses when posing for her own portrait. At a time when lesbianism was frowned upon, she lived openly with her childhood friend, Nathalie Micas. For this, her relationship with her family became strained.

By 1853, Bonheur had won so many awards at previous Salons that she no longer had to submit her work to a jury before being accepted. At the Salon that year, she first exhibited her monumental painting, *The Horse Fair*. In 1854, it was sold to a British art dealer for 40,000 French francs, which was about three times more than most contemporary male artists were earning. As the foremost French *animalier* (animal artist) of the period, she was feted as a celebrity.

MOVING TO THE COUNTRY

Bonheur did not enjoy the attention she was receiving through her fame, and in 1859 she bought the Château de By, a fifteenth-century manor house in the tiny village near Thomery, in the French department of Seine-et-Marne. Around 8 kilometres (5 miles) from

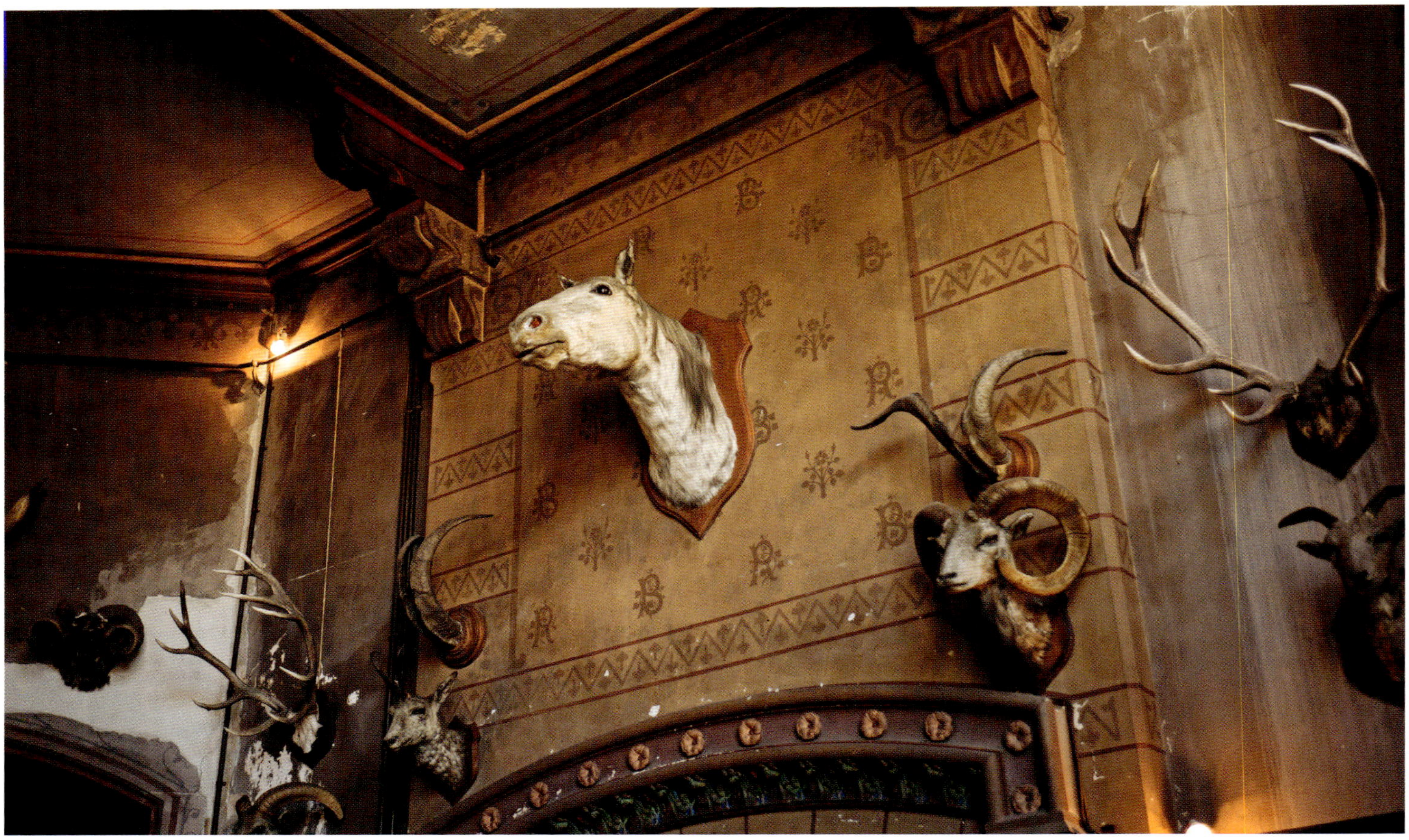

Above and opposite: Bonheur's Chateau de By was filled with both live and stuffed animals that she used as references for her work.

the town of Moret-sur-Loing, it was a peaceful location away from the bustle of Paris. There she could sketch and paint in the nearby forest, be close to the wildlife of the countryside, and house her own increasing menagerie without disturbance. As soon as she acquired the house, she began collecting animals. Eventually, she had more than 200, including sheep, goats, horses, dogs, a heifer, deer, wild boars, chickens, an otter and three lions. Most lived in the house with her or in the vast grounds of the château, where she had special pens constructed for them. In this way, she could study a diversity of individual animals close up.

Although she had servants to help her with the animals, Bonheur trained them herself. She spent hours with each of them, sitting reading her newspaper or sketching, so they became used to her and she could tame them. She drew them constantly, capturing their proportions, textures and features, breaking down their movements and musculature, and learning about their behaviour – nothing escaped her. She corresponded a lot with her veterinarian – scientific, thoughtful letters between equals. It was a remarkable achievement for a woman of her era to have been taken so seriously by a professional man.

Bonheur was thirty-seven when she moved into the château with Micas and Micas's mother, Henriette, and she immediately rebuilt it to make it comfortable. Firstly, she added a large, light-filled, Neo-Gothic-style studio. She also renovated the bedrooms, for herself, Nathalie and Henriette, and for guests and servants. The latter included those who took care of her animals, the grooms, a coachman and gardeners, as well as Etienne, the steward, and Céline, the cook, who were husband and wife. The modest kitchen that connected to the servants' rooms by stairs was modernised, and there was a pantry for food storage and a fairly large dining room. Bonheur became quite self-sufficient, growing her own fruit and vegetables, and using the eggs from her chickens. She regularly entertained small groups of friends, fellow artists, art dealers, buyers and some eminent guests, including the Empress Eugénie, Napoleon III's wife, who visited to give her the Legion of Honour in 1865; the first time it had been awarded to a woman and by a woman. As the Empress pinned the award to Bonheur's blouse, she is reported to have said, 'Genius has no sex.'

For forty years, Bonheur lived at her château. Most days followed a particular pattern. She usually began her day at dawn,

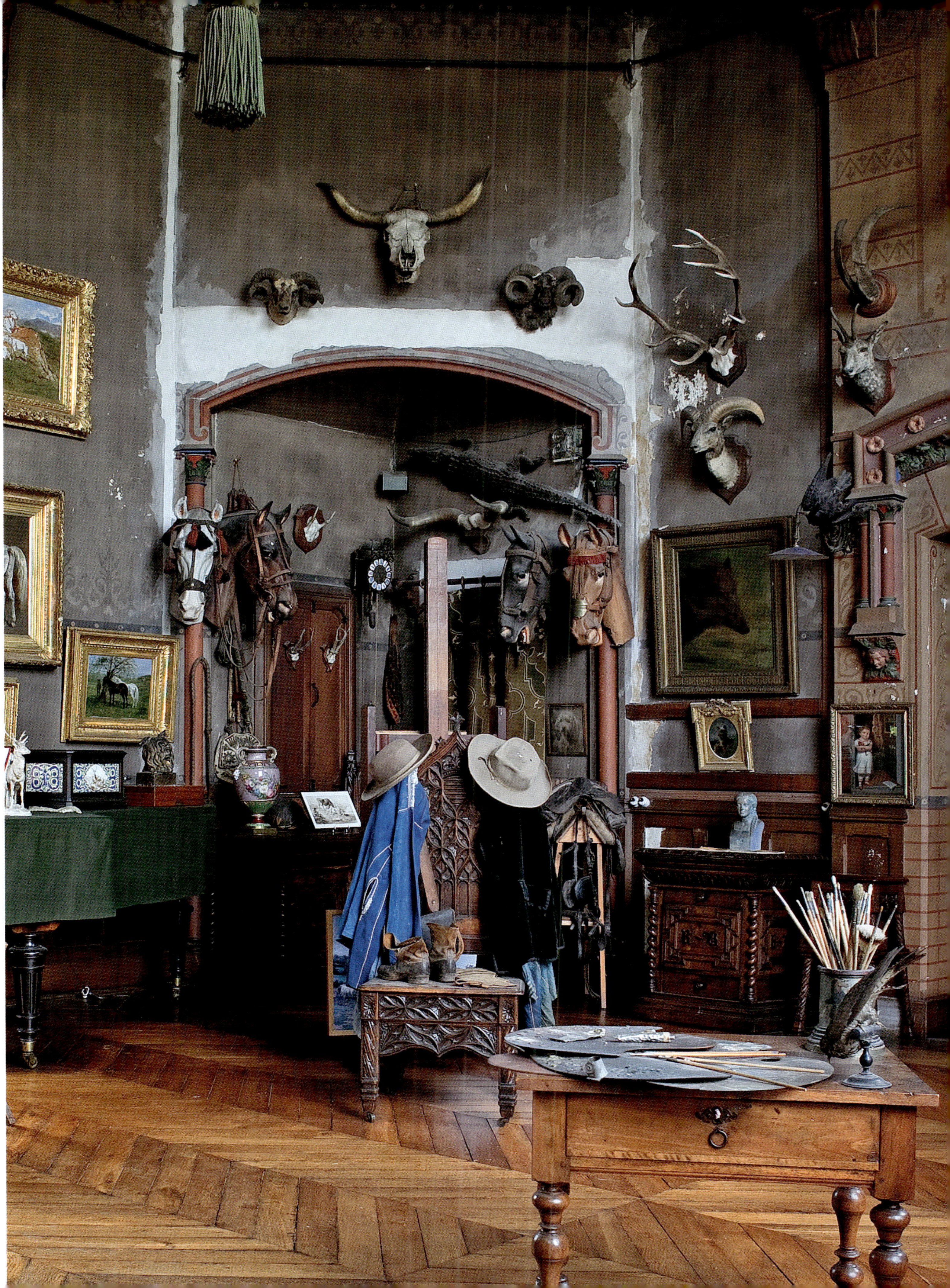

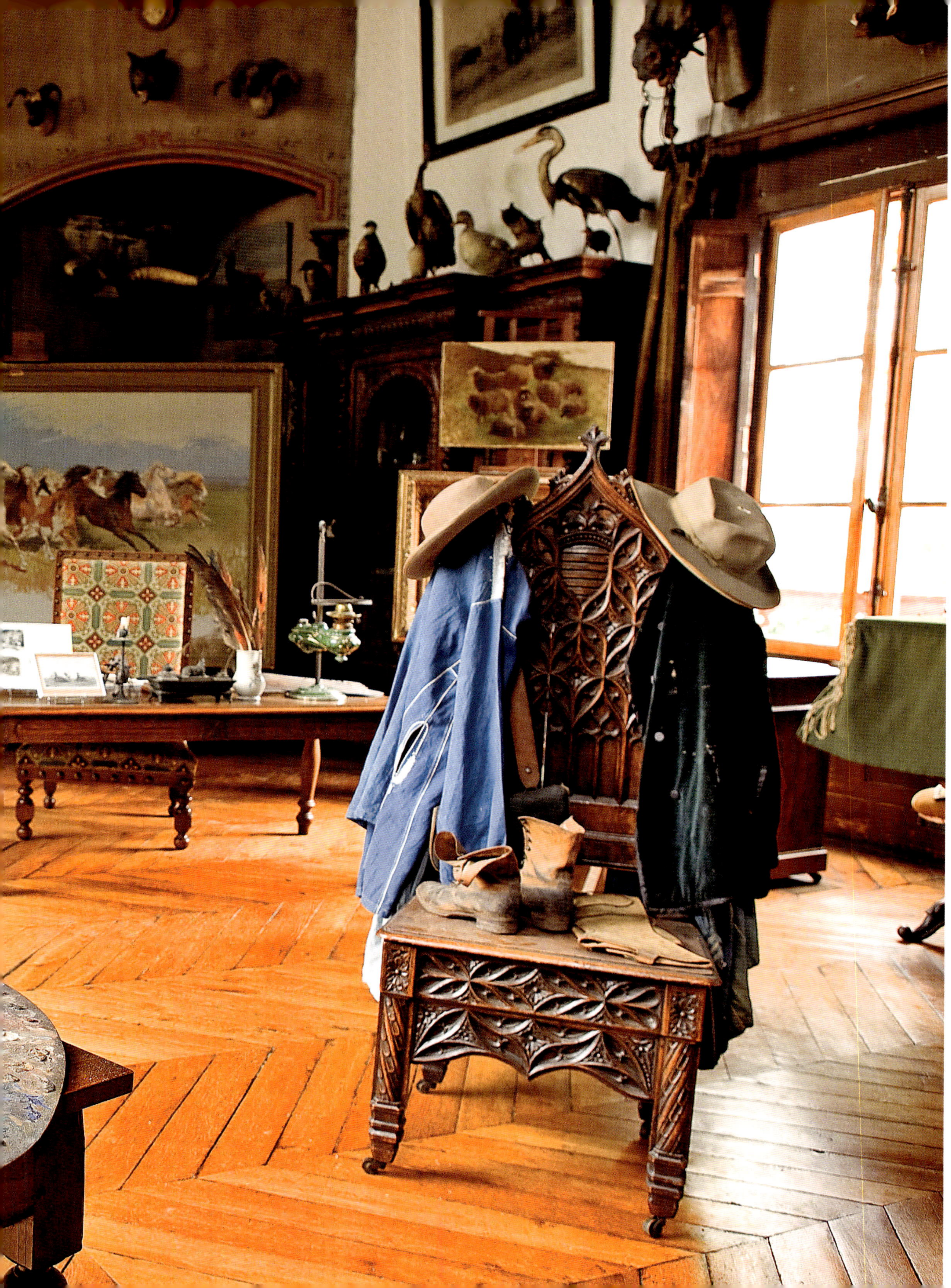

walking to find a suitable place in the forest where she could work until dusk. She saw a few fellow artists, but was mainly solitary. Only her good friend, artist Paul Chardin, regularly sketched with her. After a day making these outdoor studies, she composed her paintings in her studio. She also produced sculpture, but stopped exhibiting it at the Paris Salon in 1848, in order not to overshadow her younger brother Isidore. She continued to produce sculpture, however, and exhibit it in provincial Salons alongside Isidore's work, and they also collaborated. She maintained that sculpture allowed her to understand and study anatomy, and inform her paintings.

When Micas died in 1889, forty years after they first lived together, Bonheur was grief-stricken, but six years later, she met the American painter Anna Klumpke, who was more than thirty years younger – and three years after that, they began living together at the château. Bonheur, by then in her seventies, created a new art studio for Klumpke, who painted three portraits of Bonheur and wrote her biography. When Bonheur died, against her family's wishes, Klumpke was named as the sole heir to the estate. That year, she opened the Rosa Bonheur Memorial Art School, providing art education for women.

'If we don't always understand animals, they always understand us.'

Rosa Bonheur

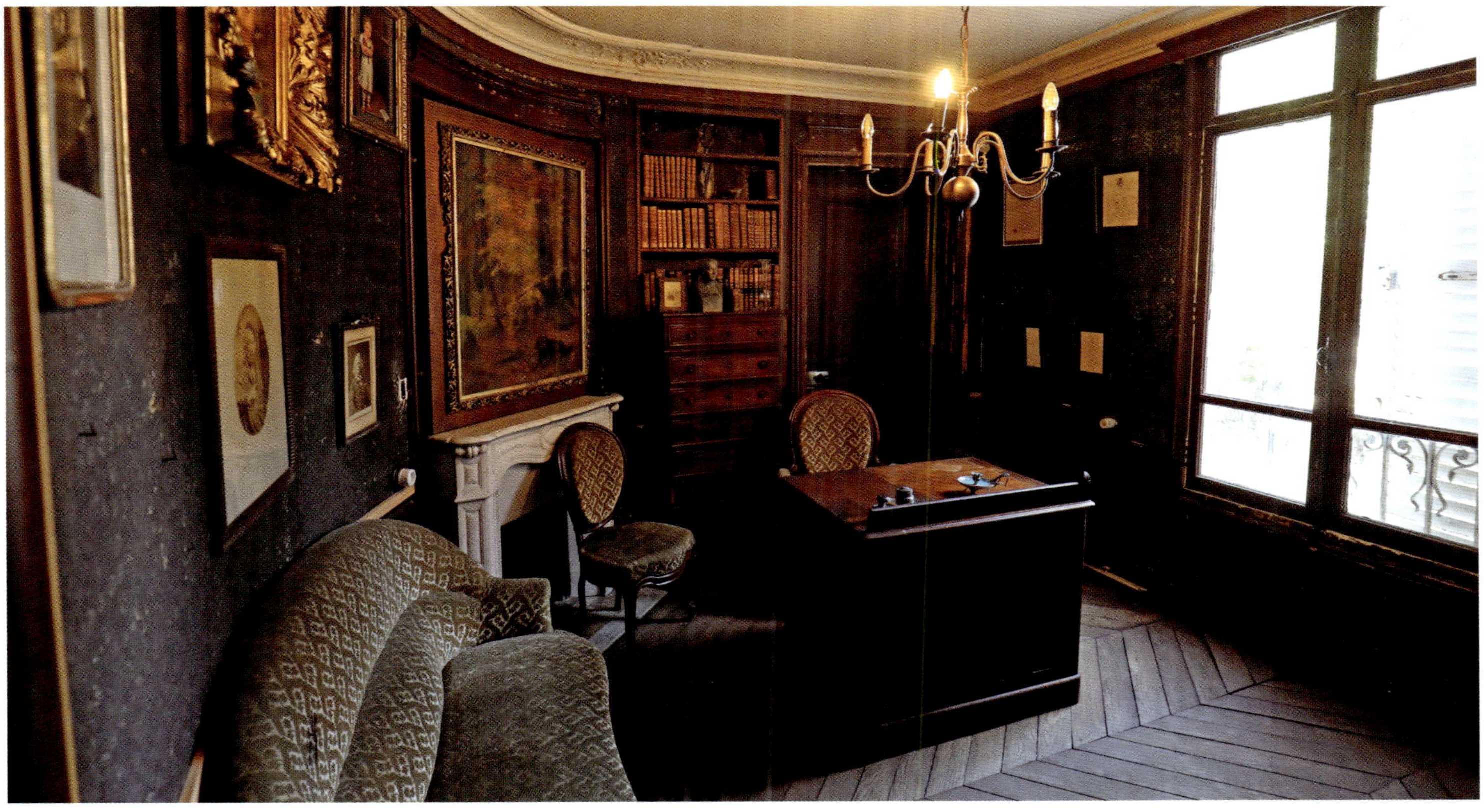

Above: Bonheur's peaceful and comfortable office was needed; it was where she organised her busy life.

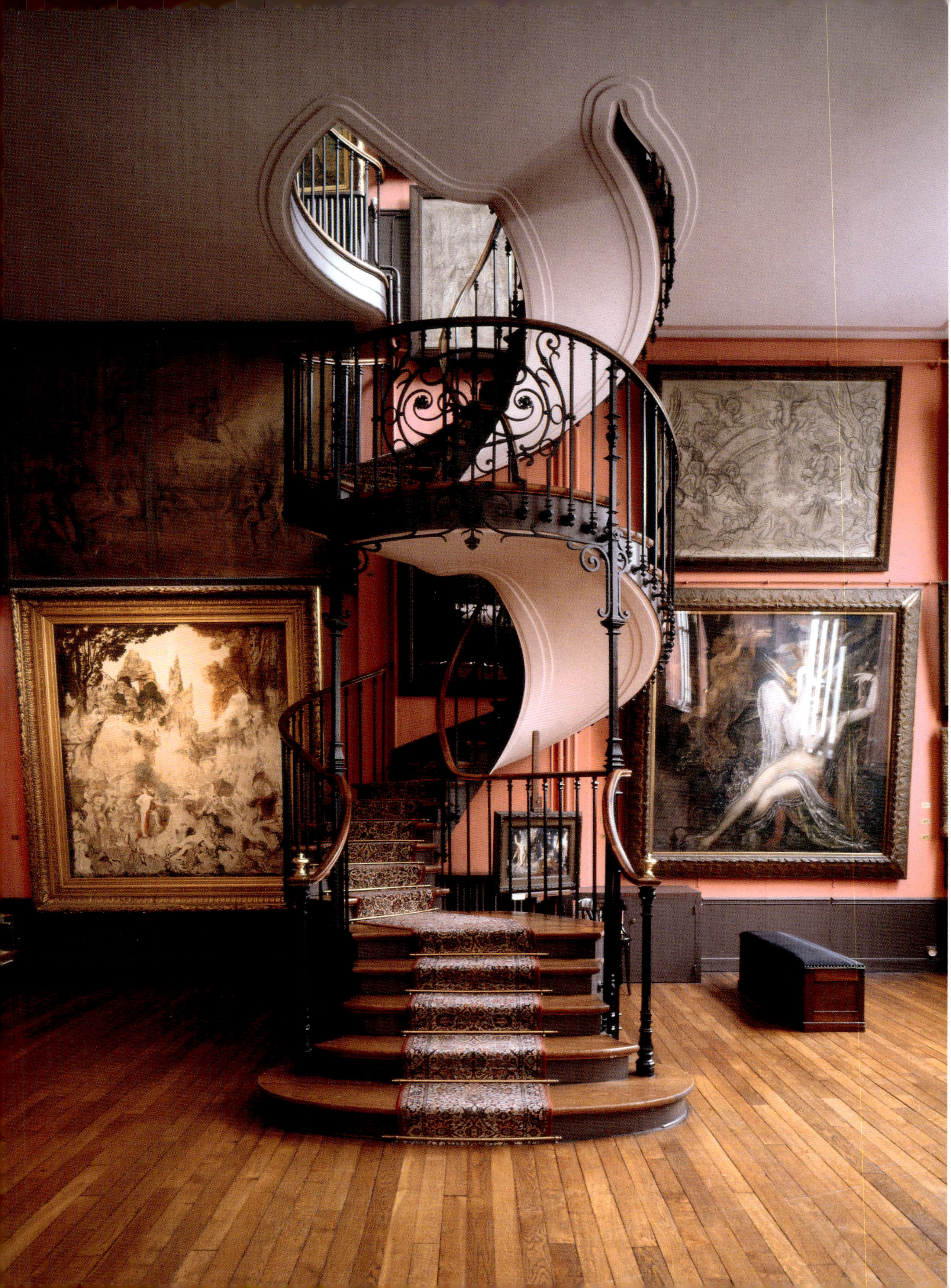

GUSTAVE MOREAU

Paris, France

In 1852, the parents of twenty-six-year-old artist Gustave Moreau (1826–98) bought a townhouse in Paris, France. They converted part of the top floor into a studio for their son, and he lived and worked in the house for the rest of his life.

Gustave Moreau produced over 15,000 paintings, watercolours and drawings, usually focusing on allegories, and biblical and mythological subjects. Categorised as both the forerunner of the Symbolist movement and one of the most important Symbolist artists, Moreau sought to express individual emotional experiences through his own invented symbols that he wove into mysterious-looking paintings.

BECOMING AN ARTIST

Growing up in Paris in a wealthy middle-class family, Gustave Moreau boarded at a respected school, but after his elder sister Camille died, his parents kept him at home. Often sick, he showed an early talent for drawing, but he also learned Greek and Latin, played the piano, and read French and classical literature in his father's library. When he was fifteen, he visited Italy with his mother and there became certain that he wanted to be an artist. Within a few years, he was studying art at the prestigious École des Beaux-Arts in Paris. He remained there for three years, but after twice failing to win the prestigious Prix de Rome, he left. Over the next couple of years, he studied and copied paintings in the Musée du Louvre, and during the early 1850s, he undertook some commissions from the French government.

In 1851, Moreau met the painter Théodore Chassériau, who had studied under the Neoclassical artist Jean-Auguste-Dominique Ingres and whose painting style was a fusion of Neoclassicism and Romanticism. Moreau became extremely influenced by Chassériau's art, and set up a studio next door to him on the place Pigalle. In 1852, for the first time, his work was accepted for the official annual Paris Salon and, in the same year, his parents bought the house at 14 rue de La Rochefoucauld. Although they occupied part of it, they put the house in his name and allowed him to establish a studio on the third floor.

At that time, Moreau began to lead the life of a dandy. Dressing in fine clothes, he would regularly visit the opera and the theatre, and often sang or played the piano at soirées in his friends' drawing rooms. Then, in 1856, Chassériau died. Seven years older than Moreau, he was just thirty-seven. His premature death deeply affected Moreau, who left Paris a few months later to travel through Italy. After two years, he returned with hundreds of copies and studies he had made of great artists' work he saw there. In 1862, his father died, and two years later, his painting *Oedipus and the Sphinx* was acclaimed at the Paris Salon, winning a medal and establishing Moreau's status in the art world. Although he was working against the dominant style of Realism in France at that time, his paintings were greatly admired. Most include Christian elements that interact with Classical and other pagan components, and his sinuous, sensuous-looking women and slender, androgynous-looking men influenced other artists, as well as the Art Nouveau design style of the period. In his enigmatic paintings, he created strange-looking visions that stressed the imperfection and impermanence of the physical world.

Throughout the 1860s, Moreau's reputation continued to rise. At the Salon of 1869, he exhibited two paintings; *Prometheus* and *Europe* (the latter also known as *The Abduction of Europa*). Prometheus won a medal, but *Europe* was criticised heavily in the press. In response, he stopped sending paintings to the Salon for seven years, and by 1880, he stopped submitting his paintings there completely. After

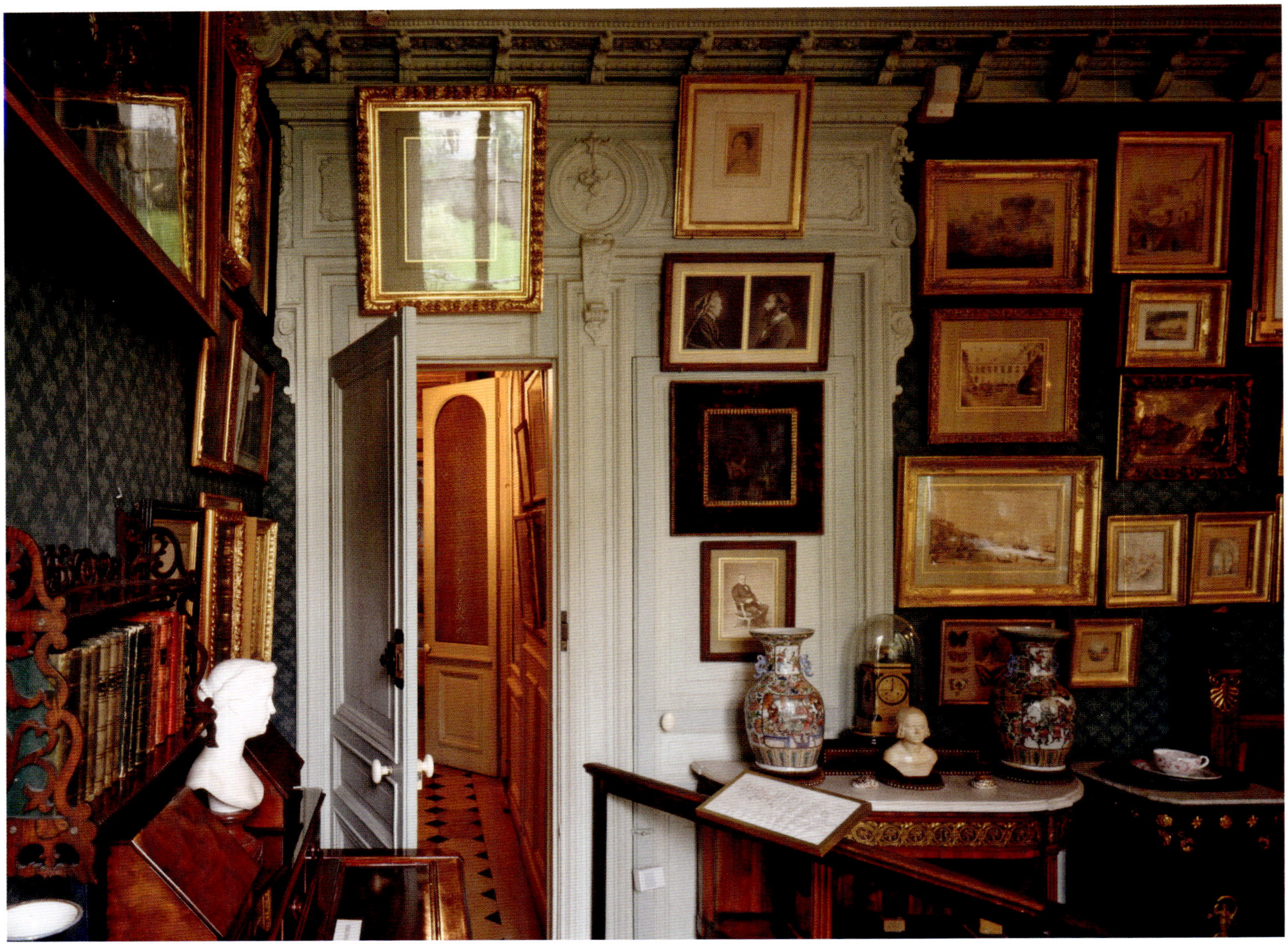

Above and opposite: Gustave Moreau's house, chock-full of his paintings.

that, he became viewed by the public and the press as a recluse. Yet in 1883, he was awarded the Legion of Honour for his art. The following year, his mother died. They had been exceptionally close and he was grief-stricken. Although he maintained his close circle of friends, he became even more withdrawn and solitary. He rarely exhibited his work anywhere, and turned down several significant offers, including, in 1887, an invitation to exhibit with the group Les XX in Brussels, where other exhibitors included Camille Pissarro, Berthe Morisot and Georges Seurat; a professorship at the École des Beaux-Arts in 1888; and the opportunity to decorate buildings at the Sorbonne in 1891. However, after one of his friends died – a fellow artist who taught at the École des Beaux-Arts – he agreed to replace him and proved to be excellent at the job. Among his many pupils there were Henri Matisse and Georges Rouault.

PRESERVED FOR POSTERITY

The house on rue de La Rochefoucauld, in the 9th arrondissement of Paris, was fairly modest. With a Neoclassical façade, it stood on an 80 square metre (861 square feet) plot, with gardens in front and behind. It was arranged on three floors, and he and his parents lived comfortably there. All three shared the first floor. Moreau's studio was on the floor above; the ground floor was rented out. The first-floor living area included a dining room, bedrooms, a drawing room, corridor and his father's office-library.

When he was sixty-nine in 1895, and had lived in the house alone for eleven years, Moreau decided to turn it into a museum for the nation after his death. However, it was not large enough, and so he gained some space by taking away the front garden and bringing

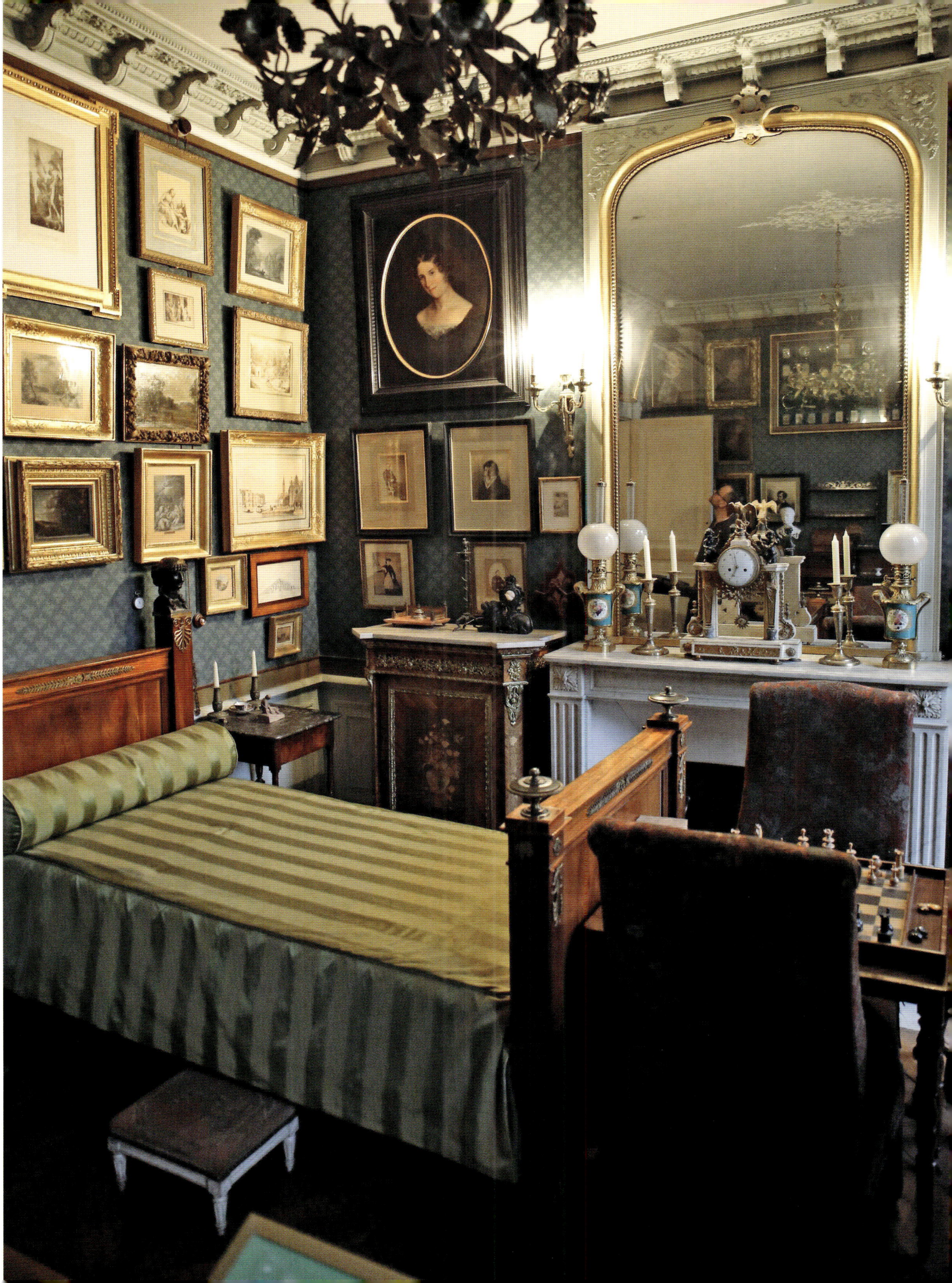

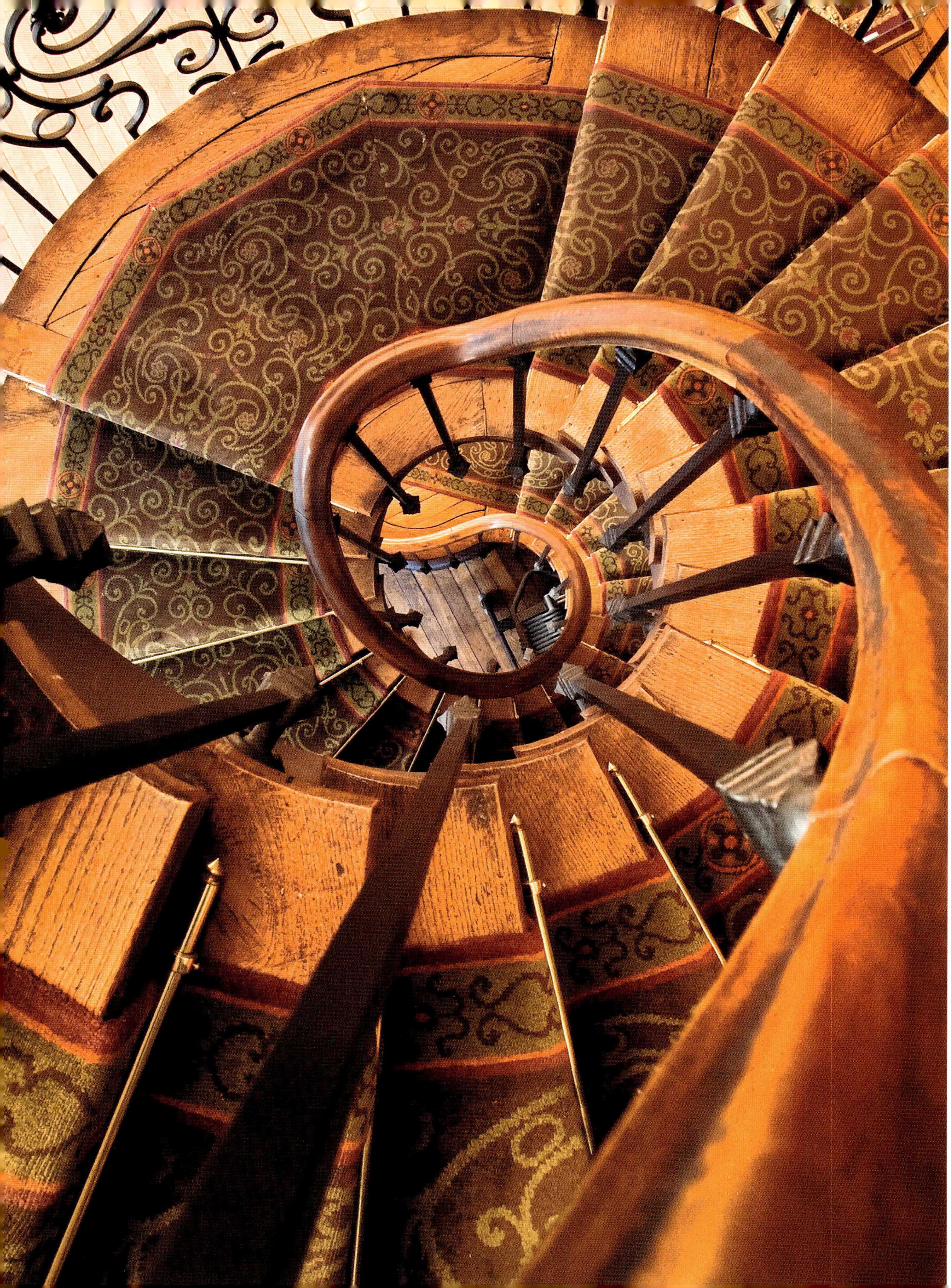

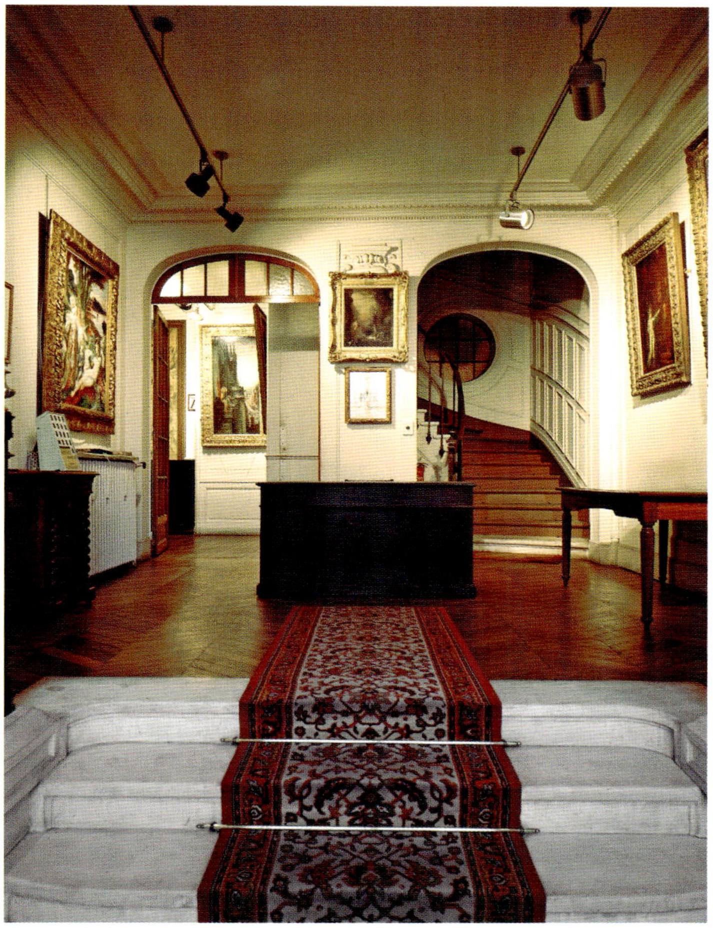

the front of the house forward, aligning it with the street. The only other way he could create space elsewhere was to build upwards. His father had been an architect, which made him particularly interested in converting the building, so he collaborated with the architect Albert Lafon in designing the museum. Above his studio, he added two spacious galleries, which linked to and from the floor below with a grand Art Nouveau-style spiral staircase.

For the three years before his death, Moreau was intensely busy, planning how and where everything would go to serve as a lasting monument to his work. For that time, he lived on the third floor, where his studio was, installing a bed, a cheval glass (tall dressing mirror) and a washstand. In the wide corridor on the floor below, he hung portraits of his friends, including Chassériau, as well as engravings, photographs and drawings. In 1898 he died of cancer and left the townhouse to the French nation in its entirety, including not just all the art in his home – comprising over 4,000 drawings, 1,200 paintings and hundreds of watercolours – but all the furniture and ornaments, as they were when he lived there.

'No one could have less faith in the absolute and definitive importance of the work created by man, because I believe that this world is nothing but a dream.'

Gustave Moreau

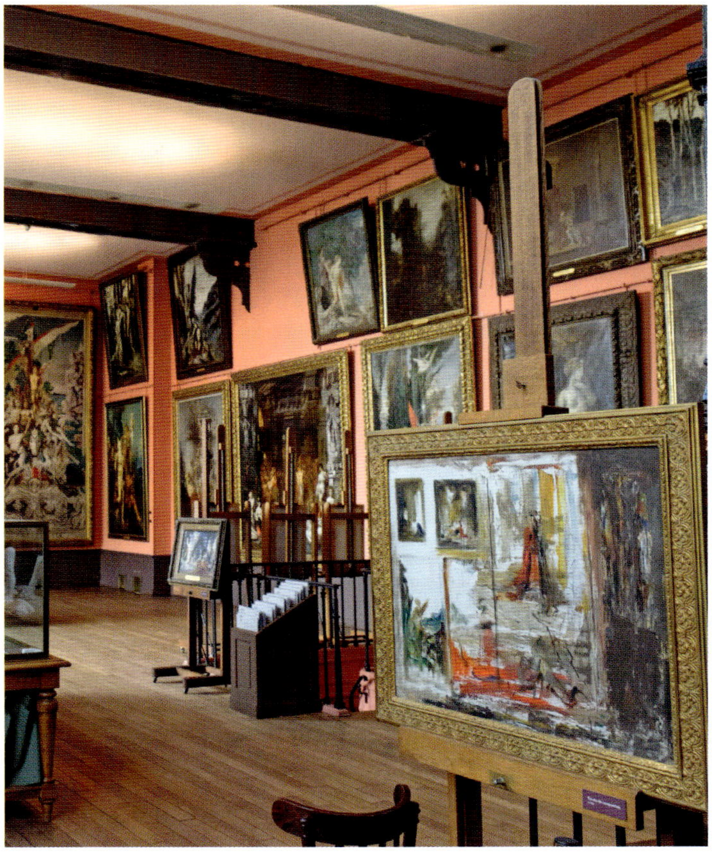

Opposite: The grand Art Nouveau-style spiral staircase.
Left, above: The wide corridor featuring several portraits among other works.
Left, below: The studio, filled with Moreau's paintings.

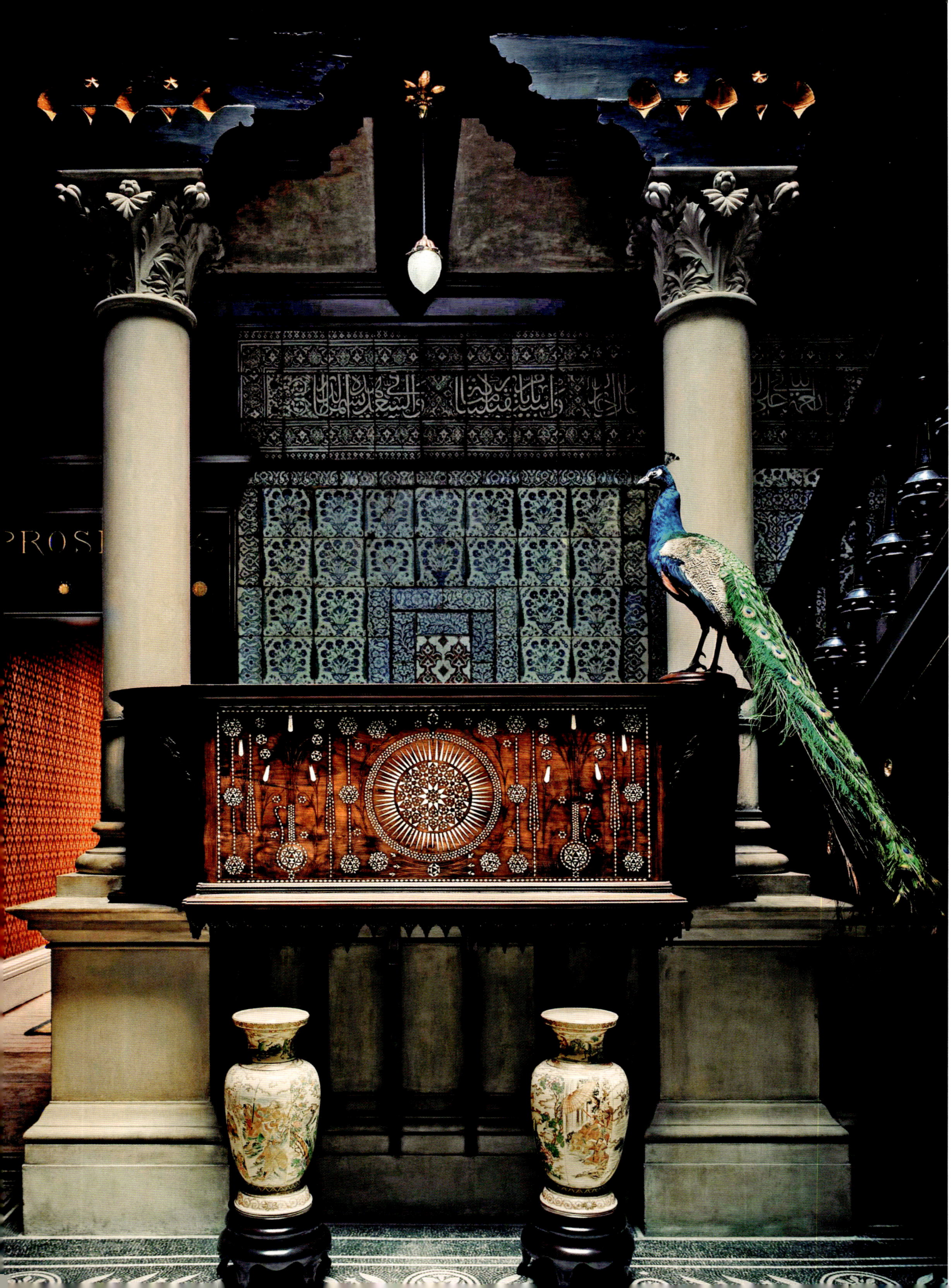

FREDERIC, LORD LEIGHTON

London, UK

The tree-dappled streets of Kensington in London have long been a haven for artists, writers and musicians, and between 1864 and 1879, the architect George Aitchison Jr. RA built a grand and imposing red brick building there, in Holland Park Road, for the painter and sculptor, and president of the Royal Academy, Frederic, Lord Leighton (1830–1896).

One of the most influential artists of the Victorian era, Leighton was born in the English seaside town of Scarborough to a well-connected family. At the age of two, he moved to London with his parents and two sisters and then they embarked on a peripatetic life around Europe for nearly twenty years. They stayed in Paris, then moved to Germany, followed by Italy. Leighton became fluent in French, German and Italian, and he studied art in Berlin, Munich, Florence, Frankfurt, Brussels and Paris. He attracted an extensive circle of friends throughout Europe, including Robert and Elizabeth Barrett Browning, William Makepeace Thackeray and George Sand.

In 1855, Leighton became friends with the painter George Frederic Watts. who had recently become a houseguest of Thoby and Sara Prinsep at Little Holland House in Kensington. The Prinseps had taken the lease on the house from Lord and Lady Holland in 1850, and Watts invited many of his avant-garde artist and writer friends, including Leighton, Thackeray, Dante Gabriel Rossetti, Edward Burne-Jones and Alfred Tennyson. Watts told Leighton that Lord and Lady Holland were selling off parts of their estate on Holland Park Road, which at the time was a fairly rural spot to the west of London. The south side of the road was bordered by gardens and stable buildings, and for Leighton, this would be a perfect location for a house and studio.

ACQUIRING THE PLOT

In the late 1850s and early 1860s, Leighton had travelled to Algiers, Turkey, Rhodes and Egypt, and some years later, to Damascus. Everywhere he went, he hunted for art and artefacts, such as ceramic tiles, mosaics, plates, jars and draperies. By the time his house was being built, he had amassed an extraordinary collection. By 1864, he was elected an Associate of the Royal Academy and his paintings began selling for huge amounts of money. At last he had the funds to build the home and studio he had always wanted.

Regularly featured in the press and opened to the public, Leighton's house was designed based on his favourite locations. Having visited several artist house-studios in Europe, including that of Eugène Delacroix in Paris, Leighton knew the type of home-studio he wanted: a place where he could welcome friends and the public, but where he could also live and work comfortably, peacefully and privately.

UNDERSTATED OPULENCE

Construction began on the house in 1864, and over the years, Leighton extended the plot, buying extra land when it came up for sale. By 1877, the Arab Hall was started.

The exterior of the house is a classical style with red Suffolk bricks and Caen stone dressings, but on stepping inside, Leighton's two-storey Arab Hall was created to an entirely different brief. Completed in 1877, the opulent hall is decorated with Leighton's collection of 1,000 tiles from Syria, Turkey and Persia. The airy space, with its grand golden dome, mosaics, tiles, sculpture, fountain, grilles, columns and pointed arches is based on a

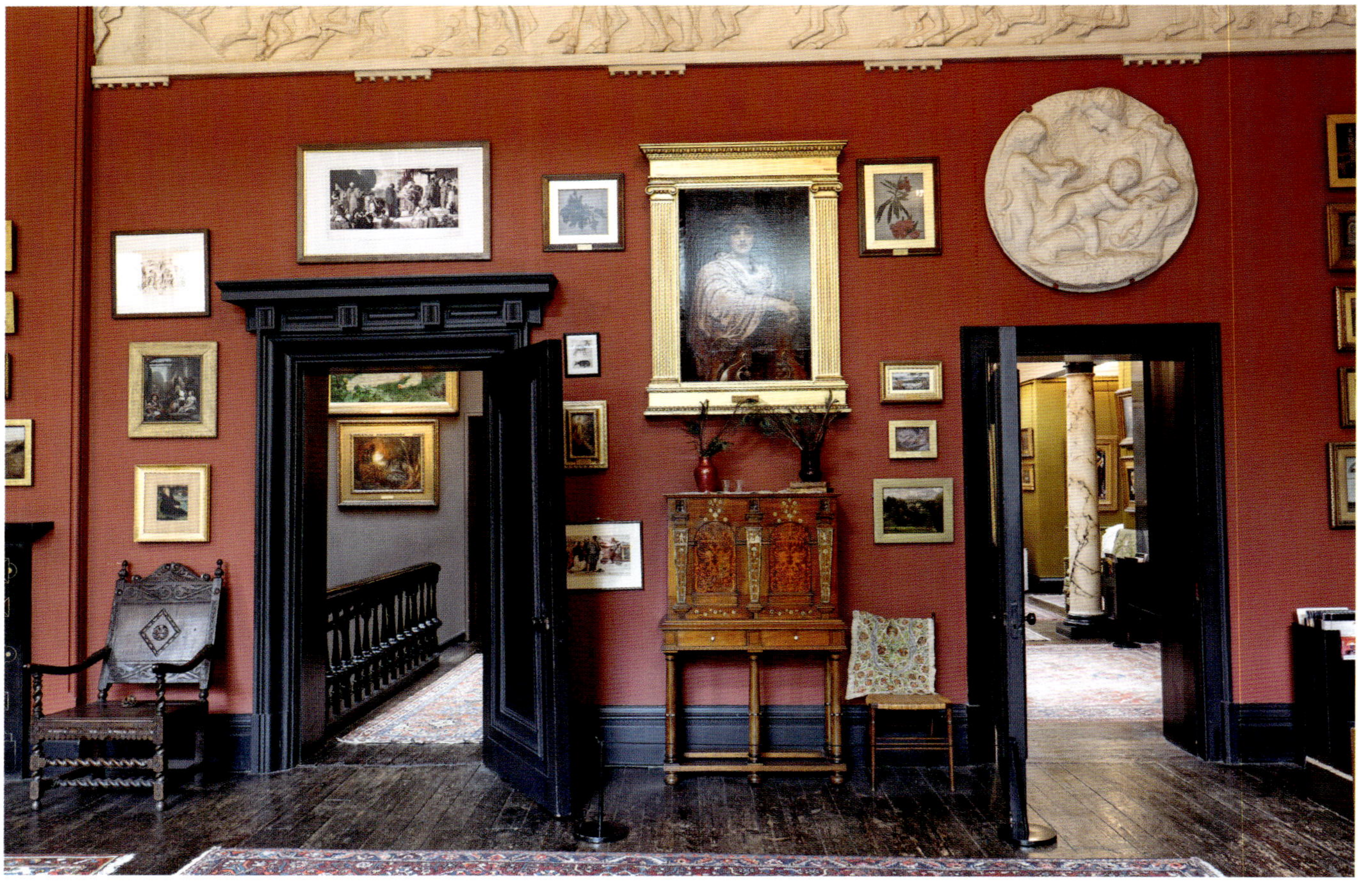

Above: Part of Leighton's huge and lavish studio. It served not only as work space but also as a reception room and the venue for musical events that he held annually. *Opposite*: The opulence of the Narcissus Hall.

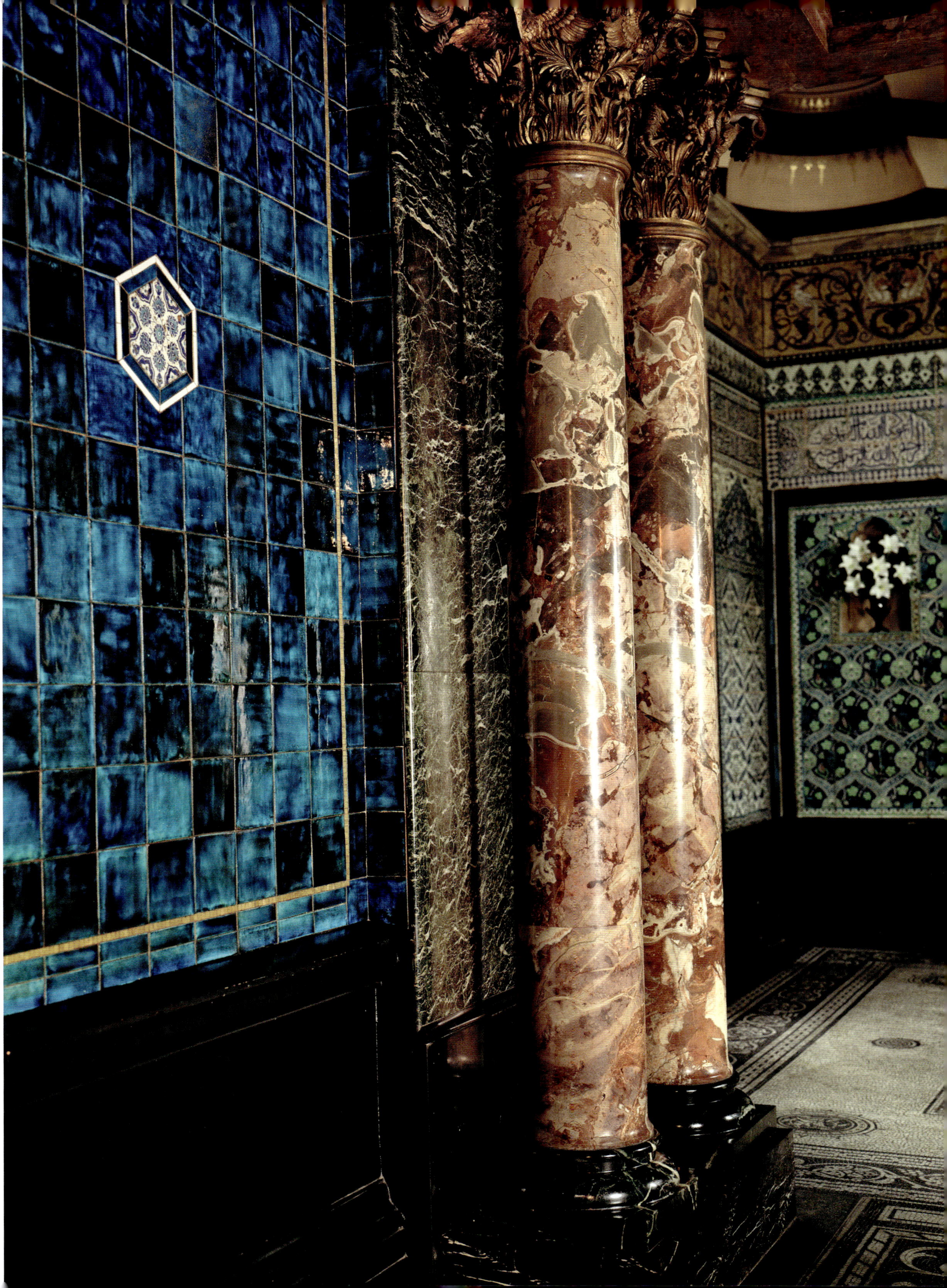

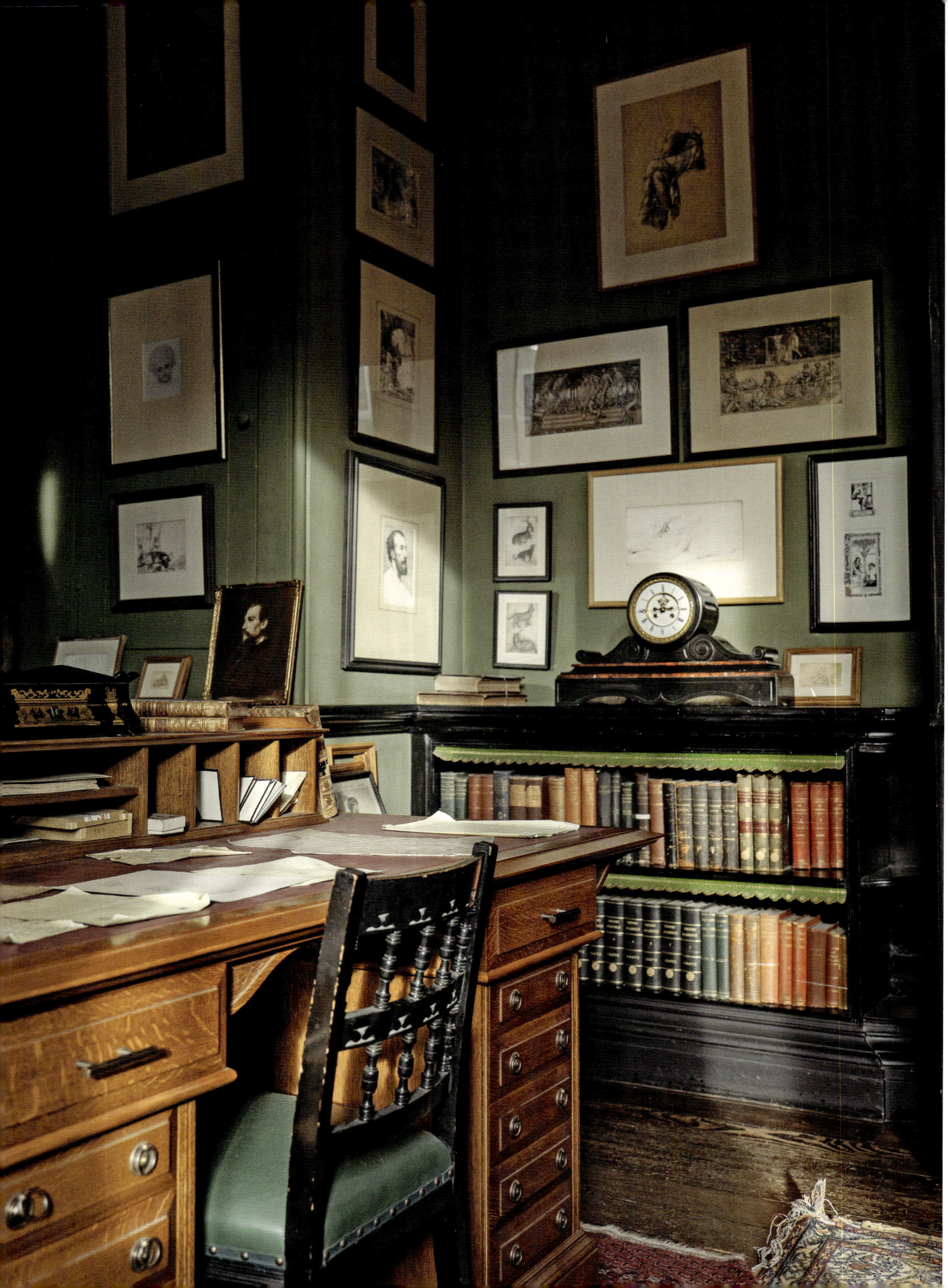

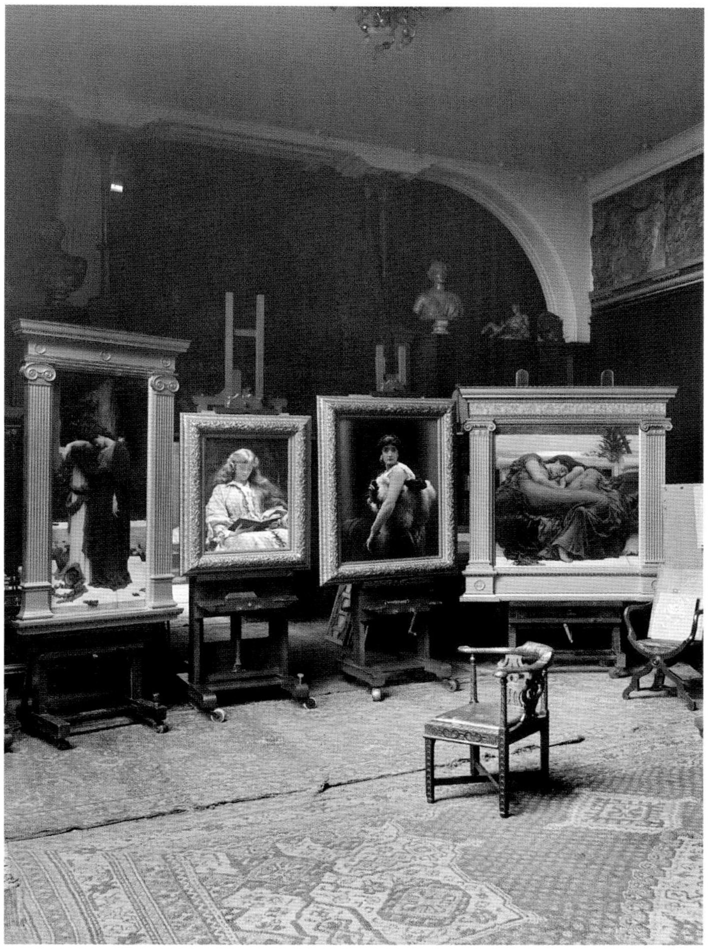

Above: A black and white photo of Leighton's studio in the 1880s.
Opposite: Leighton's office.

12th century Moorish-Norman palace in Palermo, Sicily, and mixes Arab, Norman and Byzantine influences.

Another profound influence on Leighton was Venice, and the staircase leading off the Arab Hall is based on 15th and 16th century Venetian palazzo courtyards. Nearby is the Narcissus Hall, so-called because it contains statues that were excavated from Pompeii in 1862, including an original bronze that was originally thought to be of Narcissus, but now is generally believed to represent Dionysus. Other rooms on the ground floor include an elegant Silk Room and a large drawing room with a west-facing bay window. He covered the walls of the rooms with paintings by his friends, including Watts, John Everett Millais, Edward Coley Burne-Jones and John Singer Sargent.

Leighton kept his bedroom – the only completely private room in the house – modest and simple, with walls papered in a dark blue William Morris wallpaper. The kitchen, scullery, pantry, wine cellar, butler's and servants' bedrooms were below stairs.

THE STUDIO

Largest of all the rooms, is Leighton's painting studio at the top of the house, a vast domed space flooded with light, that he filled with his work in progress, props, materials, easels, tables and chairs. Three fireplaces kept the room warm; tables were piled high with books, papers and other art materials. Chairs were placed around the room for his models and friends. It was a huge space, with two stained glass windows in a 'Moorish' style that sent splinters of glittering colour across every nearby surface. In addition, Leighton had a Winter Studio built in 1889–90, to use when daylight was poor. After his death, many sketchbooks and over a thousand sheets of studies were found there.

His working methods involved a complex process, involving a number of stages and weeks, months or years of work. Once he had decided on a subject and composition, he would make several detailed drawings from life. Then he made a highly finished drawing to establish overall composition. He would produce small colour oil sketches and larger monochrome studies, marking in areas of light, shade and volume. He carefully followed these studies as he began the final work, beginning with underpaintings that picked out the darkest tones. Finally, he began painting, building up from dark to light. He once commented that he doubted whether any other artist enjoyed the process of making a picture as much as he did. He usually worked on several paintings at once, works including commissions and submissions for the Royal Academy's Summer Exhibition.

Over his life of travel, Leighton had gathered many friends among the art and literary community of Europe, and many of these came to the house. Small groups of friends occasionally dined with him, but on a larger scale, his Sunday afternoon 'At Homes,' held between 3pm and 5pm, became renowned. Then visitors explored the interiors of his home and admired his collections. He also invited visiting groups of 'the poor.' Each year, at the end of March or early in April, on the weekend before sending-in day for the RA Summer Exhibition, the public were invited to see his paintings before they were hung in the Academy. On that 'Show Sunday', thousands passed through his house, eager to see the images that would be written about in the papers over the coming days. Another annual event he held in the house, was a musical recital for his friends. It was viewed as 'one of the real treats of the year'.

At the age of 64 however, in 1894, some thirty years after construction began on the house, Leighton's health failed. He travelled to North Africa to convalesce, and resigned his position as president of the Royal Academy. Having been made a Baronet eight years after his knighthood, he was elevated again in 1896, becoming Baron Leighton, the first painter ever to receive that honour. The following day however, he died of angina.

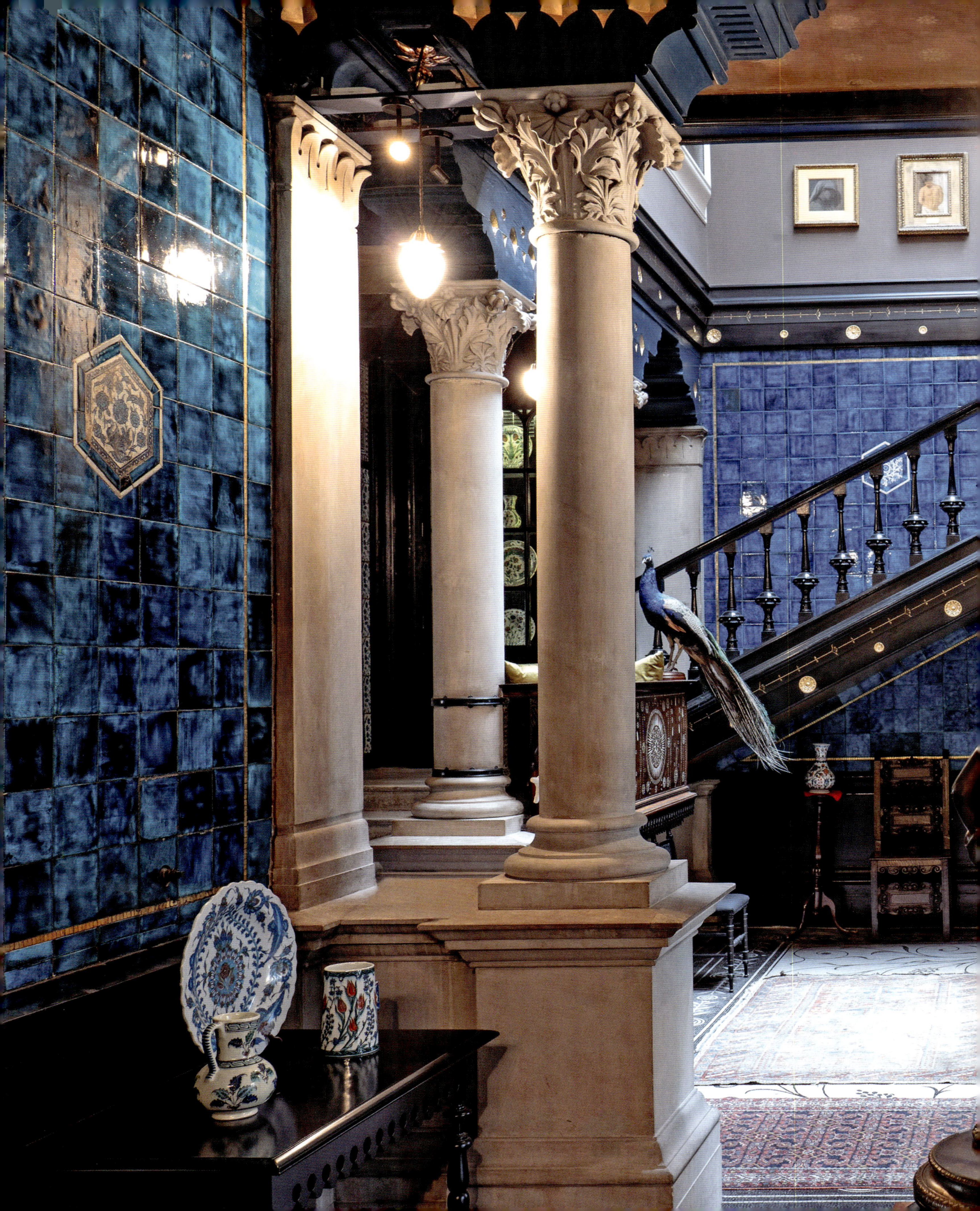

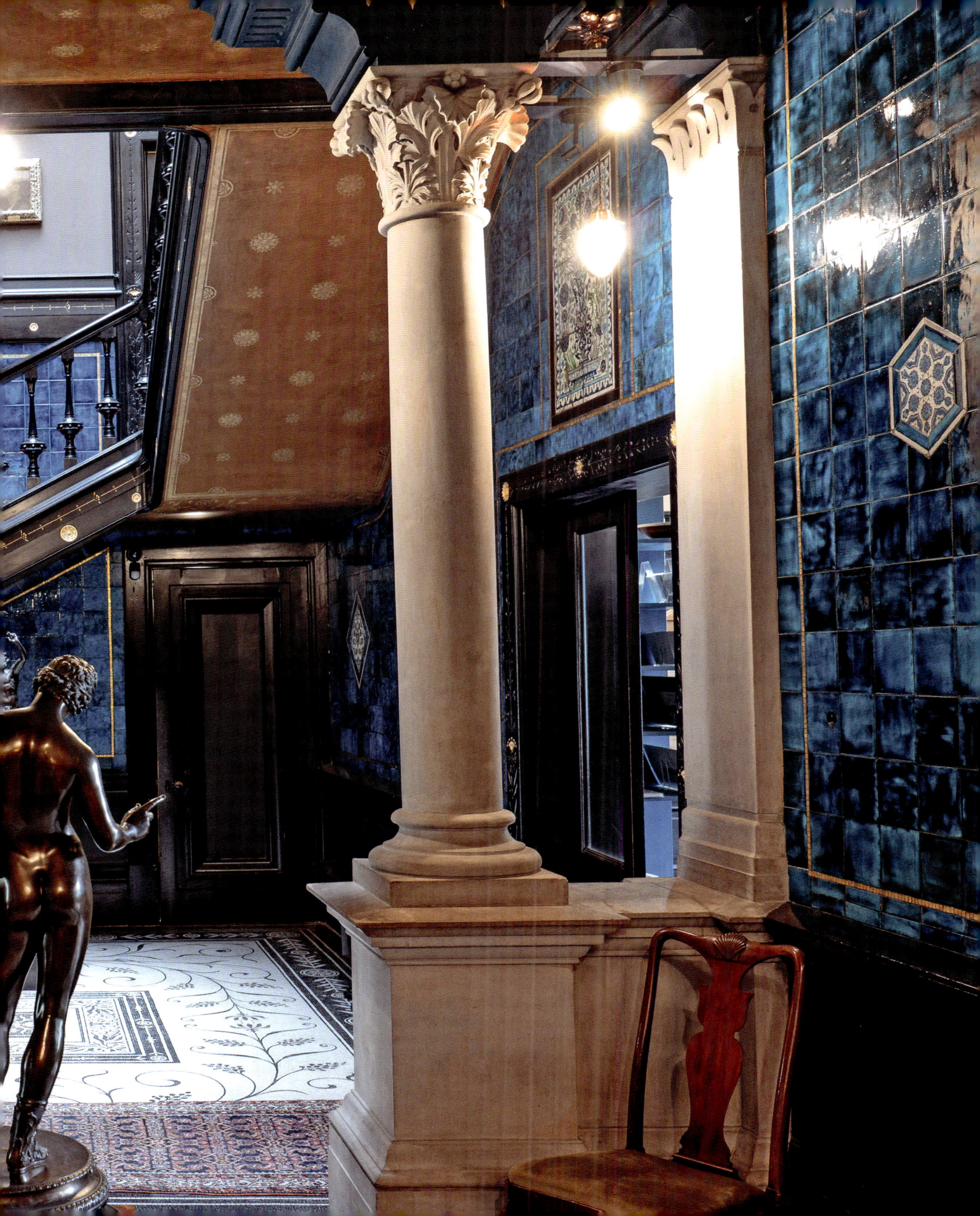

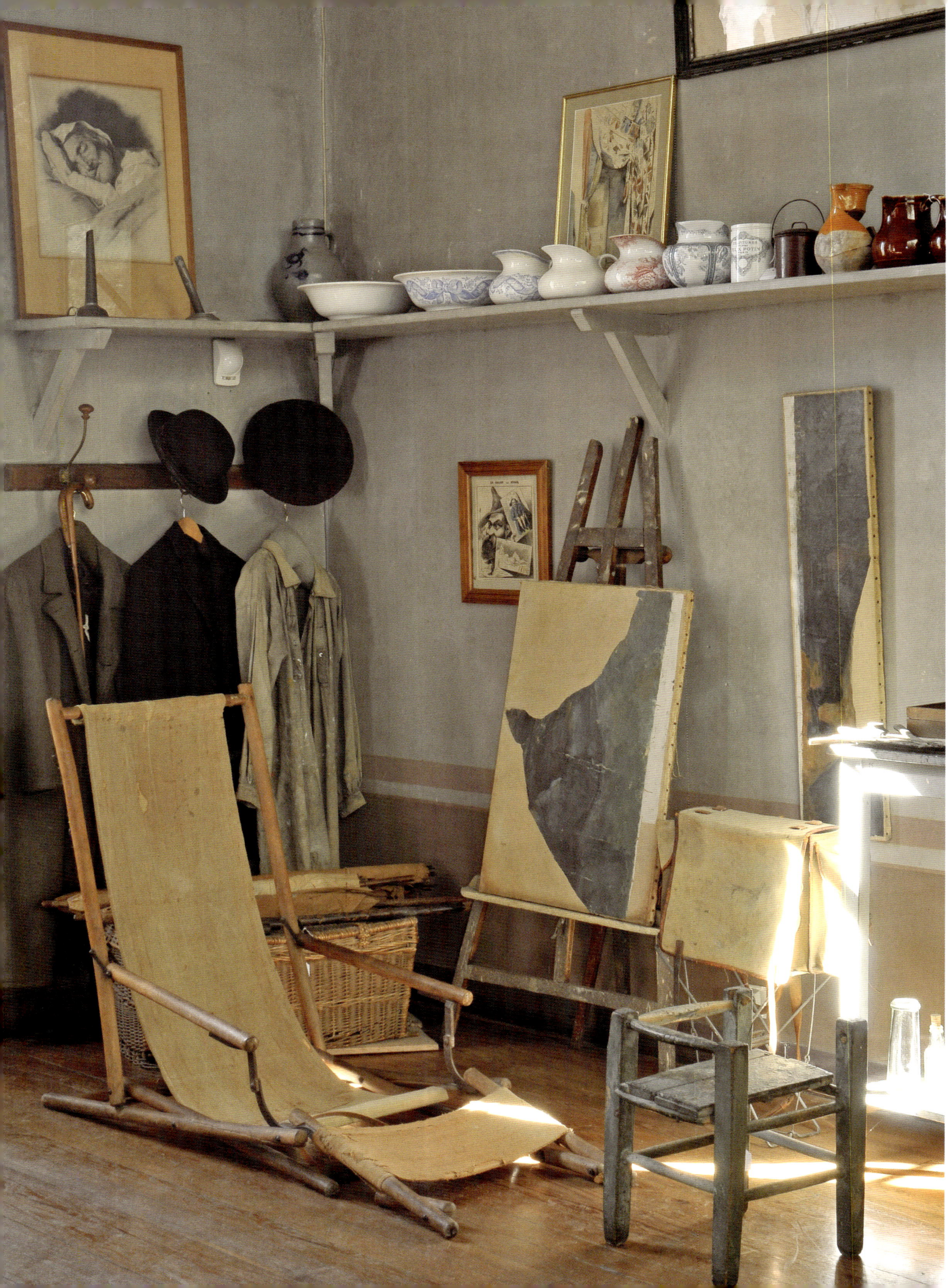

PAUL CÉZANNE

Aix-en-Provence, France

The eighteenth-century country house Jas de Bouffan in Aix-en-Provence, France, was home to the Cézanne family for forty years. Louis-Auguste Cézanne bought it in 1859, and his son, the artist Paul Cézanne (1839–1906), worked there often. It was his favourite place, where he first began painting *en plein air* (in the open air) and invented his unique approach that inspired so many subsequent artists, prompting Picasso to declare: 'Cézanne is the father of us all.'

A reclusive adult, Paul Cézanne was the eldest child of forty-year-old Louis-Auguste Cézanne and twenty-four-year-old Anne-Elisabeth-Honorine Aubert. He was five years old when his parents married, and it was unusual for the time that his father acknowledged his illegitimate child. A successful businessman who ran both a millinery business and a bank, Louis-Auguste was sixty years old when he bought the Jas de Bouffan, which had once been the home of the governor of Provence. He aimed to raise his social standing, for despite his wealth and business success, he was not respected – partly because he and Anne-Elisabeth had not married before the births of their first two children, and partly because he had made his living from millinery and money-lending, both generally perceived as dubious occupations. He decided his son should take a respectable profession, and so, by the age of twenty, Cézanne was reluctantly studying at the Faculty of Law at the University of Aix-en-Provence. In his spare time, however, he took drawing and painting lessons with a local artist.

PROVENCE AND PARIS

Built in 1750 on a vast plot of land, the Jas de Bouffan comprised a farm, outbuildings, a caretaker's house, a large pond, fountains and an orangery, and it had mature chestnut trees lining the drive. As the railway did not arrive in Aix-en-Provence until the end of the nineteenth century, the Jas de Bouffan's location was isolated and peaceful. It was there that Cézanne first painted in the open air, and where he worked out his radical approach to painting that changed the history of art.

As soon as Louis-Auguste bought the dilapidated Jas de Bouffan, renovations began. He allowed his son to use the shabby salon as a kind of bedsit and to paint four panels to decorate the room for when the refurbishments were underway. He painted colourful allegories of the four seasons and then a portrait of his father reading a newspaper. He later had a studio in the attic and over the next few years, he also completed religious paintings and portraits. By then, he had decided that painting was his vocation and he stopped attending law lectures. Although he learned some traditional painting techniques at his local municipal art college, he was largely untutored and made up his own rules. His early works often expressed sensual and morbid themes in dark colours with heavy brush marks. They were scorned by most who saw them. His friend Émile Zola began trying to convince him to go to Paris, where there were art galleries, official annual Salon exhibitions, top-quality art tuition and the company of many fellow artists. Although he was usually quite solitary, in April 1861, Cézanne travelled to the French capital. Once there, he enrolled at a private, quite unconventional, popular art studio, the Académie Suisse, but he soon realised that life in Paris was not what he had expected. The disruption caused by its modernisation and rebuilding was difficult, and the other students at the Académie Suisse teased him about his southern accent and awkward manner; so, disillusioned and despondent, he returned to Aix, where he rejoined the local school of drawing for evening classes, and painted in the tranquil surroundings of the Jas de Bouffan during the day.

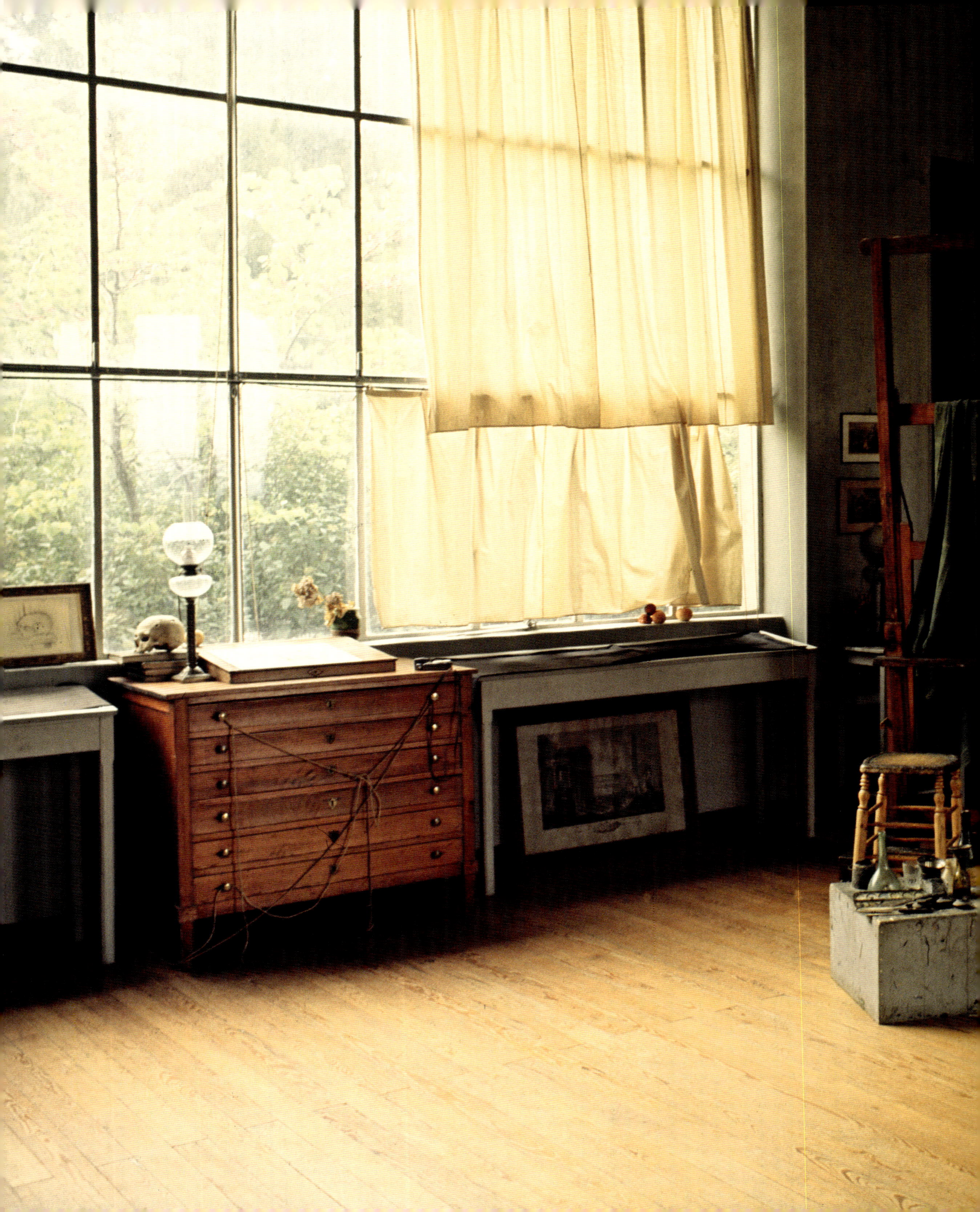

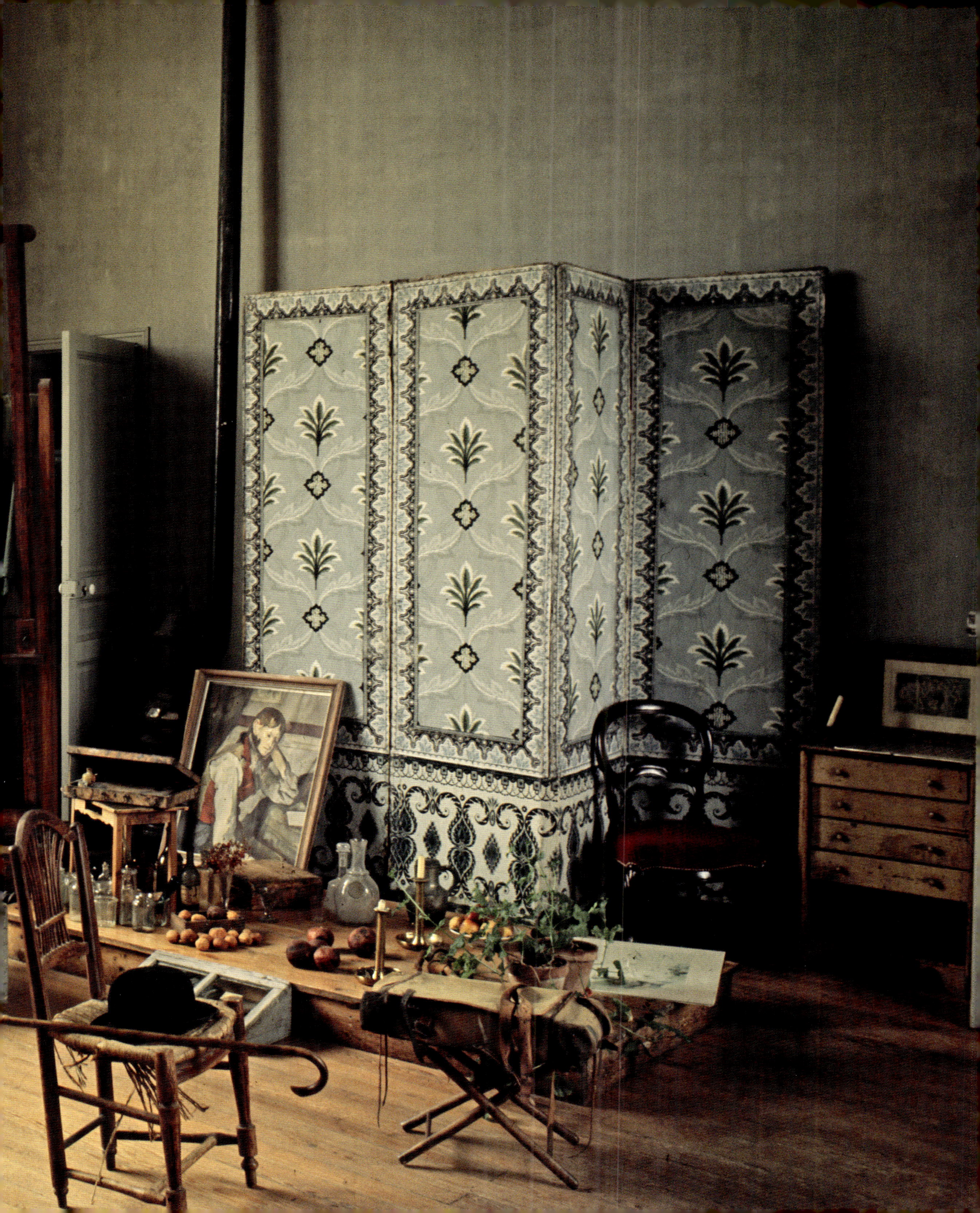

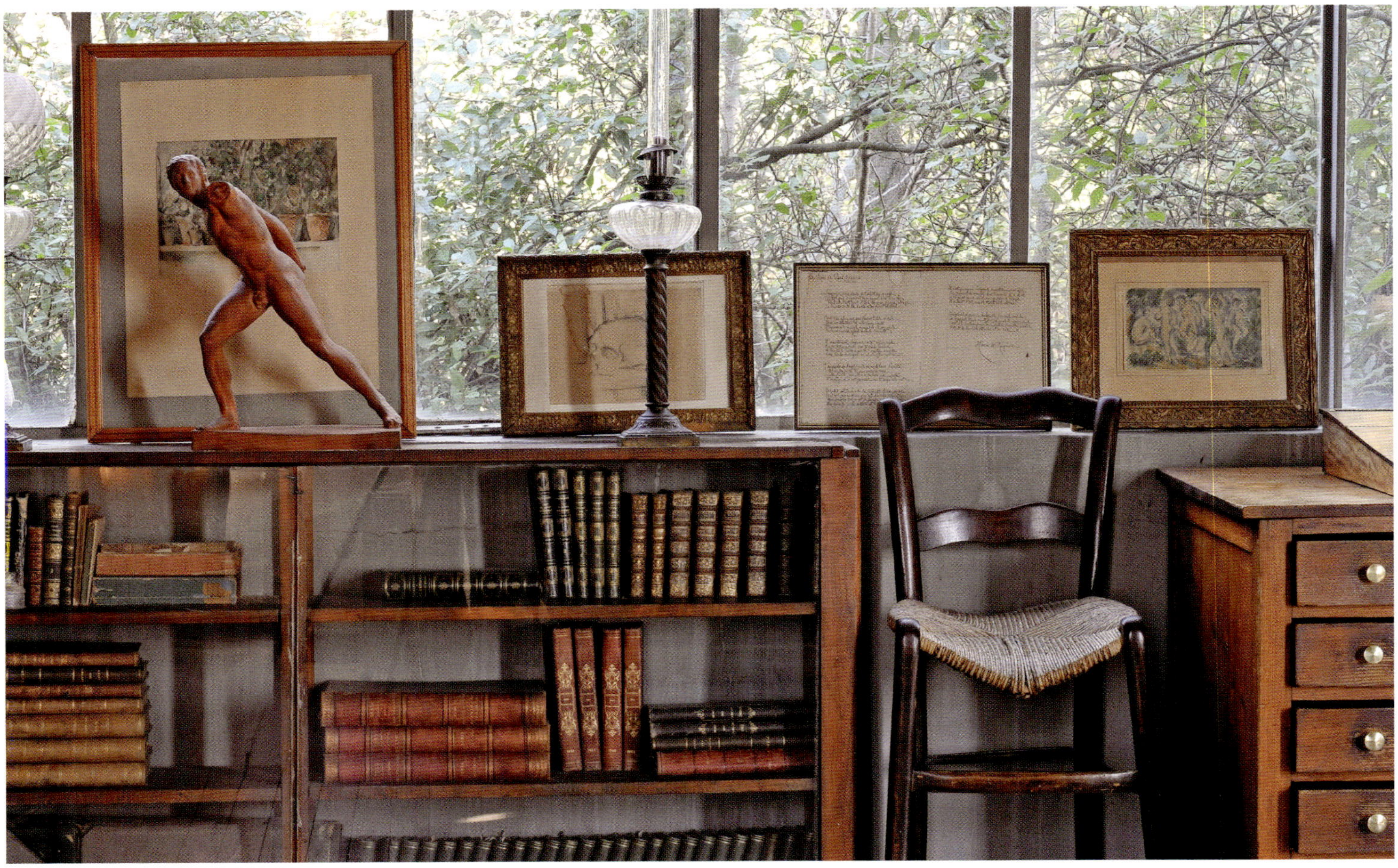

Above and previous page: The view from within the studio of Les Lauves in Aix. Beyond the large windows, olive and fig trees can be seen. From other windows was the view of Mont Sainte-Victoire.

Cézanne and his father were often at odds, but despite this he became unusually attached to his family home. The grand manor house with its vast grounds was, throughout his life, the place where he felt the most comfortable. However, determined to make more effort, he soon returned to Paris, re-enrolling at the Académie Suisse. Two paintings that he submitted to the 1863 Paris Salon were rejected and instead included in the Salon des Refusés, an alternative exhibition instigated by Napoleon III for all the artists rejected from that year's Salon. For the first time, art that did not necessarily conform to academic conventions was on public display. From then, Cézanne's painting method began to change.

NEW STUDIO

For the next few years, Cézanne spent some time in Paris but remained mainly in Aix. In the summer of 1870, as the Franco-Prussian War broke out, he painted his first version of *Mont Sainte-Victoire*. To avoid being conscripted, he hid in the Jas de Bouffan, but when the gendarmes came looking for him, he escaped to L'Éstaque, near Marseille, and stayed there for the rest of the war with his girlfriend Marie-Hortense Fiquet. After the birth of their son Paul in January 1872, he and Hortense moved to Auvers-sur-Oise, a small village north-west of Paris. There, he went on painting expeditions *en plein air* with Camille Pissarro, who inspired him to brighten his palette. Then he began looking for what he believed was the truth that lay beneath appearances, seeking to capture underlying structures and applying short marks in a patchwork style.

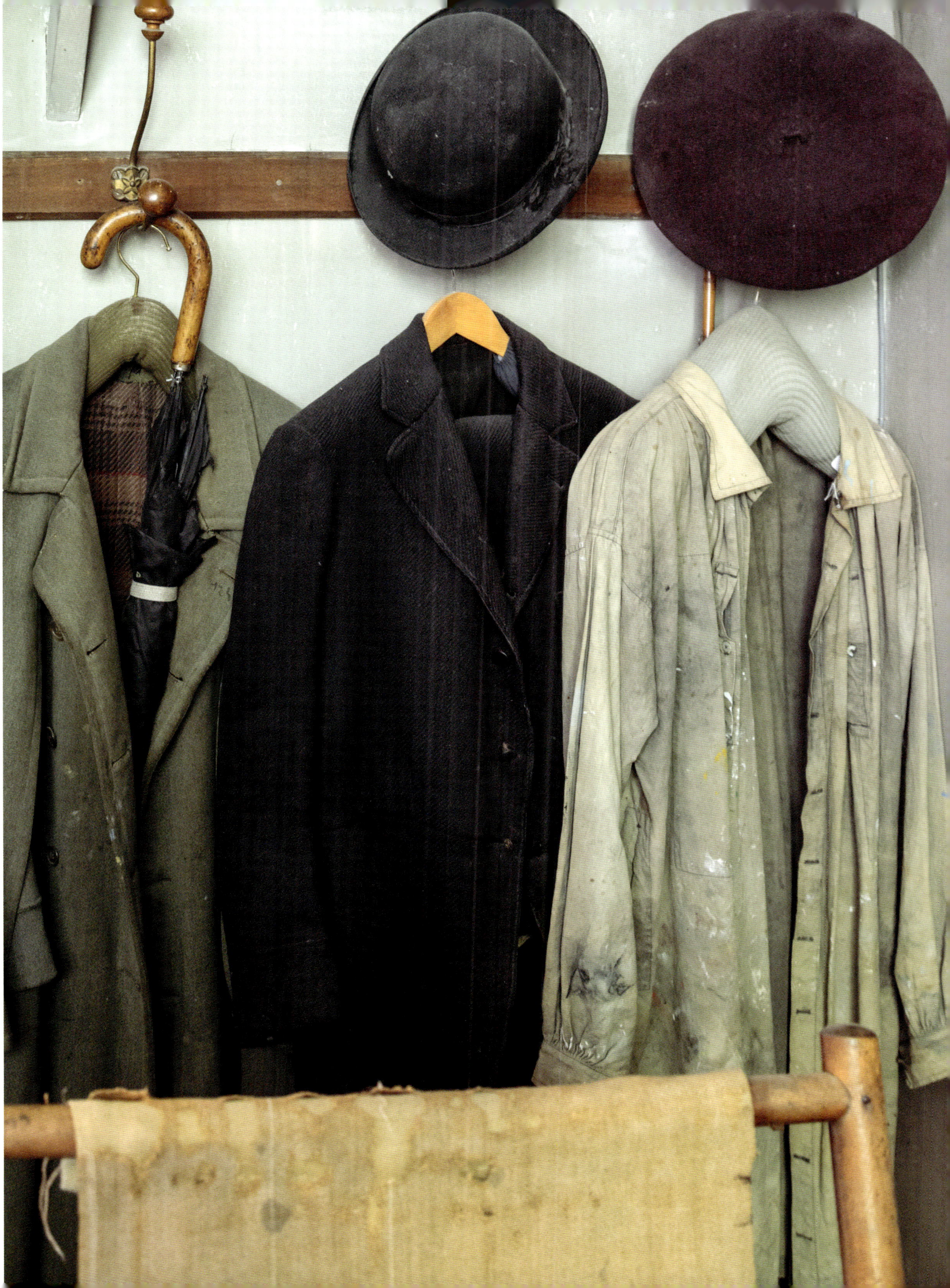

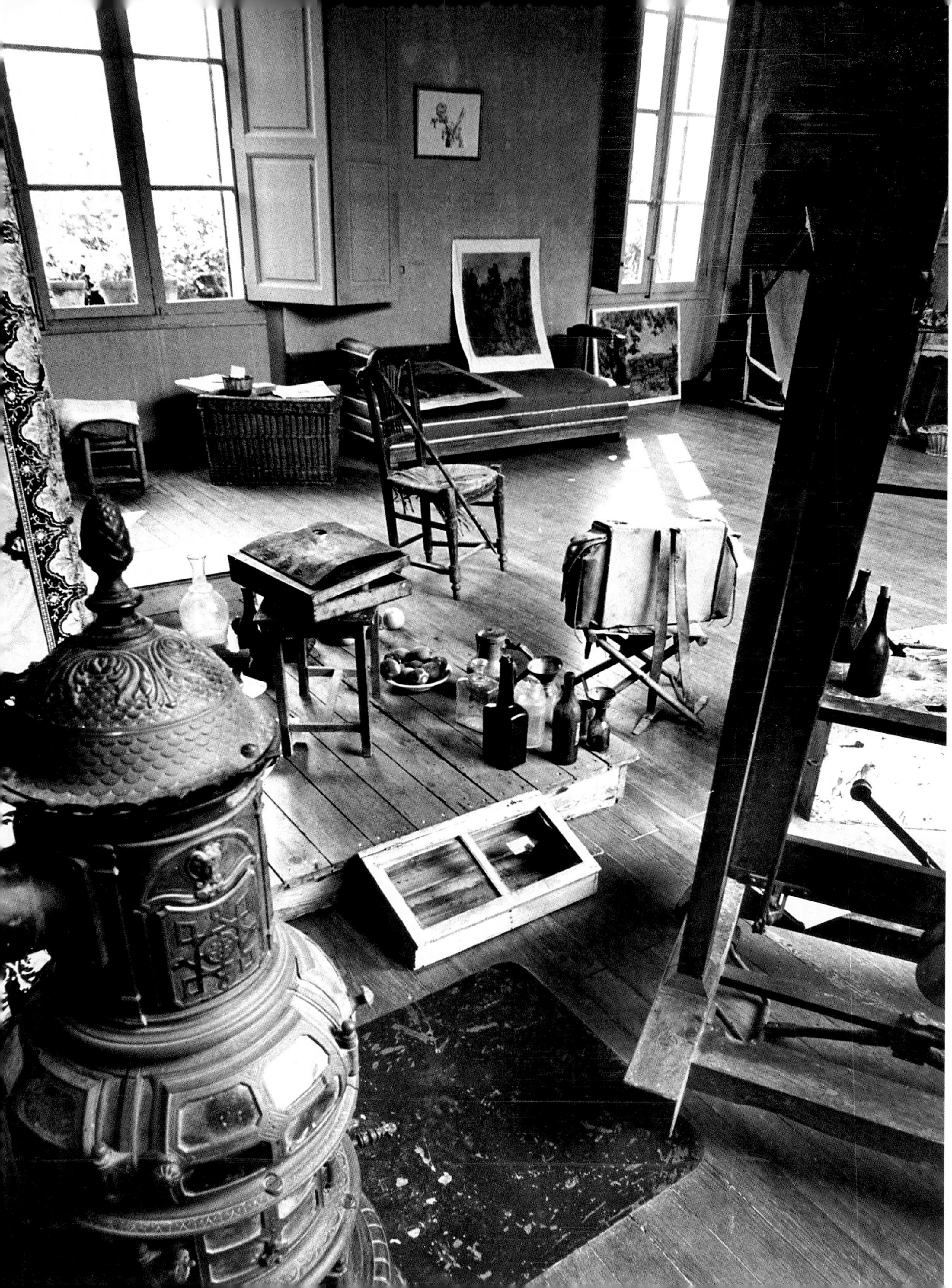

In 1886, Cézanne and Hortense married in Aix-en-Provence, legitimising their fourteen-year-old son. Later that year, Louis-Auguste died. Hortense returned to Paris with the teenage Paul, and Cézanne remained at the Jas de Bouffan with his mother. He worked in his attic studio, and in and around the grounds, painting the buildings, the land and the surrounding countryside, including Mont Sainte-Victoire, which rose up in the distance. From 1890, he also began using the estate's farmers as models. The familiarity of everything around him meant that he could concentrate on aspects beyond superficial appearances.

In October 1897, Cézanne's mother died. One of his brothers-in-law insisted on selling the estate so that the inheritance money could be split between Cézanne and his sisters; accordingly, in September 1899, the Jas de Bouffan, Cézanne's beloved home of forty years and subject of many of his paintings, was sold. The proceeds were divided between the three siblings.

Two years later, in 1901, he paid 2,000 francs for an old farm and 7,000 square metres (75,347 square feet) of land on the Lauves hill in Aix, on the other side of town from the Jas de Bouffan. Lush with olive and fig trees, and the Verdon Canal running alongside, the location gave a unique view of Mont Sainte-Victoire. Cézanne designed a simple two-storey house to be built there as his studio, and in September 1902, after ten months, Les Lauves was complete. On the ground floor are two lounges, a kitchen and a small pantry and a lavatory. Upstairs is the studio itself, lit from the south by two big windows and from the north by a glass roof. In wet or cold weather, Cézanne painted there – generally still lifes of fruit, jugs, bottles, vases, fabric, skulls and a small, plaster Cupid. In good weather, he painted outside: the surroundings and particularly Mont Sainte-Victoire.

Early each day, in any weather, Cézanne left his apartment and walked 1.2 kilometres (0.7 miles) to his studio. He worked there in the morning, then returned to Aix for lunch. In the afternoon, he returned to Les Lauves to paint until 5.30pm. One day in October 1906, while painting there, he was caught in a storm and fainted, soaked to the skin. He was taken home unconscious and died of pleurisy eight days later.

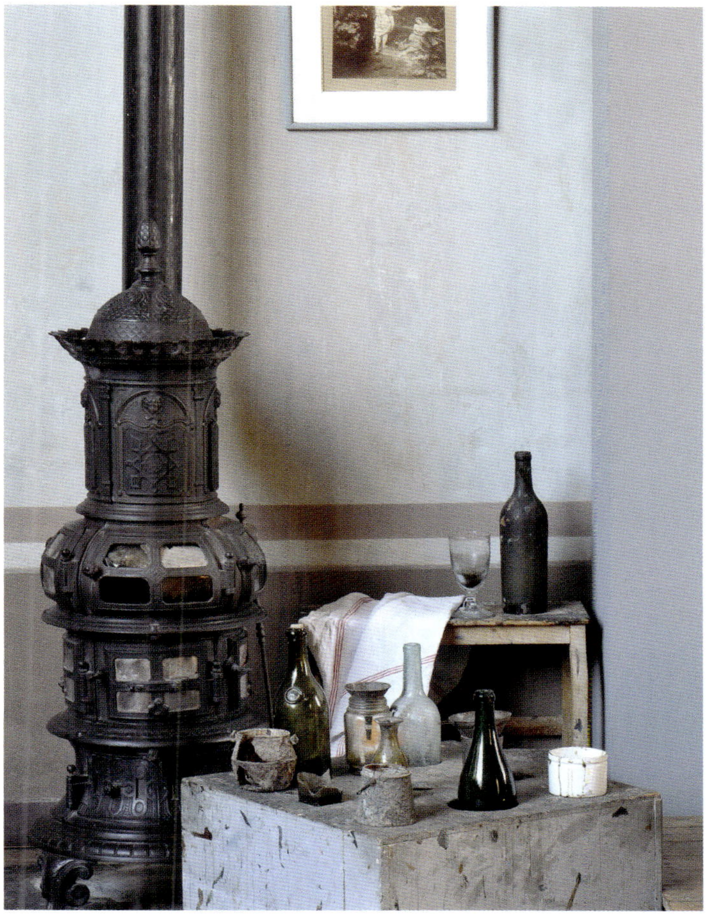

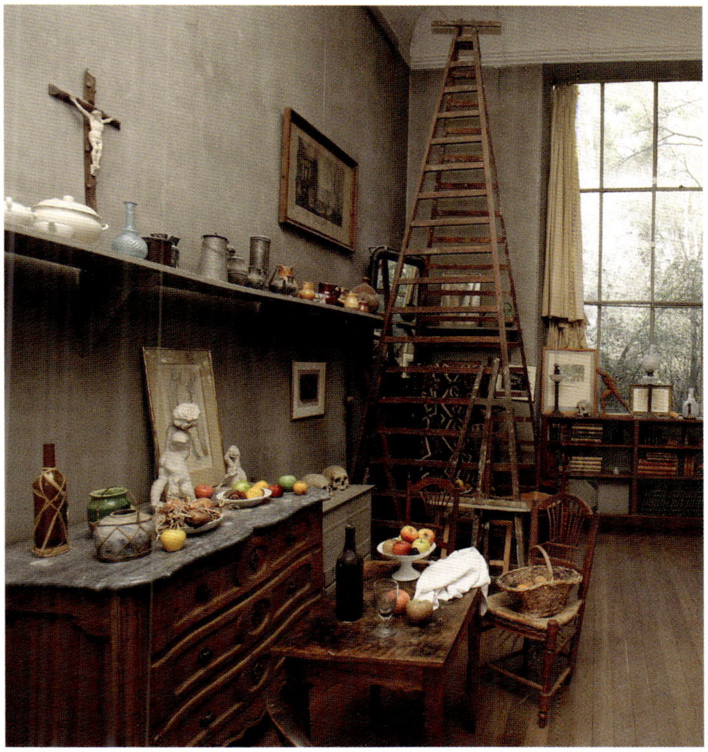

'The clear French landscape is as pure as a verse of Racine.'

Paul Cézanne

Above and opposite: Interior views of Cézanne's studio and some of the props he used. Many of the objects are familiar from his still life paintings.

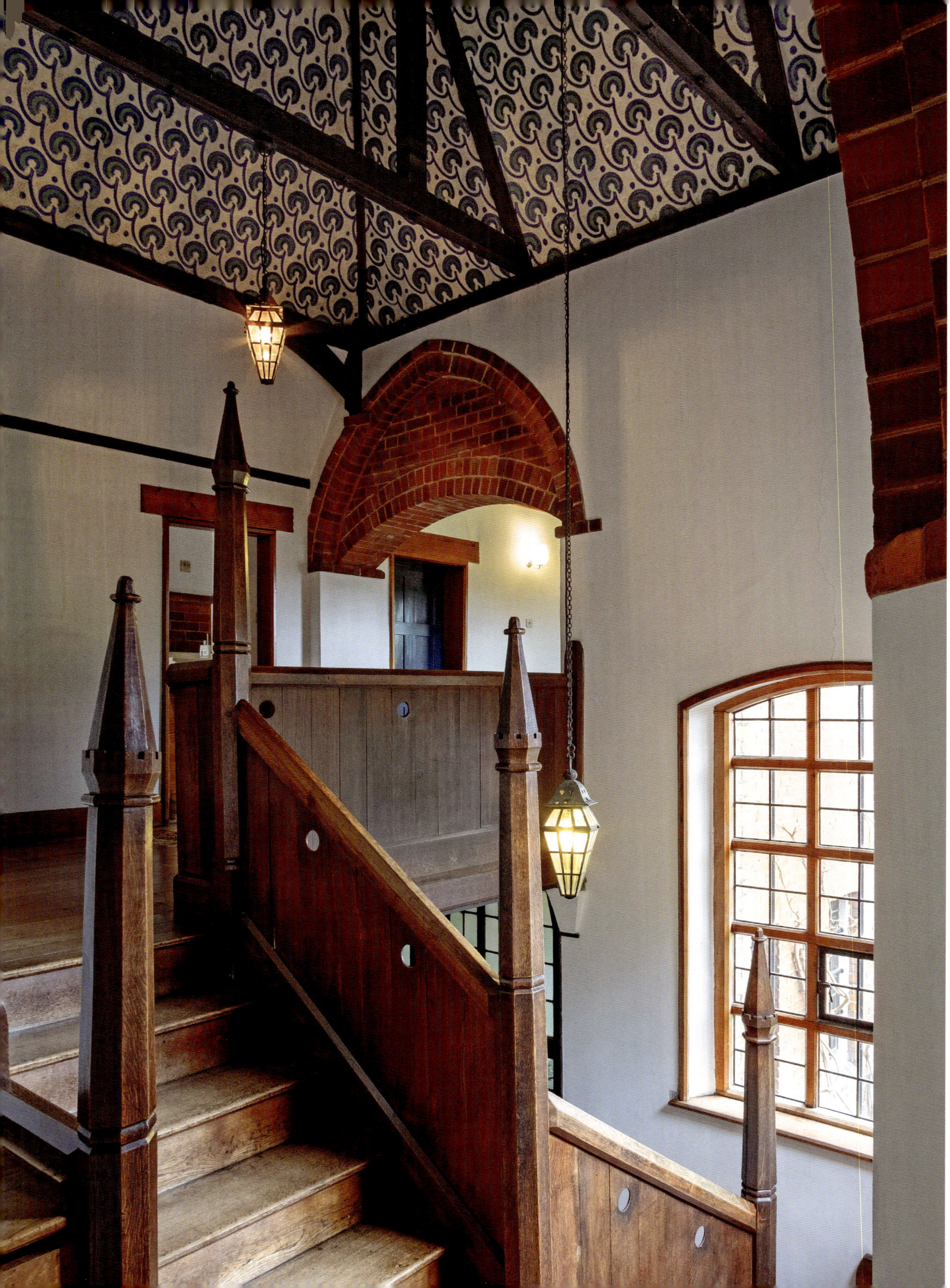

WILLIAM MORRIS

Bexleyheath, UK

Poet, painter, designer, typographer, polemicist, manufacturer and socialist William Morris (1834–96) married Jane Burden in 1859 and decided to build a home for them beyond London, but within commuting distance. He found the village of Upton – now Bexleyheath – in Kent, which suited his needs perfectly.

Strongly influenced by writer, philosopher and art critic John Ruskin, Morris was disturbed by the effects of the Industrial Revolution on the environment and society. He believed that cheap, factory-made goods had a negative effect on both those who made them and those who used them, and that good design helped to shape a better society.

Although prone to rages, and constantly challenging himself and others, Morris was a generous man with a close circle of friends. Morris, with his work ethic, concern for others, empathy with nature and the breadth of his achievements, initiated the Arts and Crafts movement that swept Britain and beyond from the mid-nineteenth century.

Using money he inherited, Morris bought an apple orchard and a meadow in the village of Upton, and commissioned his friend, the architect and designer Philip Webb, to design the house. Intending it to be both a family home and a place where he and his friends could meet and work, Morris followed his ideals that were based on his admiration for medieval art and literature. He especially strongly opposed the dehumanising effects of industrialisation, and insisted that all designs should be produced with craftsmanship and artisan skills. In this way, he believed that they would be better than those mass-produced goods that could be bought so cheaply, and they would ultimately create a happier society. Because of this belief, Morris was deeply involved with the design of his house, which became an early example of the Arts and Crafts movement.

USEFUL AND BEAUTIFUL

An imposing L-shaped building, Morris's house featured soaring gables and steeply pitched roof areas covered with red tiles, blending elements of Medieval, Tudor and Gothic architectural styles. Morris's friend, artist Gabriel Rossetti described the house as '...more a poem than a house...'

Most fashionable houses of the period were covered in stucco, but Morris's home was made of the unadorned red brick that inspired its name, Red House. Also contrasting with contemporary houses was the way it embraced natural light. Windows were sized and positioned to suit this and the designs of the rooms, rather than any external symmetry, so they included various styles, such as tall casements, hipped dormers, and oriel, sash and bull's eye windows. The asymmetrical plan gave the house an air of informality. On the ground floor were a large hall, dining room, library, morning room and kitchen, and on the first floor were the main living rooms, the drawing room, a studio and bedrooms. Also living in the house were servants, including cook, housemaid, nanny and groom – and they had their own quarters.

In June 1860, with the building complete, William and Jane Morris moved into Red House, and he set about furnishing and decorating the interiors to his own vision of beauty. Webb designed tables, dressers, chairs, cupboards, copper candlesticks and glass tableware, while Rossetti, his new wife – the artist Elizabeth (Lizzie) Siddal – and Morris's other close friends, Edward Burne-Jones and his new wife, the painter and engraver Georgiana Burne-Jones, all helped to create other aspects of the décor. They painted wall murals and furniture, stencilled the ceiling, and created embroideries, tapestries and stained glass. In reference to the medieval pilgrimage route to Canterbury, Morris called the

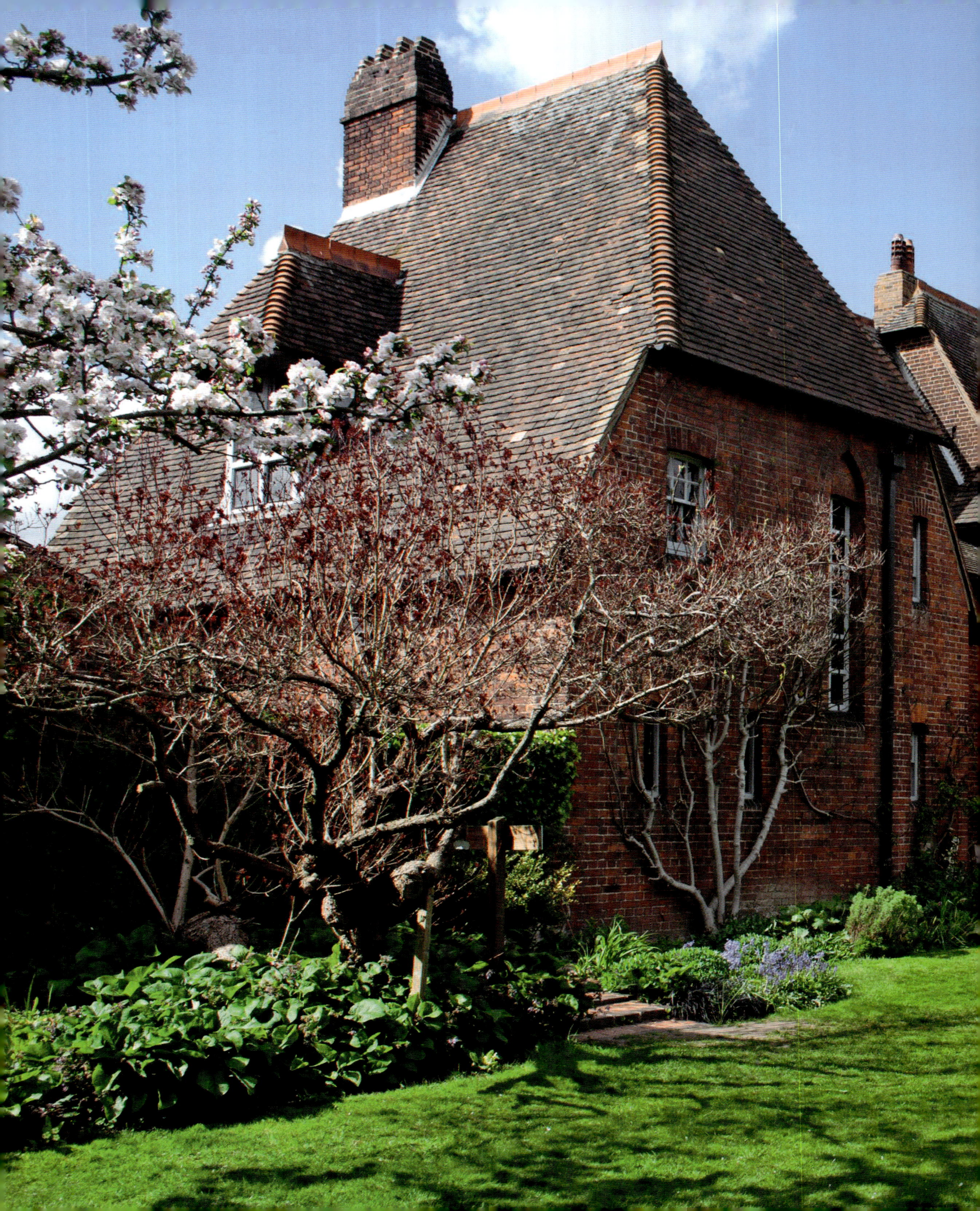

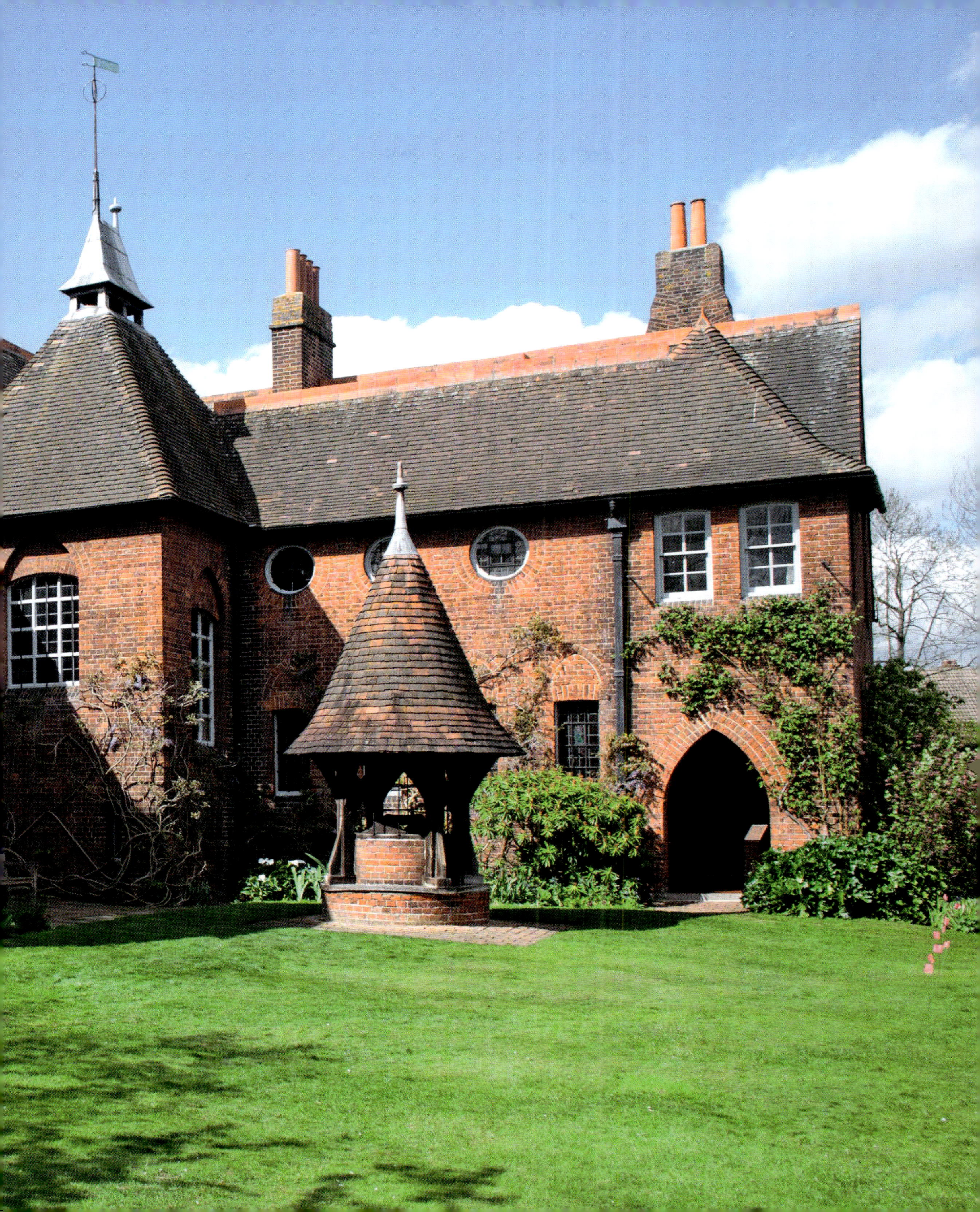

passage that connected the main hallway to the back door 'The Pilgrim's Rest'. Wrapped around the house, the garden was divided into four small squares by rose trellises. Elsewhere, there was an abundance of lavender, rosemary, lilies, sunflowers, white jasmine, roses, honeysuckle and passion flowers.

Over the next five years, Morris and his friends added to the house and garden. Not all of it was finished. The walls of the staircase were intended to feature a medieval-style mural painted by Burne-Jones, depicting scenes from the Trojan War, and the wall of the hall beneath was intended to feature a painting of warships carrying ancient Greek soldiers to Troy. On the hallway cupboard, Morris began, but never completed, a painting based on Thomas Malory's tale of Sir Lancelot, Sir Tristram and La Belle Iseult. Morris's sitters for this included Jane, the mathematician Charles Faulkner (another of his friends), the Burne-Joneses and Lizzie Siddal. In the dining room, a series of female heroines, based on Geoffrey Chaucer's 'The Legend of Good Women', were to be embroidered by Jane and her sister Bessie, but only a few were completed.

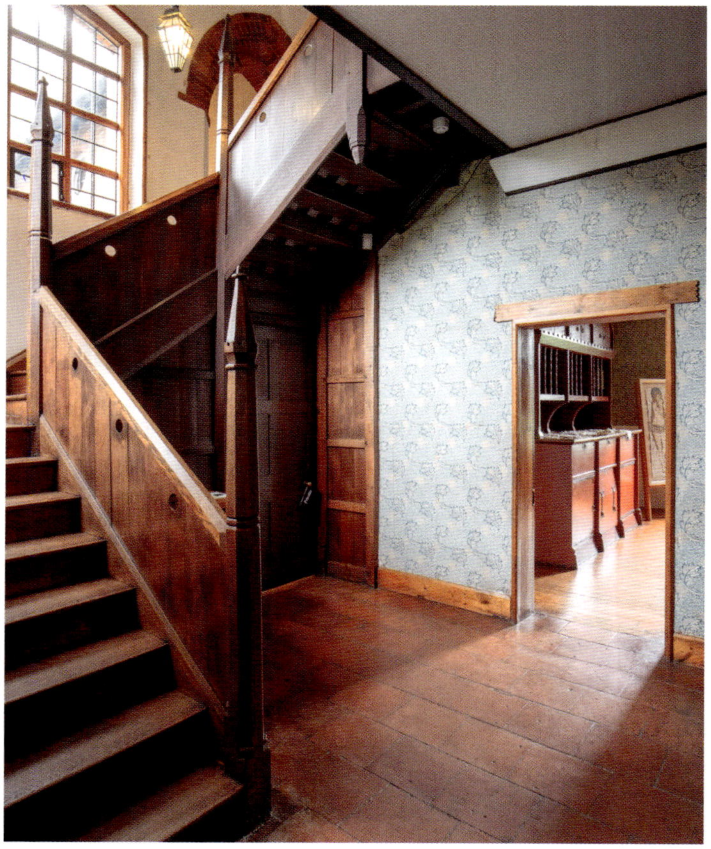

Previous page: The exterior of the house, with its unadorned red brick that inspired the name Red House.
Above: The predominantly wooden entrance to Red House, with its miniature crenelations and spires on the railings are examples of Webb's Neo-Gothic detailing.
Opposite: Side view of the settle in the drawing room at Red House.

LIGHT AND LAUGHTER

As well as light, the house was filled with laughter, as Morris's friends frequently stayed, including the Burne-Joneses; the Rossettis; Faulkner and his two sisters; Webb; the poet, playwright, novelist and critic Algernon Swinburne; artist Ford Madox Brown; engineer and amateur artist Peter Paul Marshall; and painter and illustrator Arthur Hughes. When they were not decorating the house, these friends ate, drank, played games and practical jokes, sang songs and put on plays. Despite his sudden bursts of temper that soon subsided, Morris was a warm and exceptionally welcoming host.

Soon after moving in, the couple had two daughters: Jane 'Jenny' Morris and Mary 'May' Morris, who later recalled their 'idyllic' childhoods at the house. Yet there were problems in the Morris marriage and Jane became increasingly close to Rossetti, especially after Lizzie died. It changed the dynamic of the group. Before that became apparent, however, the closeness of the friends, and their artistic experimentation and invention inspired them to found a decorative arts company: Morris, Marshall, Faulkner & Co. in 1861, which they nicknamed 'the Firm'. The partners were Morris, Marshall, Faulkner, Madox Brown, Burne-Jones and Rossetti. With premises at Red Lion Square in London, they took on commissions for murals, carving, stained glass, metalwork and furniture making, asserting the importance of artists creating designs individually with artisan skills, rather than everything being mass-produced. Other philosophies that Morris sought to follow were affordability and anti-elitism. With this in mind, when looking for additional staff, they employed boys from the Industrial Home for Destitute Boys in central London. However, the Firm did not generate large profits; the notion of being affordable to poorer people could not be realised, and Morris faced increasing financial strain.

To help with financial constraints, and to reflect their friendship, Morris and Burne-Jones devised a plan for a second wing of Red House to be constructed, so that their two families could live in close proximity and they could all enjoy the dwelling. However, Georgiana contracted scarlet fever and miscarried their second child, and the Burne-Joneses abandoned the plan. Having initially intended to spend the rest of his life there, Morris found that the house was simply too expensive to run. After only five years of living there, in 1865, he moved his family to a flat in Queen Square, Bloomsbury, and he sold Red House.

'Have nothing in your house that you do not know to be useful or believe to be beautiful.'

William Morris

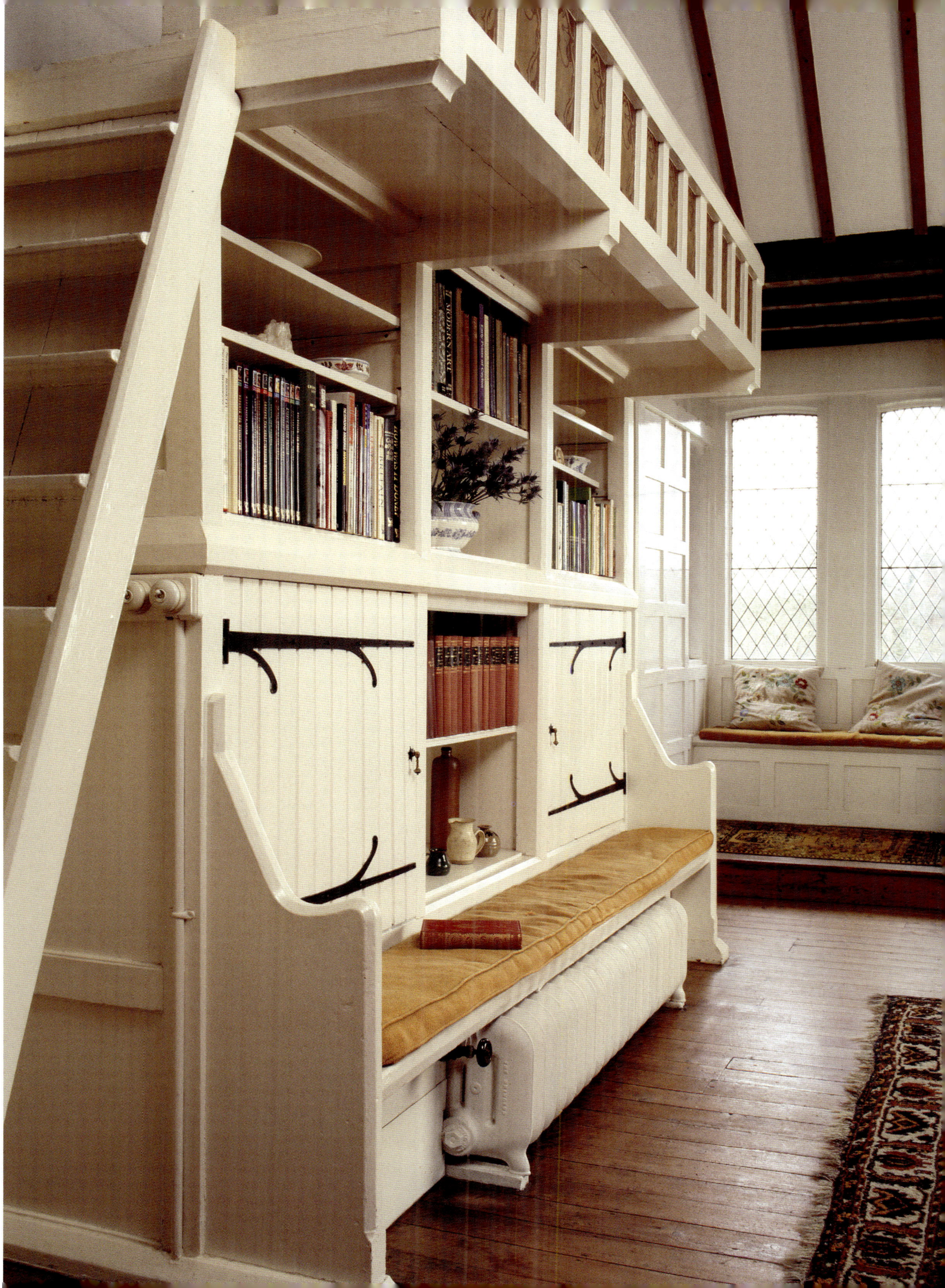

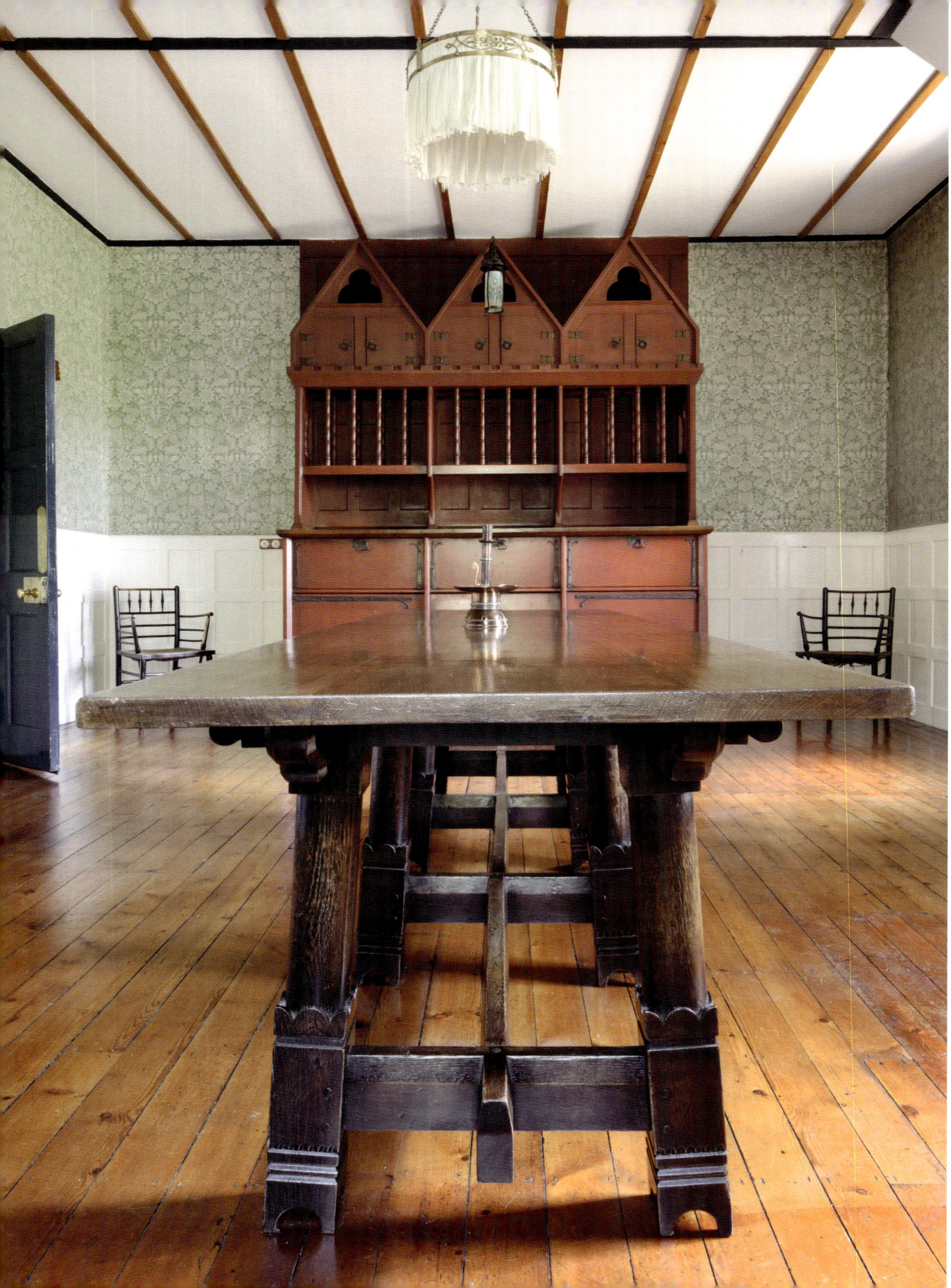

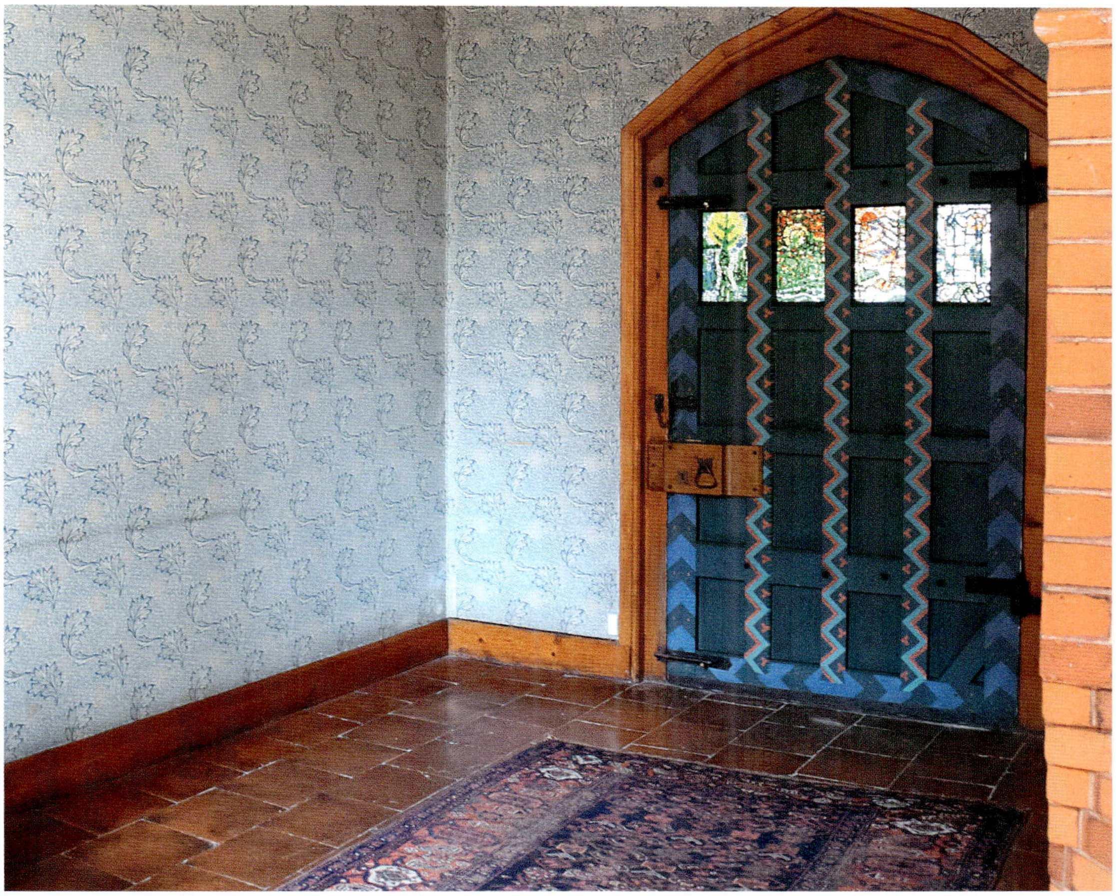

Above: The hallway intentionally communicates a sense of light and space on entry to the house.
Opposite: The table and dresser in the dining room.
Following page: Detail of a settle in the hallway at Red House, painted by William Morris.

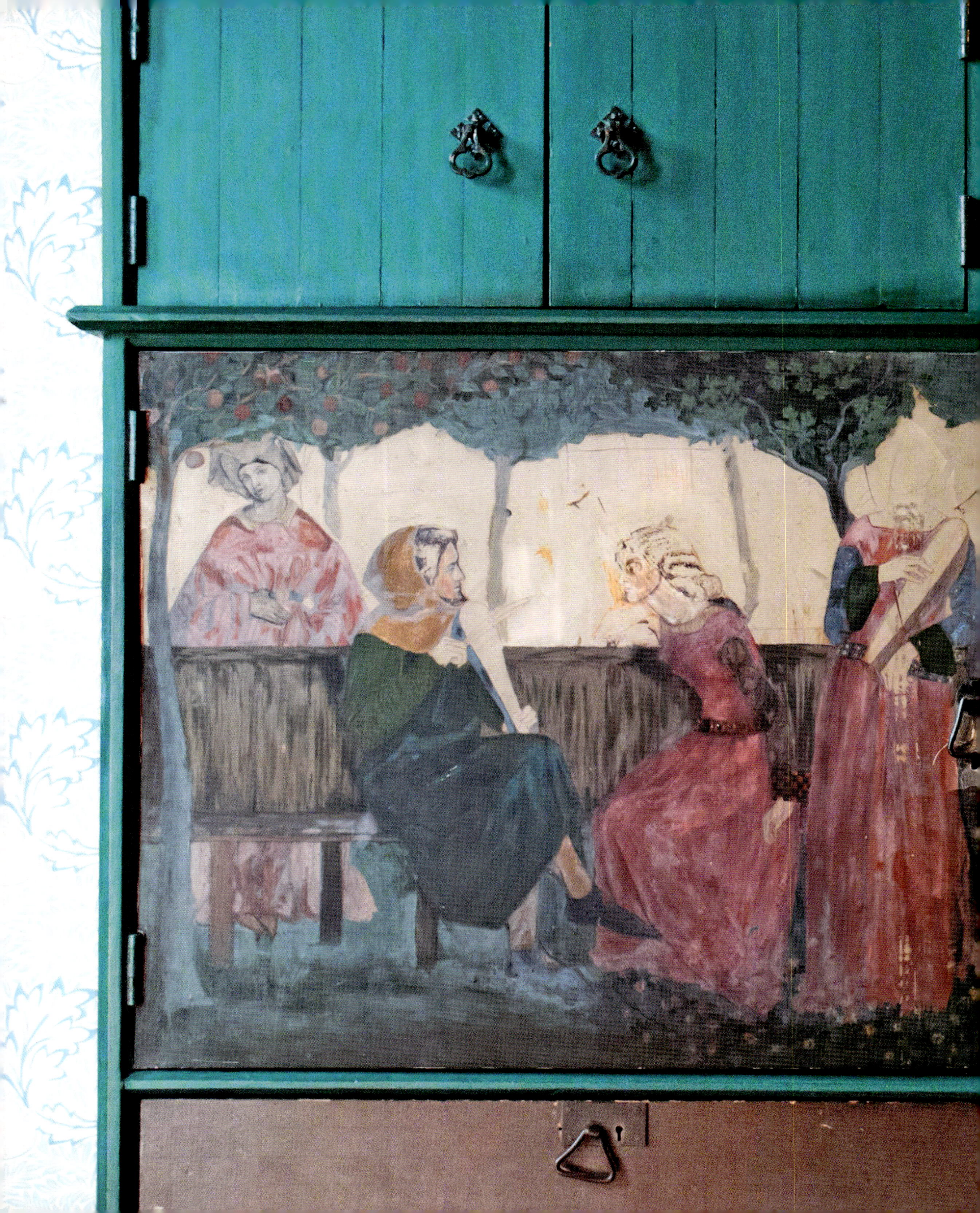

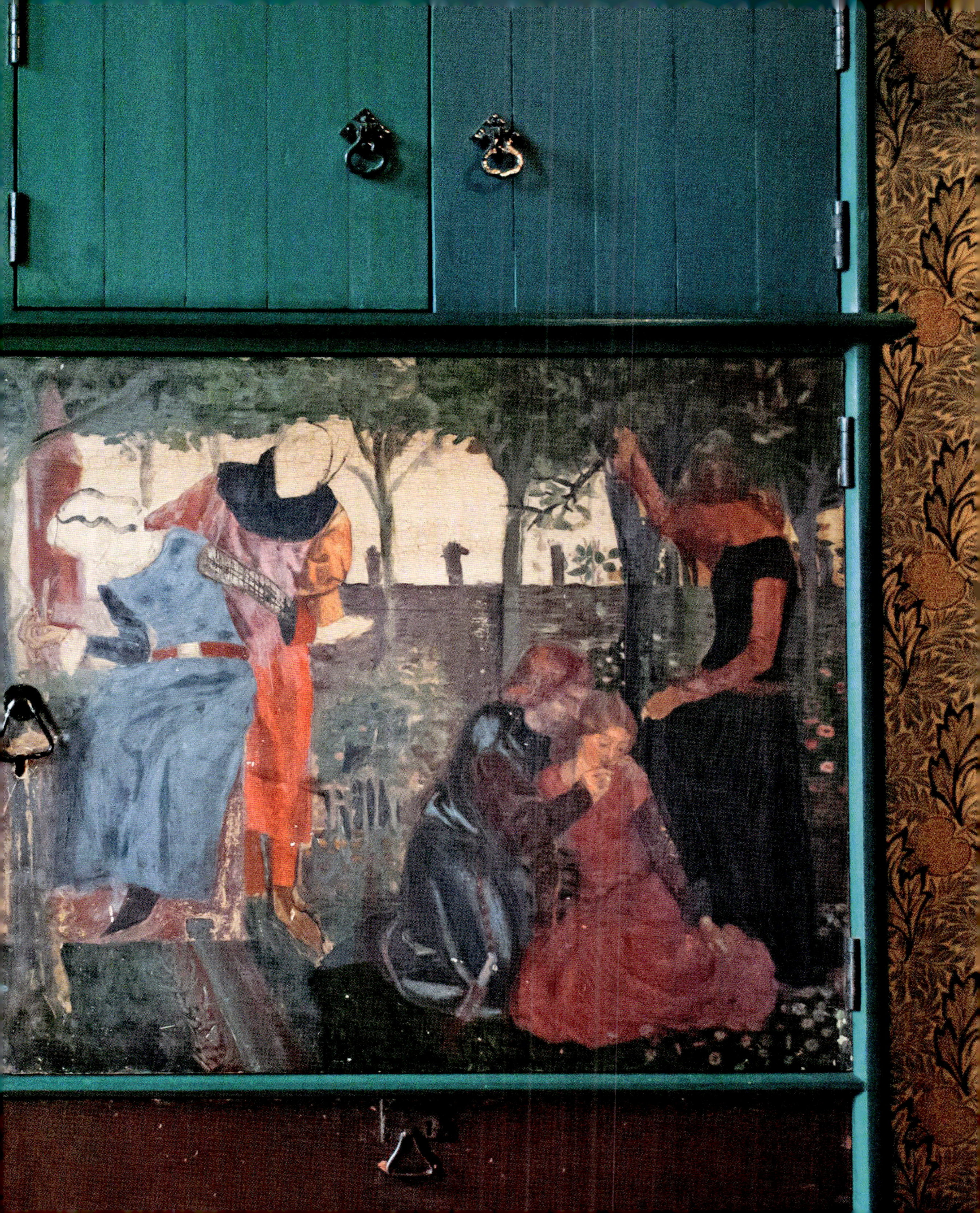

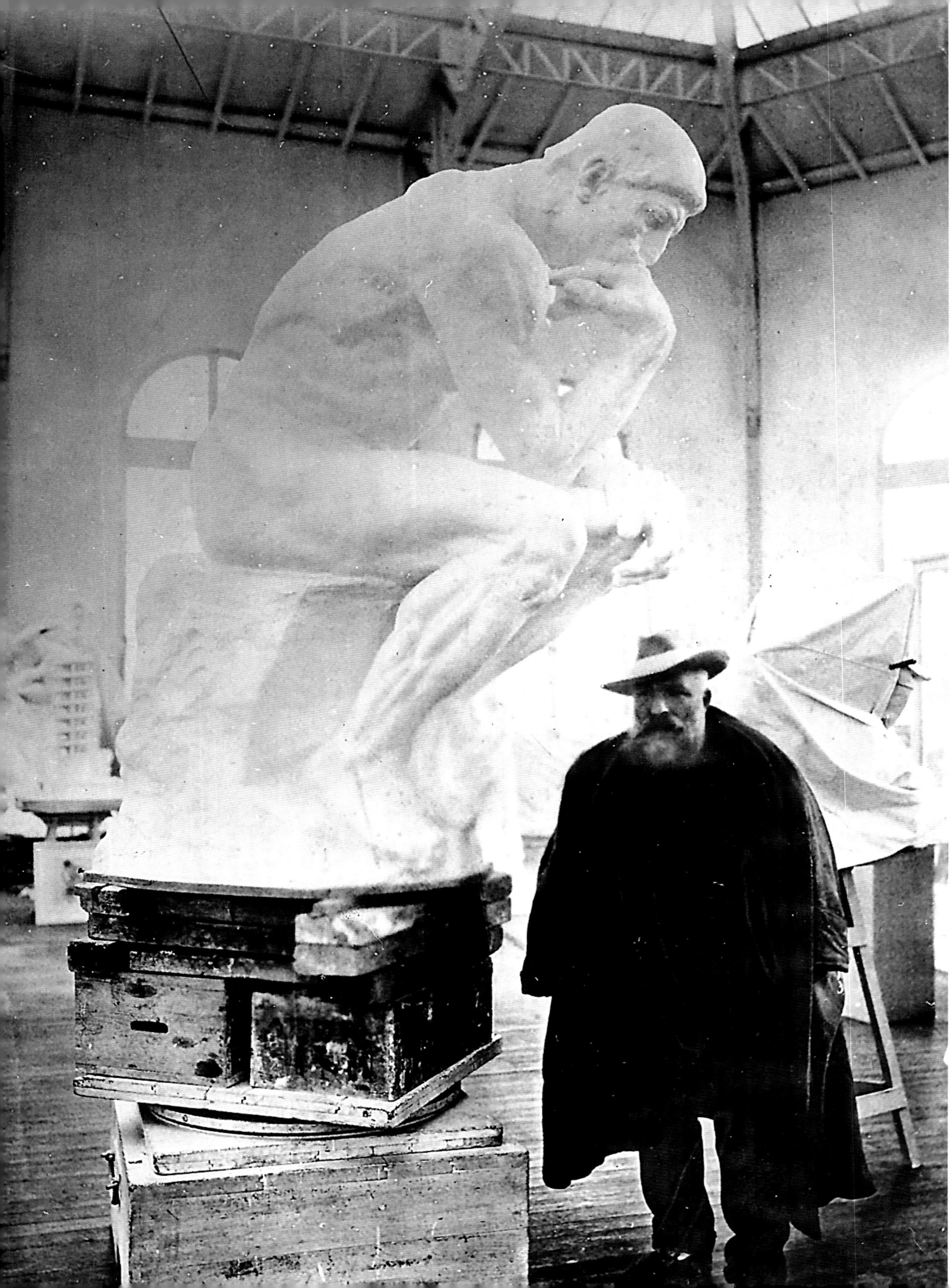

AUGUSTE RODIN

Meudon, France

Twenty minutes south-west of Paris by train, on a hill on the south bank of the River Seine, is the municipality of Meudon, where the sculptor Auguste Rodin (1840–1917) spent the last two decades of his life. In 1895, when he was fifty-five, he bought a fairly modest, tall brick-and-stone Louis XIII-style château there called Villa des Brillants.

Situated only 9 kilometres (just under 6 miles) from the centre of Paris, the Villa des Brillants was surrounded by gardens, and Rodin added a studio to the house, as he was inspired by the peaceful surroundings. From that time, he executed most of his work in Meudon, where he lived with his long-term partner Rose Beuret.

Rodin was born in a working-class district of Paris to parents of modest means and was largely self-educated. He began drawing seriously as a child, but despite his early artistic promise, he was rejected three times by the prestigious École des Beaux-Arts in Paris. So for the next two decades, he worked in various studios, mainly earning his living as an ornamental sculptor, producing decorative objects and architectural embellishments. When he finally created his first artwork in 1877, *The Age of Bronze*, it was so lifelike that he was accused of sculptural cheating, but was later cleared. He eventually became recognised for his naturalistic figures that convey warmth, movement and emotion, contrasting dramatically with the then-fashionable smooth, classical-looking sculptures of gods or muses. In time, his lifelike figures in natural poses came to be compared to the works of Michelangelo and he is still often acclaimed as the father of modern sculpture. So despite his years of struggle, by 1900, his reputation was established and he was earning vast sums of money for his art. Prestigious commissions kept coming, and while he was working on those, his many assistants produced copies of his works, as they were so much in demand. By that year, he employed almost fifty people, including studio assistants and students, and although he continued to go to his Paris studios often, his major creative work was undertaken in Meudon.

'WORK, ALWAYS WORK'

From 1905 to 1906, the Austrian poet and novelist Rainer Maria Rilke acted as Rodin's secretary, and wrote a long essay on him and his work. Rilke lived at the Villa des Brillants and wrote to his wife about it: 'The effect of the vast hall filled with light, where all these dazzling white sculptures seem to gaze out at you from behind high glass doors, like creatures in an aquarium, is extremely powerful. It makes a huge, a tremendous impression.'

Initially, Rodin allowed the estate to grow wild. Paths and the garden were overgrown, and the house itself was sparsely furnished. There was no gas or electricity, no soft furnishings – only hard chairs and trestle tables – and no paintings on the walls. The only decorations he displayed were his collection of more than 6,000 antiques that included terracotta pots, Etruscan artefacts and ancient Greek figure sculptures. One of his many visitors recounted that his home 'gives one the feeling that the act of living itself plays hardly any role for him'. He often told Rilke: 'Work, always work.' Indeed, work for him took up almost all of every day. Although his sculptures appear spontaneous and naturalistic, each was the product of a huge effort. He began with several rapidly executed life drawings, recording his models in many different poses and from various angles. To create each sculpture, he modelled clay into his desired form and then made a mould from it. Finally, he produced several casts of each original, so that he could create numerous versions. He also made plaster casts of his marble

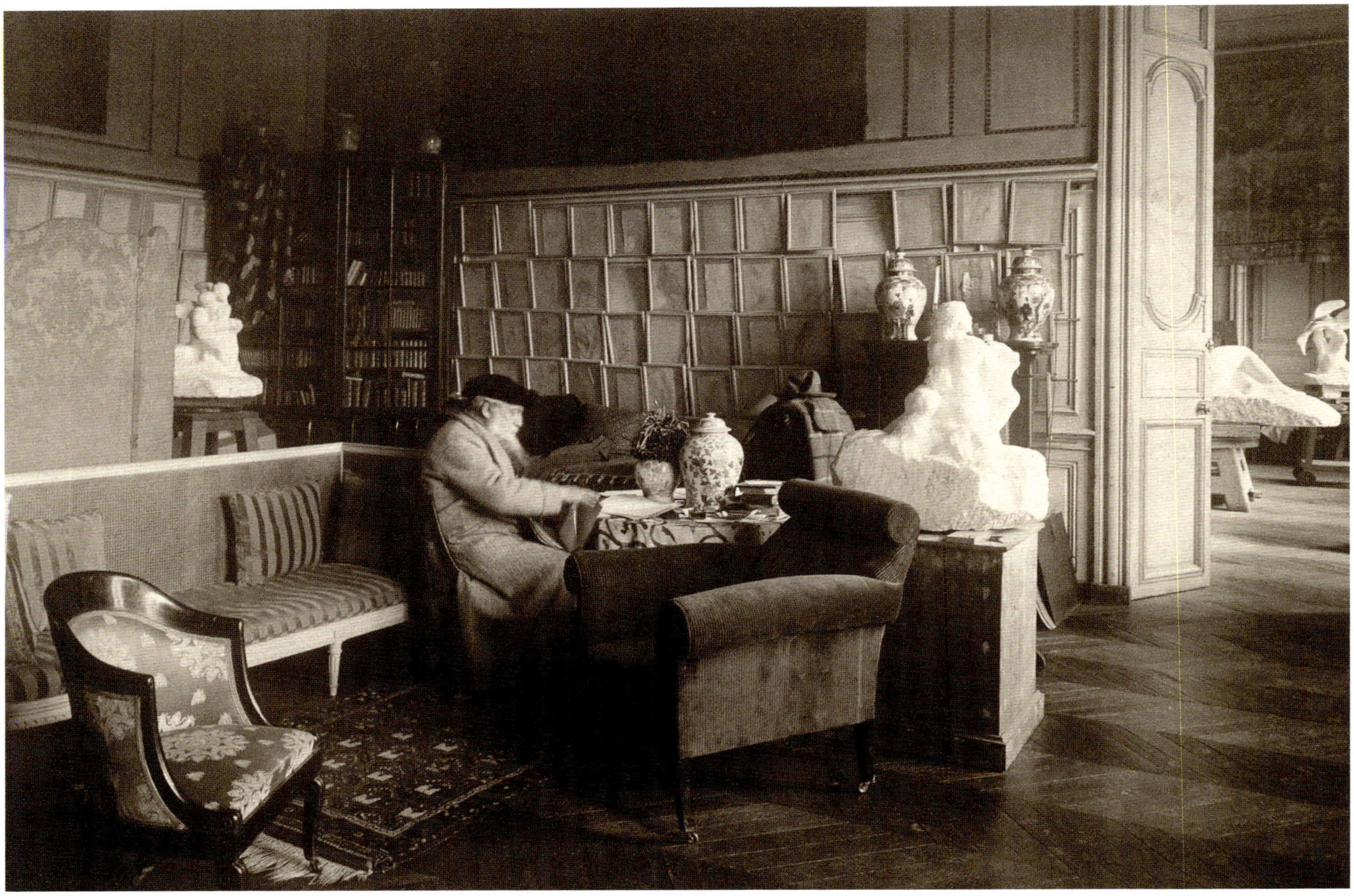

Above: Rodin pictured consulting some documents at home in 1912.
Opposite: Rodin's studio-museum at Meudon.

sculptures, so that they could be cast in bronze and for these, he used either the lost-wax method or sand casting. At first, he did all this himself, but later in life, when he became successful, his artworks were so much in demand that his assistants and students undertook much of the work, under his direction.

EXTENDING THE PLOT

Rodin spent most of the 1890s suffering with depression and was frequently unable to work, but by 1900, he had become the highest paid artist in the world. The Exposition Universelle in Paris of that year featured a pavilion that he built in front of the Alma Bridge, with money from patrons. He displayed over 150 of his sculptures and drawings there, and it attracted huge crowds and commissions from across Europe and parts of America. After the Exposition closed in March 1901, he had the pavilion dismantled and rebuilt in the grounds at Meudon.

With his increased wealth, Rodin made some improvements to Villa des Brillants. He had electricity installed and built new studios and housing for his many assistants – for a time, over forty of his assistants and friends stayed there. He also bought a neighbouring plot of land and, between 1907 and 1910, he salvaged and installed part of the façade of the Château d'Issy, a small French Baroque château that had stood on the outskirts of Paris but burned down in 1871 during the Franco-Prussian war. Rodin had it reassembled in the garden, so it looked like an ancient ruin. He also hired Jean, a handyman, and Madeleine, a cook, which lessened Rose's responsibilities, although she continued to help look after their animals, which included their horses Moca, Quinola and Rataplan; dogs Dora and Lulu; two cows – one called Coquette – chickens; swans; and a guenon (a type of monkey).

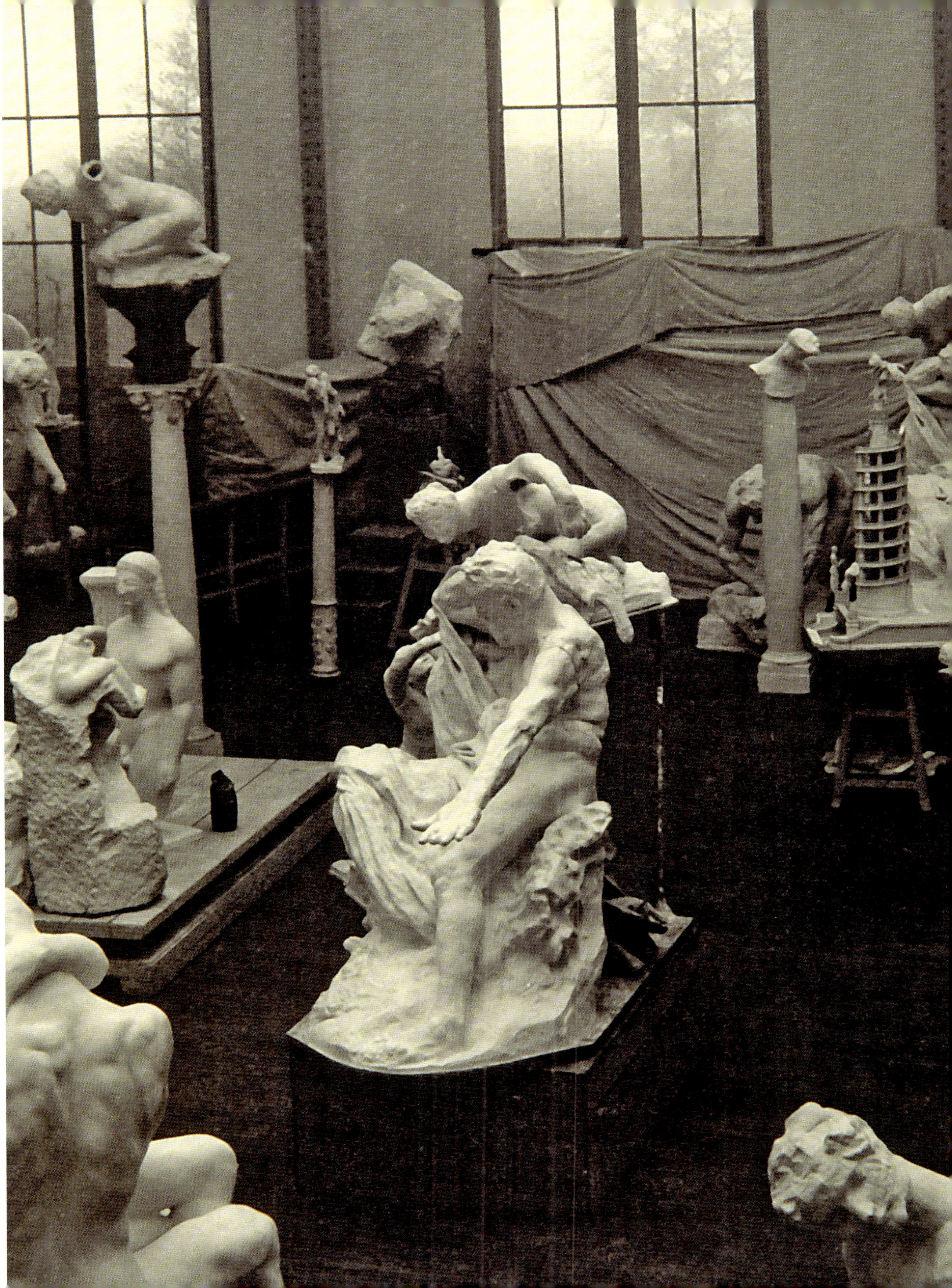

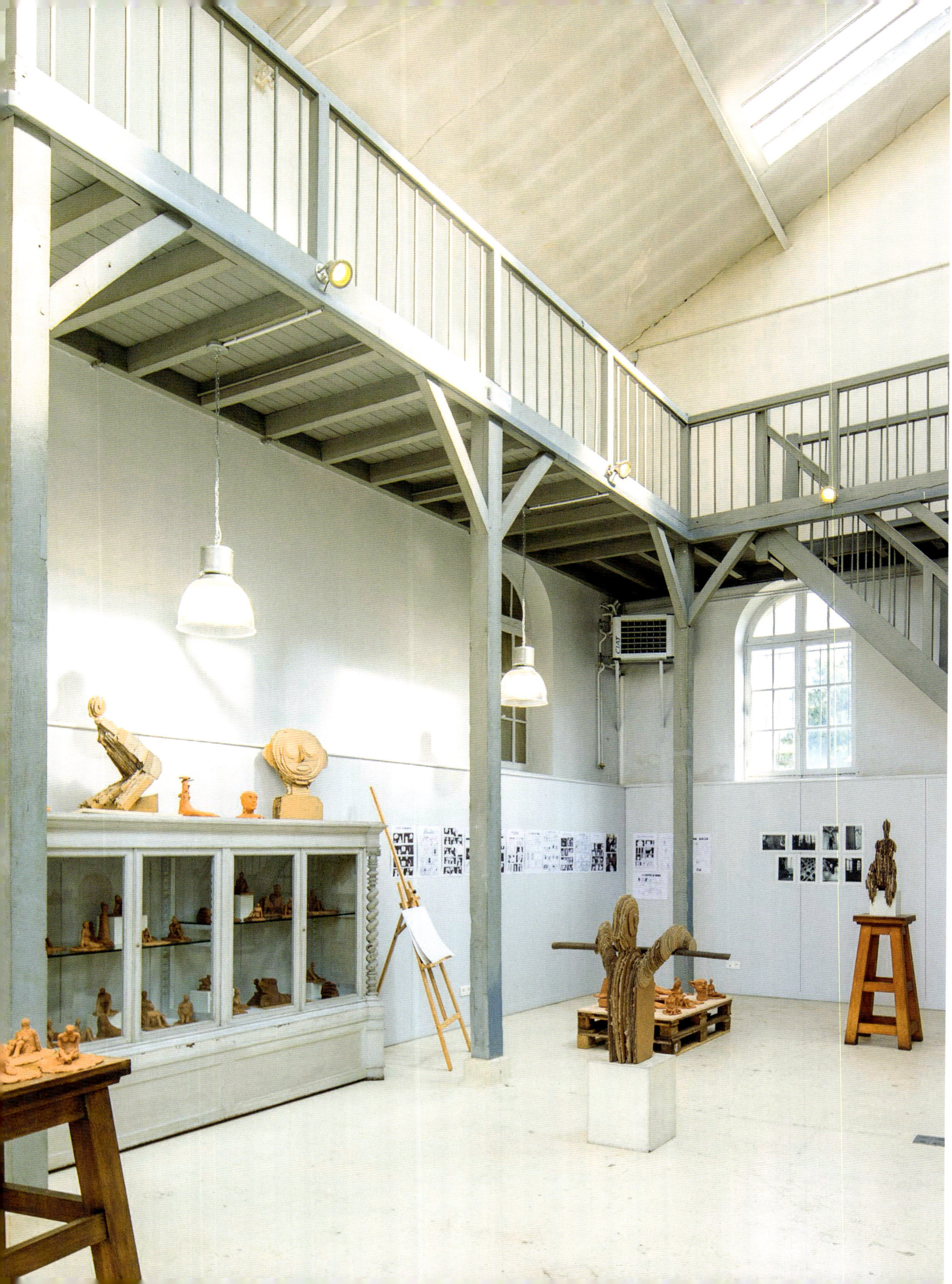

Yet despite his success, Rodin remained fairly restrained, preferring to retire to bed by 9pm rather than socialising, and he did not enjoy expensive food or belongings. On most mornings he rose at 7am and ate a light breakfast of fruit and coffee, then headed straight to his studio to work. On the mornings he left Meudon, he rose at 5am and caught a train and carriage to places such as Versailles, where he walked for hours, sometimes with Rose, or Rilke, or another of his private secretaries or friends. At other times he sat quietly by his large pond at Meudon and watched his swans.

As his fame increased, orders came in for portrait busts from France and around the world, including the United States, Germany, Austria and England. In England, in particular, he was feted and had many friends. In 1902, he was given an honorary doctorate at Oxford University and during a banquet in his honour, he was carried aloft by students. Various prominent figures visited him at Meudon and, in 1908, Edward VII of England was one of them.

'In short, Beauty is everywhere. It is not that she is lacking to our eye, but our eyes which fail to perceive her.'

Auguste Rodin

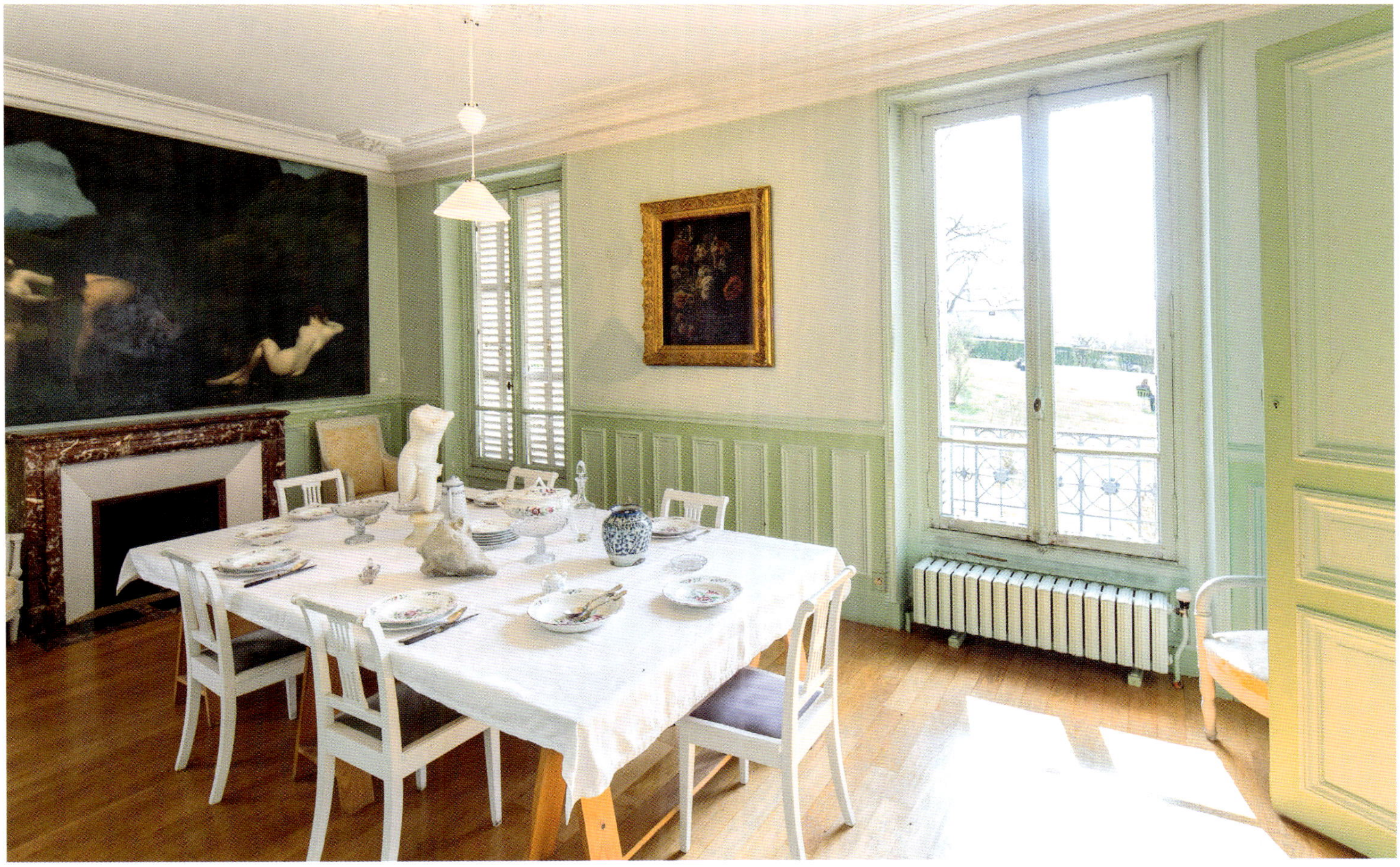

Above: In Rodin's eau-de-nil dining room is a large painting by Alexandre Falguière, and a small marble statue is on the table.
Opposite and following page: The Villa des Brillants is now a museum of Rodin's work.

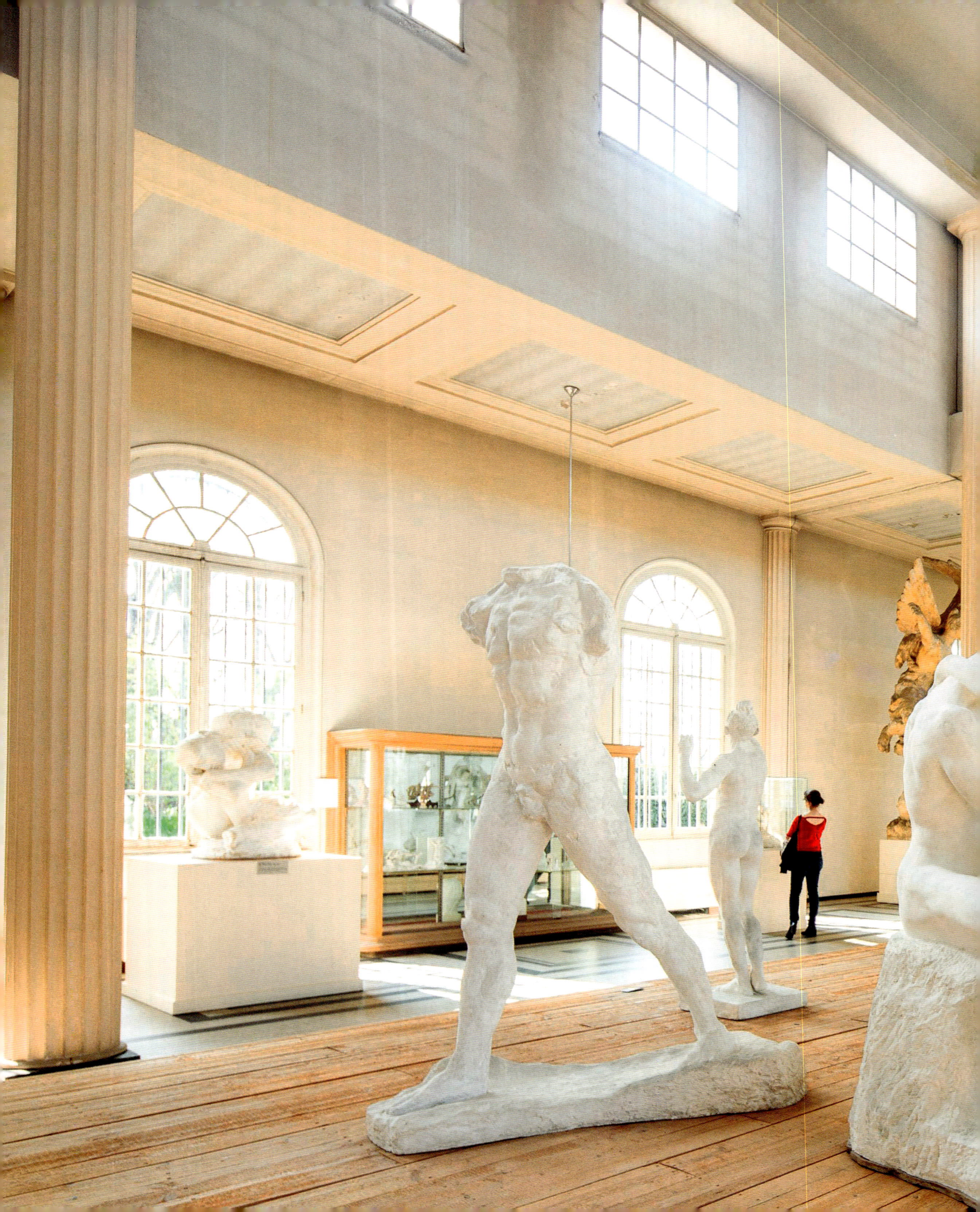

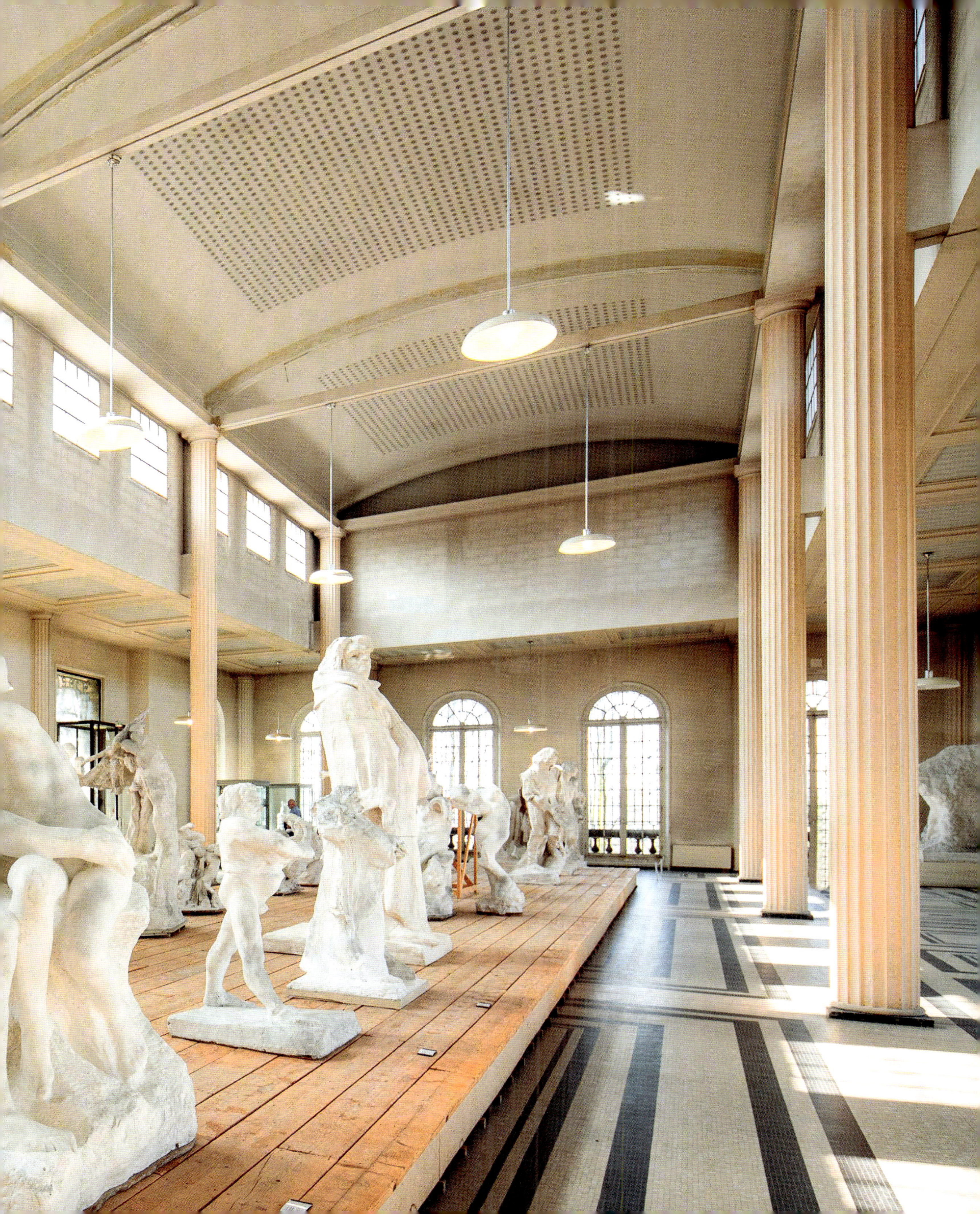

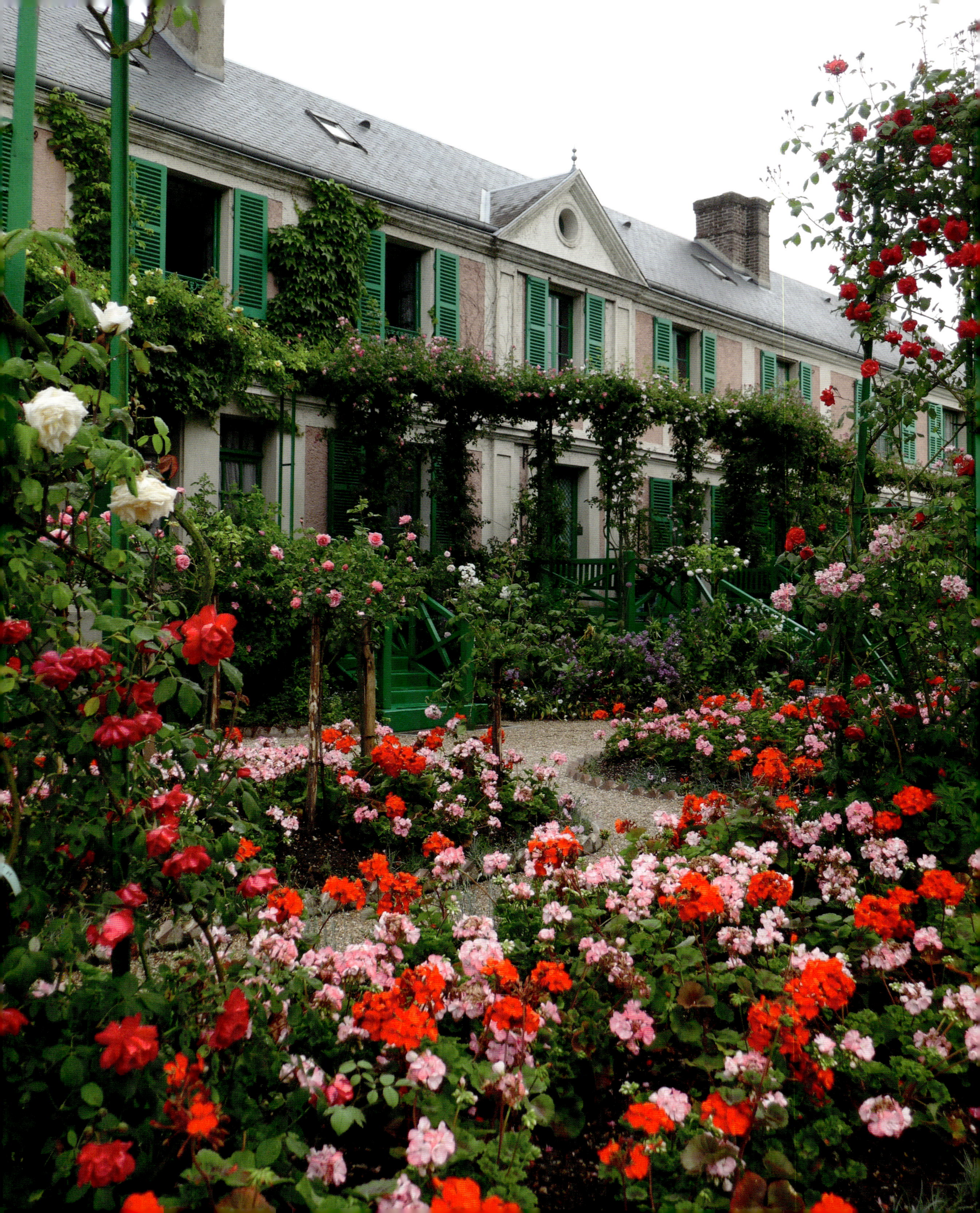

CLAUDE MONET

Giverny, France

The leader of French Impressionism, Claude Monet (1840–1926) spent exactly half his life living and working at his home in Giverny, a village 80 kilometres (50 miles) from Paris. During his forty-three years there, he created some of his greatest work.

Although Monet's upbringing was fairly middle class, he spent much of his life in poverty. For years, his paintings hardly sold. When he was twenty-five, he met Camille Doncieux, who became his model and girlfriend, and in 1870, three years after giving birth to their son Jean, they married. Money was still tight, but in 1874, a wealthy store owner, Ernest Hoschedé, began buying and commissioning Monet's art. The two families became good friends and the Monets moved into the large Hoschedé home, with Ernest, his wife Alice and their six children.

However, in 1877, Ernest went bankrupt. The house was sold, and he left Alice and the children. Monet took responsibility for both families. They moved to a house in the village of Vétheuil, where Camille gave birth to their second son, Michel, but by that time she was seriously ill, and Alice nursed her and cared for all the children. In 1879, Camille died. Alice continued to care for the children and run the household, while Monet strove to support them all financially.

They moved from Vétheuil to Poissy, a small industrial town outside Paris, but society frowned upon a widower and a married woman openly living together. By that time, Monet and Alice's relationship had blossomed into a romantic one, but there was not much they could do with little income and Ernest still living in Paris.

MOVING TO GIVERNY

In 1883, Monet, Alice and the children had to vacate the house at Poissy. Monet found a house in Giverny, in the northern French department of Eure, where the River Seine meets the River Epte, and his art dealer Paul Durand-Ruel lent him money for the rent. Attached to the house was a garden surrounded by meadows, a railway and the River Ru, a small tributary of the Epte. At the time, Giverny had just 279 inhabitants, and Monet loved the peace, the light, the poplar trees that bordered the fields, the meadows and the nearby rivers. The modest house had a long, plain façade rendered in pale pink, with grey shutters and a slate roof. A row of windows on one side faced a small orchard.

Within a year of moving in, Monet had created a studio out of a barn in the west part of the house. Wooden flooring was laid over bare earth and large windows were cut into the walls to give views of the garden. With plenty of space to keep his canvases and a range of comfortable seating, the studio doubled as a place for entertaining. He also moored his studio boat nearby and he began planning the garden so that there would be flowers to paint throughout the year.

By the 1890s, Monet regularly entertained friends in the studio, including artists, writers, intellectuals and politicians, such as Guy de Maupassant, Stéphane Mallarmé, Mary Cassatt, Paul Cézanne, Octave Mirbeau and Georges Clemenceau, who served as Prime Minister of France from 1906 to 1909 and again from 1917 until 1920.

BRILLIANT PALETTE

Towards the end of the 1880s, Monet's work began selling. Durand-Ruel had taken approximately 300 canvases to America, where viewers were receptive to his work. After that, the French also began buying. In 1892, Ernest Hoschedé died, and Monet and Alice married.

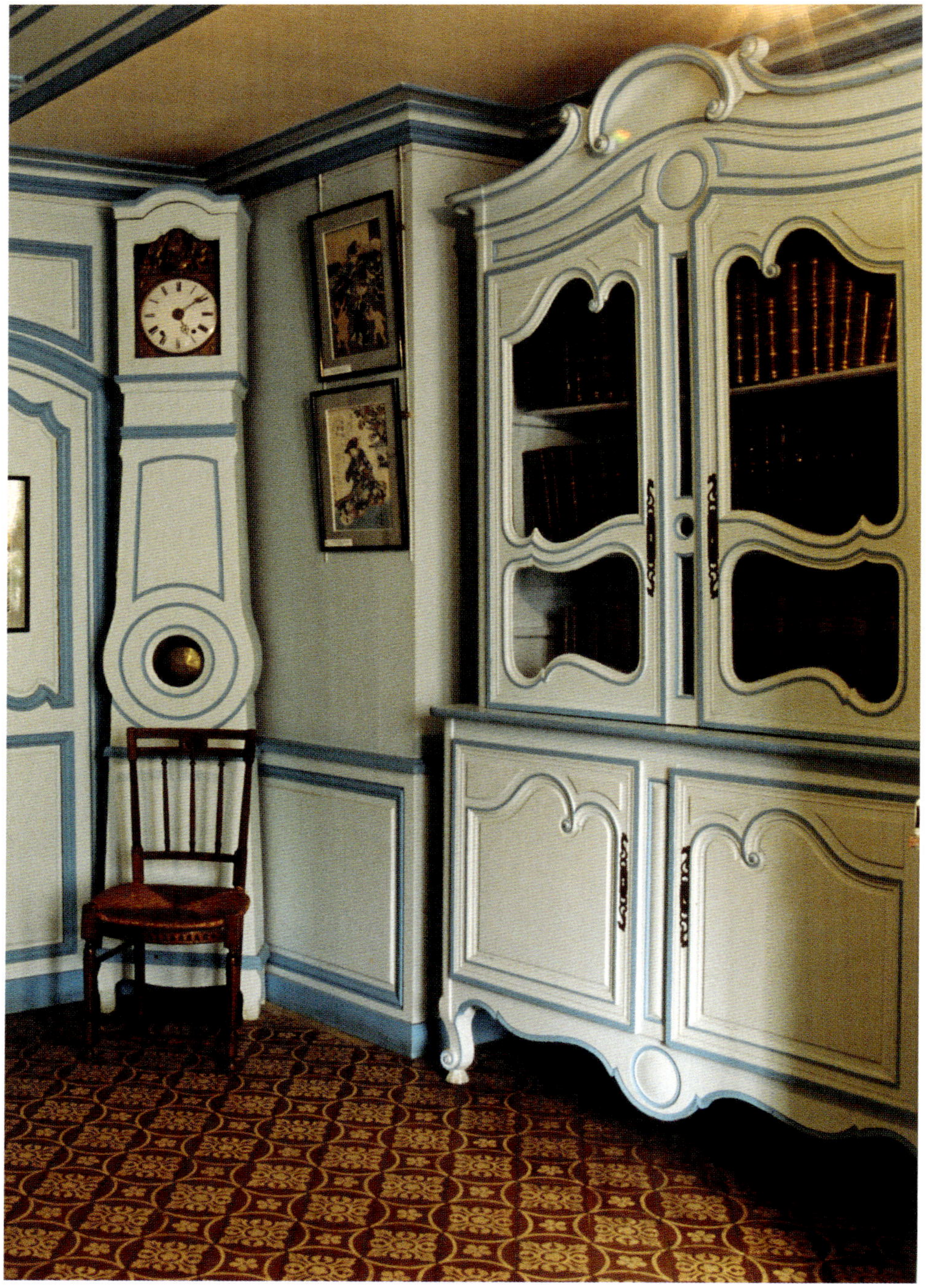

Above: A master of colour, Monet paired cobalt and light blue in his large sitting room, or salon, contrasting dramatically with the darker coloured interiors that were popular at the time.
Opposite: The colourful, patterned kitchen tiles.

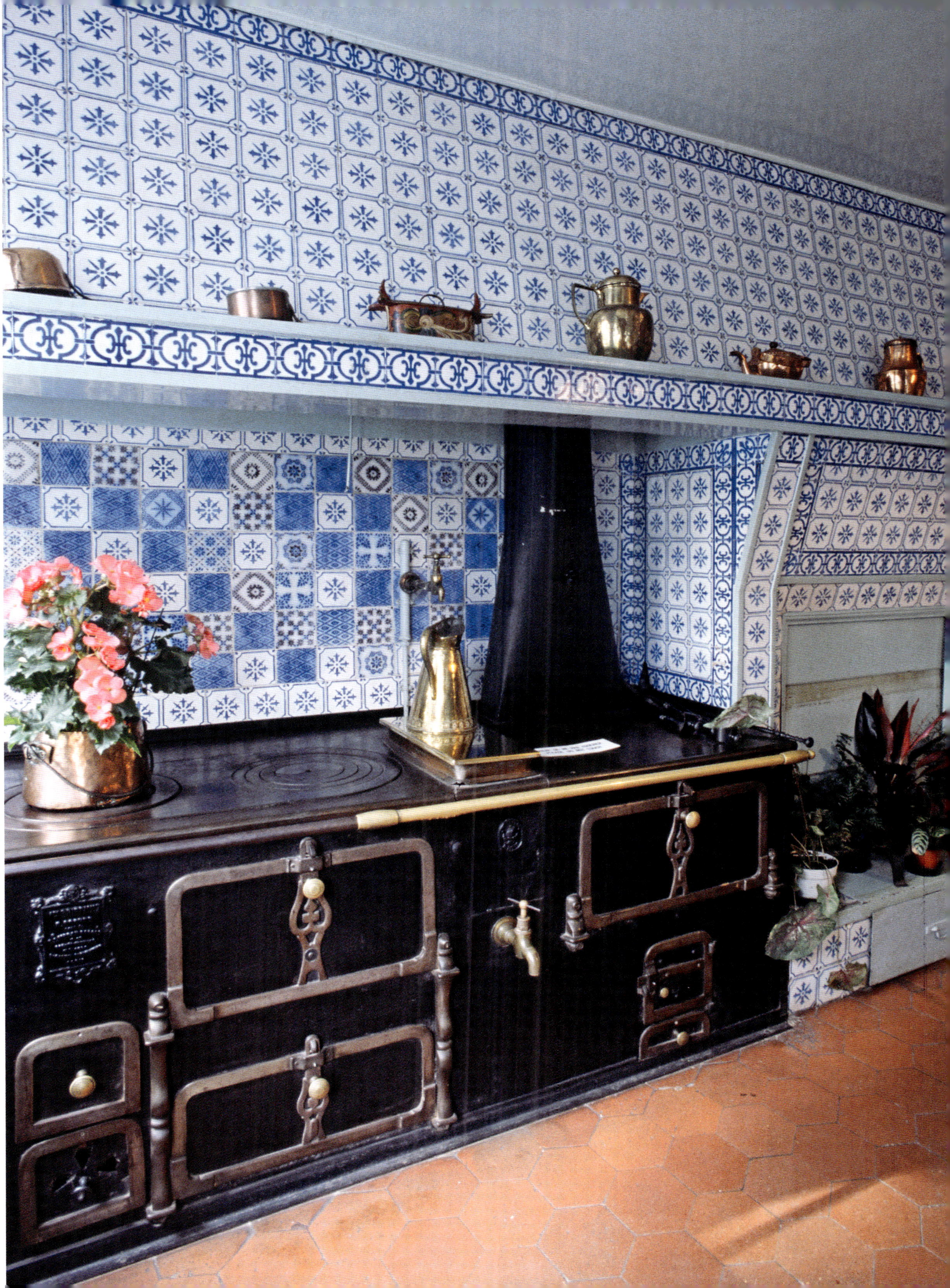

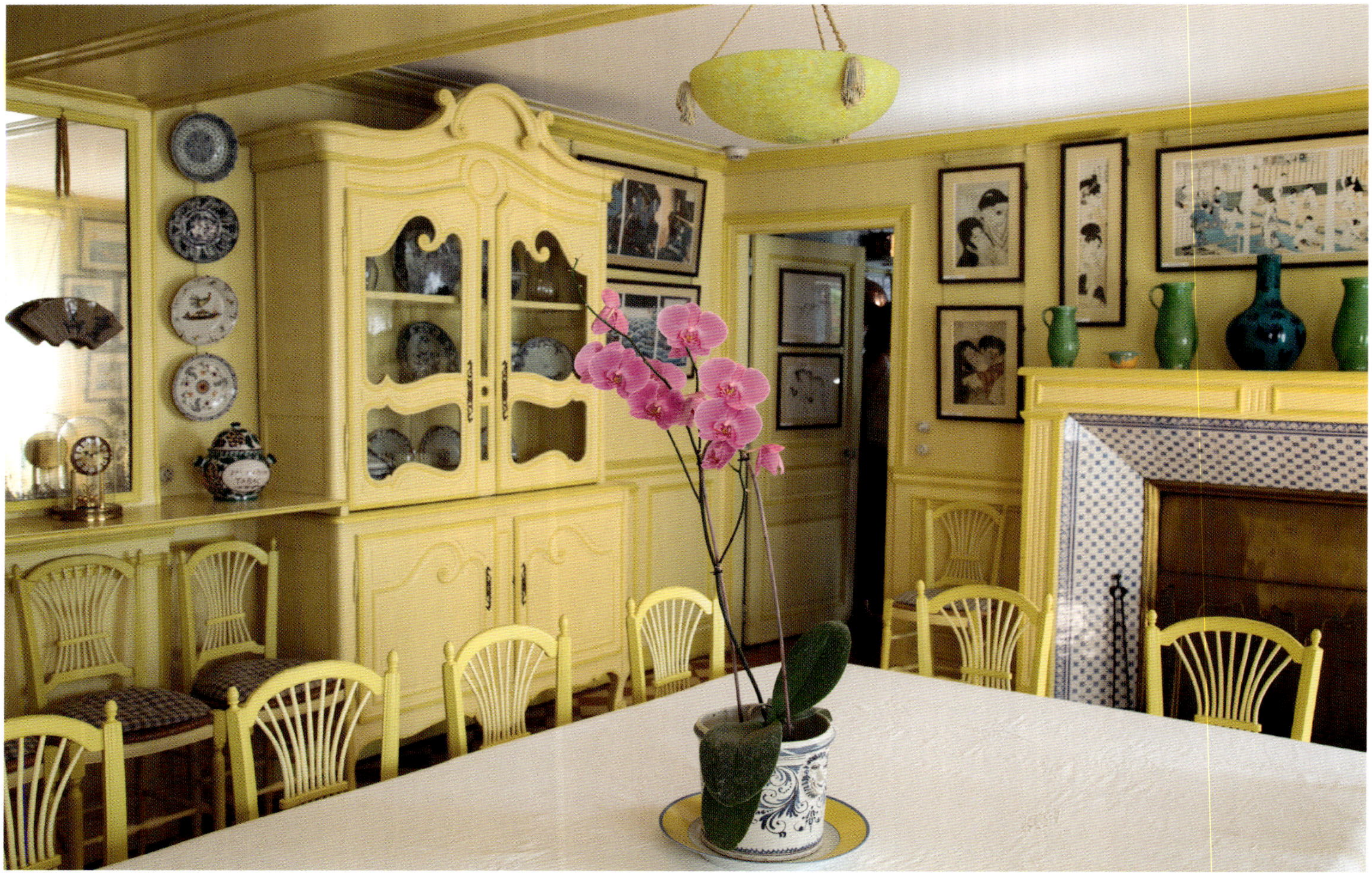

Above: The sunny yellow dining room where Monet displayed his collection of Japanese woodblock prints. The floor is equally bright, in red and white. *Following page*: The blue kitchen, adjacent to the dining room.

Monet enjoyed taking his guests on tours of the house and grounds, which he altered over the years. Double doors led from the garden to a small central hall, with interconnecting rooms leading off towards a staircase that went up to the first-floor girls' bedrooms and then the attic bedrooms of the boys. Monet enlarged and modernised the kitchen. As a master of colour, he avoided the heavy, dark décor that was popular at the time, and instead hired craftsmen to create simple furniture using local materials. He painted the walls in bright colours, and some of his furniture was also picked out in the same or similar hues. He painted the house exterior in a deeper salmon pink and the shutters in a bold Veronese green. Monet chose soft greens and blues for the hallway, and his kitchen was bright blue and yellow, with blue-and-white Rouen tiles with copper pots and utensils, two windows opening on to a veranda and a separate door leading down to the cellar. The dining room was painted in sunny yellow, its walls adorned with his collection of Japanese prints. The art critic Gustave Geffroy recalled: 'In that modest house which was nevertheless sumptuous in its décor, we derived enormous pleasure from sitting round a table where food was served in generous portions.'

Between the main entrance hall and the *épicerie* – a pale green storage room – was the Blue Salon, painted in pale and cobalt blue, with French windows leading on to the veranda. Here, Monet, Alice and the children gathered to read, sew, play card games or listen to music. From the *épicerie* another staircase led up to Monet's and Alice's bedrooms.

In 1890, Monet bought the house and continued altering it to suit his needs. Later that decade, he had a larger studio built on the north-west side of the garden: a spacious building with skylights, along with a photography darkroom, and more living rooms and bedrooms for the children who were, by then, fairly grown-up. He also had a garage built, as he and Alice became motoring enthusiasts. Finally, between 1914 and 1916, when his earnings had become considerable, he had a third studio built on the north-east

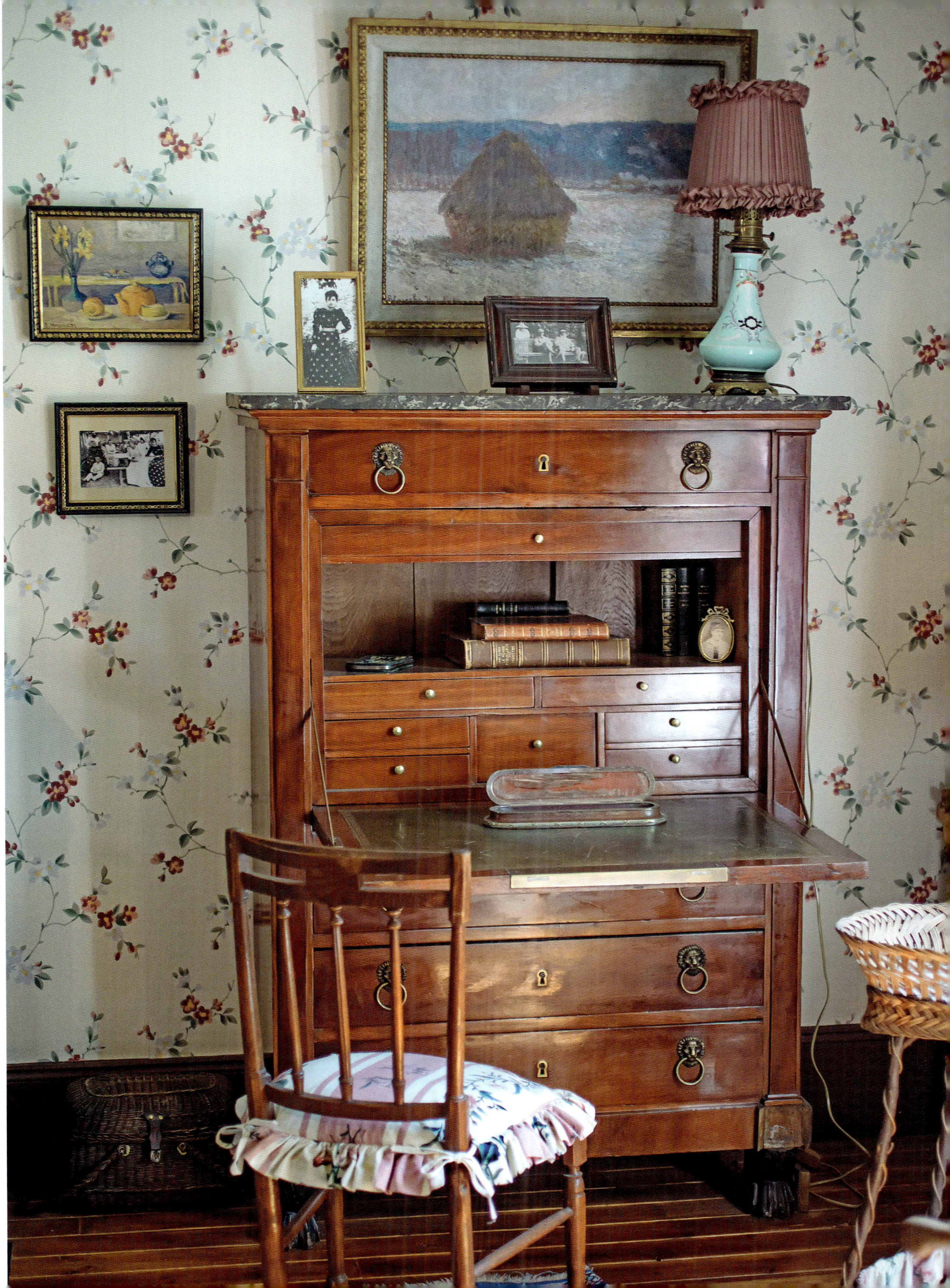

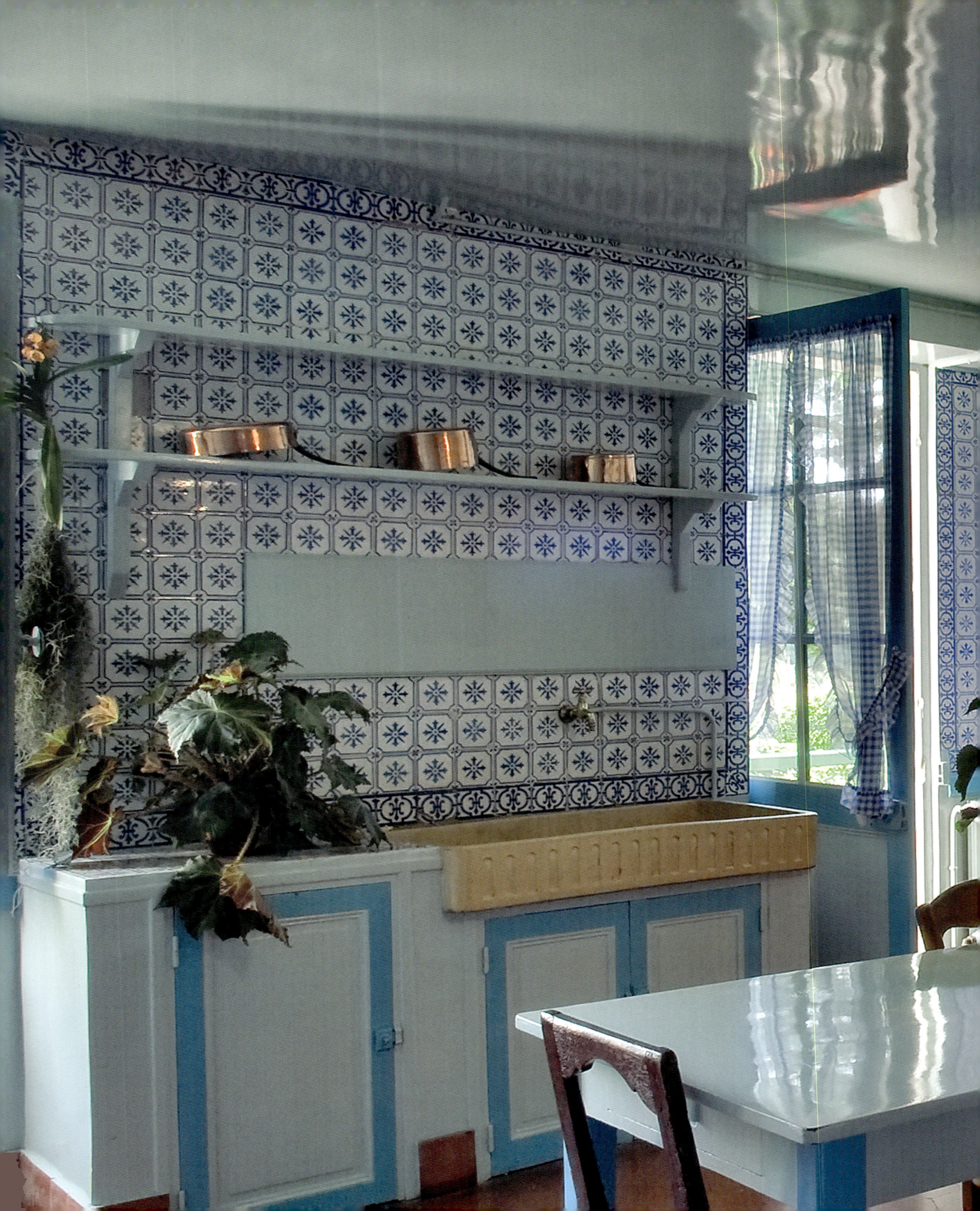

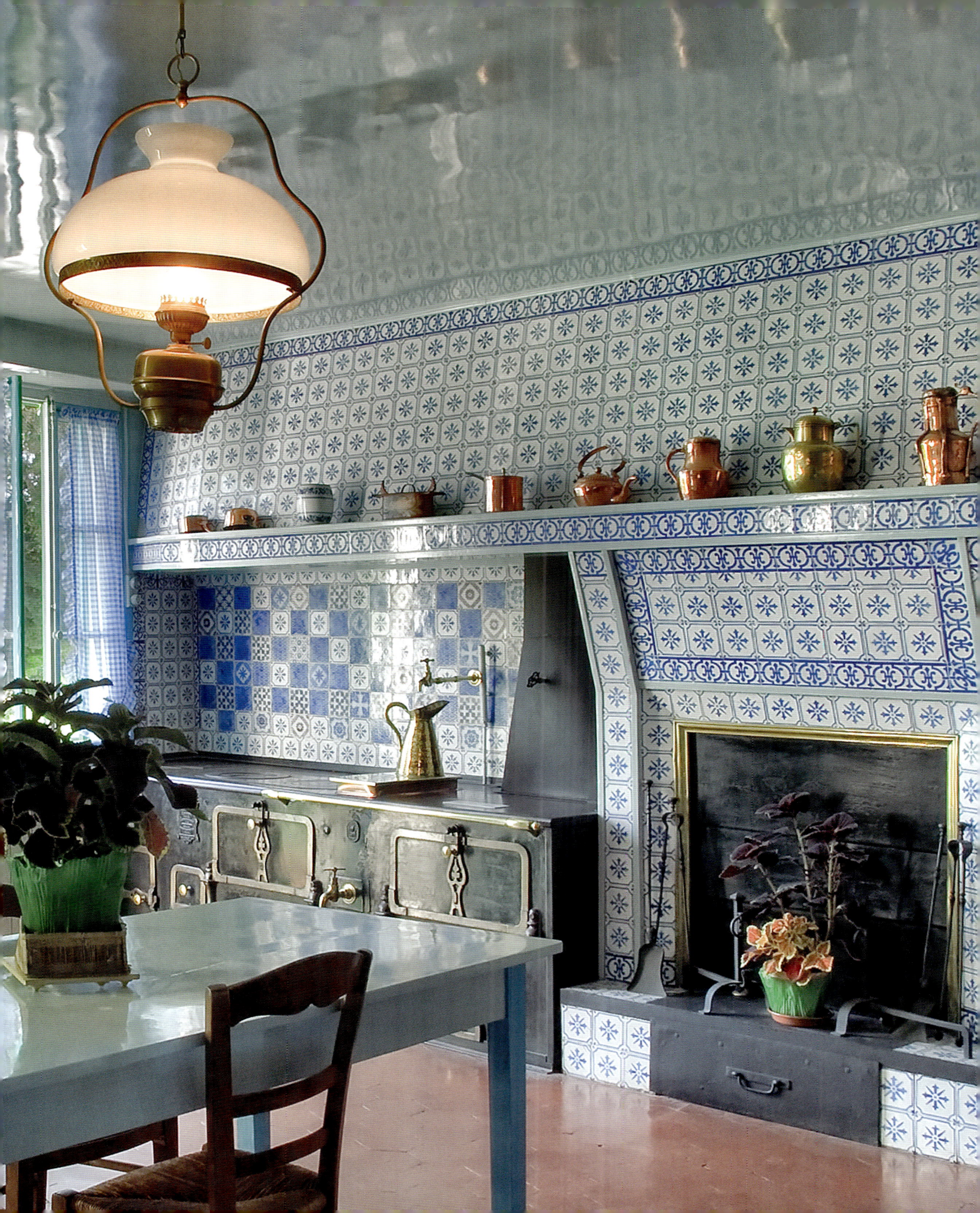

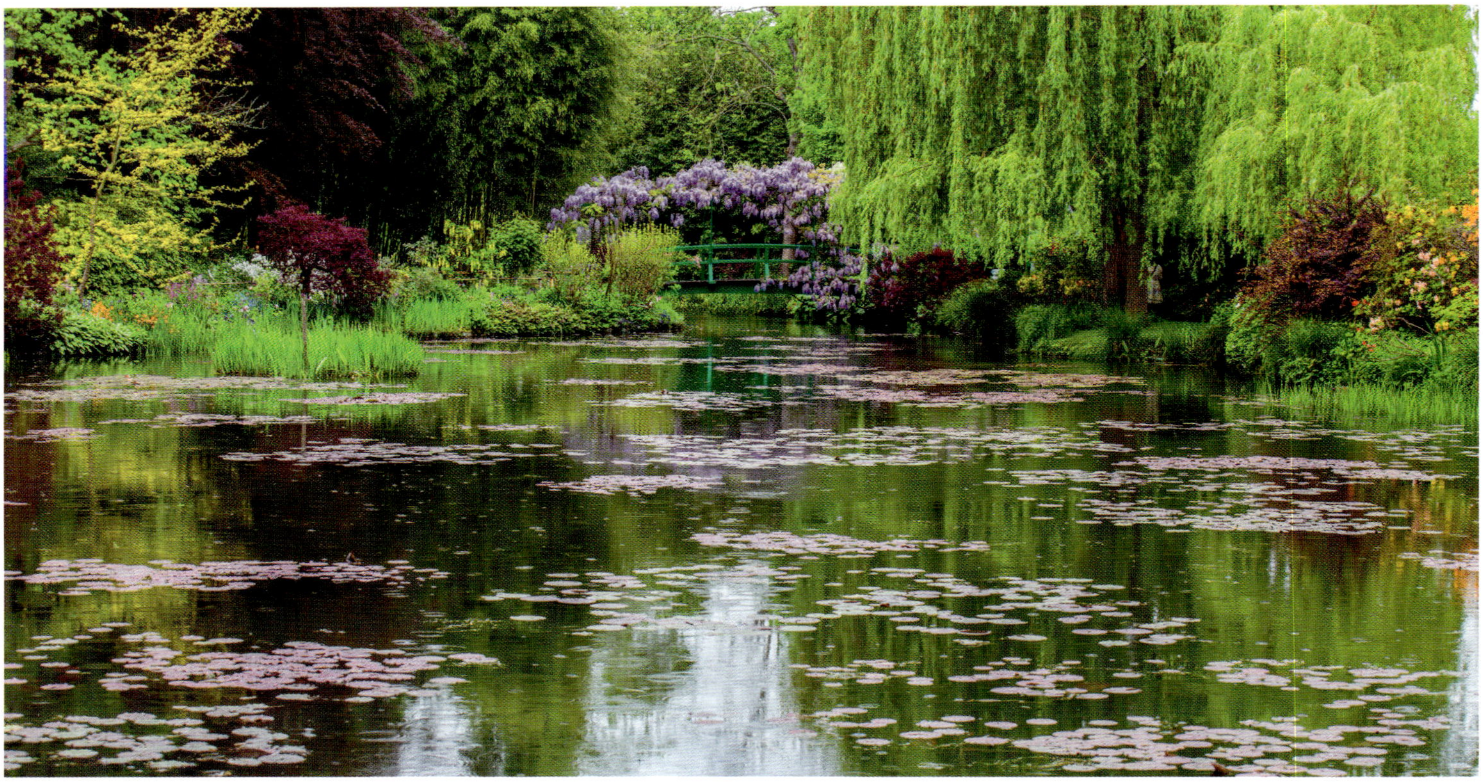

Above: For Monet, gardens offered a refuge from the world, and the idea for his vast lily pond may have occurred to him after he had seen the water garden at the 1899 Exposition Universelle in Paris created by the grower Joseph Bory Latour-Marliac, who bred the first colourful hardy waterlilies.
Opposite: Monet carefully planned the garden so that there would be flowers to paint throughout the year.

side of the garden. It was a vast construction of iron trusses, concrete and glass. By then, Alice had died, World War One had started and Monet was suffering with cataracts. Grief-stricken and troubled by the sound of fighting audible from his home, he embarked on his most ambitious project to date. The *Grandes Décorations des Nymphéas* were to be a monumental panorama of his water garden.

THE GARDEN

For the entire time he lived there, Monet's greatest source of inspiration was his garden. At first, he did the gardening himself, with help from the children, but by 1890, he could afford to hire six gardeners, and he had two greenhouses built. With his painter's eye, he selected all his flowers. He planned the walkways and trellises, including which flowers would bloom during certain months, making sure that he had the combinations of colours he wanted at all times. The garden was surrounded by a low wall and railings, so anyone passing could admire it. Monet wrote daily instructions to the gardeners, with precise designs and layouts for plantings.

In 1893, he bought a further strip of land beyond the railway line at the end of his flower garden. It bordered the River Ru, and eight years after that, he obtained permission from the local authority to divert the stream so that he could enlarge an existing pond and create an extensive water garden. He surrounded it with weeping willows, poplars, lilies, azaleas, rhododendrons and roses, and built a green Japanese-style bridge across it, over which he trained white and mauve wisterias. It was from this that he painted his *Grandes Décorations des Nymphéas* that occupied him for the rest of his life and became his bequest to the French nation.

'I am in raptures; Giverny is a splendid place for me.'

Claude Monet to Théodore Duret.

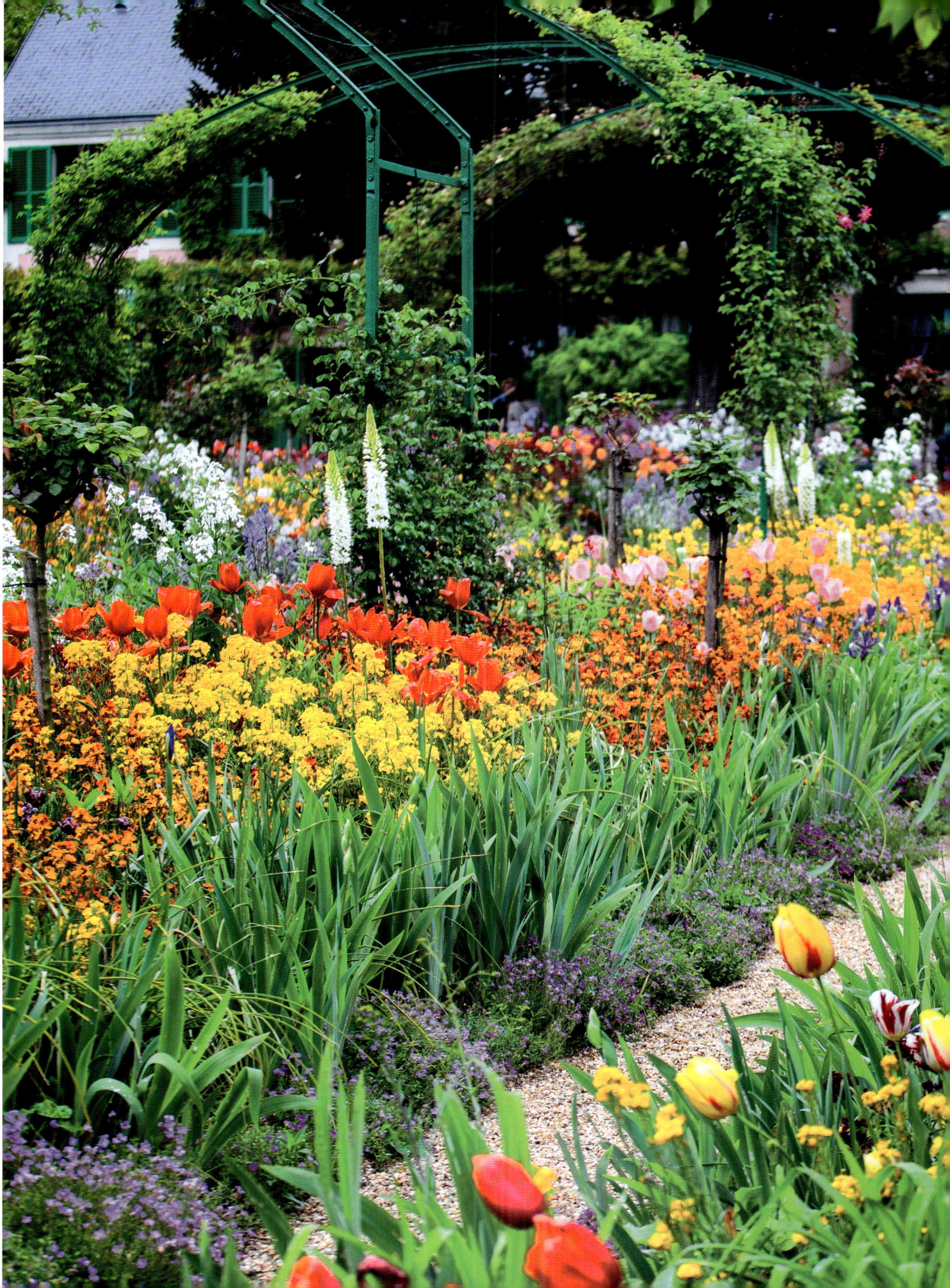

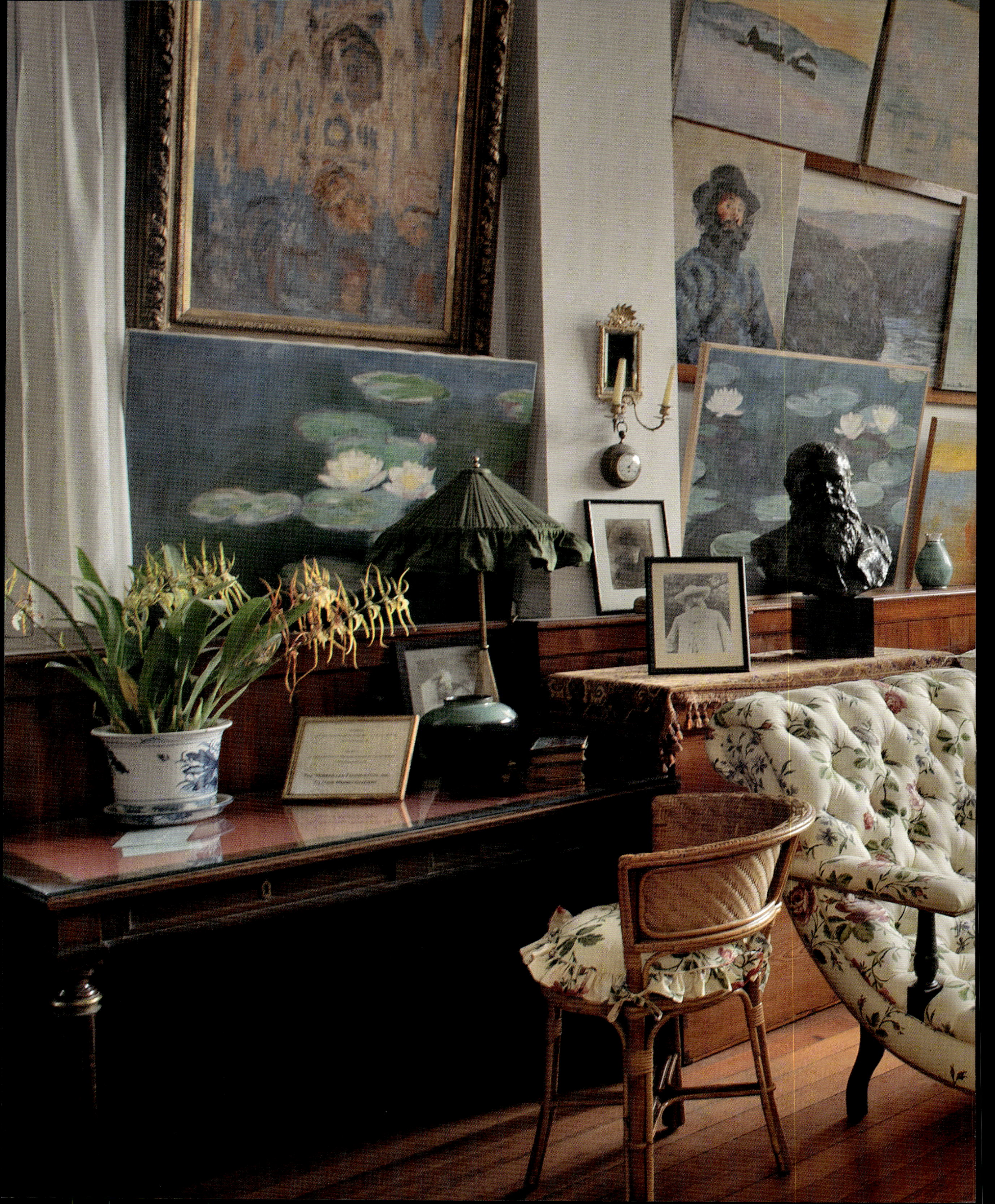
The Versailles Foundation Inc.

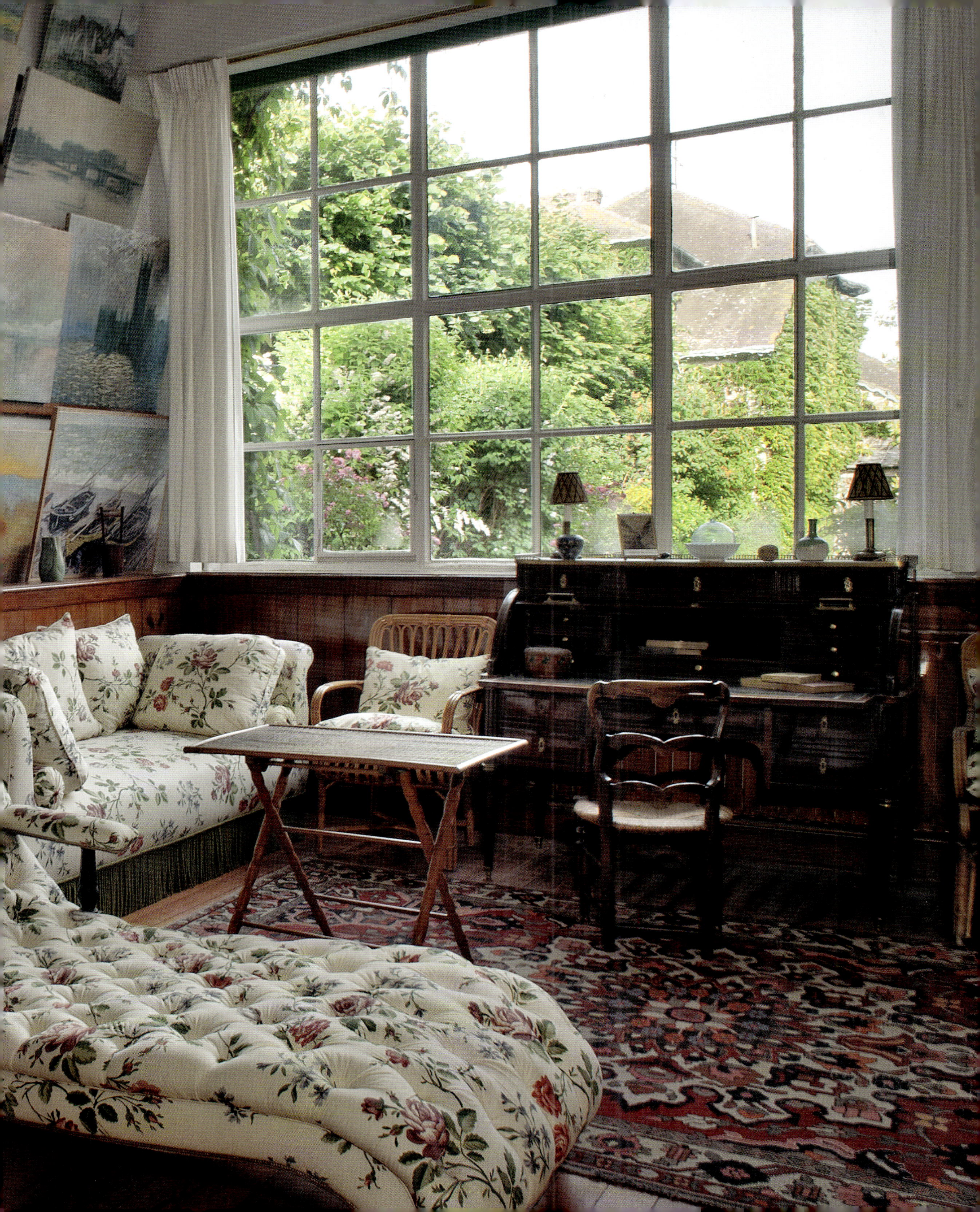

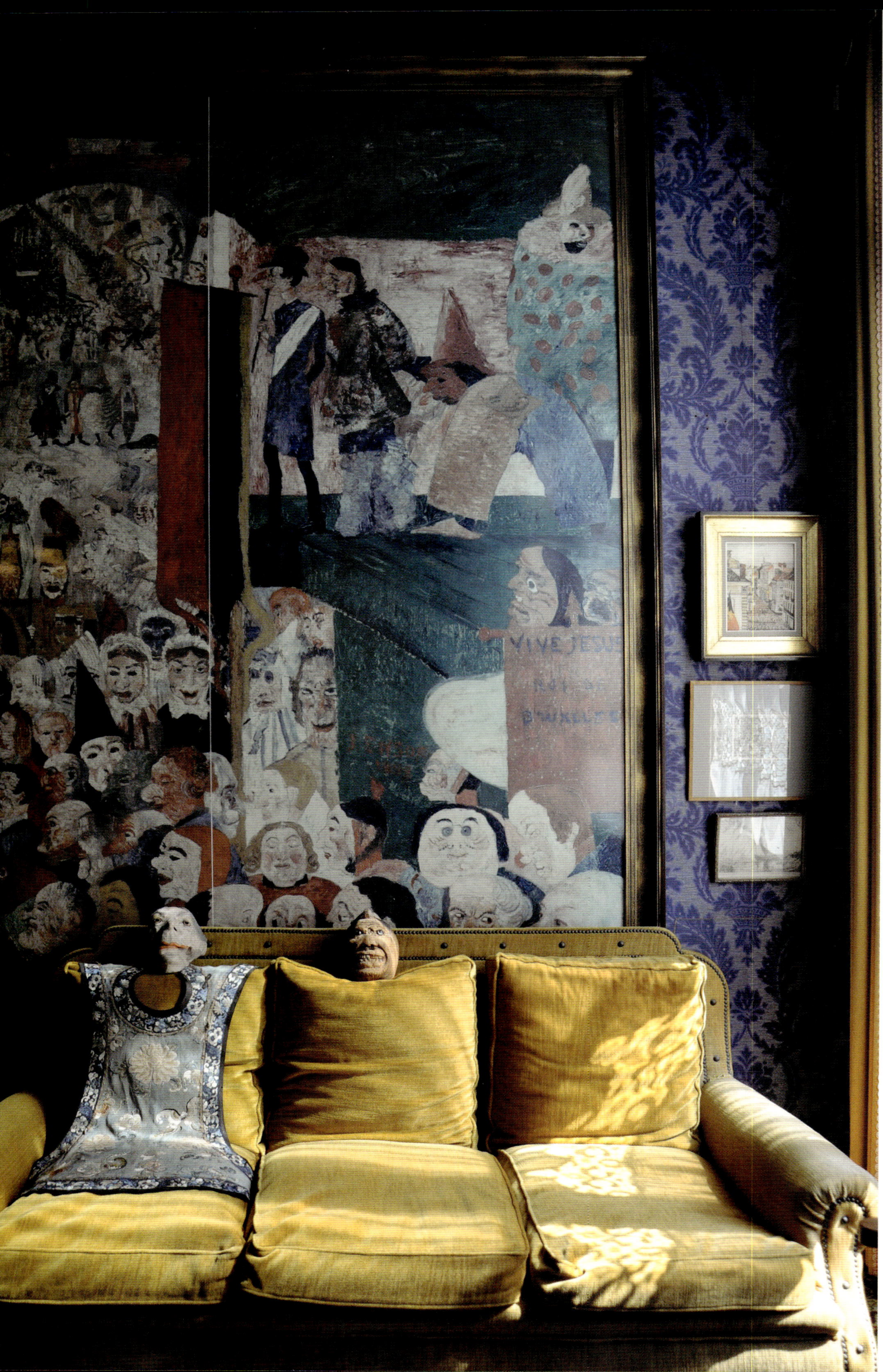

JAMES ENSOR

Ostend, Belgium

Born in Belgium to English parents, the artist James Ensor (1860–1949) inherited his house from his uncle Leopold Jean Haegheman in 1915. His family had sold shells and souvenirs in a small shop on the ground floor of the house, and while he lived there, Ensor kept the shop as it had always been, but he never opened it to the public again.

Despite his traditional artistic training, throughout his career, James Ensor produced unconventional images that expressed his own somewhat cynical views of the world. Probably because of his family shop that sold souvenirs and curiosities relating to the seaside, carnivals, festivals and parties, he was always particularly fascinated by masks and the grotesque, often featuring these in his paintings as ways of conveying what he saw as the underlying truths of society. At first, his art was disliked and even ridiculed, but he ended up being the highest paid artist in Belgium, and many of his ideas greatly influenced the Expressionists and the Surrealists.

CHANGING OPINIONS

In the Belgian tourist town of Ostend, James Ensor's parents and aunt and uncle sold carnival novelties and seaside trinkets in a family shop inherited from Ensor's grandparents. At school, Ensor was not academic, did not enjoy most subjects and left at the age of fifteen. By then, he had shown an aptitude for painting, and he began studying with two local watercolourists. He soon enrolled at the Brussels Academy of Fine Arts, but later disregarded much of the conventional tuition he received, instead finding other ways to express himself with paint and describing the academy as 'an establishment of the short-sighted'. While studying there, however, he befriended several other like-minded artists, including Fernand Khnopff and Théo van Rysselberghe. Together, they founded an art group that comprised painters, sculptors and designers. Aiming to be independent and unrestricted, they called themselves Les Vingt (or Les XX). As well as holding exhibitions that broke away from the mainstream, they wrote articles on their beliefs about the future of art and invited other innovative artists from abroad to exhibit with them, such as Seurat, Pissarro, Renoir and Vincent van Gogh. At their first show in 1884, Ensor exhibited six works, but critics lambasted them all.

From 1880 until 1917, Ensor worked in a studio in the attic of his parents' house and rarely left Ostend. Over his lifetime, he only took a few brief trips to France, the Netherlands and London. For about five years, he painted fairly mundane subjects, including interiors, self-portraits and still lifes, which later became known as his 'sombre period'. For the following fifteen years, he painted objects relating to carnivals and masks. However, his work was not appreciated and the rest of the Les Vingt group decided it was too outrageous, even for them, and so began rejecting his submissions to their exhibitions and deriding his paintings. Even his mother and aunt criticised him for his art. Depressed, he moved to Brussels, where he befriended local intellectuals, artists and free-thinkers who encouraged and inspired him. These friends wrote admiring assessments of his work in local magazines, which prompted further new, positive appraisals of his work.

Gradually, Ensor won acceptance and acclaim, and in 1901, he became a founding member of the Free Academy of Belgium. In 1903, he was made a Chevalier of the Order of Leopold. Yet as his reputation flourished, his own enthusiasm began to diminish, and he became depressed and dispirited. He began working in what later became called his 'crystalline period' that lasted until the end of his life. These paintings comprised vibrant colours in loose,

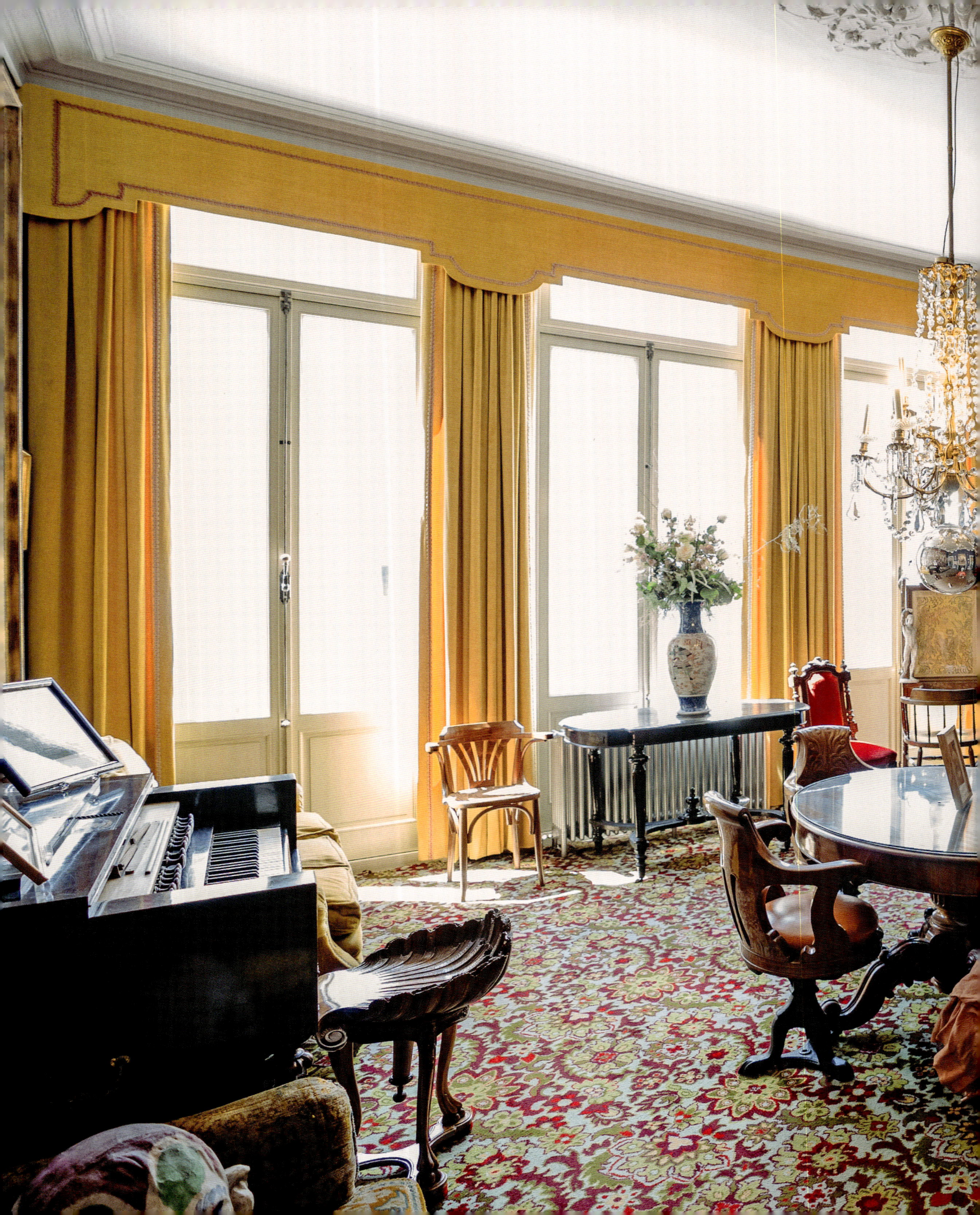

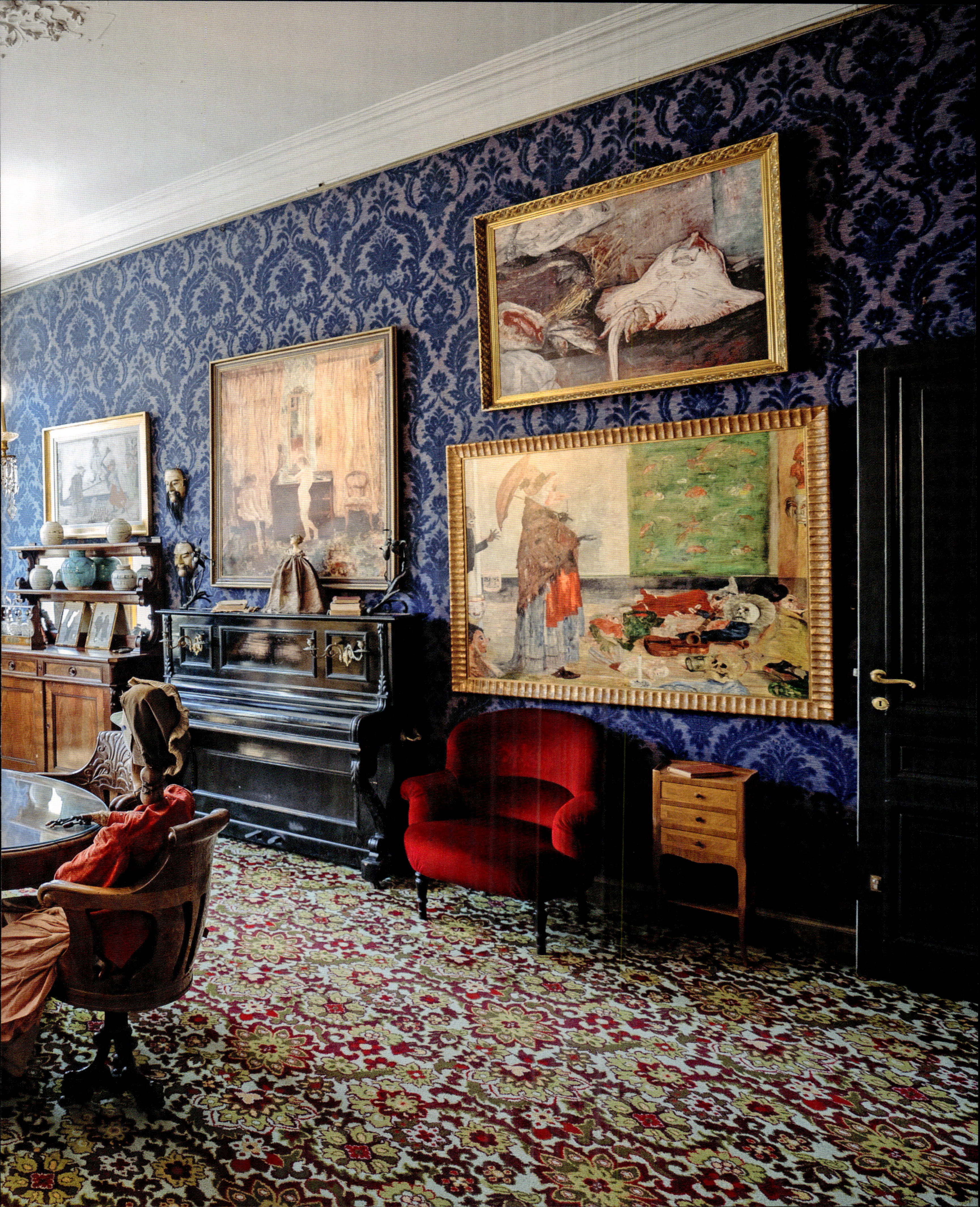

sketchy marks. He continued to be given many prestigious awards and accolades, including being made a baron in 1929 by King Albert I of Belgium, being awarded the Legion of Honour, having a bust of him carved by Belgian sculptor Edmond de Valériola and a work of music dedicated to him, created by Belgian composer Flor Alpaerts. However, he continued to withdraw and his output decreased, while his paintings commanded higher prices than any other living Belgian artist.

When Ensor was twenty-eight, he had met Augusta Boogaerts, who was eighteen and the daughter of an Ostend hotel owner. She was working in the family souvenir shop and became Ensor's closest companion, remaining close to him until his death. She never lived with him, yet she was the only woman, apart from his mother and sister, with whom he was on intimate terms. His nickname for her was 'La Sirène'. Both families opposed the relationship and, in an effort to end it, her family sent her to England to study; later in life, she was often away working as a governess, but their relationship lasted. When he became successful and yet depressed and lethargic, Augusta stepped in, effectively becoming his office manager: arranging models for him and helping with other subjects for his art. She made an inventory of his studio and decisions on the printing of his etchings, and promoted the sales of his work.

INHERITANCE

In 1915, Ensor inherited his uncle's narrow townhouse in the Vlaanderenstraat, which is perpendicular to the seafront promenade. Two years later, he moved out of his parents' house across the street, and into the townhouse, where he lived and

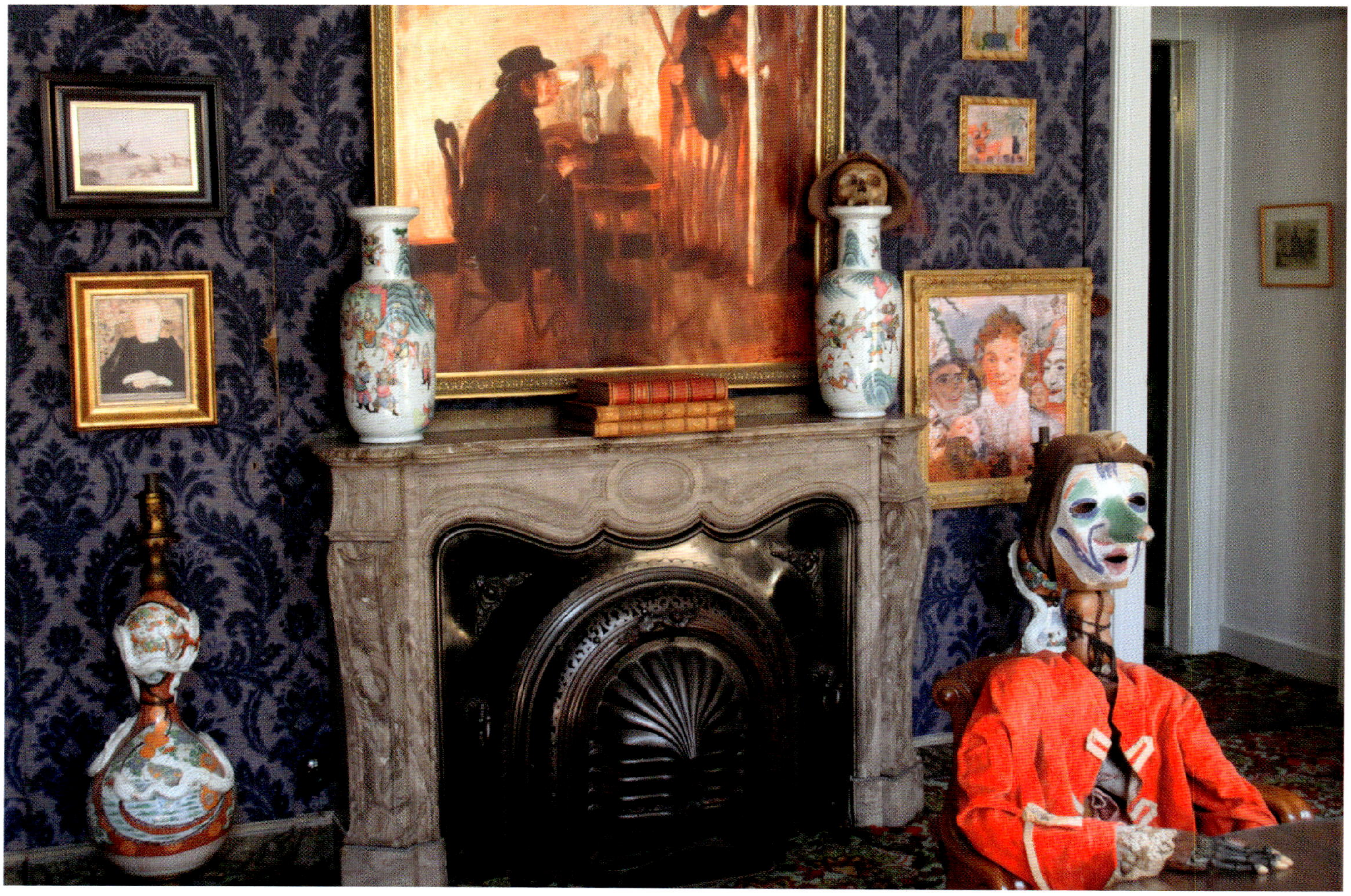

Above: The fireplace in Ensor's blue living room (*het blauwe salon*).
Opposite: Some of the curios inside Ensor's house, including papier-mâché masks.

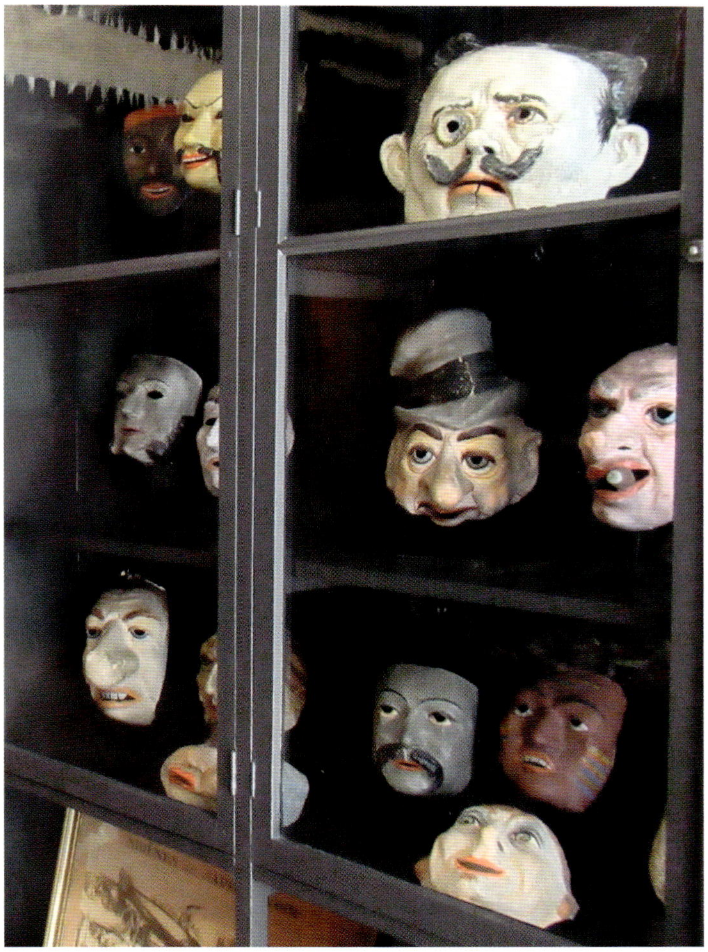

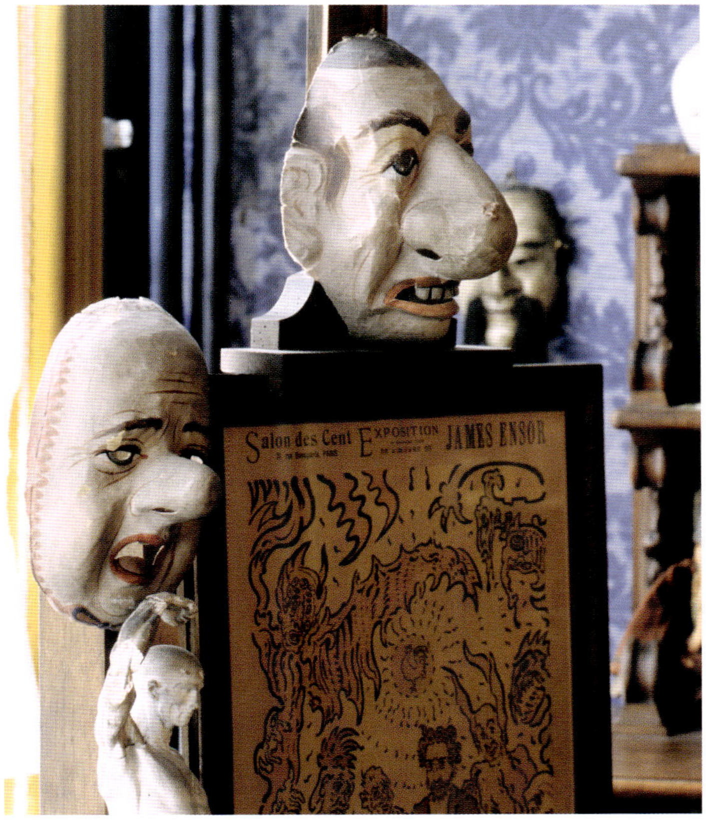

worked for thirty-two years, until his death in 1949. Built in 1865, the house required numerous renovations when he moved in, and he took great care of it, putting it in order and keeping it that way, even throughout World War Two. The ten rooms, plus an attic and a cellar, comprised four or five bedrooms, a parlour – decorated with highly patterned carpets and wallpapers, an upright piano, chandelier and filled with ornaments and other decorations – and the 'Blue Salon' that was Ensor's studio, where he spent most of the last thirty years of his life. There was no bathroom. With the shop taking up the ground floor, all living rooms were on the first and second floors. Ensor lived there with his faithful manservant August Van Yper (called Guustje) and his maid Ernestine Mollet, Guustje's long-term girlfriend. The couple had entered Ensor's service in 1915 and all three became especially close. Guustje would often accompany Ensor on long walks and Ensor's will stated that the pair were allowed to remain in the house until their deaths.

Ensor kept the souvenir shop on the ground floor as it had been when his uncle, aunt and parents ran it; multiple wooden cases were filled with nick-nacks, including shells, toy boats, varnished, long-dead shellfish, toy mermaids and gaudy papier-mâché masks which had sold particularly well during Ostend's springtime carnival. Ensor described himself as a forerunner of numerous art movements, including Luminism, Fauvism, Cubism, Expressionism, Futurism and Surrealism. Additionally, he wrote musical productions; for instance, in 1911, the libretto for a ballet called *La Gamme d'Amour* (The Love Song). He also designed the scenery and costumes and produced a painting with the same title. With so many diverse interests and skills, he attracted many friends, who regularly visited him at his house, including artists, art buyers, intellectuals, musicians, the nobility and even King Albert of Belgium himself.

'In our house, all you hear is groaning.'

James Ensor

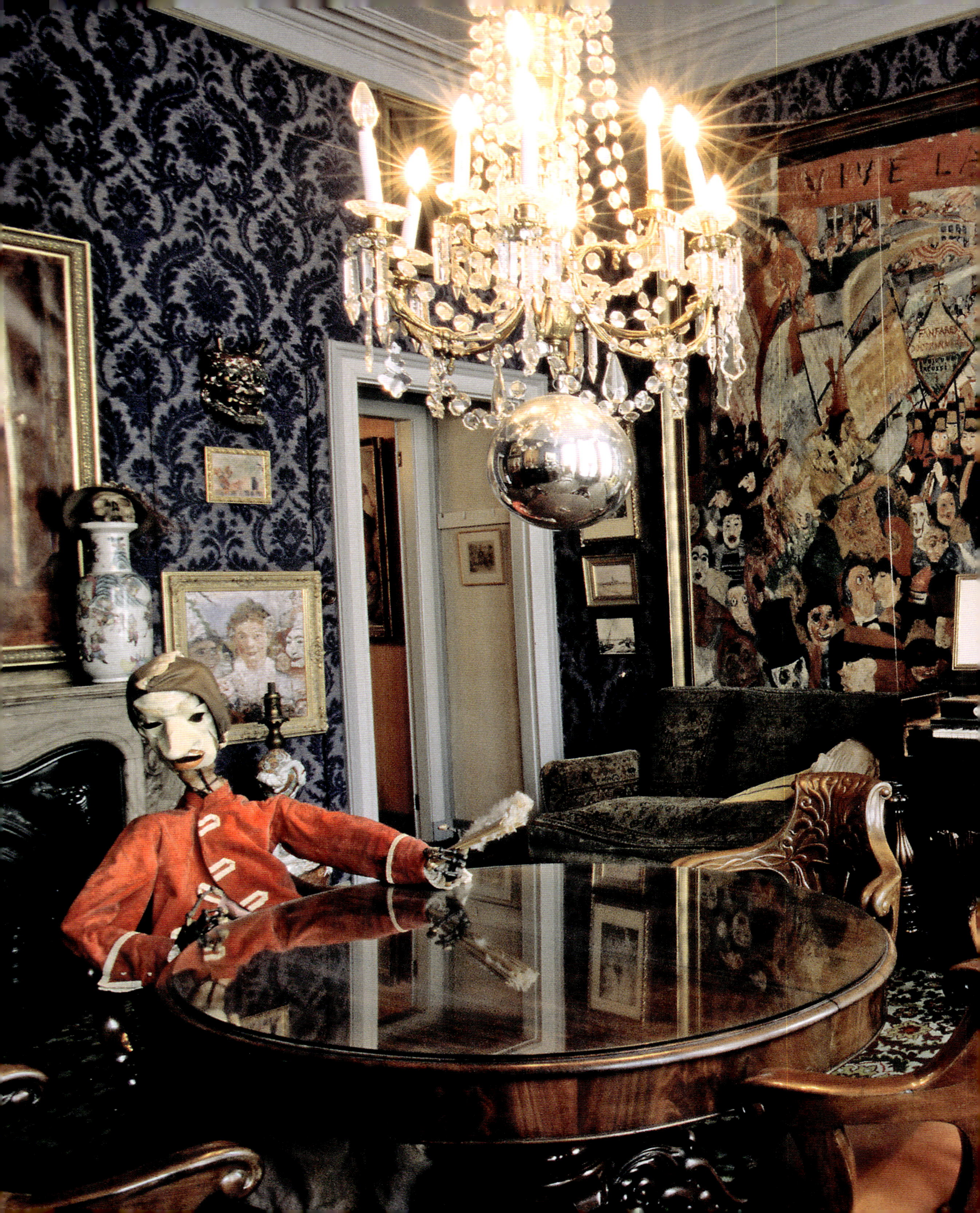
VIVE LA

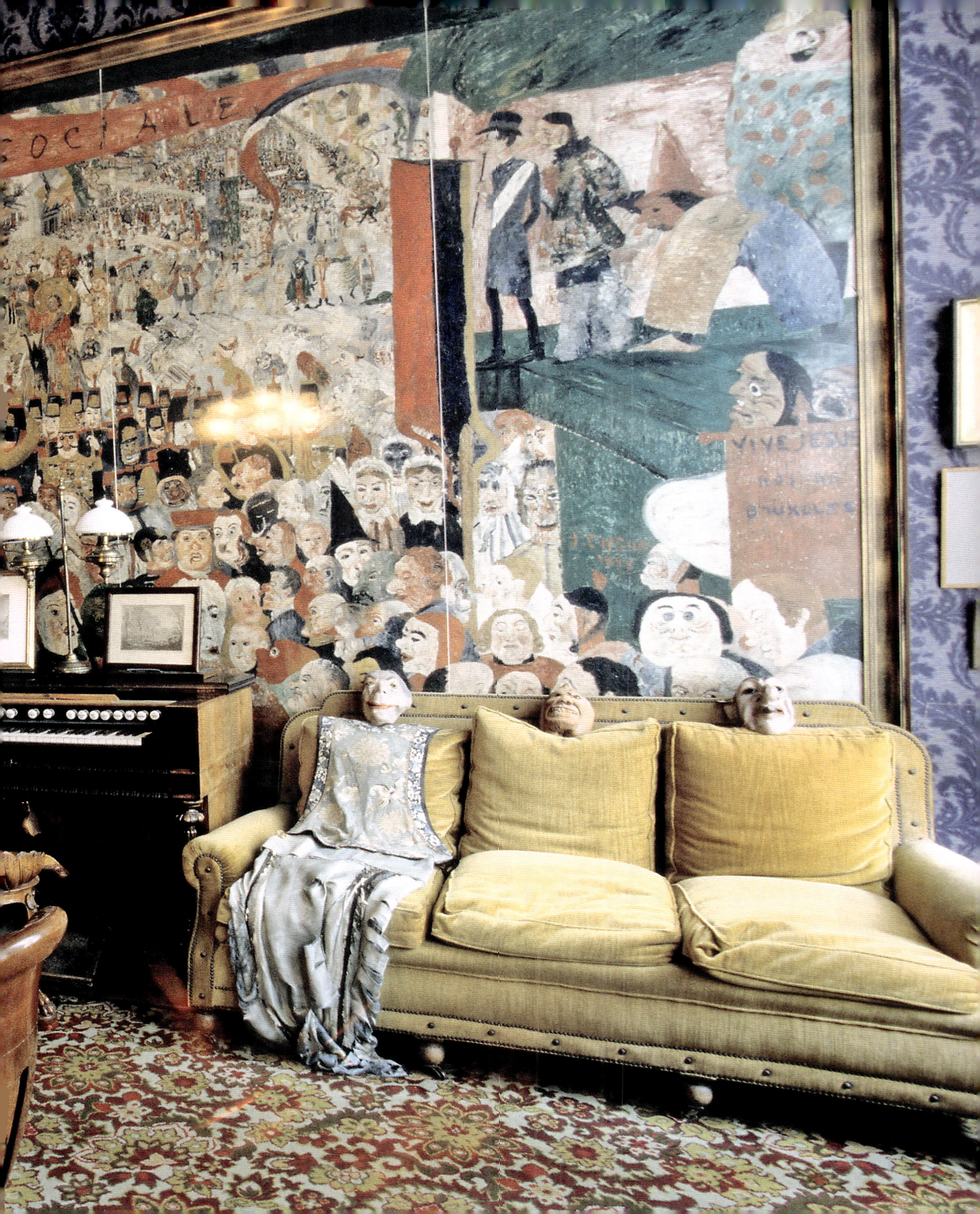
VIVE JESUS

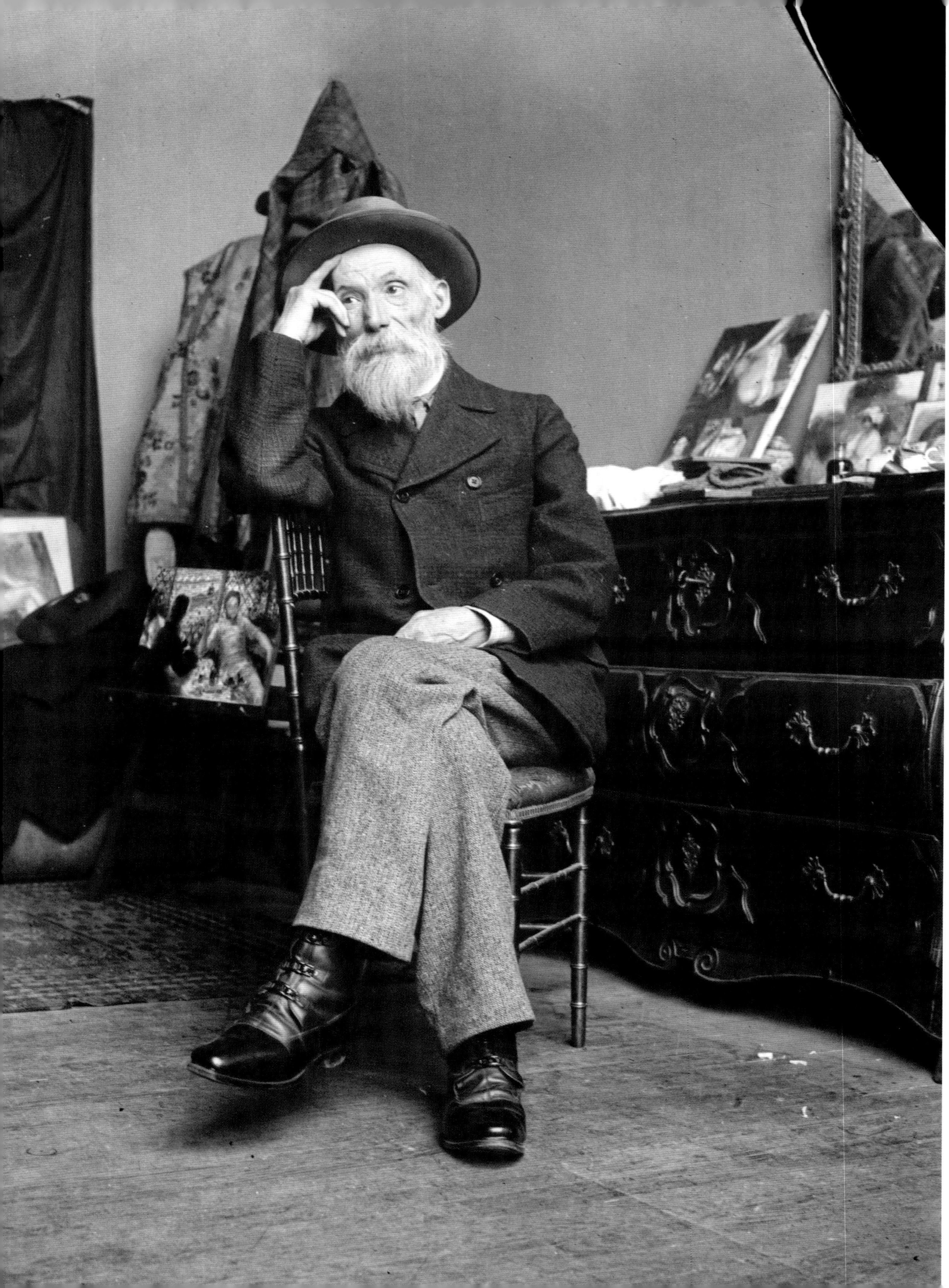

PIERRE-AUGUSTE RENOIR

Essoyes, France

From 1896 until 1907, one of the original Impressionists, Pierre-Auguste Renoir (1841–1919), lived in the small village of Essoyes in the Champagne region of north-central France. Just over 190 kilometres (118 miles) south-east of Paris, Essoyes sits quietly on the banks of the River Ource, a tributary of the Seine, slightly under 50 kilometres (30 miles) south of Troyes.

Over the course of his adult life, Renoir had rented many homes, mainly in northern France, and had also spent time staying with friends, but he had not yet bought a home of his own. His wife, Aline Victorine Charigot, had been born in Essoyes and had tried for years to convince him to move there, as she believed he would relish the peace. Twenty years Renoir's junior, Aline had modelled for several of his paintings, including *Le Déjeuner des Canotiers* (*Luncheon of the Boating Party*) of 1881. When they married in 1890, they already had a son, Pierre. Two more sons, Jean and Claude, followed.

In the summer of 1888, Aline managed to persuade Renoir to stay in Essoyes for the first time. He loved it. Everything appealed to him: the trees shading the banks of the Ource, the meadows, vineyards and woods, the small alleyway (the Chemin des Laveuses) where young washerwomen worked. He loved the peace and relaxed pace of life, the local wine, fruit, bread and butter. Although they thought him a little eccentric, the locals liked him, too. He wrote to a friend that he was pleased to 'get away from expensive Parisian models... [and to paint] laundresses, or rather washerwomen on the riverbanks.' He, Aline and three-year-old Pierre returned in the autumn and stayed for several weeks.

After that first stay in 1888, the Renoir family spent most summers or autumns in Essoyes. Unlike most of the other Impressionists, Renoir had earned some money for his art from the start of the movement in the early 1870s, although he did not earn much until he was in his sixties. By the late 1880s, he was able to support his family modestly. In December 1895, he rented a house in Essoyes and the following year, he bought it.

LIFE IN ESSOYES

From 1895, the unpretentious stone house in Essoyes became home for the Renoirs, usually for the summer. After Claude was born, the three boys grew up relishing their summers in the village. A year after they moved into the house, Renoir and Aline employed a local girl and one of her distant cousins, Gabrielle Renard, as nanny to Jean and then Claude. When the boys were older, Gabrielle remained with the family as housekeeper, and Renoir painted her repeatedly. Initially, an upstairs sitting room doubled as Renoir's workspace, and for the first ten years they lived there, only a screen separated his easel, paints and models' costumes from children's toys and other family belongings. In 1902, he extended their home by incorporating the house next to it, and in 1906, he had a studio built at the end of the garden to give him space away from the bustle of family life. As well as painting there, with the help of sculptor Louis Fernand Morel, he tried out sculpture. Meanwhile, back at the house, on the second floor were the attic and bedrooms for the boys and servants. On the floor below was Renoir's bedroom, with its polished wooden bed, and adjoining that, Aline's, decorated with pink wallpaper. Downstairs in the kitchen was a large, wooden family table, a wooden dresser and a large cooker in a tiled recess. Aline loved to cook for the family and for their many guests, and often produced picnics, which Renoir also painted. In the garden was a vineyard, and Aline – and the gardener, Clément – grew fruit, vegetables and flowers. Often, Renoir would paint some of the fruit, and then Aline would make it into a pie.

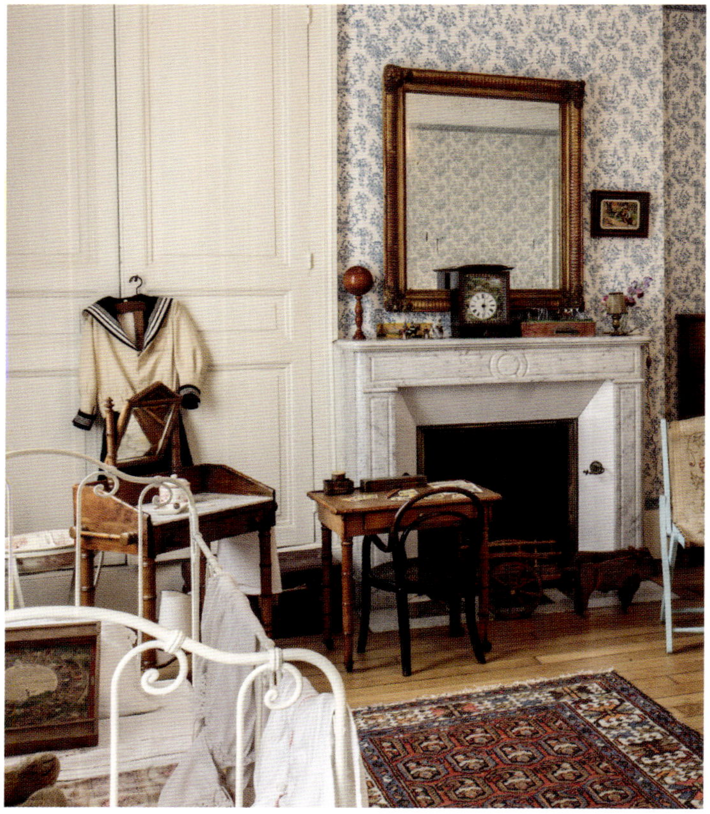

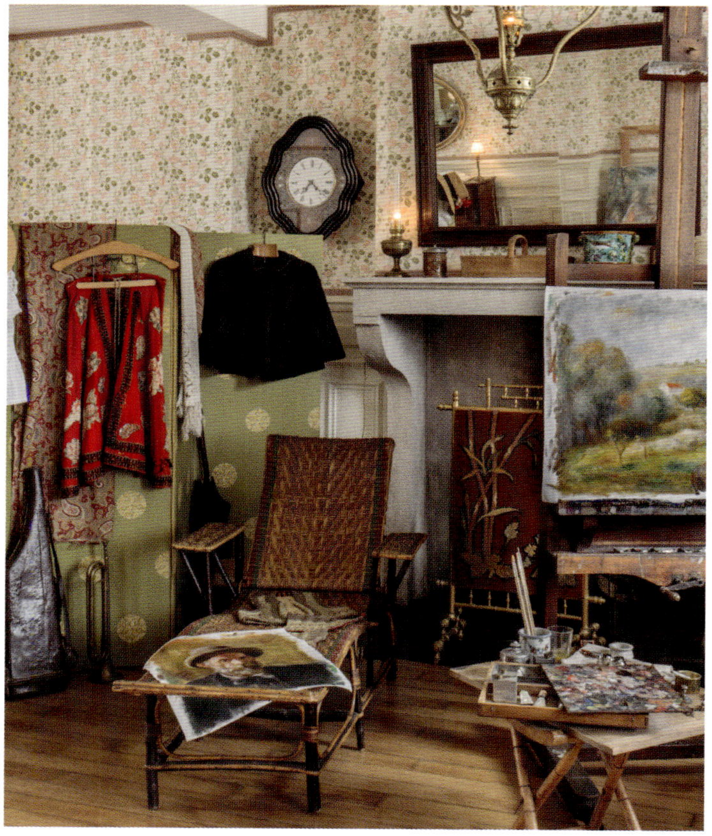

Above: The upstairs sitting room, where a screen separated Renoir's workspace from the rest of the room before he built a dedicated studio space in the garden.
Opposite: The exterior of the stone house in Essoyes.
Following page: The kitchen with its wooden family dining table.

As a doting father, Renoir would use only wax candles, not tallow, as he believed the light was better for them all; he would not allow a slow-burning stove in the house for fear of fire, and when he was not travelling for his art, he tucked the boys into bed each night. An extremely sociable man, he frequently welcomed his friends to the house, including the family of Gustave Caillebotte, who had died of a stroke at the age of forty-five, art dealers Paul Durand-Ruel and Ambroise Vollard, Monet, Rodin and Albert André. Despite an age difference of nearly thirty years, Renoir and André had become good friends after meeting in 1894 at the Salon des Indépendants. All his friends came with their families, and Renoir thoroughly enjoyed showing them around his little village.

In 1897, riding his bicycle on a rainy September day, Renoir skidded in a puddle and onto a pile of stones, breaking his right arm. He had broken the same arm seventeen years previously, so he was practised in painting with his left hand, and from then on, he painted with either hand, as it suited him. However, the accident exacerbated his rheumatoid arthritis, which had started in the early 1890s. While his arm was in plaster, he continued teaching at his house. His students were: Julie Manet, the daughter of Berthe Morisot and Eugène Manet; Julie's orphaned cousins, Jeanne and Paule Gobillard; and Jeanne Baudot, the daughter of his doctor.

MOVE TO THE SOUTH

By his late fifties, Renoir's rheumatoid arthritis was beginning to dominate his life, and in 1898, he decided that the dry, warm climate of the south of France might help to alleviate the painful, debilitating symptoms. He discovered Cagnes-sur-Mer, a seaside town in south-eastern France on the Mediterranean coast. Surrounded by hills, it nestles on a sweeping bay between Antibes and Nice. Part of it, Haut de Cagnes, is 90 metres (295 feet) above sea level, overlooking the sparkling blue sea in the distance, with a breathtaking view of the Cap d'Antibes. Early in 1899, Renoir travelled there again to receive treatment for his condition. He was accompanied by Jeanne Baudot, his pupil and the daughter of his doctor. She stayed with him for two weeks while he underwent his medical treatment, and after she returned home, he remained there until May. Years later, in 1907, he moved with his family to Cagnes-sur-Mer, into Les Collettes, an old farmhouse with a balcony, surrounded by olive and orange groves. From 1911, during the summer months, the Renoir family lived in their apartment in Paris, always returning to Les Collettes for the winter.

> 'I need to feel the excitement of life stirring around me'
>
> *Auguste Renoir*

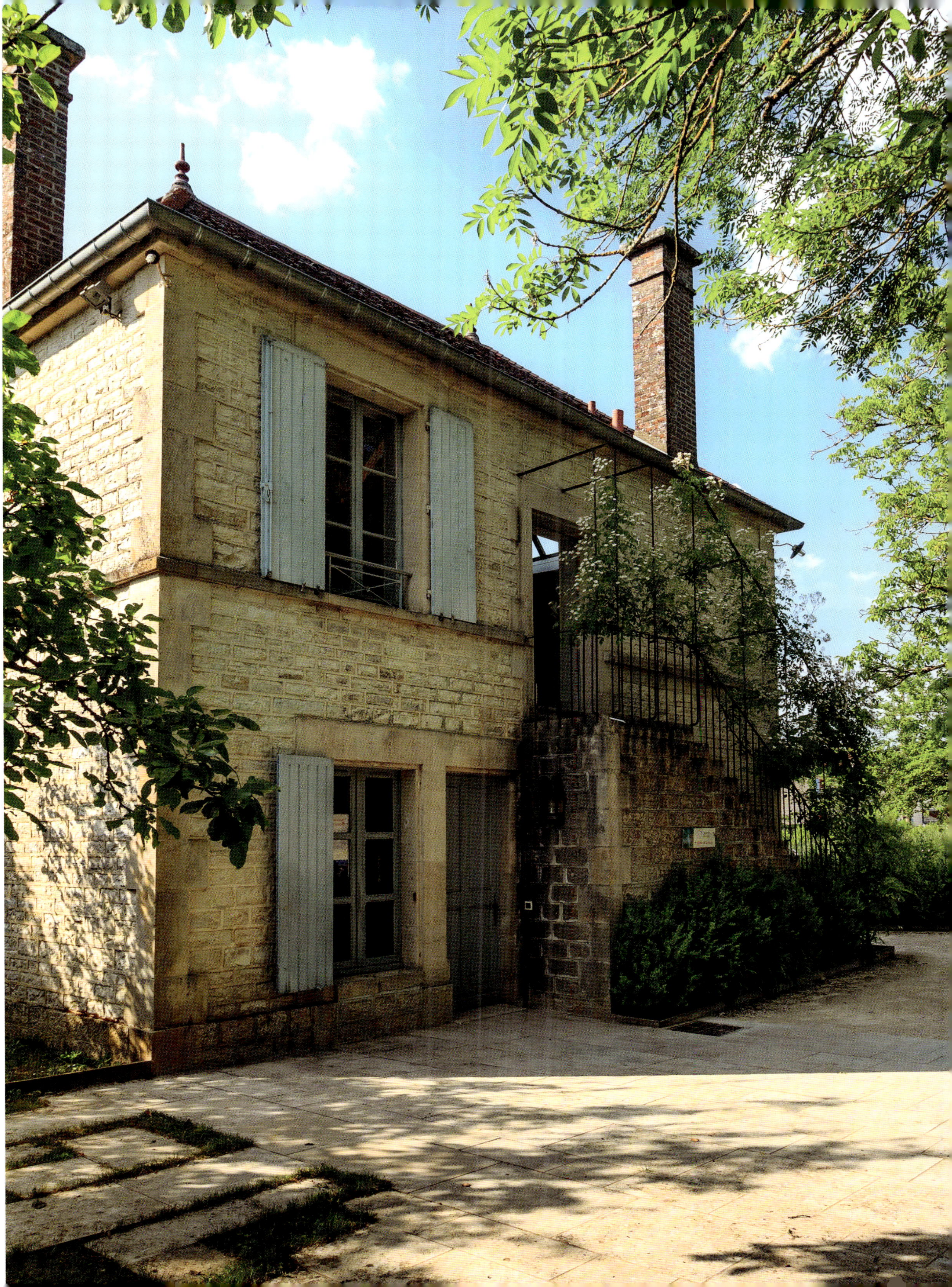

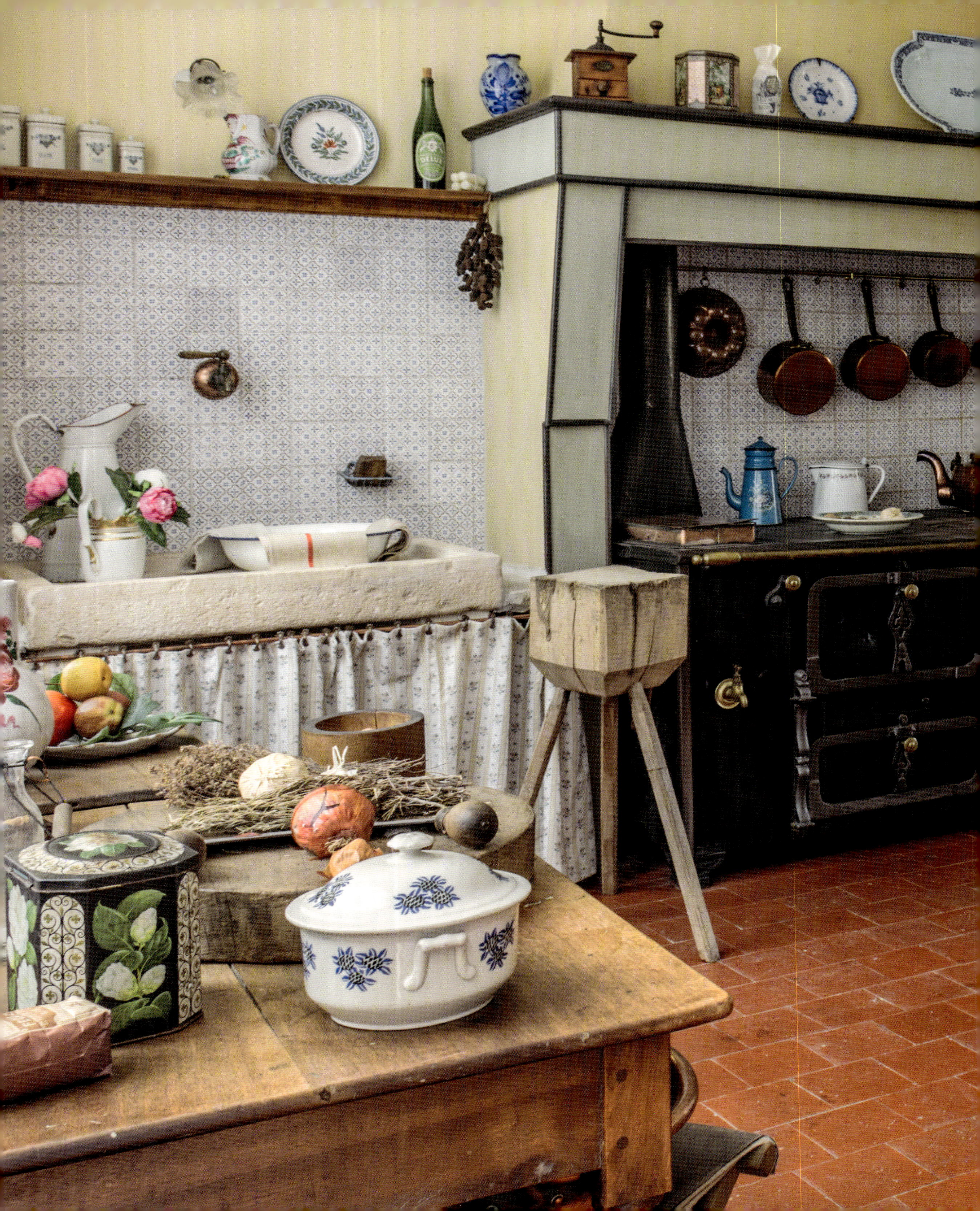

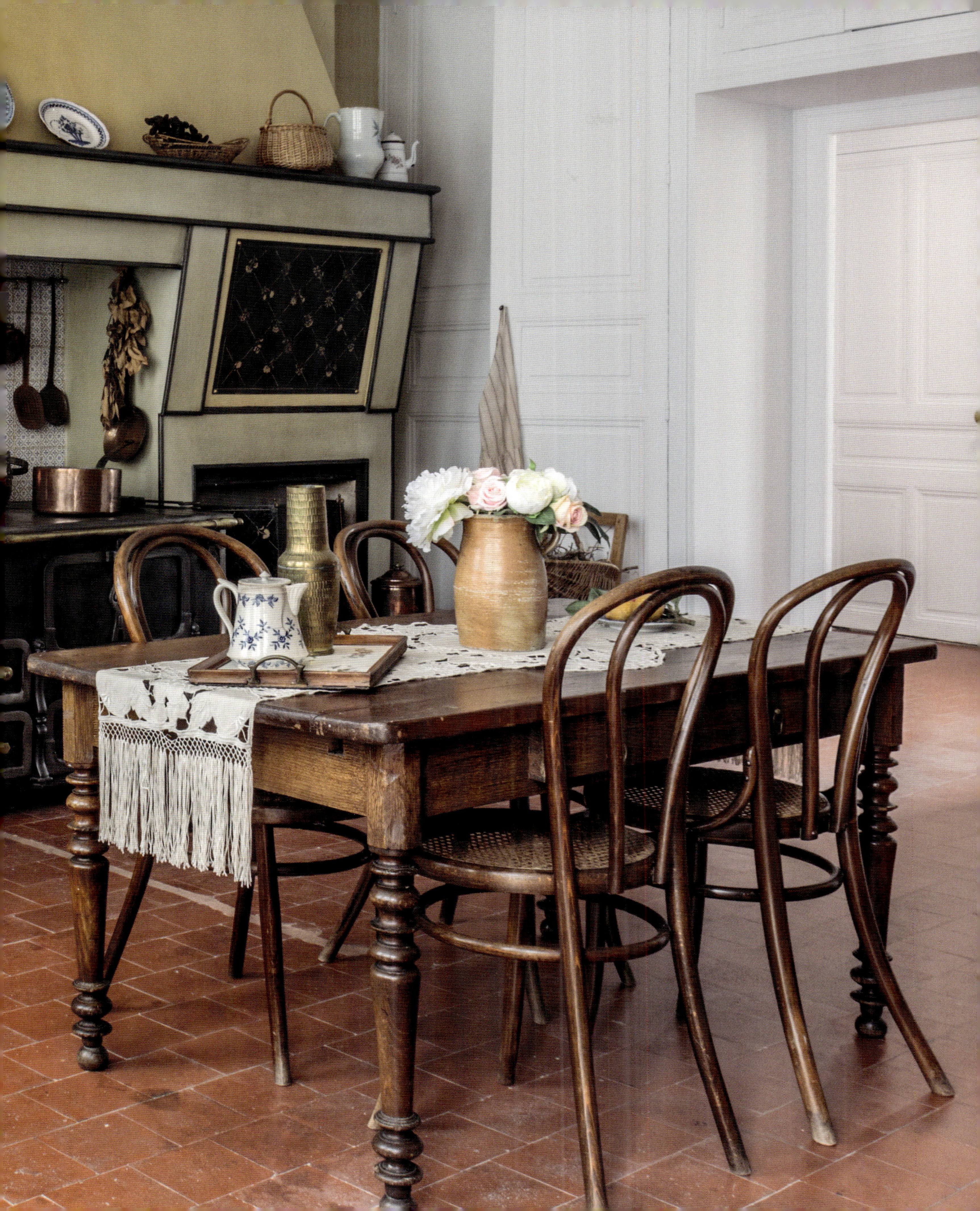

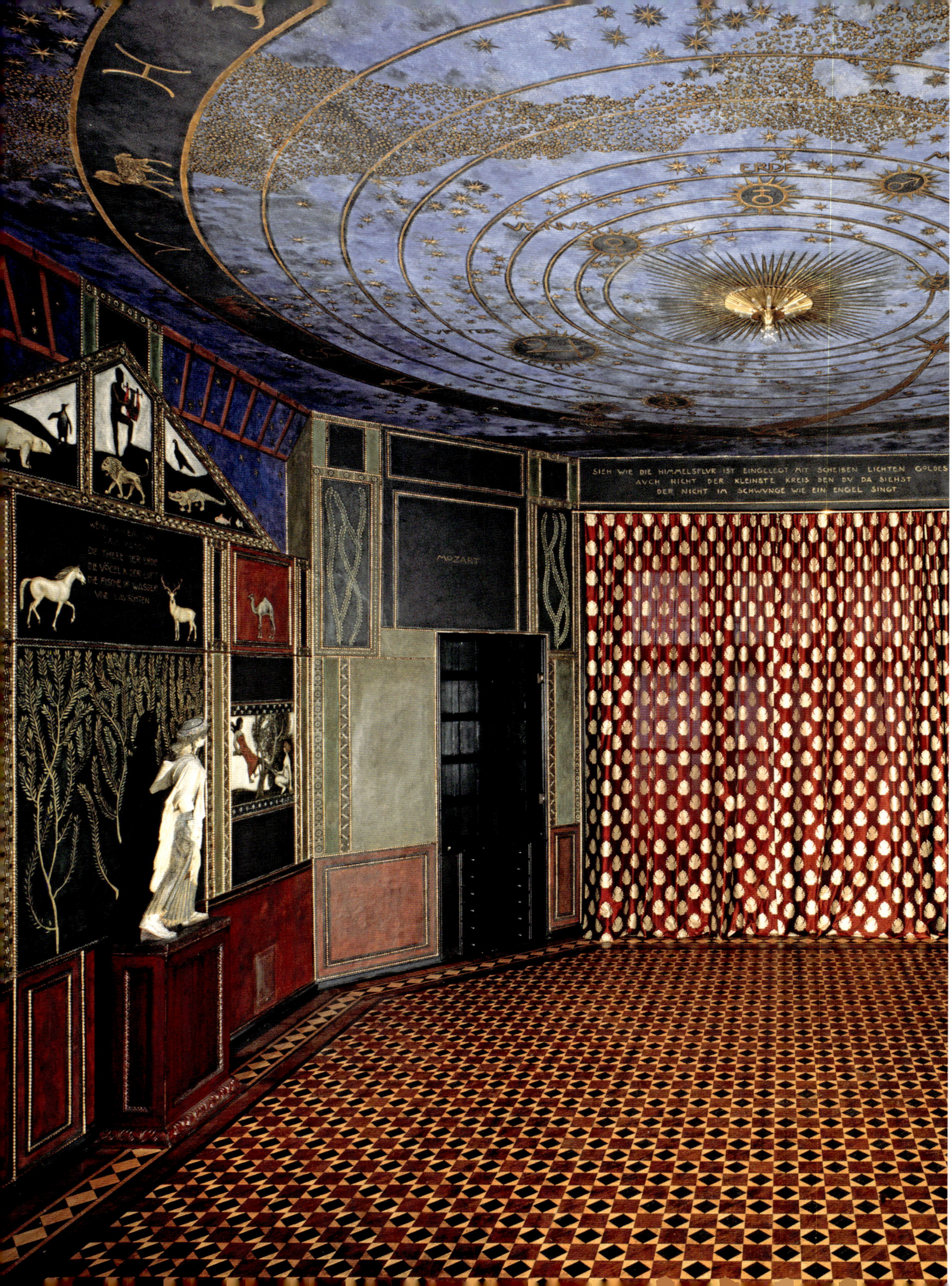
ERDE
MOZART
SIEH WIE DIE HIMMELSFLVR IST EINGELEGT MIT SCHEIBEN LICHTEN GOLDES
AUCH NICHT DER KLEINSTE KREIS DEN DV DA SIEHST
DER NICHT IM SCHWVNGE WIE EIN ENGEL SINGT

FRANZ VON STUCK

Munich, Germany

Soon after marrying American widow Mary Lindpaintner in 1897, Franz von Stuck (1863–1928) designed a palatial residence as their marital home, with a studio. Villa Stuck was distinctive and eclectic, drawing on many varied sources, especially Classicism and Art Nouveau.

Painter, sculptor, printmaker and architect, Franz Stuck was born in the Bavarian village of Tettenweis, the son of a miller. Later in life, he became famous for his paintings of mythological subjects in a sensual, sinuous Art Nouveau and Symbolist style. When he was in his early forties, he was awarded the Order of Merit of the Bavarian Crown and, from that time, he was known as Franz Ritter von Stuck.

With precocious talents in drawing as a child, Stuck knew that he wanted a career in art. As a teenager, he moved to Munich where, at the time, more artists lived than in Vienna and Berlin put together. Initially, he studied at the School of Decorative Arts, and then, from 1881 until 1885, he attended the Munich Academy of Fine Arts to study painting. He began his career drawing cartoons for *Fliegende Blätter*, a satirical weekly magazine that was published in Munich between 1845 and 1944, and he also created illustrations and designs for programmes and books. In 1889, he exhibited his first paintings at an annual exhibition at the Munich Glass Palace and won a gold medal for his monumental work *The Guardians of Paradise*. He soon came to be in great demand as a portraitist, and he began producing sculpture.

BREAKING AWAY

In 1892, Stuck helped to co-found the Munich Secession, an association of young artists who broke away from the official Munich Artists' Association, which was opposed to many new ideas and contemporary trends in art. Stuck and other progressive artists called for changes in beliefs about what constitutes art, and they wanted artists to have the freedom to present their work directly to the public rather than only be allowed to enter official exhibitions.

Around that time, one of Stuck's first sculptures was *Athlete*: an idealised, detailed bronze figure that reflects ideas of antiquity as well as contemporary styles, with his own self-portrait for the face, which was received with general approval. The following year, he participated in the Munich Secession exhibition, showing his painting *The Sin*, which brought him further critical and public acclaim. During the same year, at the World's Columbian Exposition in Chicago, he was awarded another gold medal.

In 1895, Stuck was appointed a Professor at the Academy of Fine Arts in Munich, and there, he inspired many pupils who later became prominent artists, including Paul Klee, Wassily Kandinsky and Josef Albers. When he married at the age of thirty-four, Stuck began designing the residence as an opulent, elegant and spacious home that moved markedly away from his humble origins, and reflected both his creative skills and his success.

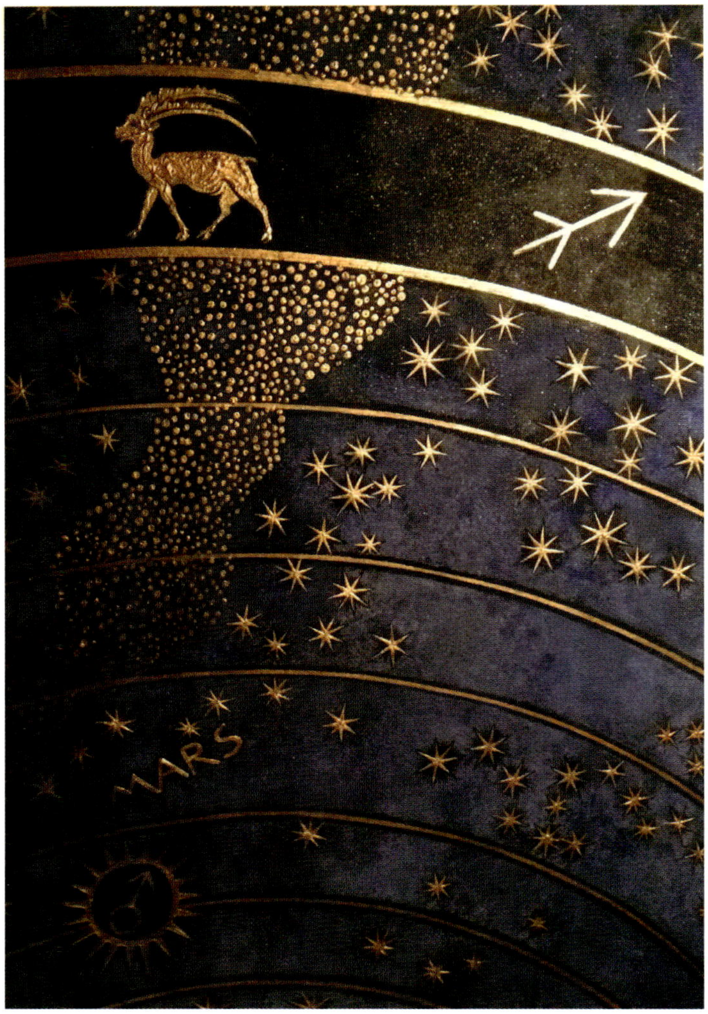

Above: Detail of the zodiac ceiling.
Opposite: Villa Stuck's music room, where Stuck and Mary often held concerts.
Following page: The exterior of Villa Stuck on Prinzregentenstraße.

GESAMTKUNSTWERK

Intending the building to be a 'Gesamtkunstwerk' (total artwork), Stuck aimed for his home to amalgamate life, architecture, art, music and theatre in one space. He designed everything from the architecture to the interior finishes, as well as the furniture and furnishings. He was awarded another gold medal for the furniture at the 1900 Exposition Universelle in Paris.

The three-storey villa was built on Prinzregentenstraße (Prince-Regent Street), one of four prestigious royal avenues in Munich. Throughout the building, Stuck worked with extravagant and lavish materials, drawing inspiration from a wide range of styles, including antiquity, Byzantine, Neoclassicism, the High Renaissance and Art Nouveau. From the outside, the grand façade, with its balanced, geometric shapes and large windows, reflects both Neoclassical and Art Nouveau elements. It is painted cream, with two driveways that lead up to a bronze entrance where a sculpture of Medusa's head is located beneath a portico. After it was built, Stuck added several gold-coloured rectangular panels to decorate this façade. Until 1914, his studio was in the centre of the house, but by 1915, he had added a construction to the side, to incorporate a larger studio as a separate building. The new space features a wide window that overlooks Prinzregentenstraße.

Inside the house, Stuck decorated the rooms with tapestries, carpets, curtains, paintings, murals, sculpture and upholstered furniture. Many were panelled with wood, some of this delicately carved. Many of the walls were hung with his own paintings, and pediments and recesses display his marble or bronze statues. Some rooms are large and spacious, others more intimate; most have high ceilings. Throughout, straight lines are counterbalanced with curves, including rounded archways and domed ceilings, arched recesses, and circular, oval and gridded patterns on some walls, floors and ceilings. Many walls and ceilings feature carvings or paintings, depicting images, or symmetrical or asymmetrical designs. Many of the rooms feature parquet flooring, or small or large ceramic tiles, set in patterns that complement the décor of each room. For example, a Neoclassical-style vestibule – or lobby in cream and gold – is decorated with antique ornaments, reliefs and sculptures. Black-and-white floor mosaics are adorned with animal symbols, and black and ochre lines embellish the white walls. Large floor tiles and a latticed ceiling pattern in relief, plus several small paintings and a marble statue, amplify the Neoclassical appearance. The gold and brown hall includes a carved gilt Greek-style frieze, a large mirror, marble, silk, gilded mosaics, mahogany furniture, a fireplace and bronze busts. Similarly inspired by ancient Greece, a waiting room features a marble sculpture, and contrasting fabrics and wall decorations, all in subtle cream and green. A smoking room is lined in red damask and features a mirror with a moulded and hand-carved frame. Elsewhere in the villa are a library, bedrooms, a dining room, and a large stairwell where the ceiling is carved in the form of a shell.

Stuck and Mary regularly entertained their friends, who included some of the most prominent figures of the time. They held dinner parties, grand celebrations, and earnest talks and debates. Mary was a talented singer, and they often held concerts in the music room, which features animal figures and sculptures depicting the ancient Greek sagas, with a ceiling painted as a night sky. Friends also joined them at times in their garden to the back of the villa: a peaceful space designed on Renaissance and Neoclassical lines, with marble arches and columns, statues representing figures such as ancient Greek and Roman gods, plus paths, walkways, flower beds and mature trees.

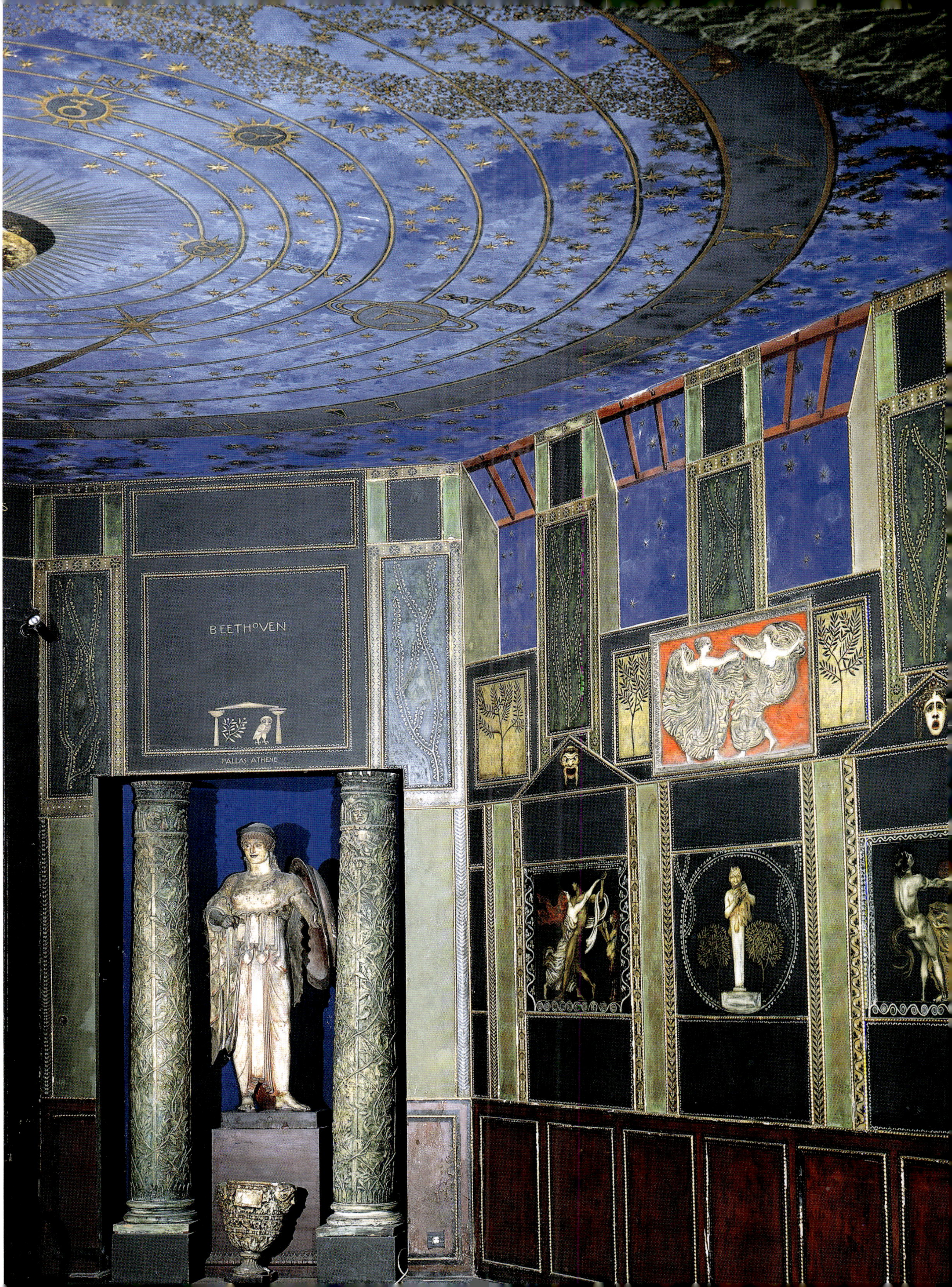

MARS
SATURN
BEETHOVEN
PALLAS ATHENE

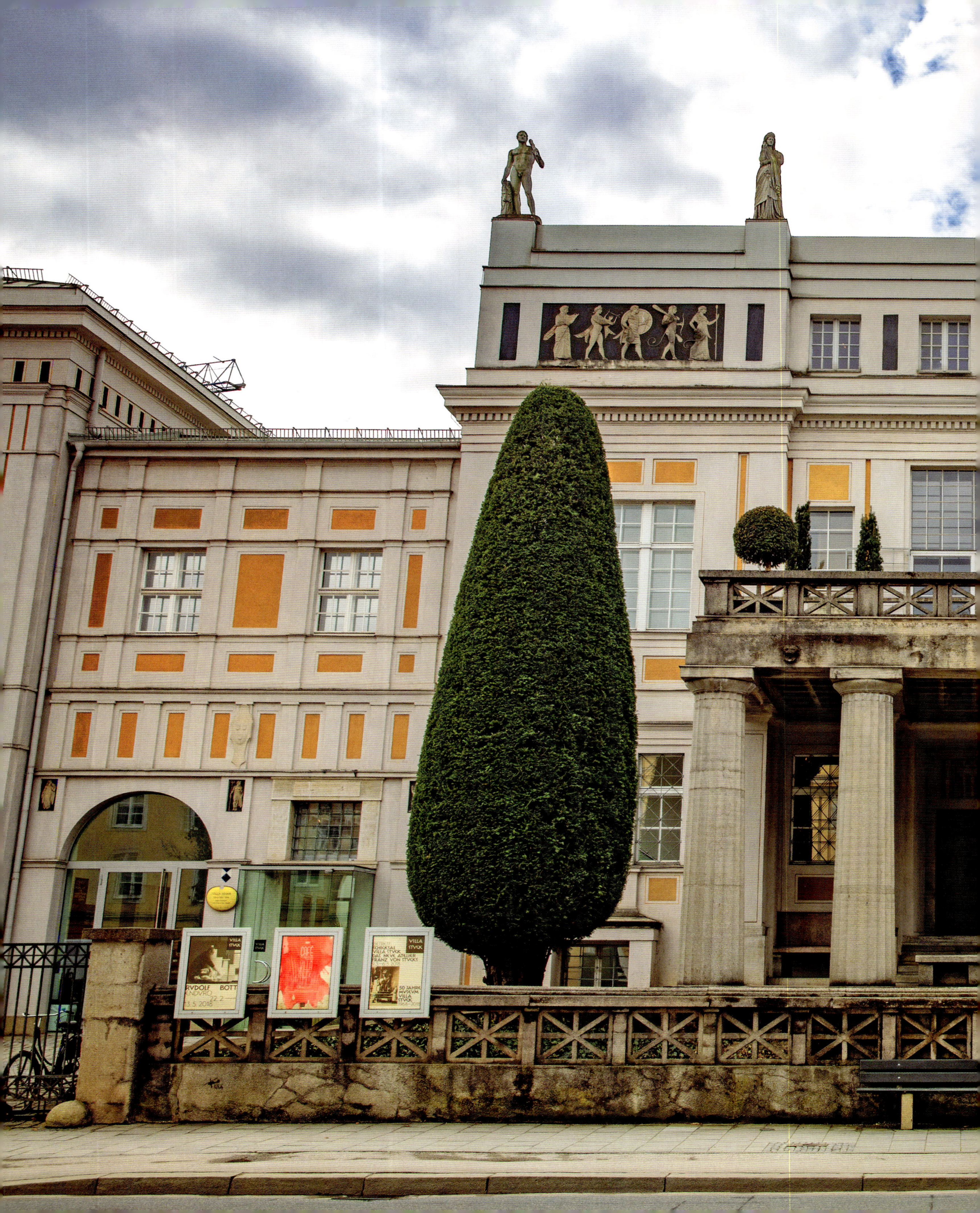
VILLA STVCK
RVDOLF BOTT
ENDVRO
22.2
13.5.2018
VILLA STVCK
CAFÉ
VILLA STVCK
SCHICKSAL
VILLA STVCK
DAS NEVE ATELIER
FRANZ VON STVCKS
50 JAHRE
MVSEVM
VILLA
STVCK

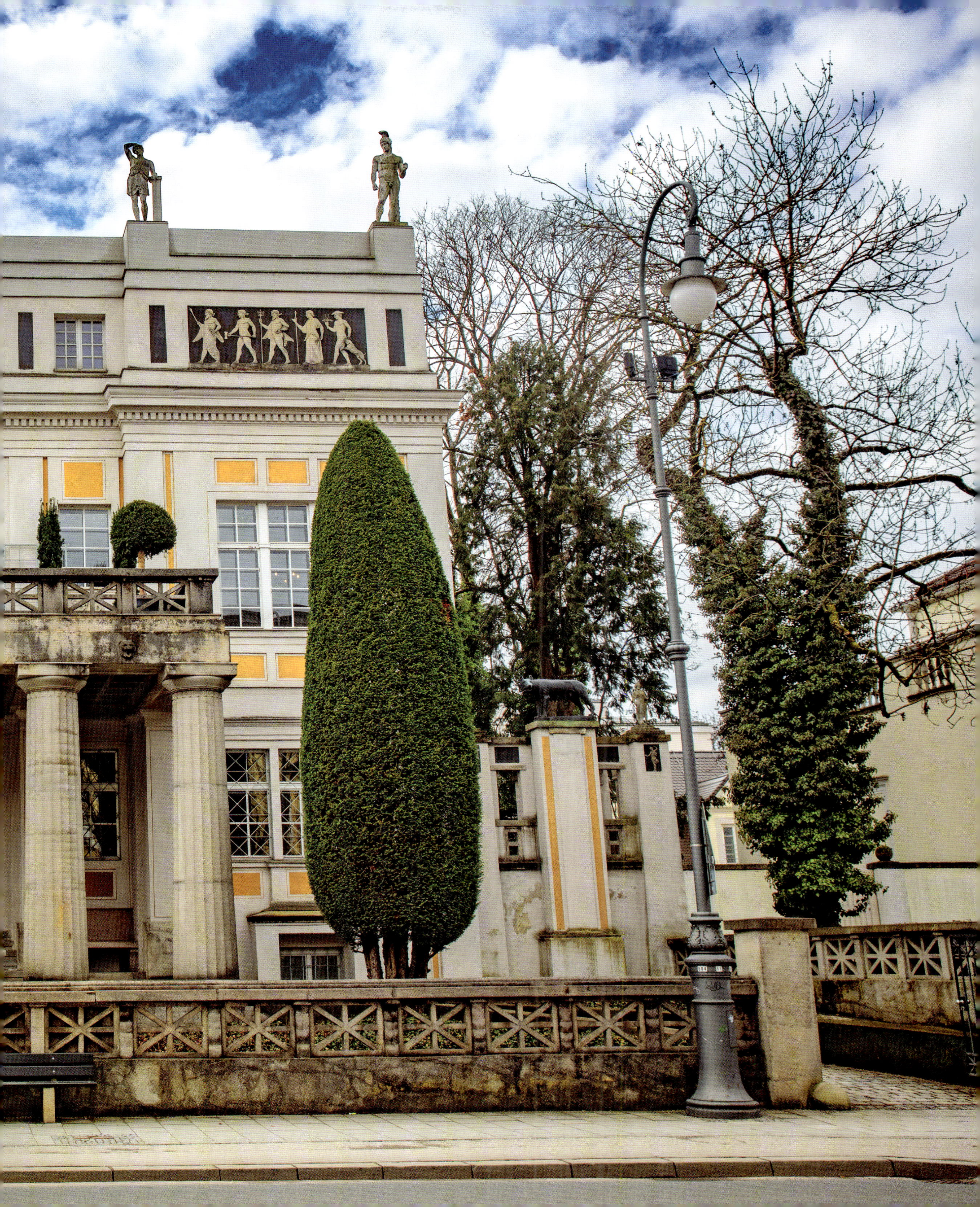

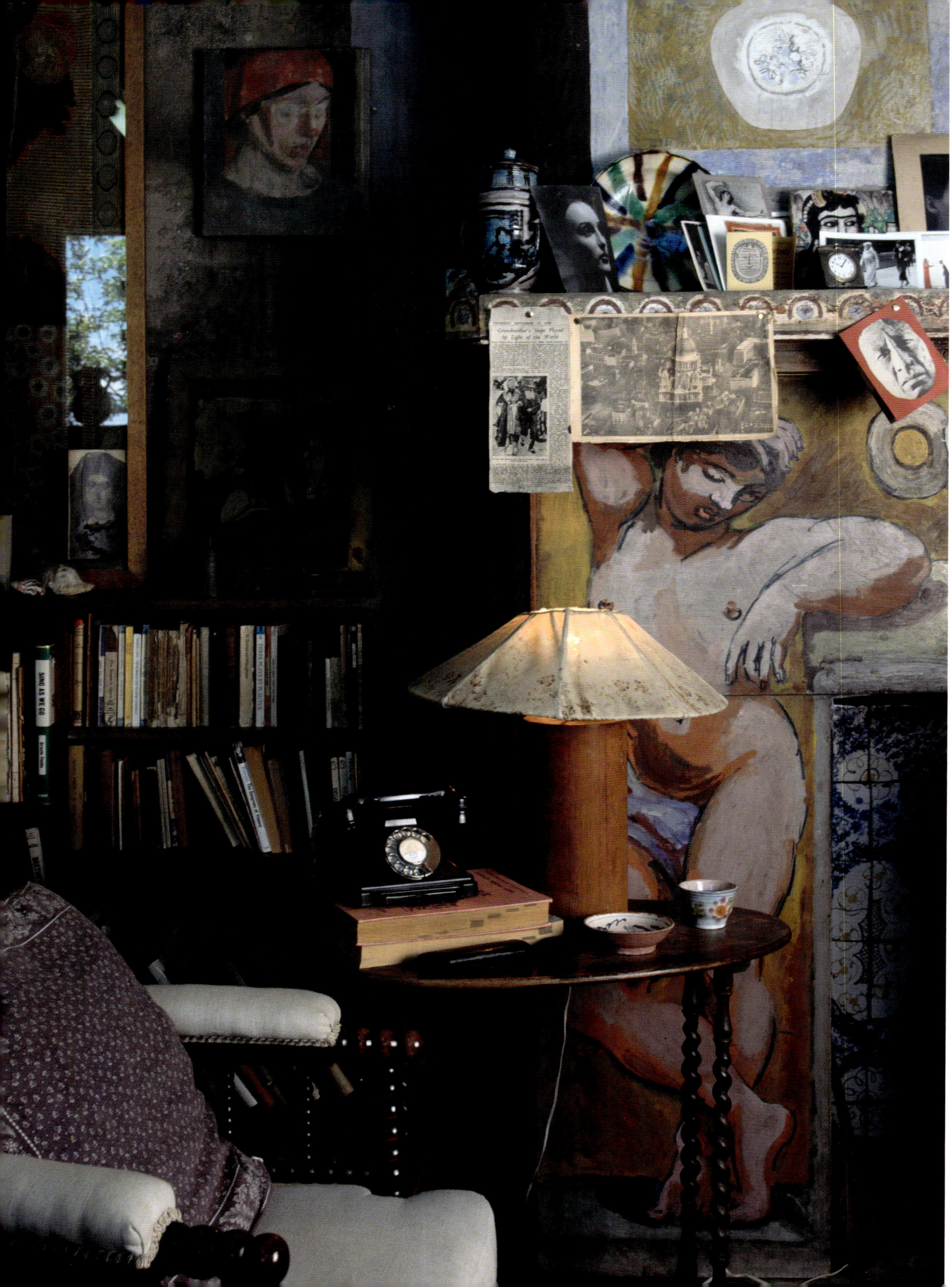

VANESSA BELL AND DUNCAN GRANT

Charleston, UK

In 1916, the English painter and interior designer Vanessa Bell (1879–1961) moved into Charleston, an eighteenth-century Sussex farmhouse. Twelve years earlier, after the deaths of both of her parents, when she was twenty-five, she had moved from Westminster to Bloomsbury in London, with her younger sister Virginia, and brothers Thoby and Adrian.

In November 1906, just two years after they had moved to Bloomsbury, Thoby died of typhoid fever. Less than three months later, Vanessa married Thoby's friend, the art critic Clive Bell. They had two sons – Julian and Quentin – and they formed the Bloomsbury group, which comprised artists, writers and intellectuals, including her siblings Virginia and Adrian, the writer Lytton Strachey, critic Desmond MacCarthy, economist John Maynard Keynes, novelist E. M. Forster, painter Duncan Grant (1885–1978), and painter and art critic Roger Fry. In 1910, Vanessa saw the first major exhibition of Post-Impressionist painting in England, organised by Fry: *Manet and the Post-Impressionists*. As well as establishing the name Post-Impressionists, the exhibition had a profound influence on Vanessa's art. From that time, she began using brighter colours and more abstracted, simplified forms.

In 1911, after her two sons were born, Vanessa and Fry embarked on what became a two-year affair. Despite the demands of motherhood and conventions for women of the period, she continued to work, and two years later, with Fry and Duncan Grant, she founded the Omega Workshops. This aimed to reduce divisions between design and art, and prove that artists could design, create and sell their own works, and that writers could also be their own printers and publishers. Producing pottery, painted furniture, murals, mosaics, stained glass, clothes and textiles, plus entire interior design schemes, the Omega Workshops was sought-after for six years, with their pared-down, colourful designs. However, after World War One, their styles became unfashionable, and Omega Workshops closed in 1919.

In 1914, Vanessa and Grant began a relationship. Even though he was also homosexual and continued liaisons with men, the pair lived together for more than forty years. They had a daughter, Angelica, whom Clive Bell raised as his own to avoid scandal. Angelica only discovered her father's true identity when she was eighteen.

MOVING TO CHARLESTON

Three years after the formation of the Omega Workshops, and two years after the start of World War One, Vanessa moved to Charleston. Arriving at the gravel-fronted porch with her were her sons Julian, then aged nine, six-year-old Quentin, Grant, his lover David 'Bunny' Garnett, Grace Higgens, and Henry the dog.

Described by Grant as 'the angel of Charleston', Grace Higgens had worked for Vanessa and the family since June 1920, as housemaid, nurse and cook, and then at Charleston as cook, housekeeper and artists' model. Exuberant and witty, she was an essential part of the running of the household. She was later joined by her husband and, for a time, by Miss Eva Edwards and then Mrs Brereton, the boys' governesses. A few other members of staff came and went, but Grace Higgens remained.

Grant, Garnett and Clive Bell were all conscientious objectors to the war, and to avoid conscription, they all had to find farm work. Bell spent the war years in Oxfordshire; he and Vanessa never formally divorced or separated, and he often visited Charleston for long periods, usually with his girlfriend. The house became a centre of artistic and literary activity for the Bloomsbury group,

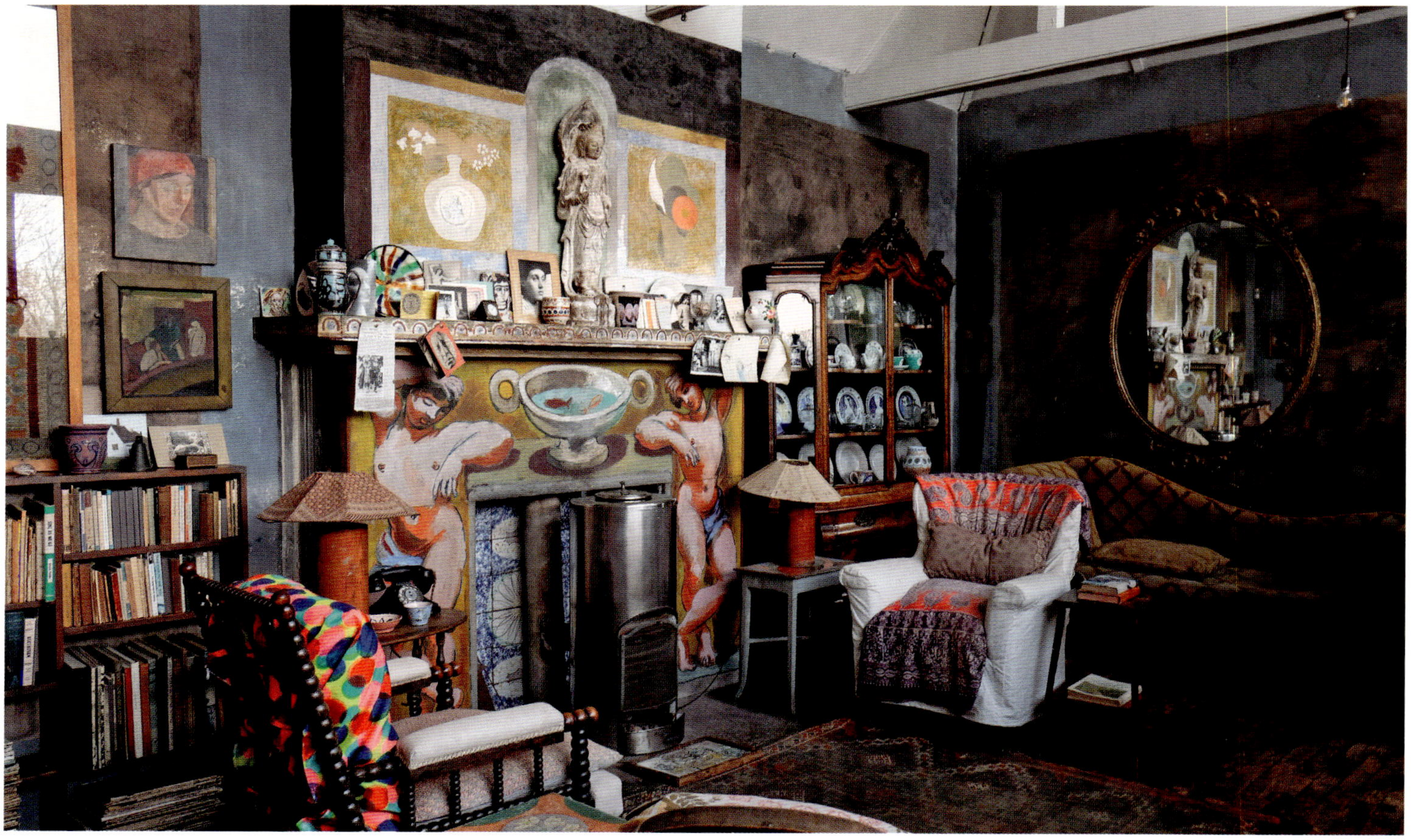

Above: Duncan Grant's colourful studio and sitting room at Charleston, with the fireplace painted by him and Vanessa.
Opposite: Detail of door and bookcase painted by Duncan Grant in the library at Charleston.

who travelled there from London. Charleston was a gathering point for the radical artists, writers and thinkers of the group, the place where they discussed their progressive social, political, literary and artistic ideas. Among the visitors were Strachey, who was Grant's cousin, MacCarthy, Keynes, Forster and Virginia and her husband, the author, publisher and civil servant Leonard Sidney Woolf. When Keynes married Russian ballerina Lydia Lopokova, they moved to a house nearby. Before they moved in, Virginia wrote to Vanessa of Charleston: '...it has a charming garden, with a pond, and fruit trees, and vegetables... The house is very nice, with large rooms, and one room with big windows fit for a studio... There is a w.c. and a bathroom, but the bath only has cold water. The house wants doing up.'

Almost as soon as they had unpacked their things, Vanessa and Grant began painting every surface, transforming it into a living work of art. They painted the furniture and fireplaces, and murals on the walls and doors; they displayed their paintings and drawings throughout the house, and used their own Omega Workshops textiles and pottery. Vanessa also designed the gardens, growing flowers, fruit and vegetables. She worked on commissions for the Omega Workshops, and designed book jackets for all her sister's books, which were published by Virginia and Leonard Woolf's publishing company, the Hogarth Press.

LIFE AT CHARLESTON

As soon as World War One had ended, Vanessa moved back to London with her two sons and baby daughter. Two-storey Charleston, with its large sash windows, then became the family summer home. In 1924, she negotiated a longer lease and building work began. There were bedrooms for each of them: the children, Vanessa, Bell, Grant, Keynes and the staff. There was also a library, a spare bedroom for guests, a study for Bell, studios for Vanessa and Grant, a pottery room, a garden room, a sitting room for Grace, plus a dining room and kitchen. In 1925, an alcove in the dining room was opened up, and an especially large studio was constructed. Beyond that, the old chicken run became 'Grant's Folly' and a pottery, and Fry designed a walled garden. Vanessa and Grant stencilled the walls of the garden

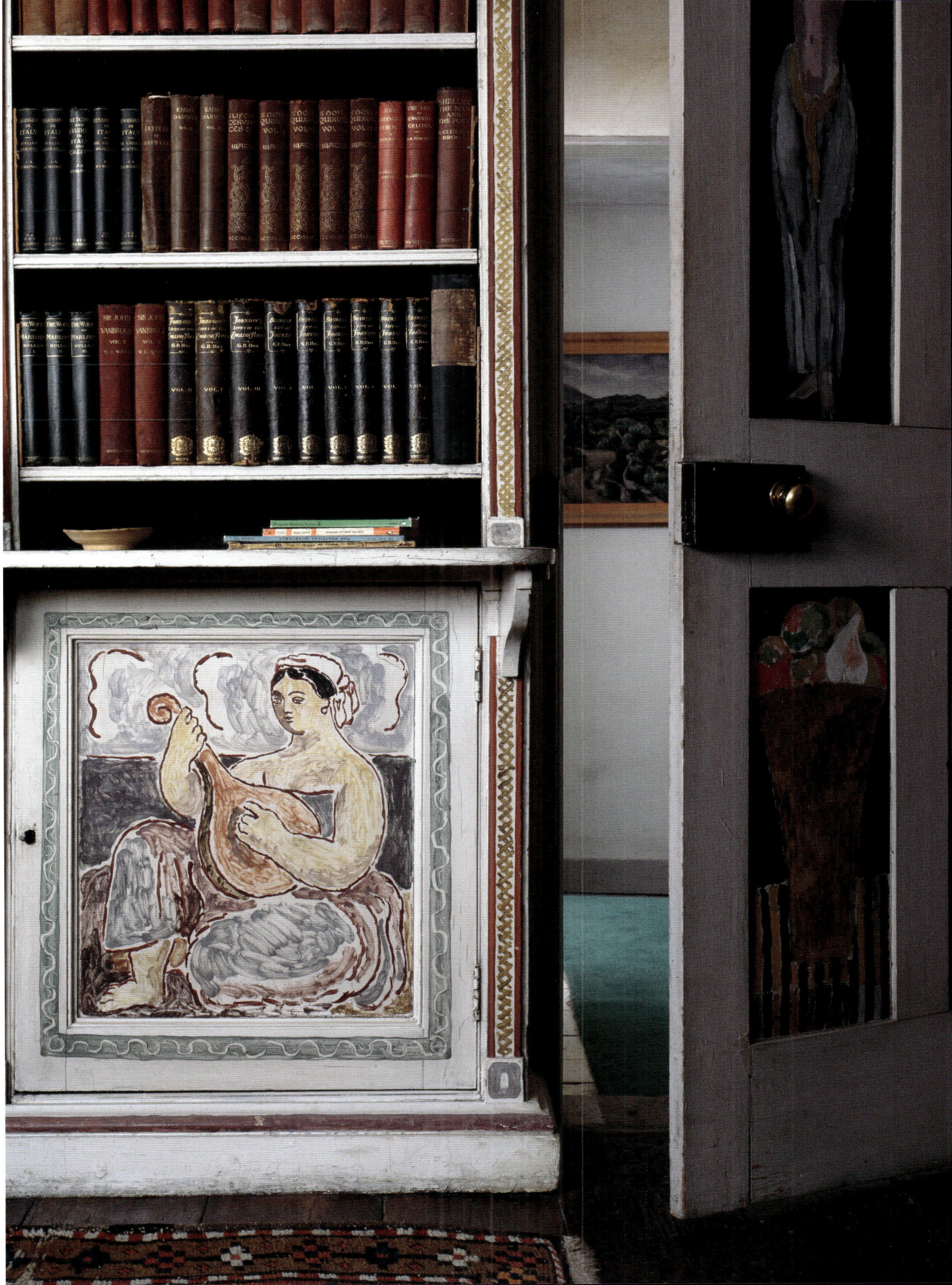
JOHNSON'S LIVES OF THE ENGLISH POETS
G.B. HILL
VOL. III

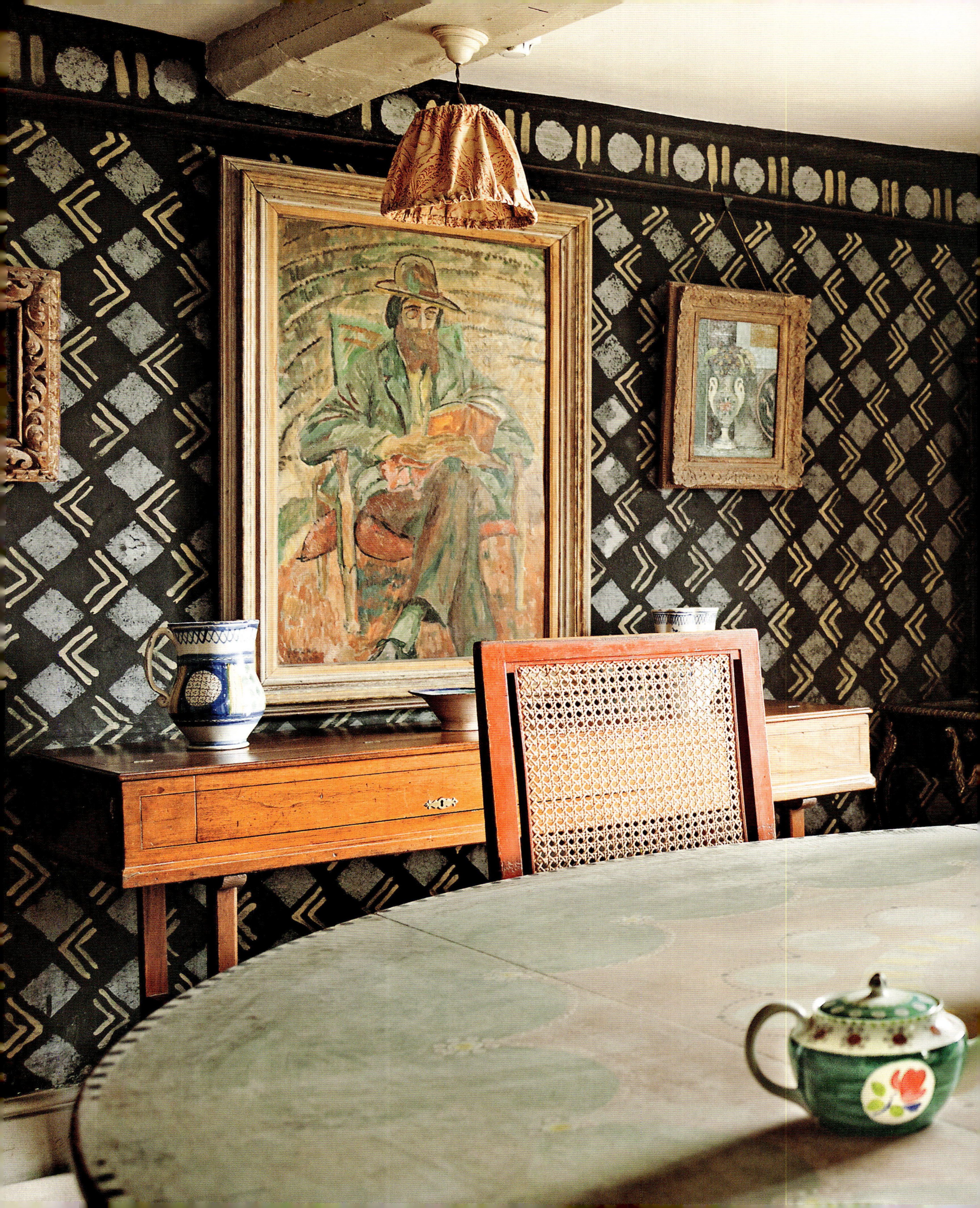

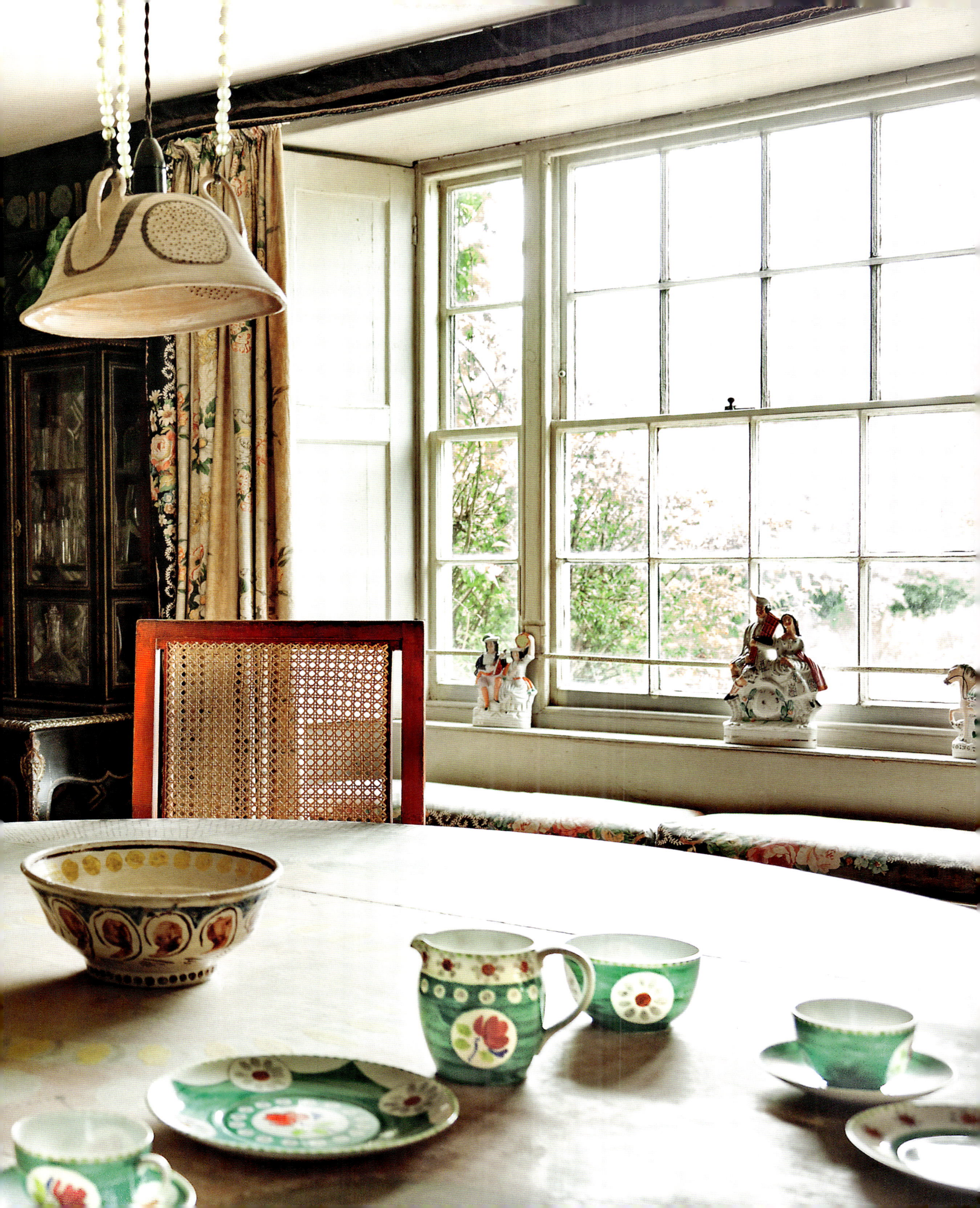

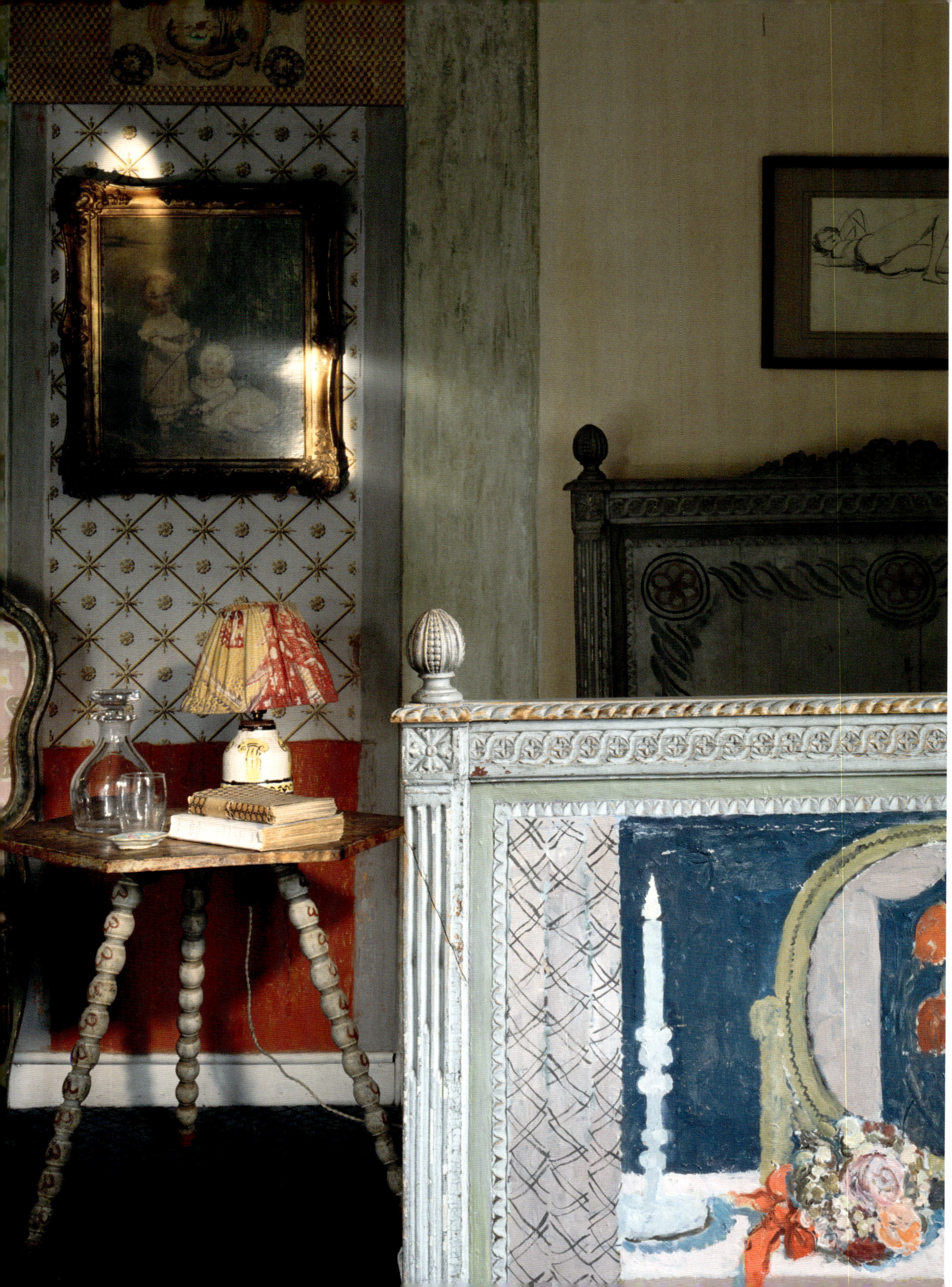

room in a paisley design with freehand flowers. As they did in the other rooms, they also created the curtains and cushions. Bell's study was originally used as a schoolroom for Julian and Quentin, until he moved his books and furniture there in 1939. Through the years, more visitors joined them, including the philosopher G. E. Moore, the poet, publisher, playwright and critic T. S. Eliot, and French film director, screenwriter, actor, producer and author Jean Renoir.

Breakfast was informal and relaxed, as people waited for the postman and paper boy. During the day, most inhabitants of the house wrote or painted individually. Vanessa worked in her studio or garden. Lunch was generally light and also fairly informal, but in the evenings, everyone gathered firstly in the garden room, for a drink, and then they ate and chatted around the large dining table.

The happy days of discussion, painting, writing, eating and laughing, however, came to an abrupt end in 1937, when Julian was killed in the Spanish Civil War. At twenty-nine, he had become increasingly empathetic with the Spanish Republicans, but both his parents and his aunt Virginia tried to dissuade him from travelling there to fight. Nonetheless, he went, and rather than fighting, he worked as an ambulance driver. He had been in Spain for just over four weeks, when he was fatally hit by bomb fragments. World War Two began two years later, and Charleston once again became a refuge for the artists, writers and thinkers of Vanessa's circle. She, however, remained grief-stricken over the death of her child. Four years after Julian's death, in 1941, Virginia drowned herself. Vanessa wrote to a friend: 'I shall be cheerful, but I shall never be happy again.'

In 1941, she and Grant were commissioned to paint murals for nearby Berwick Church, and their complex relationships continued. The following year, Angelica married Garnett; they had four daughters. Quentin married and had three children: a son and two daughters. As well as from her remaining children and grandchildren, and her enduring relationship with Grant, Vanessa continued to find serenity and solace in her painting – and Charleston.

'One discovered that one was, after all, in love with nature.'

Vanessa Bell

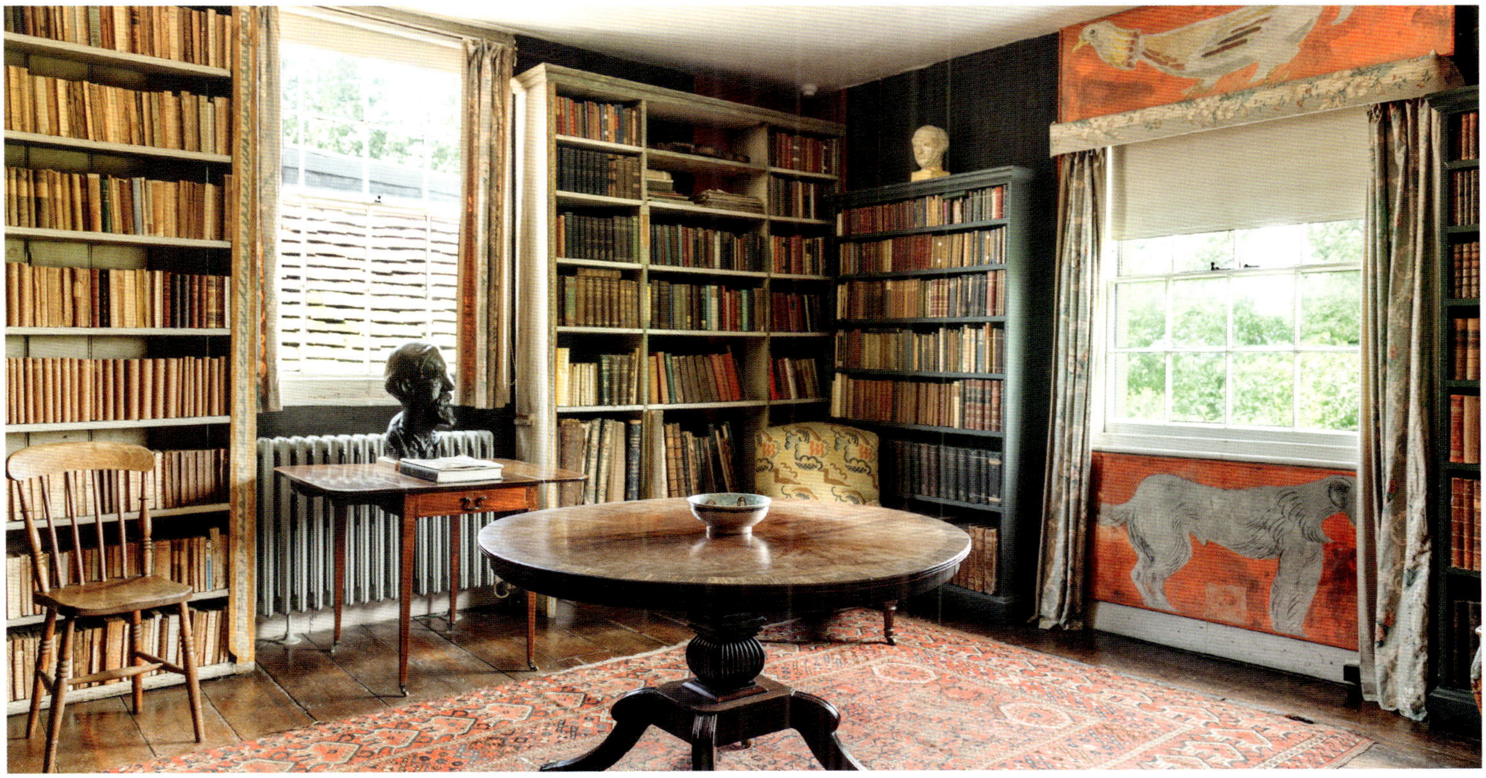

Above: The library at Charleston was a hub for the Bloomsbury Group in the early 20th century
Opposite: Clive Bell's bedroom.

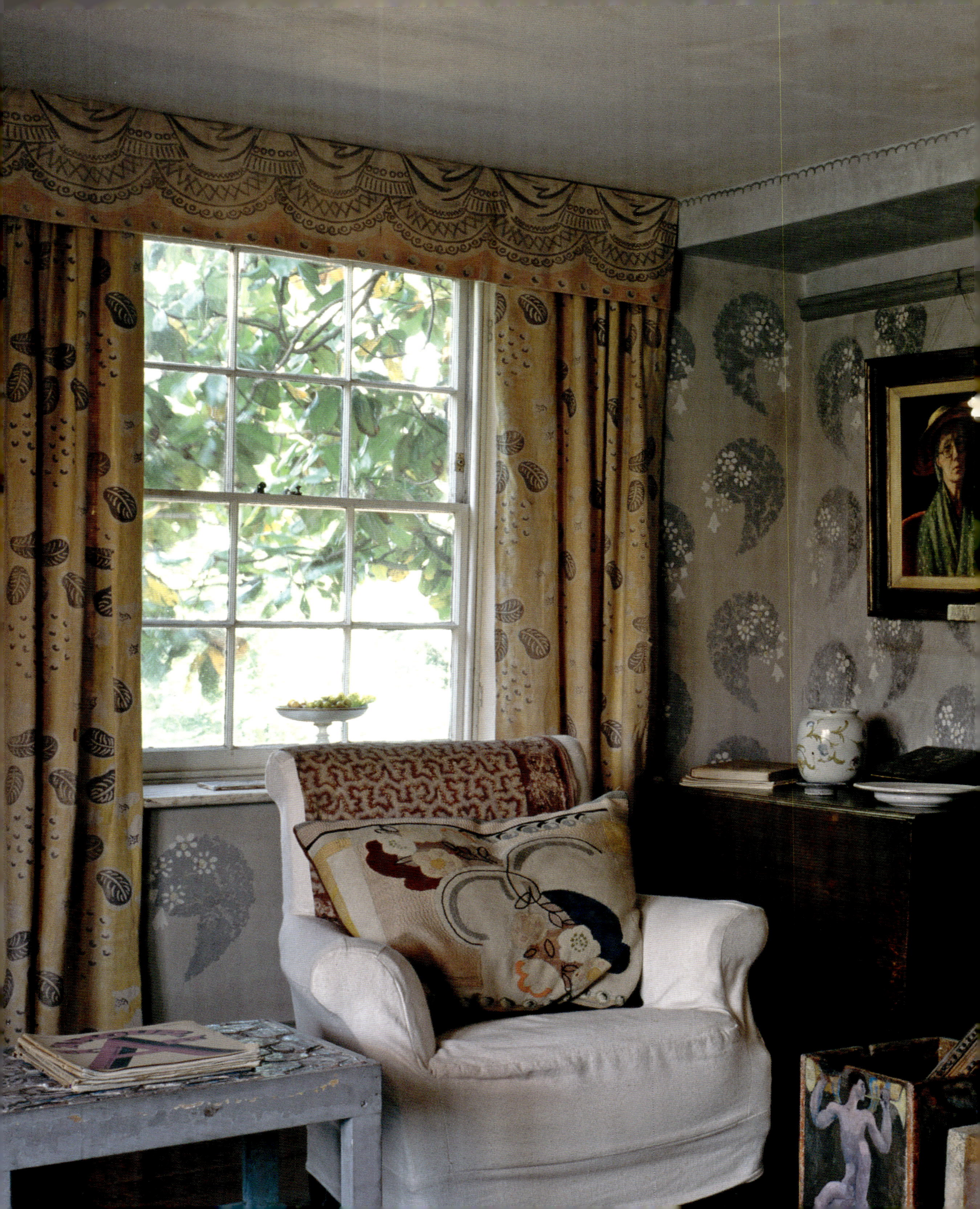

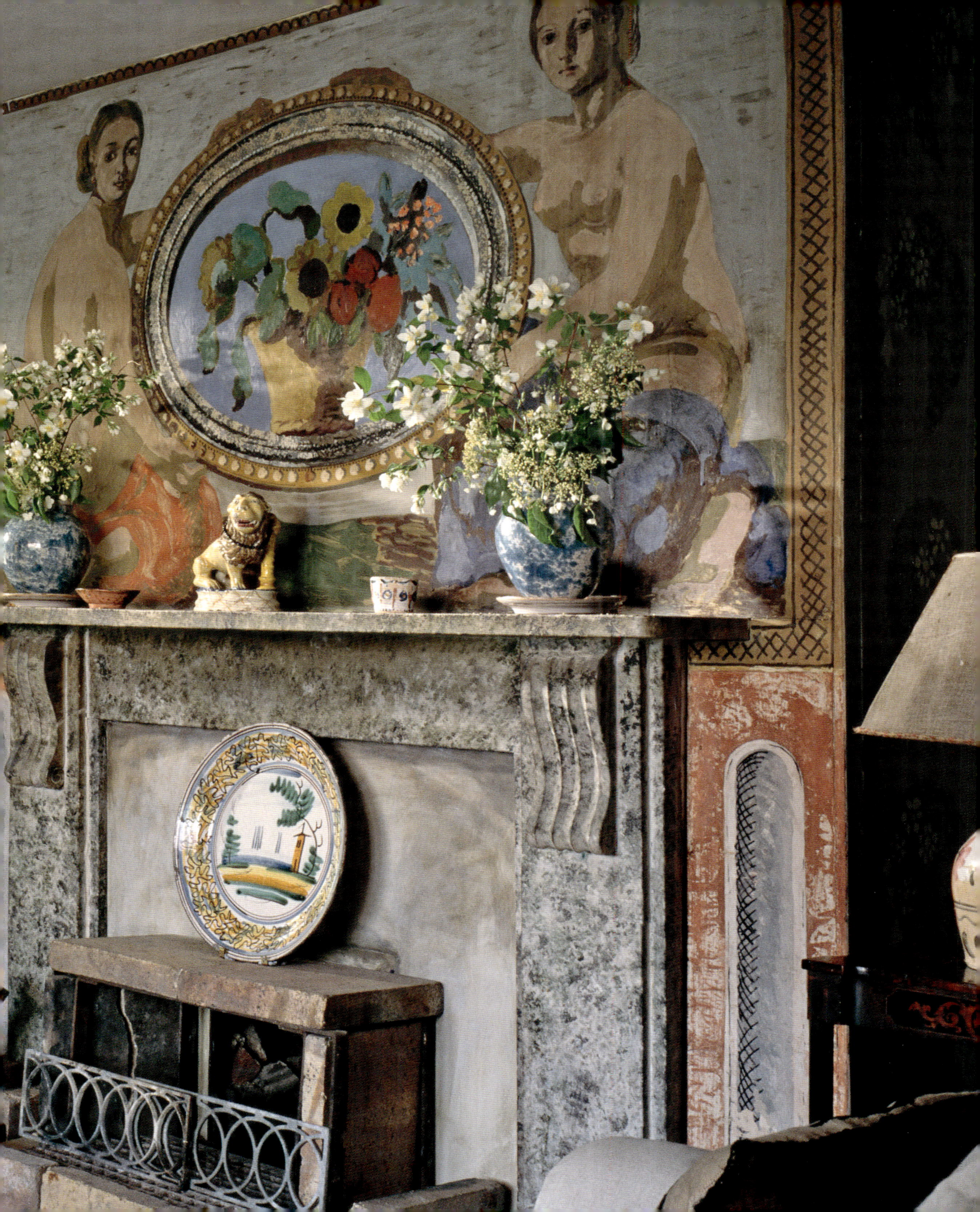

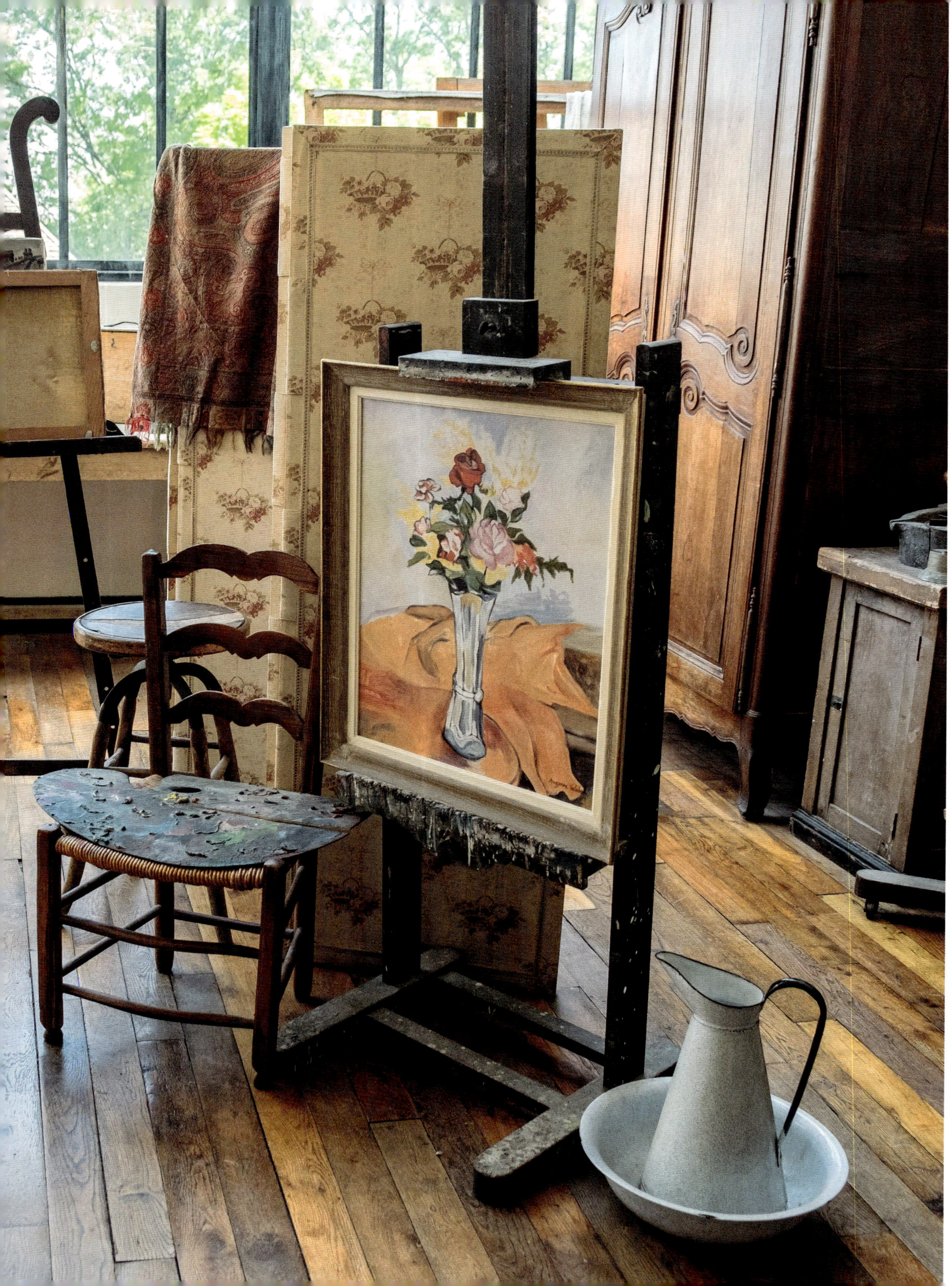

SUZANNE VALADON

Paris, France

Close to the summit of Montmartre, tucked away behind the place du Tertre and the imposing Sacré-Cœur, is the rue Cortot. Once known as rue Saint-Jean, it appeared on the first street map of Paris in 1672, and after 1859, it was renamed after the Parisian Neoclassical sculptor Jean-Pierre Cortot.

During the late nineteenth and early twentieth centuries, Montmartre was a bohemian and vibrant quarter favoured by artists and writers, and with just twenty buildings, the steep, cobbled rue Cortot was where many of them lived and worked. In particular, numbers 12–14 became a meeting place, home and studio to among others, Pierre-Auguste Renoir, Émile-Othon Friesz, Raoul Dufy and Émile Bernard. Suzanne Valadon (1865–1938) used it as her apartment and studio from 1896–1905 with her first husband, and from 1912–1926 with her second husband.

WATCHING THE ARTISTS

Born in a small town in western France, Marie-Clémentine Valadon and her mother moved to Montmartre when she was five. From the age of eleven she worked in various jobs, including in millinery and floristry, at a vegetable market and, when she was fifteen, at the Cirque Molier as a gymnast, equestrian and trapeze artist. However, after falling from a trapeze and injuring her back, she had to leave. Through her gregarious spirit and fascination with art, she became acquainted with several artists who also lived in Montmartre and she began modelling for them. As a beautiful young woman, small, extrovert and with dark hair and blue eyes, she was popular with artists including Pierre Puvis de Chavannes, Berthe Morisot, Renoir and Henri de Toulouse-Lautrec. Lautrec nicknamed her Suzanne from the biblical story of Susanna and the Elders, because she had affairs with several of the older male artists. She began using Suzanne as her painting name, although her friends continued calling her Marie.

While she posed, Valadon watched the artists working and several gave her advice about painting, drawing and printmaking. For example, Edgar Degas, impressed with her bold drawings and colourful paintings, advised and encouraged her. He taught her to etch and engrave, showed her how to use pastels and introduced her to the influential art dealers Paul Durand-Ruel and Ambroise Vollard. Valadon and Degas remained lifelong friends and she referred to him as 'the Master.' In 1883, when she was eighteen, she began painting seriously, and in the same year, gave birth to a son whom she called Maurice. Although his paternity is uncertain, her friend and former lover Miguel Utrillo signed papers recognizing the baby as his son. Speculation abounded that the real father could have been perhaps Puvis de Chavannes or Renoir, and when Utrillo signed the paternity papers when Maurice was eight, he allegedly declared: 'I'll sign my name to the work of any of those men'. As he grew up, Valadon trained her son to paint. In 1894, she became the first woman to be admitted to the Société Nationale des Beaux-Arts.

During the 1890s, she met and married wealthy businessman Paul Mousis. Before their marriage, they lived with Utrillo and Valadon's mother at number 2 rue Cortot, then moved to a house in the country, but Mousis also rented her a studio with living accommodation at 12–14 rue Cortot. It was an airy space, high above Paris, with a leafy orchard garden. They lived there until 1905, but by then, Valadon was having an affair with a friend of her son; the painter André Utter, who was over twenty years younger than her. She divorced Mousis in 1909 and married Utter five years later, but lived with him from 1912, in the studio and apartment in rue Cortot with Utrillo and her dogs, cats and a goat. Despite the three being

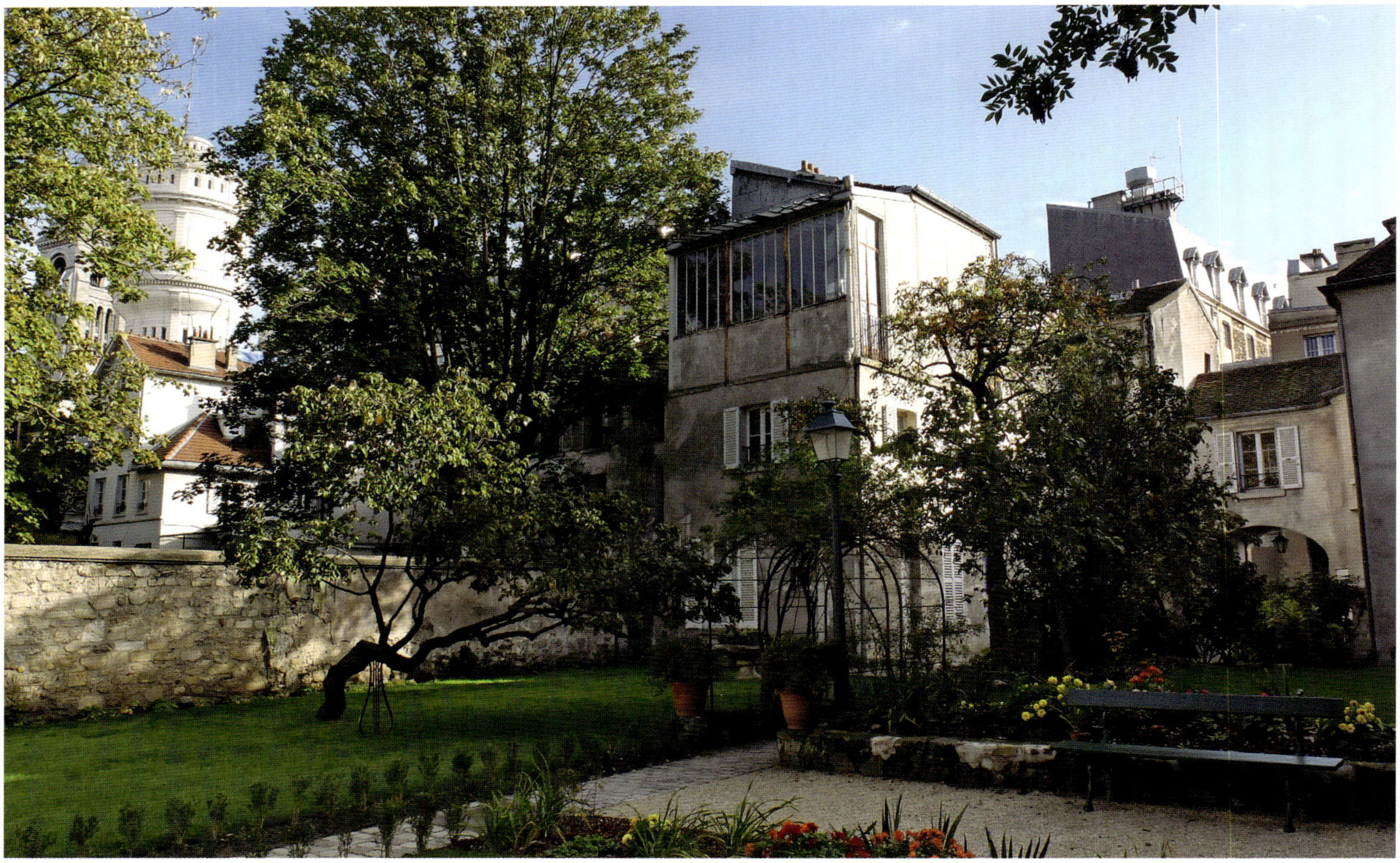

Above: A view of Valadon's second floor studio from the garden.
Opposite: A jumble of paint boxes and canvases in the studio.

fairly volatile – Utrillo was an alcoholic and depressive, which led to frequent arguments between Valadon and Utter – Valadon spent the most productive years of her life at rue Cortot. The three artists became known as 'Le Trio Infernal'.

SECOND FLOOR STUDIO

The studio at 12–14 rue Cortot was in a grand seventeenth-century building, one of the oldest in Montmartre, which had been divided into rooms and studios. When Valadon arrived at the street entrance, she walked through a huge arched doorway, greeted the concierge and then walked up a wooden stairway to her workplace on the second floor. Each day, her confidence grew as she sat and drew or stood at her easel, and she worked prolifically. She had employed a housemaid, Catherine, since her days with Mousis, and this allowed Valadon time to paint. She continued to socialize with the inhabitants of Montmartre and first thing each morning, either she or Catherine would descend the wooden staircase to take her dogs – usually wolfhounds, and for a while five of them – for walks. Occasionally, her close friends, Degas and Amedeo Modigliani would visit and sit and chat with her as she worked. Or her art dealer Vollard would come and view her latest works. She was exceptionally generous, empathetic and passionate, and as her success rose, she would often drop 100-franc notes from her studio window to young urchins in the street below. She also gave money to any vagrant she passed while walking through the streets of Montmartre.

In the studio, she painted brightly coloured still lifes, portraits, flowers, landscapes, candid nudes, her dogs and Catherine. She also painted many nude self-portraits, depicting her body as it aged. Her earliest large oils related to sexual pleasure, and included some of the first paintings to convey a man as an object of desire by a woman, for example in *Casting the Net* (1914). Because of her bohemian lifestyle, and her close friendships with the male artists of Paris, she

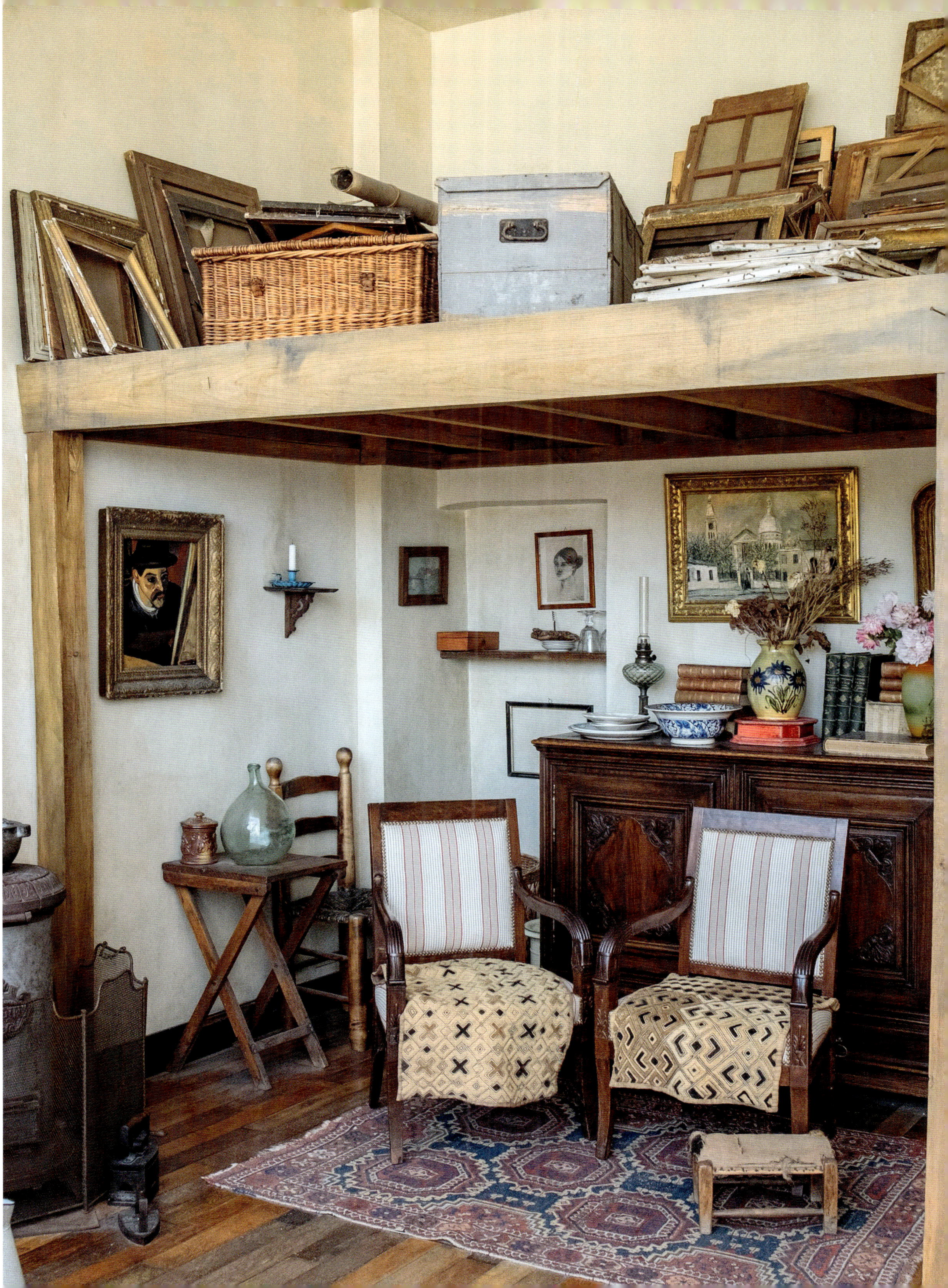

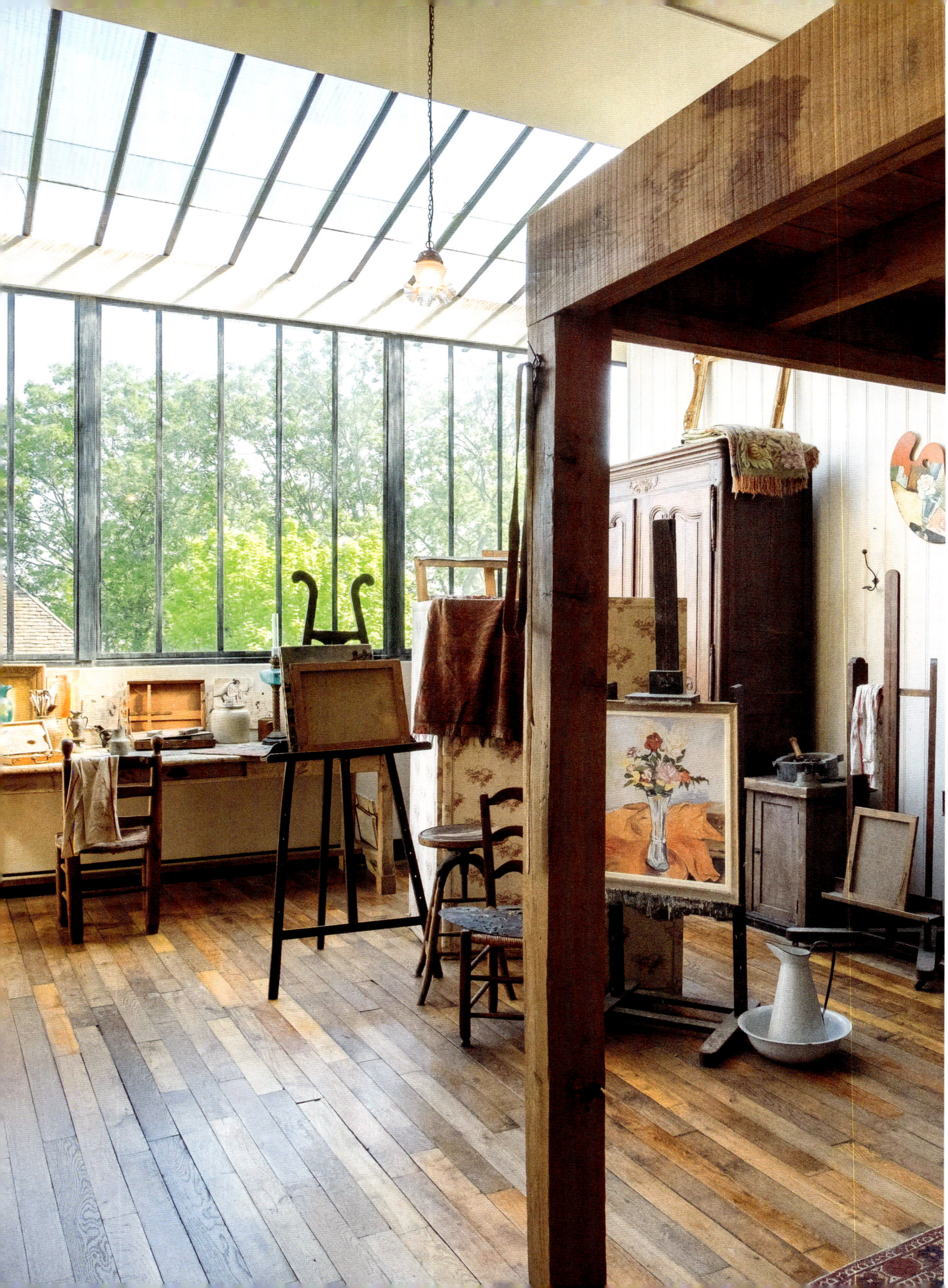

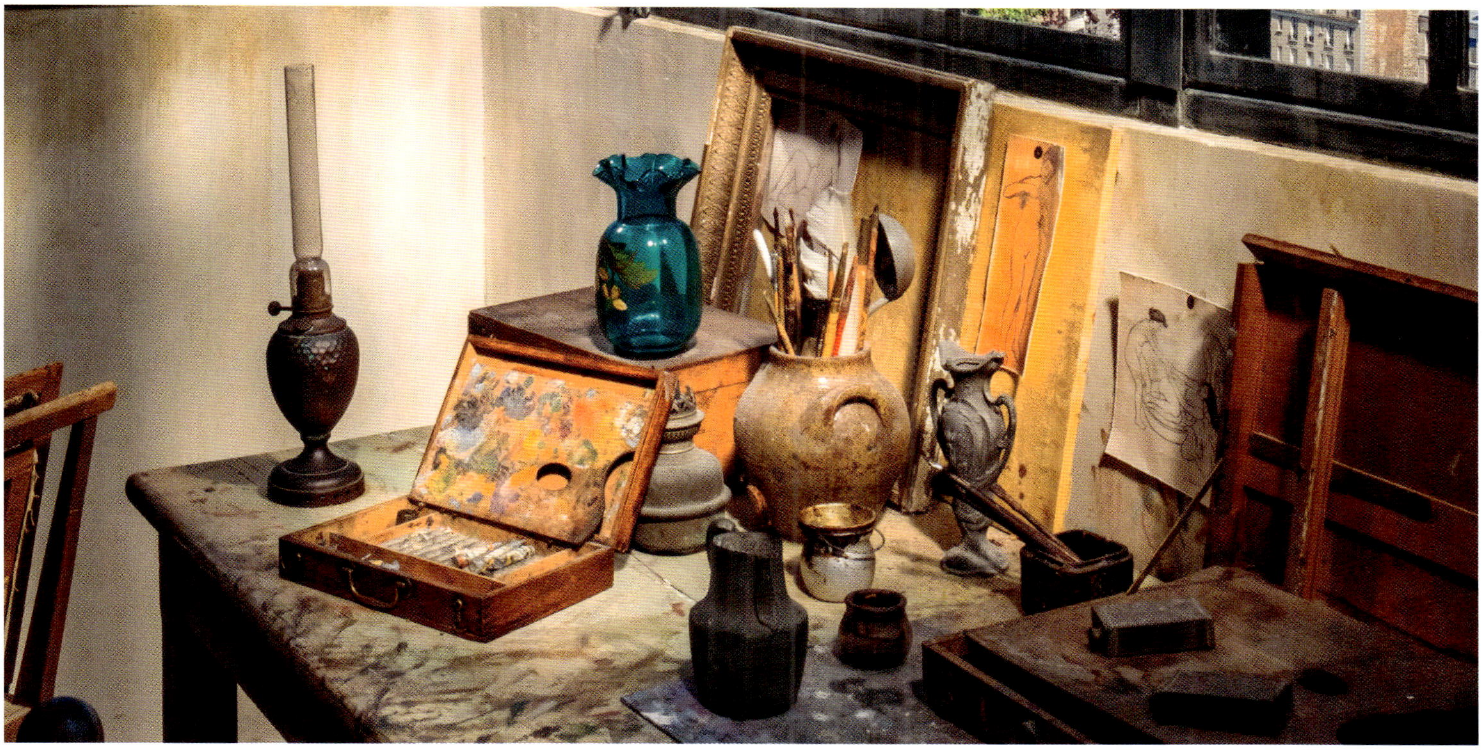

Above: The corner of a table laden with Valadon's materials and some of her props.
Opposite: Part of Valadon's studio in rue Cortot.

became the first woman to paint male nudes, using the same models her male contemporaries hired. However, the three male figures in *Casting the Net* were all posed by Utter. Comprising rich colours and animated brushwork, all her paintings explore themes that digressed from contemporary trends and expectations of academic art. She developed a signature dark outline to her subjects, rejecting the more usual and accepted light and feathered 'feminine' brushstroke, instead experimenting with decisive lines and colours. Her themes, too, were exceptionally bold and unconventional for any artist, let alone a woman. Her portraits were based on real emotions and solid, thoughtful women, and her approach with bright colours, animated brushwork and visible brush marks contradicted the requirements and expectations of the official art world. Unlike many conventional artists, she always mixed her own colours and kept her palette simple, as she said 'So that I don't have to think about it'.

PANORAMIC VIEWS

With its creaking, narrow, shadowy passageways, the living quarters of Valadon's apartment comprised small, dimly lit rooms, albeit with breathtaking panoramic views of Paris out of the modestly sized windows. The tall windows and skylights of the studio however, created an airy sense of space and light. This bright studio had wooden panelled walls, high ceilings, a wooden mezzanine and a small stove. A rug covered part of the floor, and a long table stood under the vast window that rose up vertically on three sides to the top of the building and horizontally spanned part of the ceiling. As well as her jumble of paint boxes and canvases, Valadon kept a screen, a wardrobe, a chests of drawers, easels and an assortment of wooden chairs, upon which she would place jars of turpentine, coffee cups, tubes of paint, brushes and palettes.

Unfortunately, as he grew up, Maurice's depression, wild rages and alcoholism worsened. This infuriated Utter, while Valadon made excuses for her son, which riled Utter even more. The three artists often worked together, but in different areas of the studio – sometimes companionably chatting or in comfortable silence, but sometimes exploding into fiery rows, when they would shout and hurl objects at each other, including paint tubes, brushes, plates or cups. At other times, Valadon would work frenziedly, anxiously waiting for Maurice to return from a drinking binge, to emerge from a depressive period in his room, or to hear that he had been arrested once again for violence or disorderliness. When things were calm however, she and Utter would leave the studio and spend a happy evening at the nearby Lapin Agile; a cabaret club in Montmartre and one of Picasso's favourite haunts.

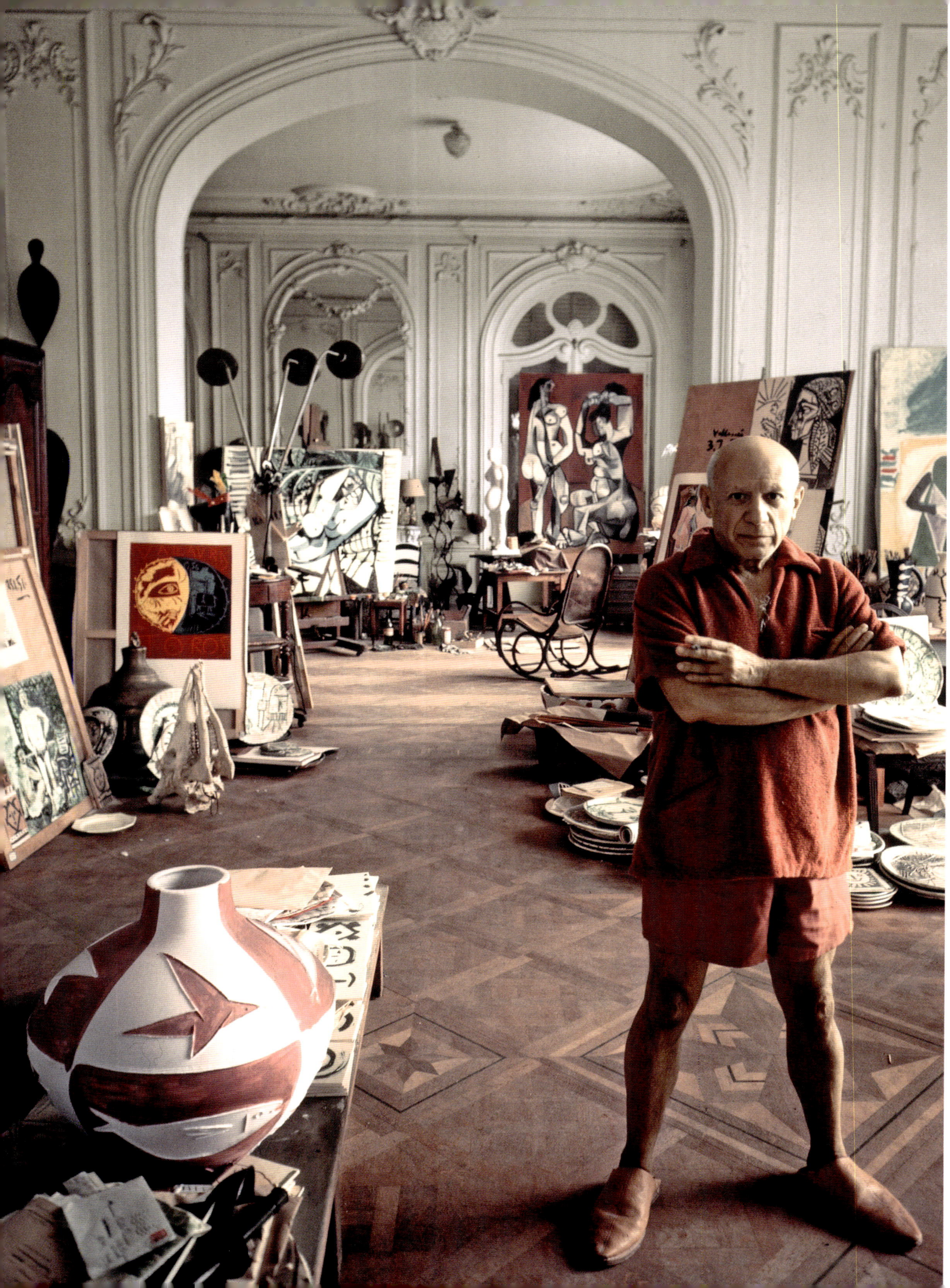

PABLO PICASSO

Cannes, France

After World War Two, Spanish artist Pablo Picasso (1881–1973) decided to leave Paris, and in 1946, he moved to the south of France. Nine years later, he bought Villa La Californie in Cannes and moved in with his girlfriend, Jacqueline Roque, and her daughter Catherine. He lived and worked in Villa La Californie for six years.

The most dominant and influential artist in the world during the first half of the twentieth century, Pablo Picasso helped to invent Cubism with Georges Braque and, throughout his life, he innovated artistically, changing the direction of art history. A painter, sculptor, printmaker and ceramicist, he grew up in Barcelona, Spain, learning initially from his art teacher father, and then later excelling at art college. In 1900, he moved to Paris and, for the next few years, moved between France and Spain, before finally settling permanently in France in 1904.

Having painted in a naturalistic way while growing up, as soon as he moved to Paris, Picasso began experimenting with original artistic approaches and materials, and within a short time, his art began to be noticed by influential patrons. His fortunes changed quickly from poverty to prosperity. Many of his works were groundbreaking. For example, in 1907, he painted *Les Demoiselles d'Avignon*, which ultimately initiated Cubism, and in 1937, he produced *Guernica*: a monumental, black-and-white painting that is one of the world's strongest statements against war.

EXPANSIVE TALENTS

Picasso was born in Málaga, Spain, and from the age of about seven was taught to draw and paint by his artist father. His mother claimed that his first word was *piz*, a shortened version of *lapiz*, or pencil. Demonstrating extraordinary artistic talent in his early years, he painted in a naturalistic manner through his childhood and adolescence. When he was thirteen and much younger than the other students, he enrolled in the School of Fine Arts in Barcelona. Three years later, he entered the Real Academia de Bellas Artes de San Fernando in Madrid. However, he disliked the classes there, preferring to spend his time visiting museums and galleries to study art on his own, and he left the school after a short time. When he was seventeen years old, in Barcelona, he began frequenting the café Els Quatre Gats, where he met bohemians and radicals, and fairly soon after, he began experimenting with different theories, techniques and styles. By the time he moved to France, his art had started to change, from his Blue Period, which was triggered by the suicide of his friend, to his Rose Period. After 1906, Matisse's Fauvist paintings motivated him to explore more radical styles and instigated an enduring rivalry between them. From then, he explored Cubism, Surrealism, Classicism and more, working with paint, sculpture, ceramics and prints. He became one of the first Western artists to be influenced by African and ancient Iberian art, and over his career, he produced more than 20,000 works, changing the way art was both made and perceived. His changes in artistic style can be correlated to each of his romantic relationships. In addition, he designed stage sets for the Ballets Russes, and produced posters and book illustrations. Even during his lifetime, entire museums were dedicated to his work.

During World War Two, Picasso remained in Paris while it was occupied by German troops. Generally, he was left alone, but the war nonetheless affected him badly. The Nazis confiscated his paintings and some of his closest Jewish friends were killed. Once the conflict was over, he no longer wanted to remain in Paris, and he moved to Vallauris in the south of France with his partner, artist Françoise Gilot. In 1953, however, Françoise left him and returned to Paris with their children, Claude and Paloma. That same year, he

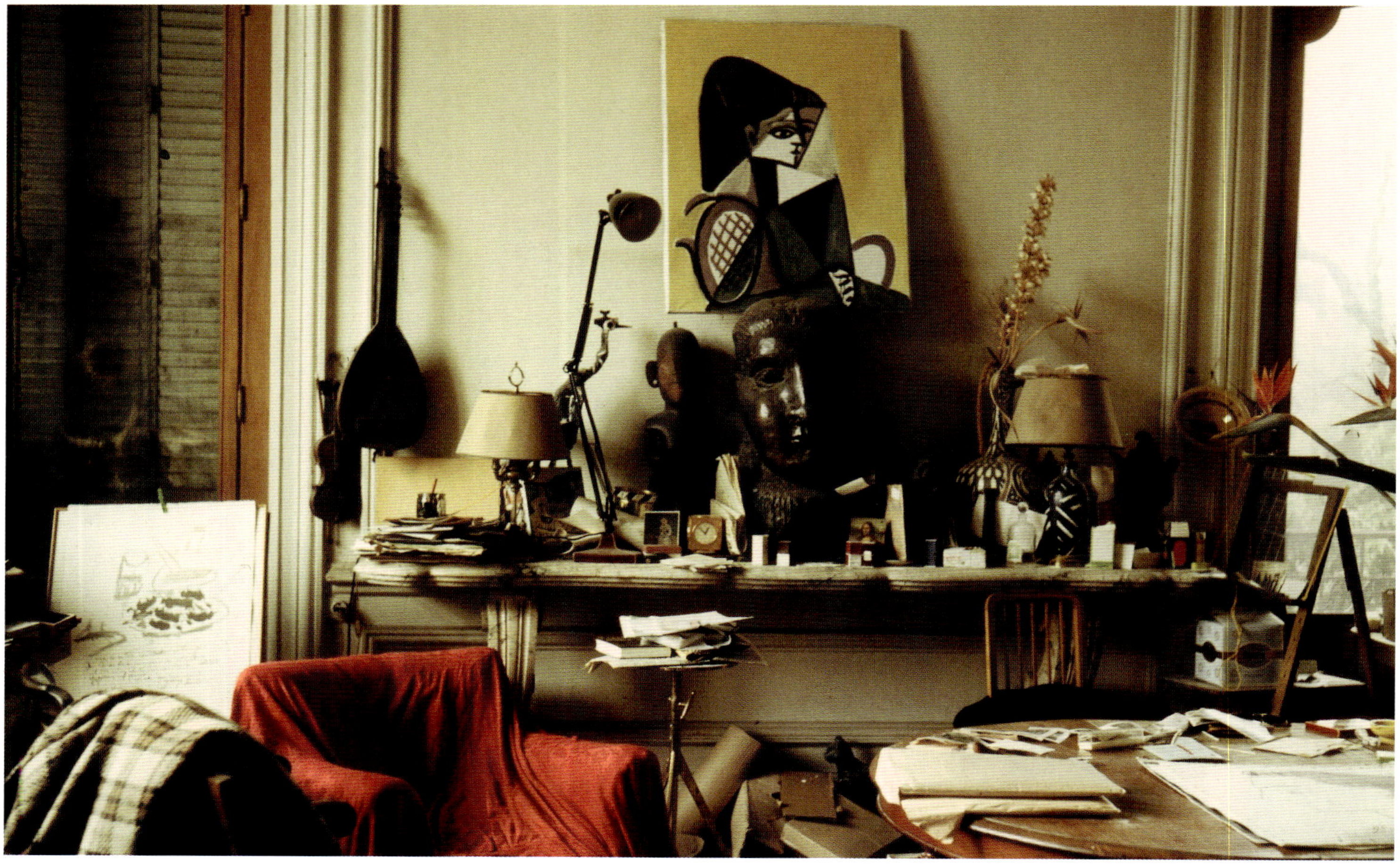

Above and following page: Every room of Villa La Californie was taken over by Picasso's art and every surface filled with his props and materials.

met Jacqueline Roque at the Madoura Pottery where he made his ceramics. Jacqueline was twenty-six and he was seventy-two. They married eight years later in 1961, and during their time together, he created over 400 portraits of her – more than he had of any of his other loves. One evening in 1955, he and Jacqueline saw a large and lavish villa in Cannes, called 'La Californie'. He decided to live there.

LA CALIFORNIE

Villa La Californie, originally known as Villa Fénelon and now called Pavillon de Flore, is a house in avenue Coste Belle, in Cannes. Located in the quarter of La Californie, it was built in 1920, and features several ornate fixtures and fittings, including a wrought-iron staircase and somewhat fussy, stylised carvings around the windows. However, despite the heaviness and ostentation, the high-ceilinged rooms were light and spacious, which appealed to Picasso. Also, a high black-iron fence spanned the terraced gardens, which was important for him now that he was so famous. Within a short time of moving in, Picasso cleared the villa of curtains, carpets, grand pianos and the furniture that had belonged to the previous owners. He was a hoarder and the house soon felt quite chaotic. The mirrored doors of the entrance halls were obscured with cases of his belongings, including canvases, easels, paints, bronzes, ceramics and furniture. He turned the kitchen into a workshop for his lithography and engraving, and left the rest of the house as it was, with no new decoration, although he made the bedrooms comfortable, but did not replace the rugs and curtains. On the walls, he displayed unframed canvases, sketches, photos and odd notes. Although disorderly, the house was welcoming; everywhere there was evidence of his work, including sketchbooks, half-finished bronzes and canvases, portfolios packed with drawings, children's toys and prints in progress.

The ground-floor rooms were interlinked by wide doors and large French doors that opened onto the tree-filled garden, which included palms and a giant eucalyptus. Warm southern light poured

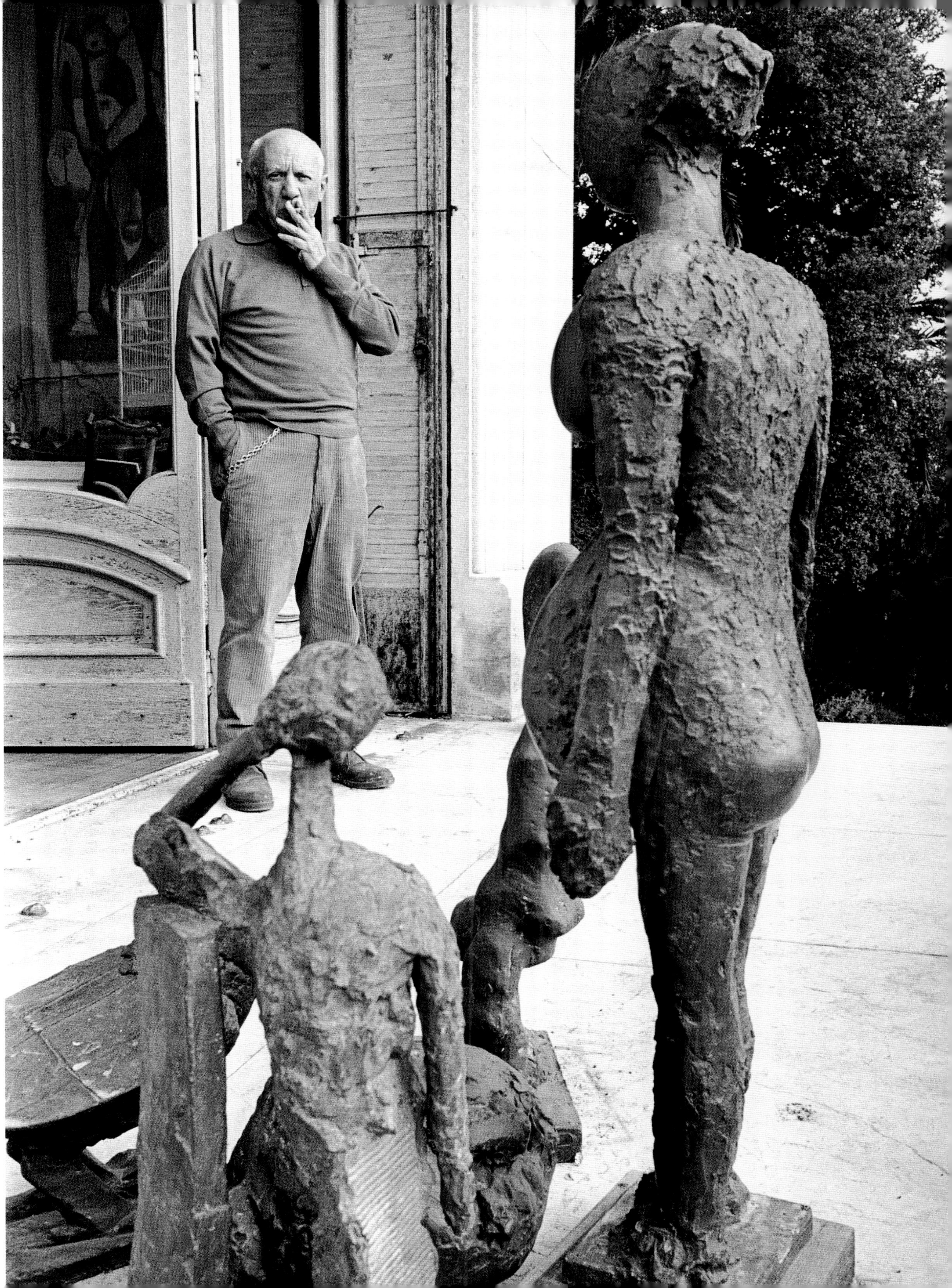

Caption

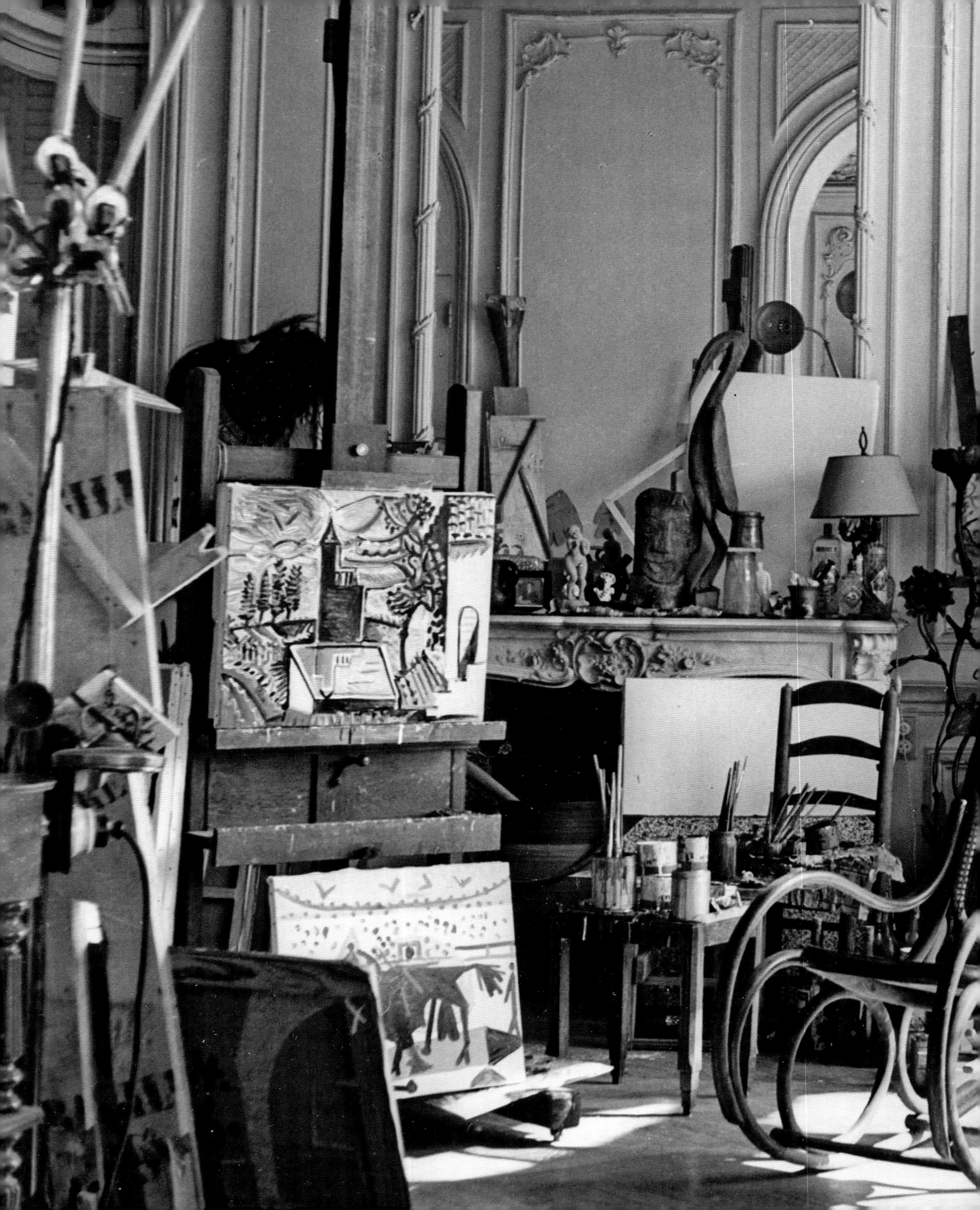

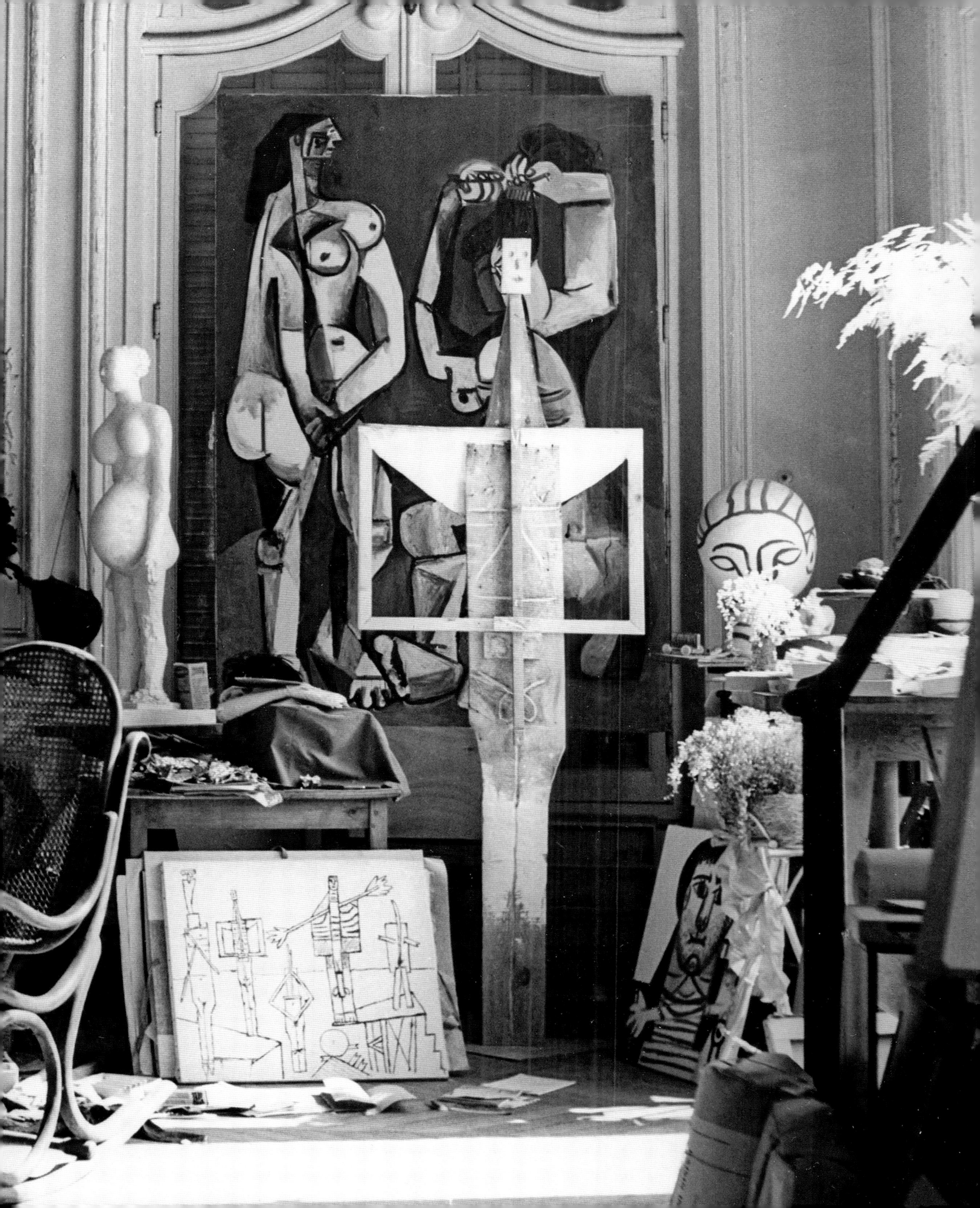

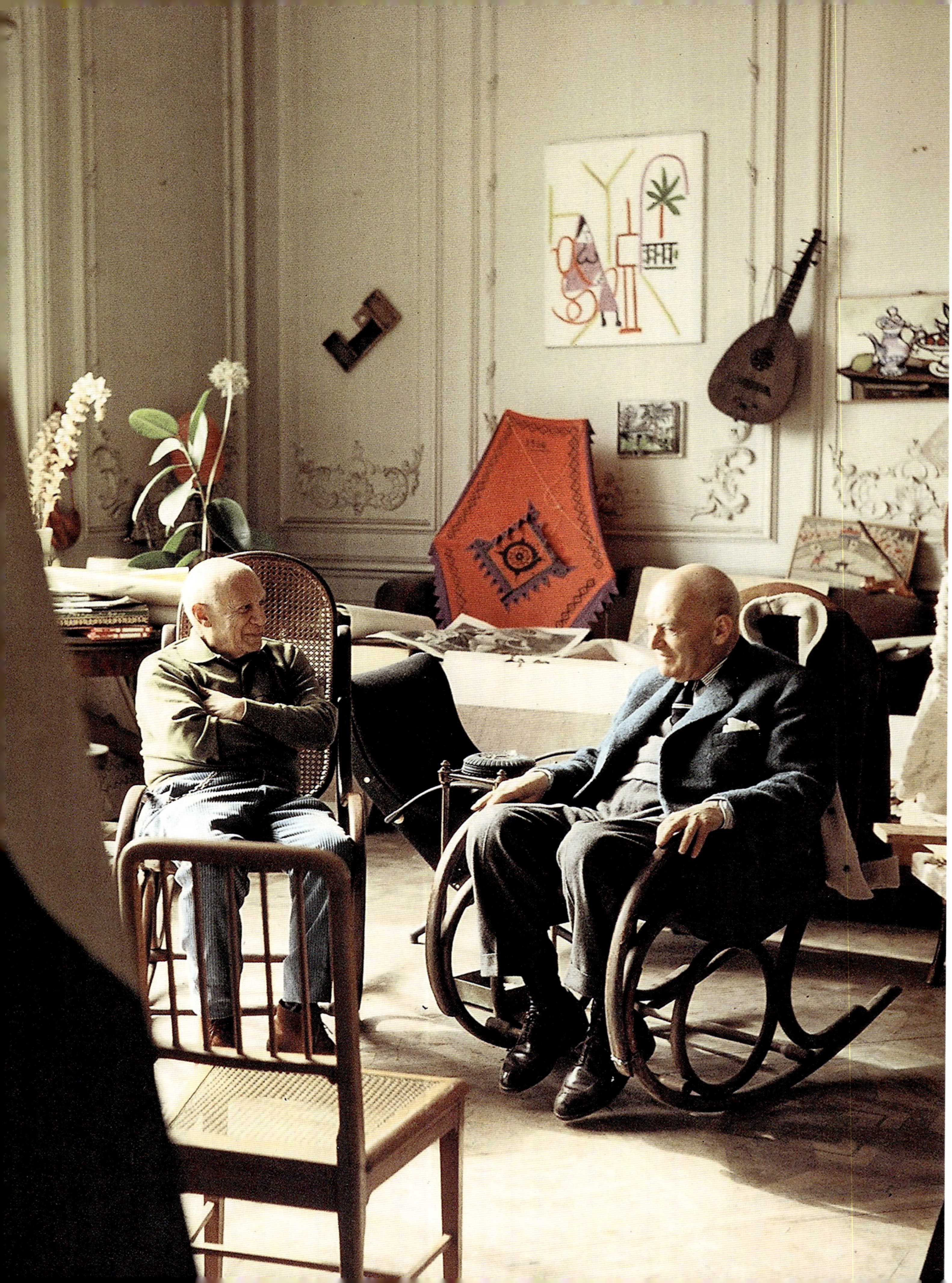

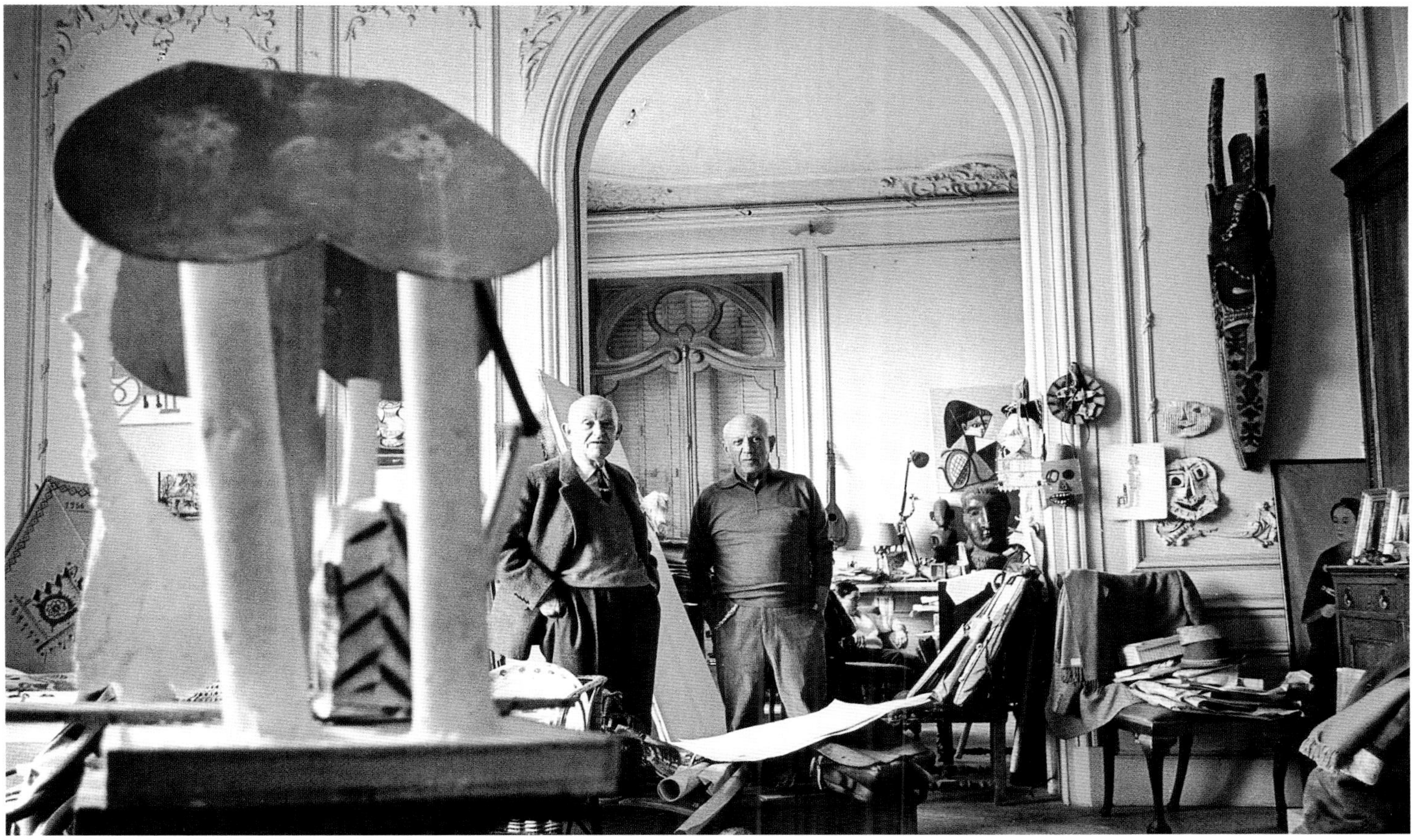

Above and opposite: Picasso and his art dealer Daniel-Henry Kahnweiler in his studio at La Californie in 1957.

through the tall windows, sometimes filtering through the palm trees, while the lofty ceilings made everywhere feel bright and airy. Picasso was inspired by everything around him and he worked in almost every room. In those same rooms, he ate, slept, worked, entertained friends and played with his pets, which included mice, birds, a dog and goats. Nowhere was separate: his work was completely entwined with the rest of his life. For example, he worked on the dining room table and when he needed to eat, it was cleared.

Jacqueline took great care of him; she cooked and played music. When his mood changed, she quickly altered plans, and she guarded the property against intruders or unwanted visitors. While Picasso worked, she and her daughter Catherine amused themselves. She learned to be an observant photographer. Many of the paintings that Picasso produced at La Californie were portraits of her. In some, she wore a Turkish dress; in others, he focused on her large brown eyes. In the winter of 1955–56, he produced several paintings of her that continue his Cubist ideas: angled and distorted, showing several viewpoints at once. She was intensely involved with his work and would often sit for him for hours, sometimes on a rocking chair or on one of the eighteenth-century English chairs that his father had given him.

In 1956, Picasso produced a series of paintings depicting the interior of his studio at La Californie and in 1958, he painted the Bay of Cannes from the garden. By 1961, however, the construction of a new building obscured his sea view, so he and Jacqueline left Villa la Californie and moved to Mougins, 7.5 kilometres (4.7 miles) from Cannes, where he stayed for the rest of his life.

'I'd like to live as a poor man with lots of money.'

Pablo Picasso

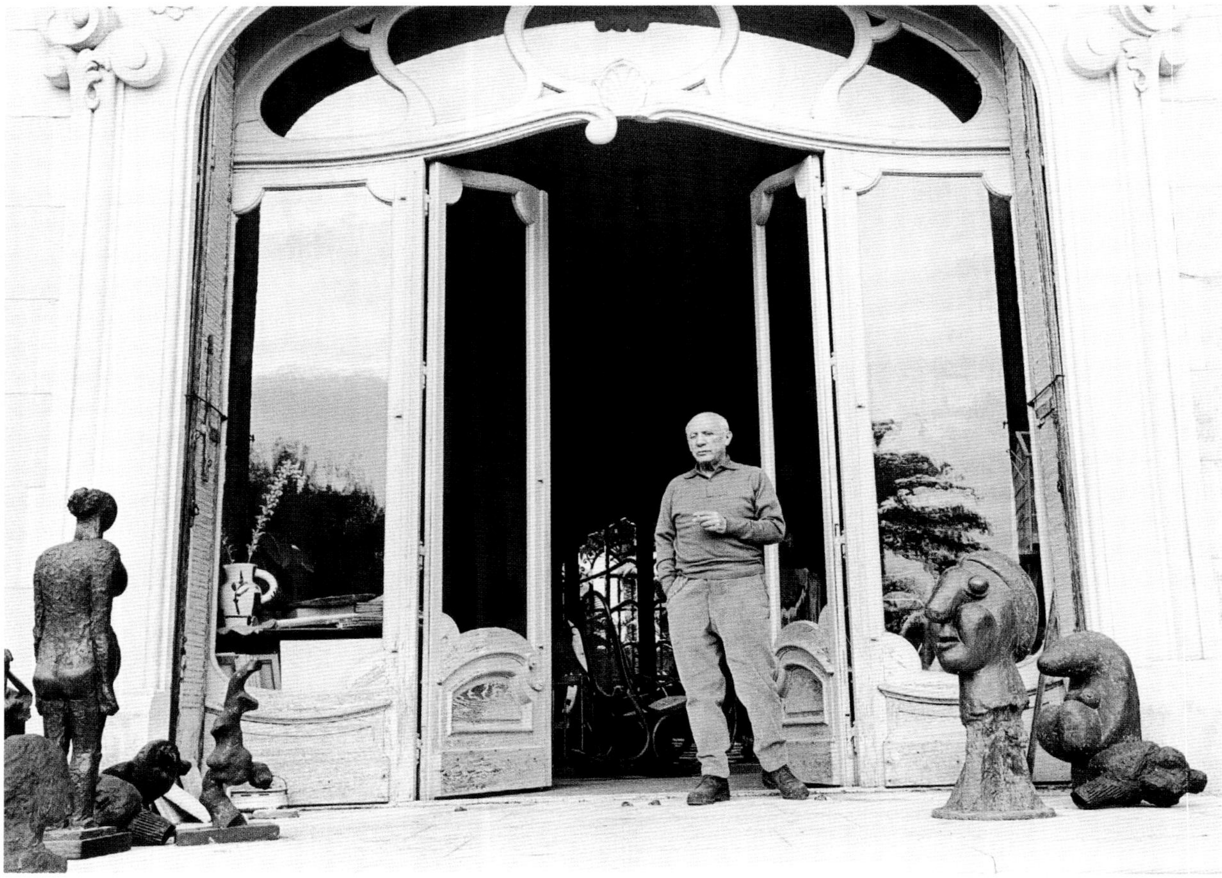

Above: A relaxed Picasso standing outside his studio, surrounded by several of his works.

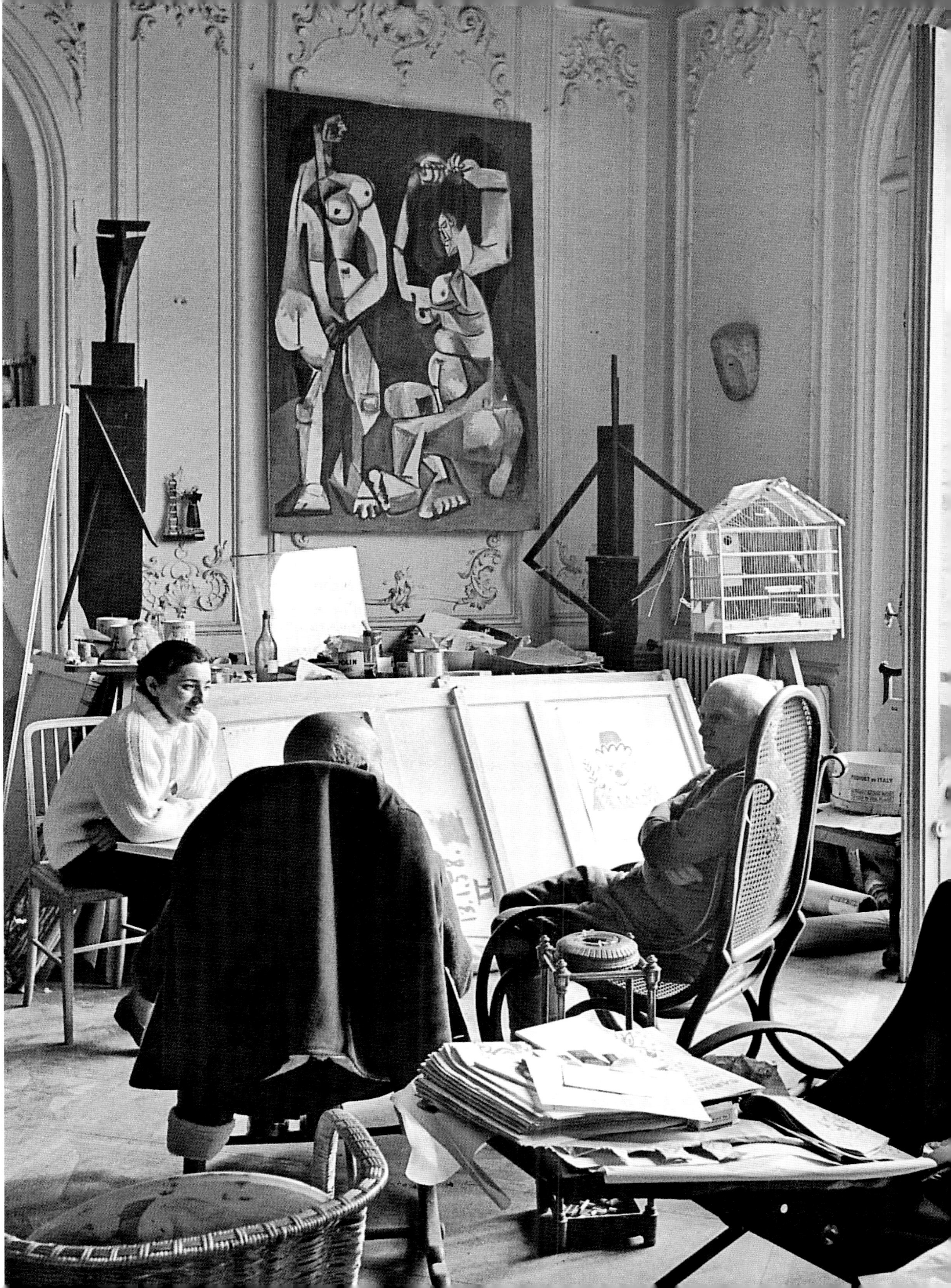

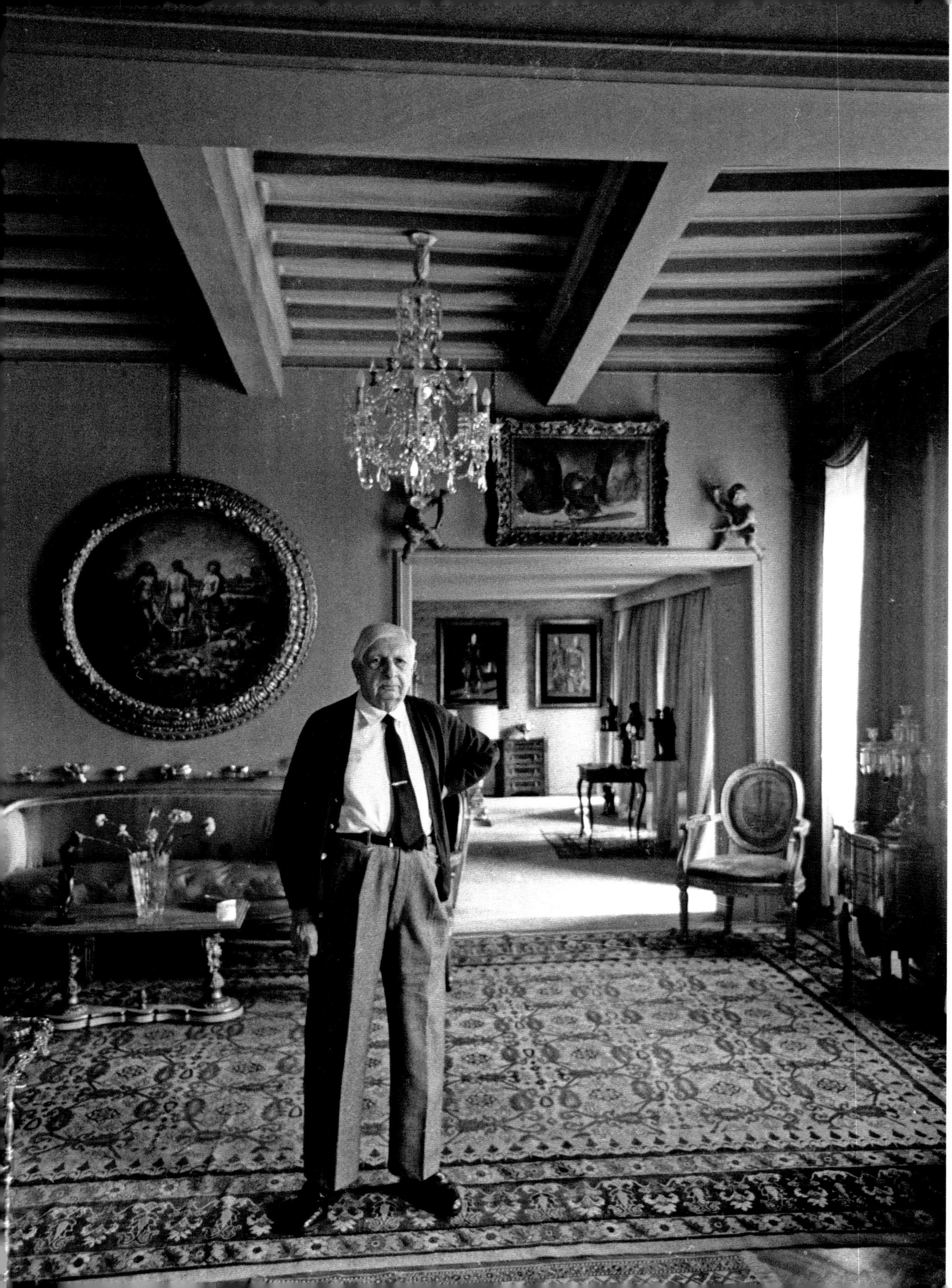

GIORGIO DE CHIRICO

Rome, Italy

A precursor of Surrealism and the leader of the Metaphysical Painting movement, Giorgio de Chirico (1888–1978) bought the seventeenth-century Palazzetto del Borgognoni in Rome three years after the end of World War Two, when he was sixty. He lived and worked there for the last thirty years of his life.

Giorgio de Chirico was influenced by his childhood experiences of growing up in Greece with Italian parents; his mother had Genoese origins and his father, a railway engineer, descended from both Sicily and Greece. As a young teenager, Giorgio began studying drawing and painting in Athens, but when he was seventeen, his father died and the family relocated to Germany. He studied for a while at the Academy of Fine Arts in Munich, and then stayed in Milan for six months. By the age of twenty-two, he was living in Florence, where he painted the first of his *Metaphysical Town Square* series, with strange juxtapositions, Roman architecture and dramatic perspectives that evoke a sense of suspense, discord and often melancholy. Featuring arches, streets, squares, long shadows, statues and an uncanny sense of silence, they convey irrationality and incongruity.

In July 1911, de Chirico spent a few days in Turin on his way to Paris, and was greatly taken with the architecture there, especially the archways and piazzas that he described as 'metaphysical'. A couple of years later, the French poet and art critic Guillaume Apollinaire became his champion; he wrote a review of a small exhibition that de Chirico put on, using the term 'Metaphysical painting' about his dreamlike, disorienting and enigmatic scenes, and praising his work: 'The art of this young painter is an interior and cerebral art which bears no relation to that of the painters of recent years.'

During World War One, de Chirico enlisted for the Italian army, but was declared unfit and instead assigned to the hospital in Ferrara. There he met fellow artist Carlo Carrà and together they established what they called the Pittura Metafisica (Metaphysical Painting) movement.

PITTURA METAFISICA

The Metaphysical Painting movement lasted for approximately ten years, from 1909 to 1919. Although de Chirico and Carrà met in 1917 and established the style as a movement then, de Chirico had already been painting in the metaphysical style for several years. At first, de Chirico's subjects were static views of empty and sinister-looking town squares inspired by Italian city architecture, with exaggerated perspective. Then he began adding unexpected objects to his imaginary locations. Unlike any other art being produced in Europe at the time, de Chirico's painting style was influenced by the writings of German philosopher, cultural critic and philologist Friedrich Nietzsche, and the movement had a powerful influence on the development of Surrealism a few years later.

From November 1919, de Chirico changed his style, replacing his perplexing images with more classically inspired paintings, influenced by the art of the High Renaissance. He also began to openly criticise modern and contemporary art. In the early 1920s, the Surrealist writer André Breton discovered one of de Chirico's metaphysical paintings on display in Apollinaire's Paris gallery and became fascinated by it. Led by Breton, the Paris Surrealist group based many of their ideas on de Chirico's metaphysical painting style. In 1924, de Chirico visited Paris and was accepted into the group, but when some of the Surrealists publicly disparaged his new work, his relationship with them soured. He moved away from them and instead continued with his new painting style, as well as

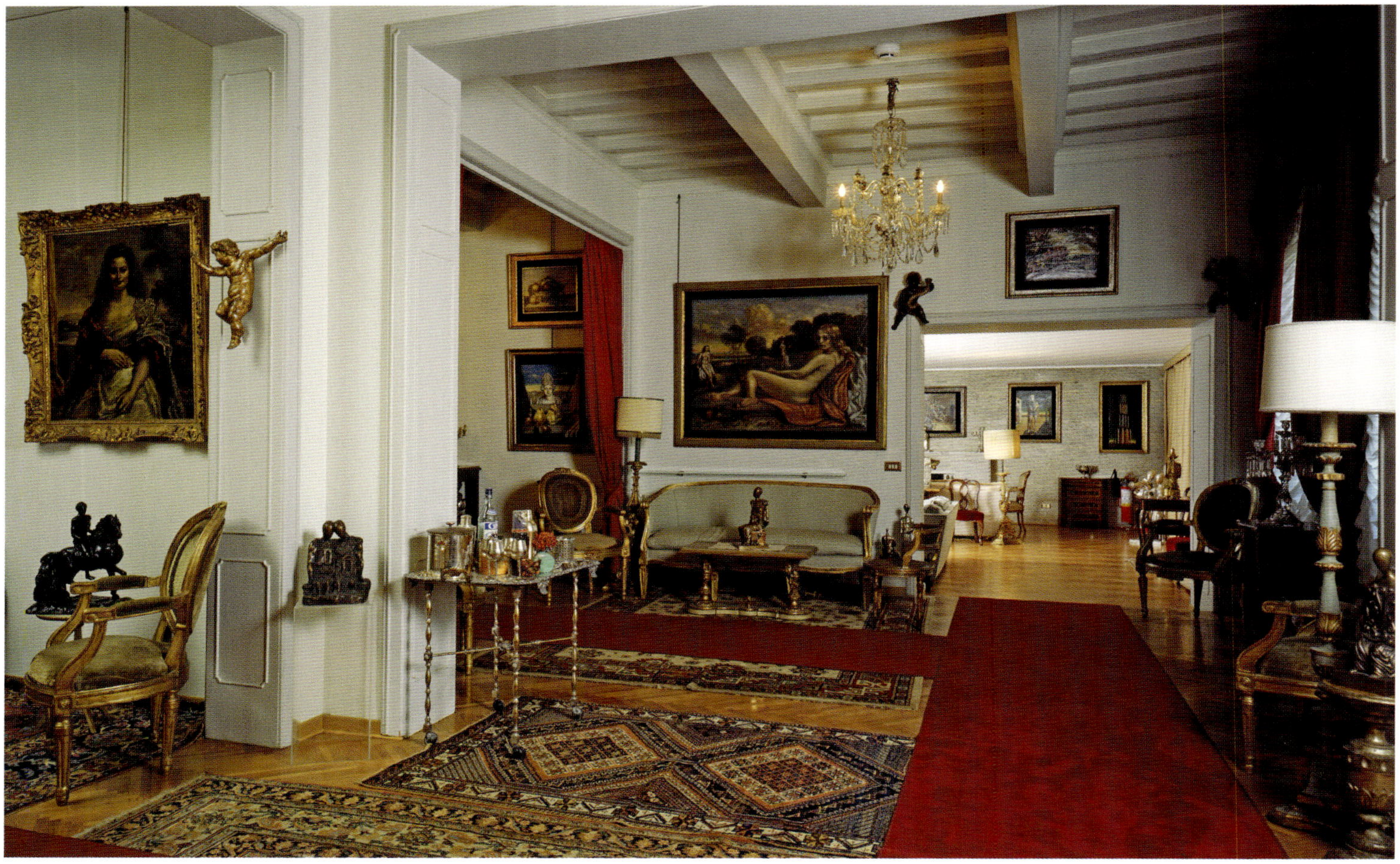

Above: Part of the de Chirico apartment inside the 17th century Palazzetto del Borgognoni in Rome.
Opposite: de Chirico in his kitchen.

writing essays, publishing a novel and making stage designs for the art critic and founder of the Ballets Russes, Sergei Diaghilev. In 1930, de Chirico met his second wife, Isabella Pakszwer Far. Two years later, they moved to Italy and then to New York in 1936, where they stayed until 1938. They returned to Europe and, in 1939, he began painting in a style that was strongly influenced by Peter Paul Rubens. He finally settled in Rome in 1944, published his memoirs in 1945 and three years later, he and Isabella rented an apartment on three floors in the Palazzetto del Borgognoni.

BAROQUE

After years of moving almost constantly, living in different cities in Europe and America, de Chirico finally settled down in what he called 'the centre of the centre of the world'. Located in the cultural and artistic centre of Rome, he occupied the three top floors of the Baroque Palazzetto del Borgognoni, at number 31, Piazza di Spagna, situated at the bottom of the Spanish Steps (Scalinata della Trinità dei Monti). From there, he had direct views of the church of the Santissima Trinità dei Monti and the Mannerist Villa Medici, both located at the top of the 138 Spanish Steps, on Pincian Hill. The Palazzetto del Borgognoni was a perfect place for de Chirico to live and work, in the heart of his favourite city. Initially, he rented the apartment, but in 1968, twenty years after moving in, he bought it. During the 1960s, the Italian architect Massimiliano Fuksas worked for him in his studio at the Palazzetto del Borgognoni and designed an extension.

On the lower floor of the three-storey apartment was a large main entrance, leading to airy living and dining rooms. The entrance was a welcoming reception area for de Chirico's numerous guests, as he held many gatherings there. With high ceilings, the dining and living rooms were furnished to suit his lavish taste: parquet flooring, heavy red velvet curtains, paintings with ornate golden

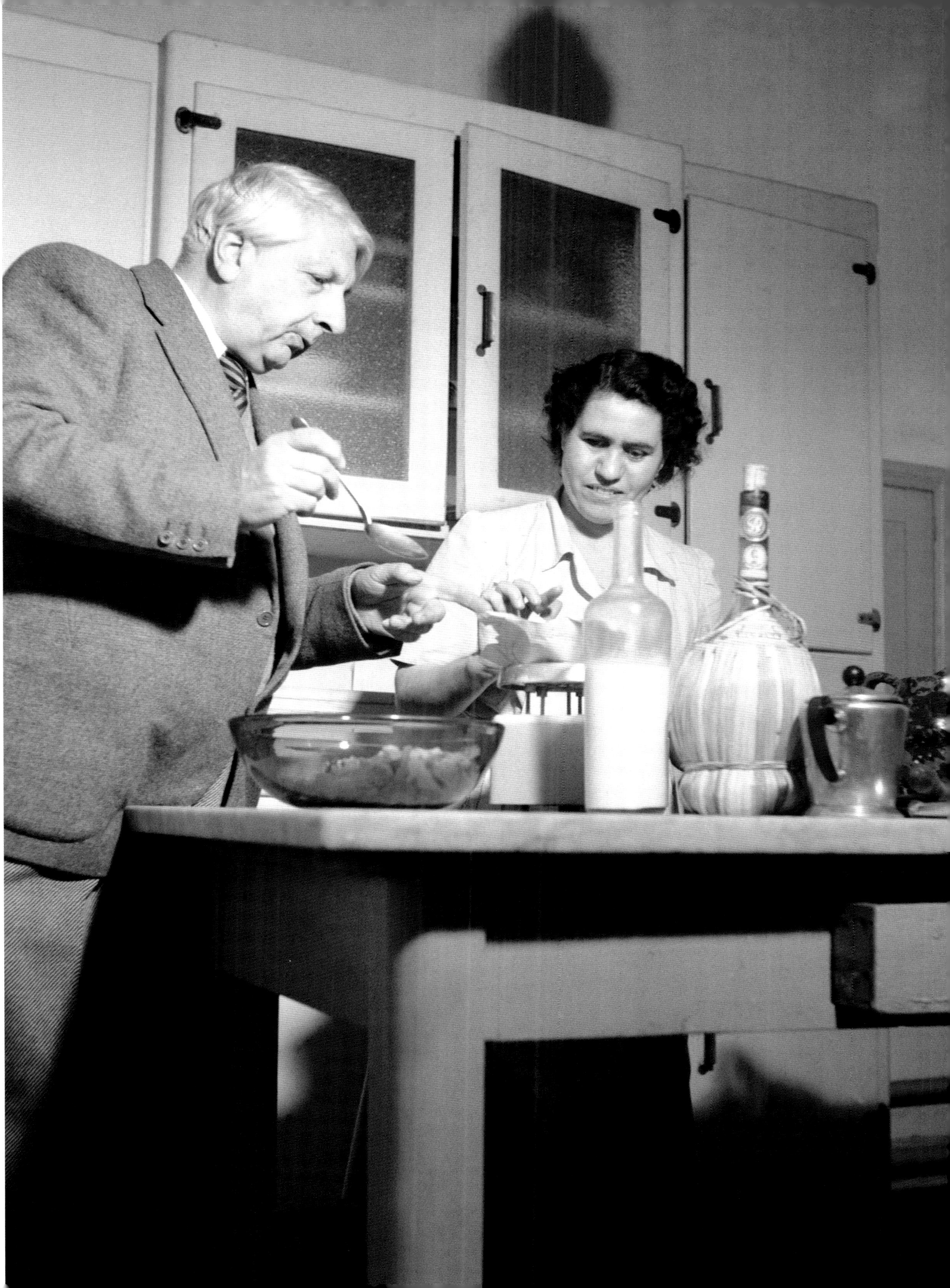

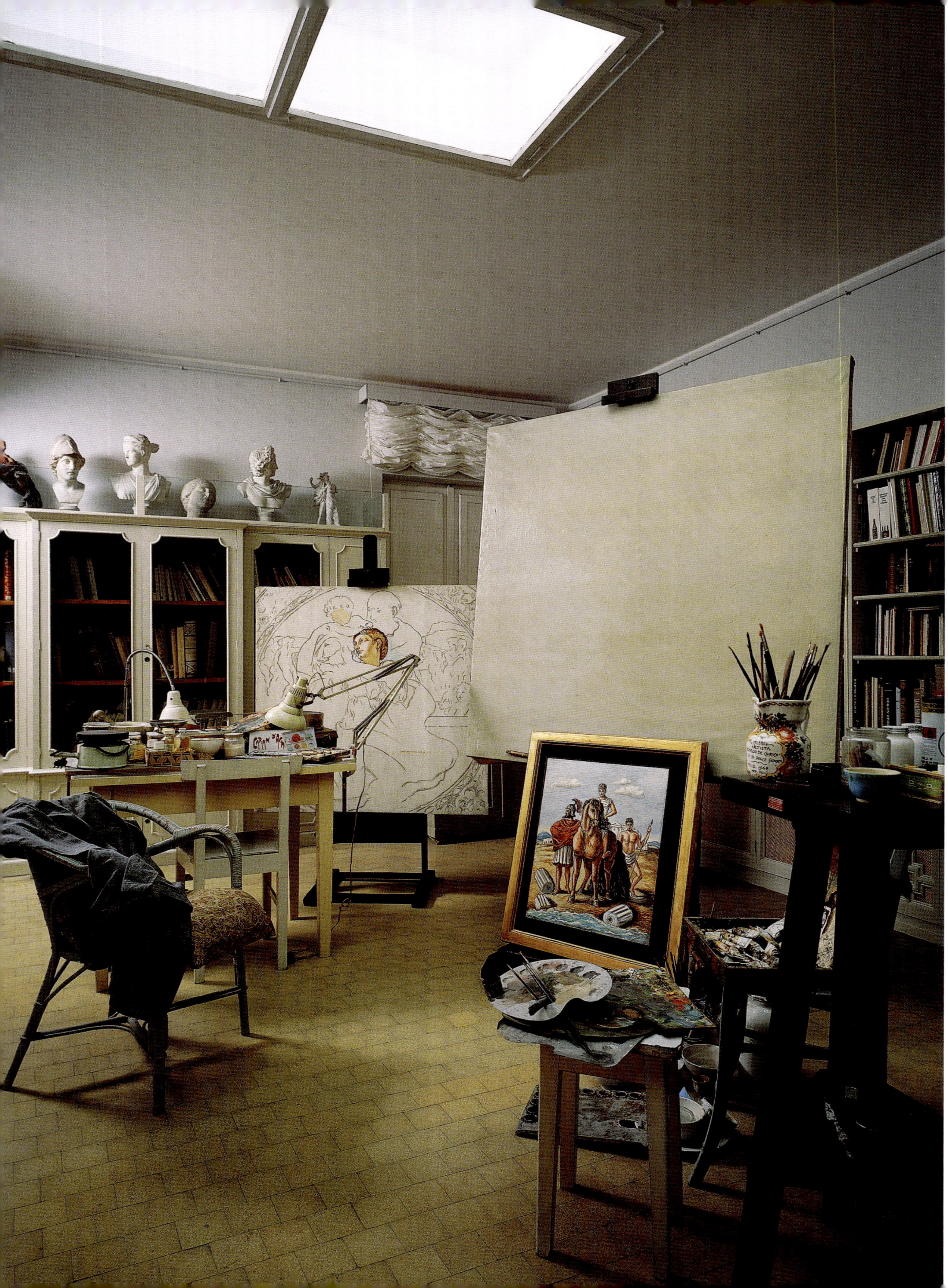

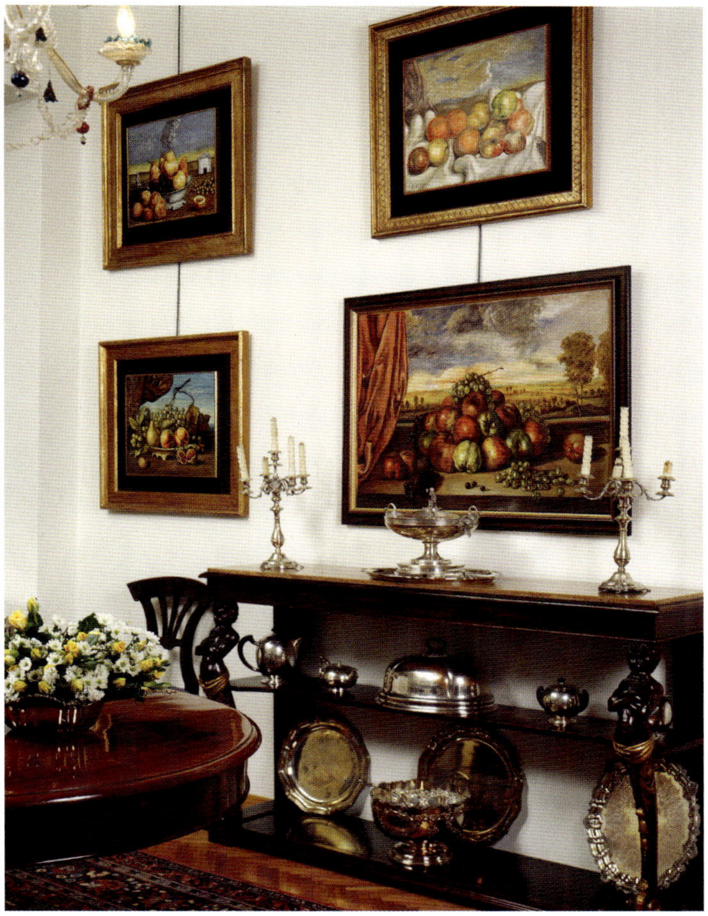

Above: Opulence, ornaments and art fill the large and airy apartment, which de Chirico believed was at 'the centre of the world'.

'They say that Rome is at the centre of the world and that Piazza di Spagna is in the centre of Rome, therefore, my wife and I, would indeed be living in the centre of the centre of the world.'

Giorgio de Chirico

frames, wooden cherub sculptures, polished mahogany furniture, silverware, simple fireplaces and cream Louis XVI-style armchairs. This décor emulates the opulence of the Baroque architecture of the building and the style of art that de Chirico particularly admired. Large, open, rectangular archways give open, spacious views of the rooms that link with each other. On the second floor were the bedrooms and de Chirico's light-filled studio. As with all the other rooms in the apartment, this features high ceilings. Here, light poured through a wide skylight in the ceiling, illuminating the space where de Chirico painted each day, often puffing on his pipe, until he was ninety. Next to this studio was his personal reference library, filled with books including large monographs on several great master artists, such as Rubens and Antoine Watteau. On the third floor was the kitchen, and a wide and spacious terrace, where de Chirico brought his friends and also took breaks during the day to sit and admire the spectacular views around him. Right up until the end of his life, de Chirico remained extremely prolific and, in 1974, he was elected to the French Académie des Beaux-Arts.

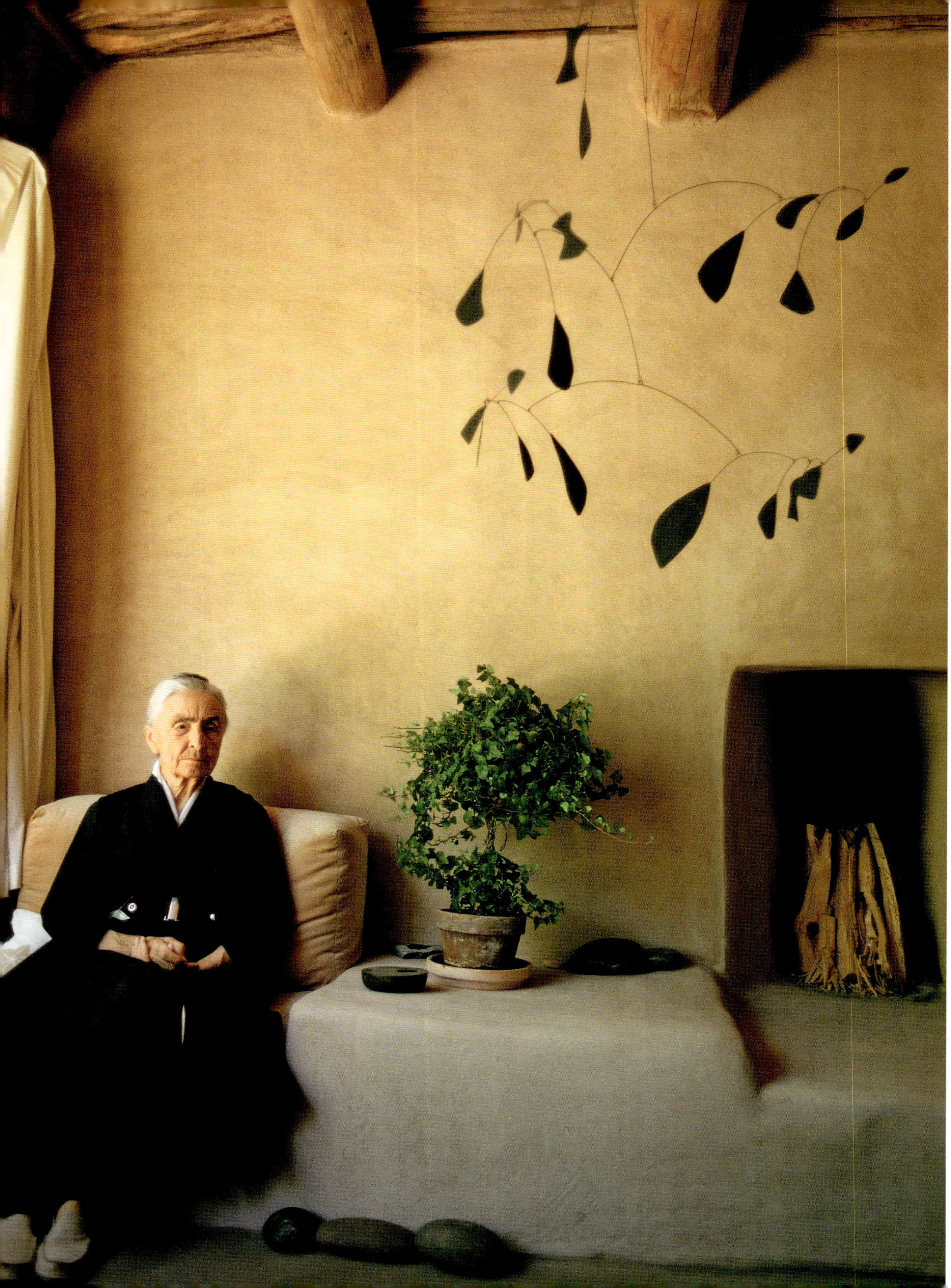

GEORGIA O'KEEFFE

Abiquiú, New Mexico, US

Surrounded by open skies and dramatic rock formations, the tiny village of Abiquiú in Rio Arriba County in the north-central region of New Mexico was once the start of the trade route of the Old Spanish Trail that connected New Mexico to California. In the mid- to late-twentieth century, Georgia O'Keeffe (1887–1986) lived there for over forty years.

Despite being a female artist in a male-dominated world, O'Keeffe became famous during her lifetime, and played a key role in the development of American modernism. She worked as an artist for more than seven decades, with much of her art depicting aspects of the world from close-up or from unexpected viewpoints, capturing a sense of emotion and power. That emotion and power became essential to the art she produced in New Mexico.

Abiquiú is approximately 85 kilometres (53 miles) north of Santa Fe, and the name means 'wild choke cherry place' in the Tewa language. In 1742, twenty-four Tewa Pueblo families were the first settlers there, led by a Roman Catholic priest as part of a Spanish plan to defend New Mexico's borders against Native American tribes.

Almost two centuries later, O'Keeffe discovered the area and was enthralled by it. When she was forty-one, in the summer of 1929, she travelled with friends to Taos in New Mexico for the first time, and she was captivated by the light, the rugged landscape, the Native American and Hispanic cultures of the region, and the spiritual atmosphere. One aspect she particularly admired was that she could see clearly over vast distances, and she became inspired to begin a new direction in her art. She wrote to a friend: 'As soon as I saw [New Mexico], it was my country. I'd never seen anything like it before, but it fitted to me exactly. It's something in the air, it's just different. The sky is different, the stars are different, the wind is different.'

GHOST RANCH

O'Keeffe began spending her summers in New Mexico. She first visited Abiquiú in 1931, and in 1934 she heard of Ghost Ranch, a 21,000-acre dude – or guest – ranch, 12 miles from the village. From the summer of 1936, she rented a house on Ghost Ranch, called Rancho de los Burros, which stood on 12 acres at the edge of the property. Situated at the base of cliffs and facing distant mountains, Rancho de los Burros was an adobe (mud brick) hacienda with a patio. In 1940, O'Keeffe bought the house, as well as its acres of land. For years, she spent only the summer months there, returning in the winter to her home in New York and her husband, the photographer and modern art promoter Alfred Stieglitz. While in New Mexico, she painted almost constantly. In 1942, she wrote to her friend, fellow artist Arthur Dove: 'I wish you could see what I see out the window; the earth, pink and yellow cliffs to the north, the full pale moon about to go down in an early morning lavender sky ... pink and purple hills in front, the scrubby fine dull cedars and a feeling of much space. It is a very beautiful world.'

Enclosed within a rattlesnake fence, Rancho de los Burros is a single-storey dwelling, built in a U-shape, with pueblo-style adobe walls in common with many of the houses in the location. It also features large picture windows that look out at the magnificent landscape, including the rock formations, green scrubland and blueish-purple mountains in the distance. She kept the house plain, with whitewashed walls and sparse furnishings, including a few chairs, a table made of a couple of planks of plywood, basic kitchen amenities and a hand-carved wooden ladder leading up to the roof, where she often slept beneath the stars. She lived there modestly, rarely seeing anyone, spending her days collecting objects from the desert – rocks, bones, skulls and gnarled branches – and she

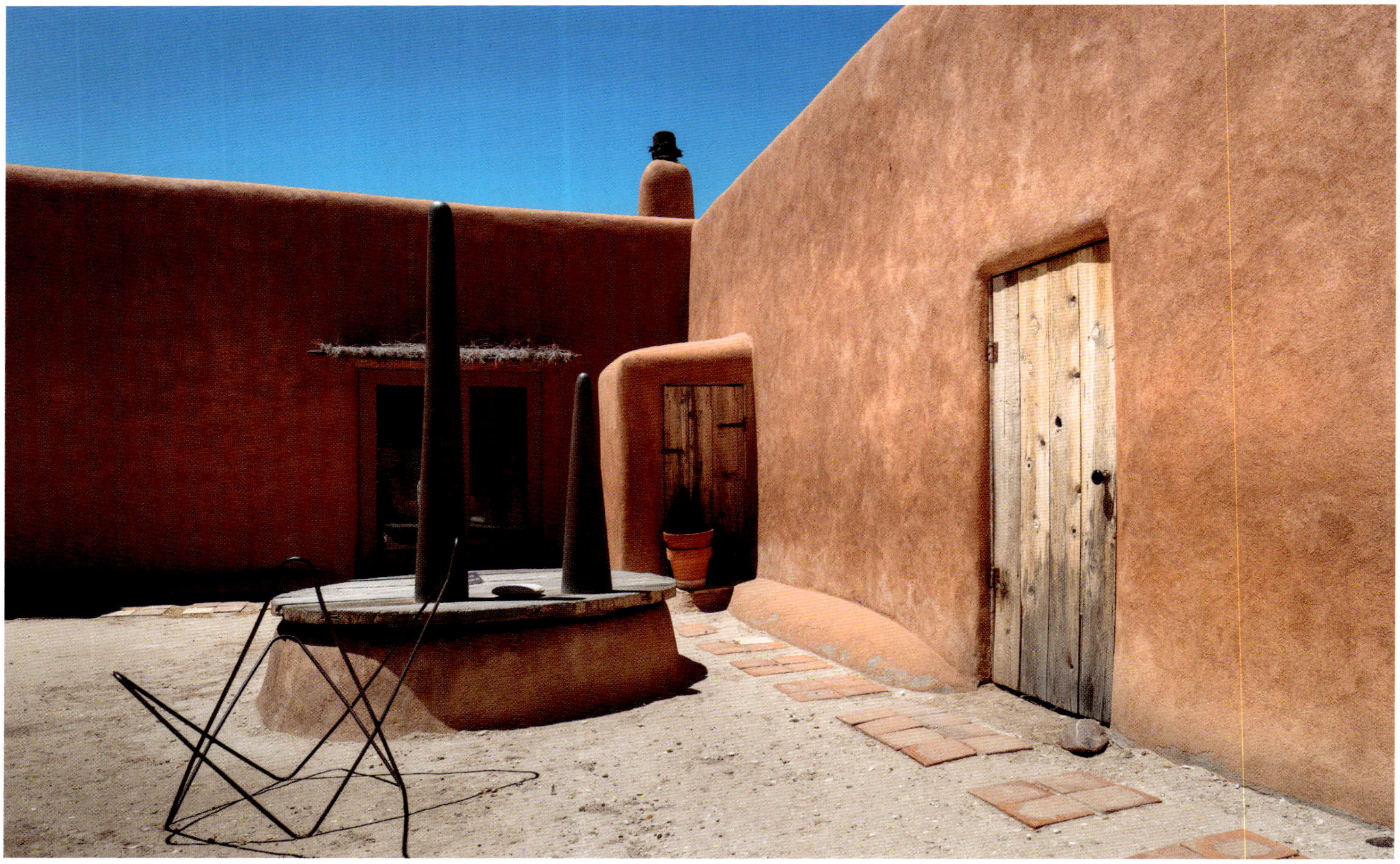

Above and opposite: The rich colours and clear light of Ghost Ranch appealed to O'Keeffe from the moment she first saw it.

painted these and the landscape over and over again, emphasising the curving forms, rich colours, strong shadows and clear light. Although she had magnificent vistas from every window, her favourite view was of the flat-topped mountain, Cerro Pedernal, directly in front of her open courtyard. She loved it, and wrote: 'It's my private mountain. It belongs to me. God told me if I painted it enough, I could have it.' In another letter, she wrote to a friend: '...I have the most beautiful adobe studio – out the very large window to a rich green alfalfa field – then the sage brush and beyond – a most perfect mountain – it makes me feel like flying.'

O'Keeffe loved Rancho de los Burros. The surroundings inspired her smooth, often almost abstract, atmospheric paintings. She reflected: 'Such a beautiful, untouched lonely-feeling place, such a fine part of what I call the "Faraway". It is a place I have painted before... even now I must do it again.' However, it was in the desert, and not suitable for the winter months. She wanted a home for the winter and a garden.

DIFFERENT HOMES

O'Keeffe had seen another house that she wanted in Abiquiú. Situated on a ridge, with a spectacular view of the Chama River Valley, it was an abandoned, uninhabitable 460 square-metre (5,000 square foot) hacienda owned by the Catholic Church. Its courtyard had first caught her eye. She recalled: 'As I climbed and walked about in the ruin, I found a patio with a very pretty well house and bucket to draw up water. It was a good-sized patio with a long wall with a door on one side. That wall with a door in it was something I had to have.' It took her years to convince the church to sell her the property, but she managed it in 1945. As soon as she bought it, she began renovating it, and for the next four years, she supervised its restoration, carried out by her friend, Maria Chabot. O'Keeffe had originally escaped to New Mexico to distance herself from her husband's infidelities. In 1946, he suffered a stroke and died soon after. She stayed with him and then spent most of the next three years in New York, settling his estate. In 1949, she was

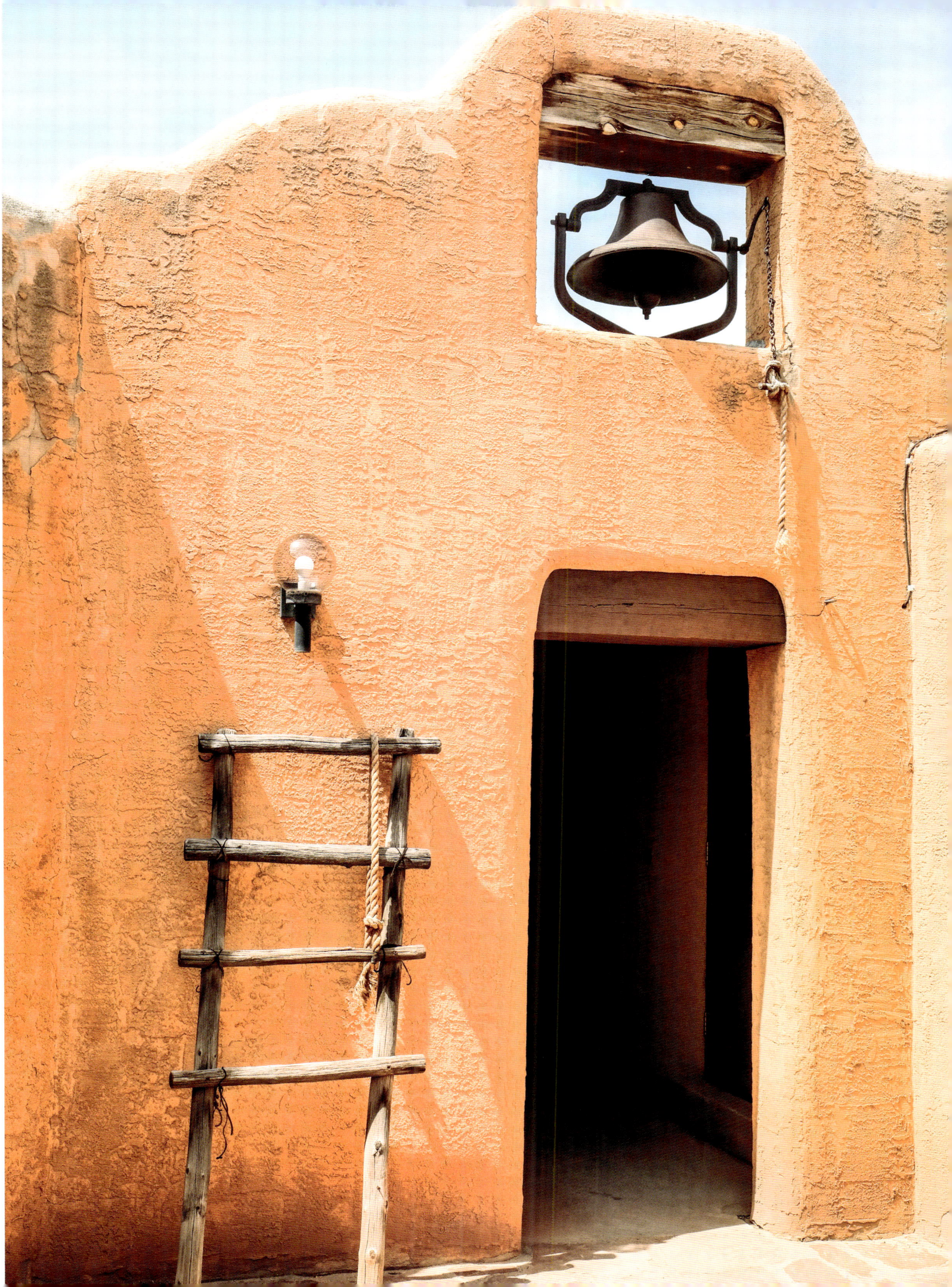

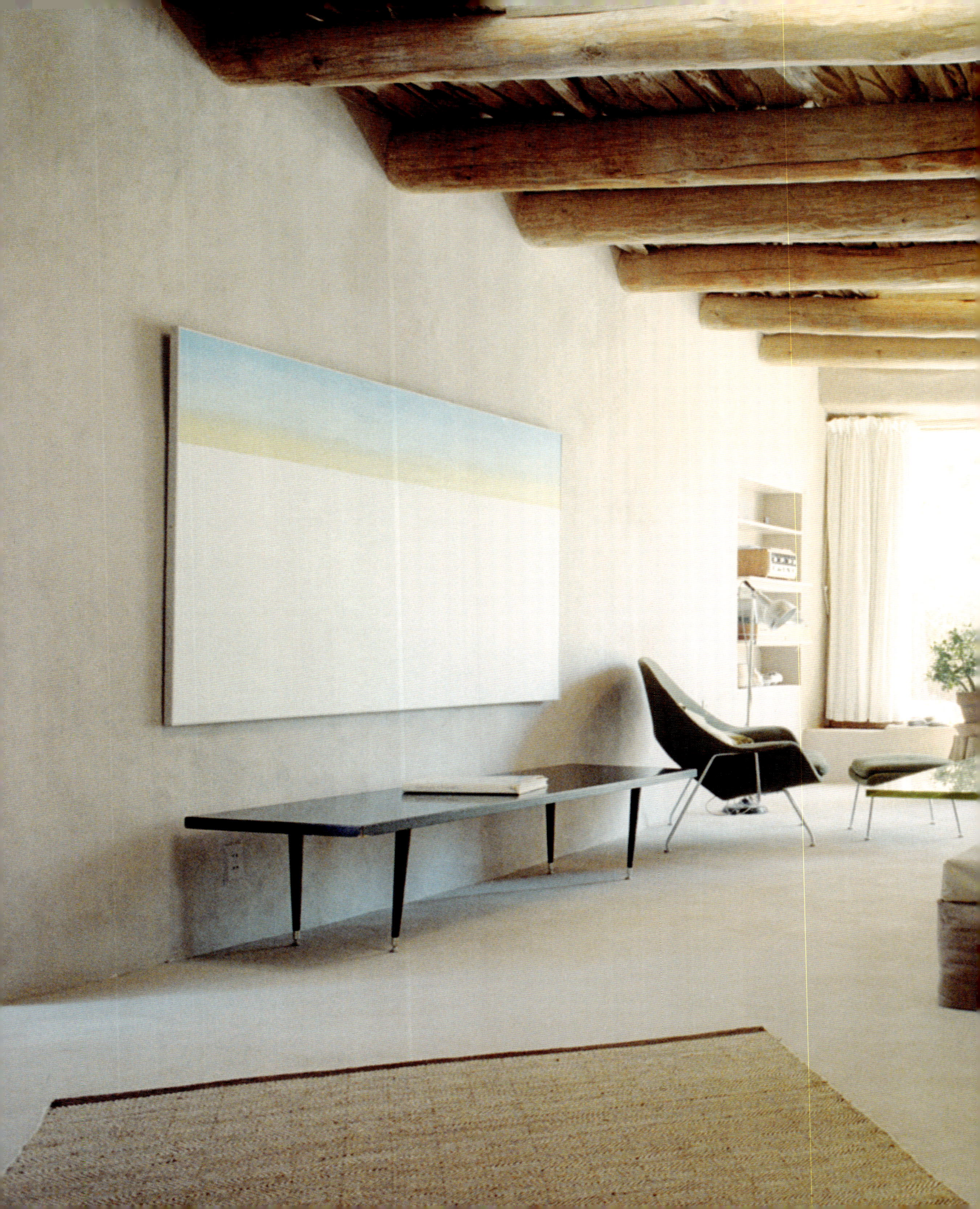

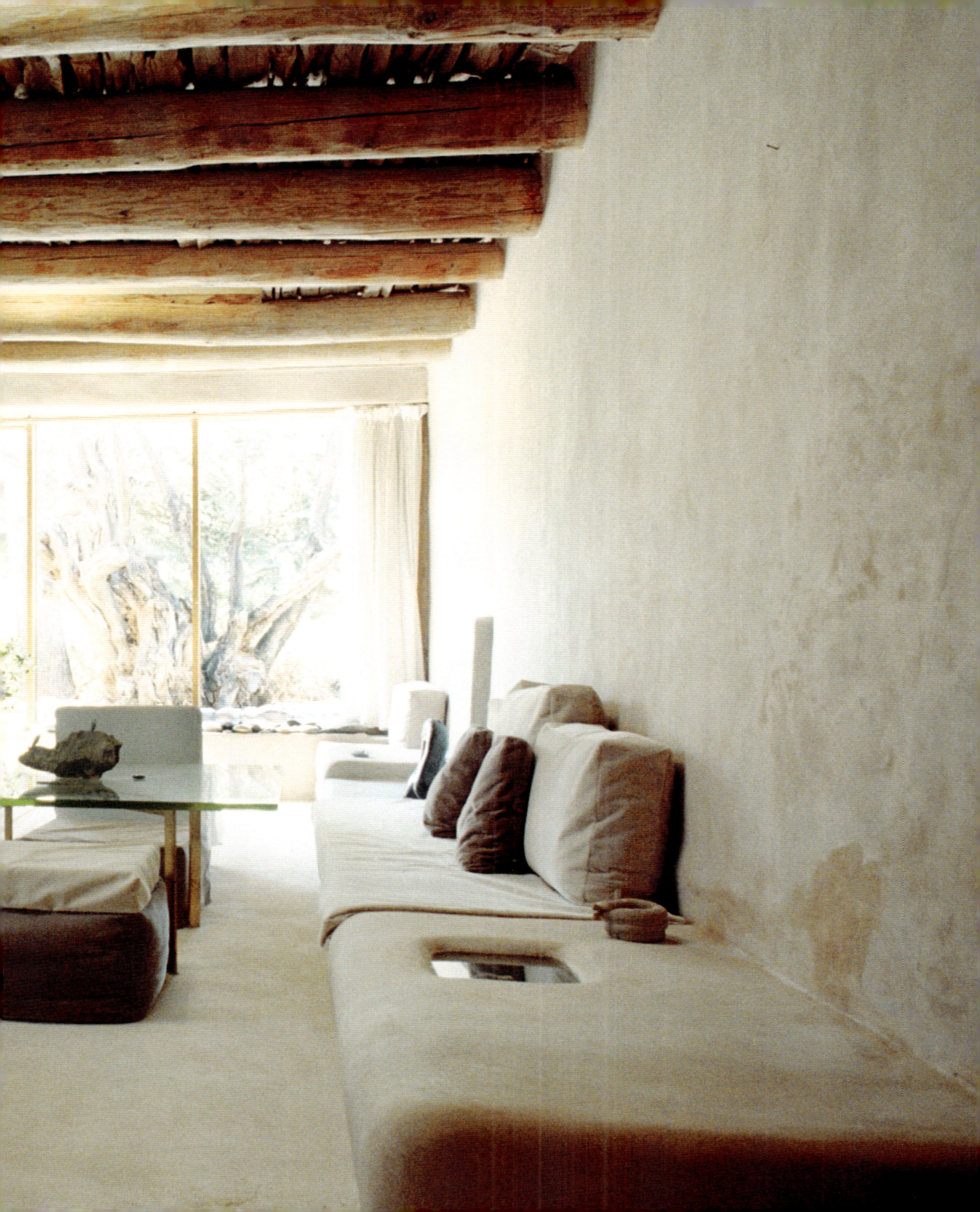

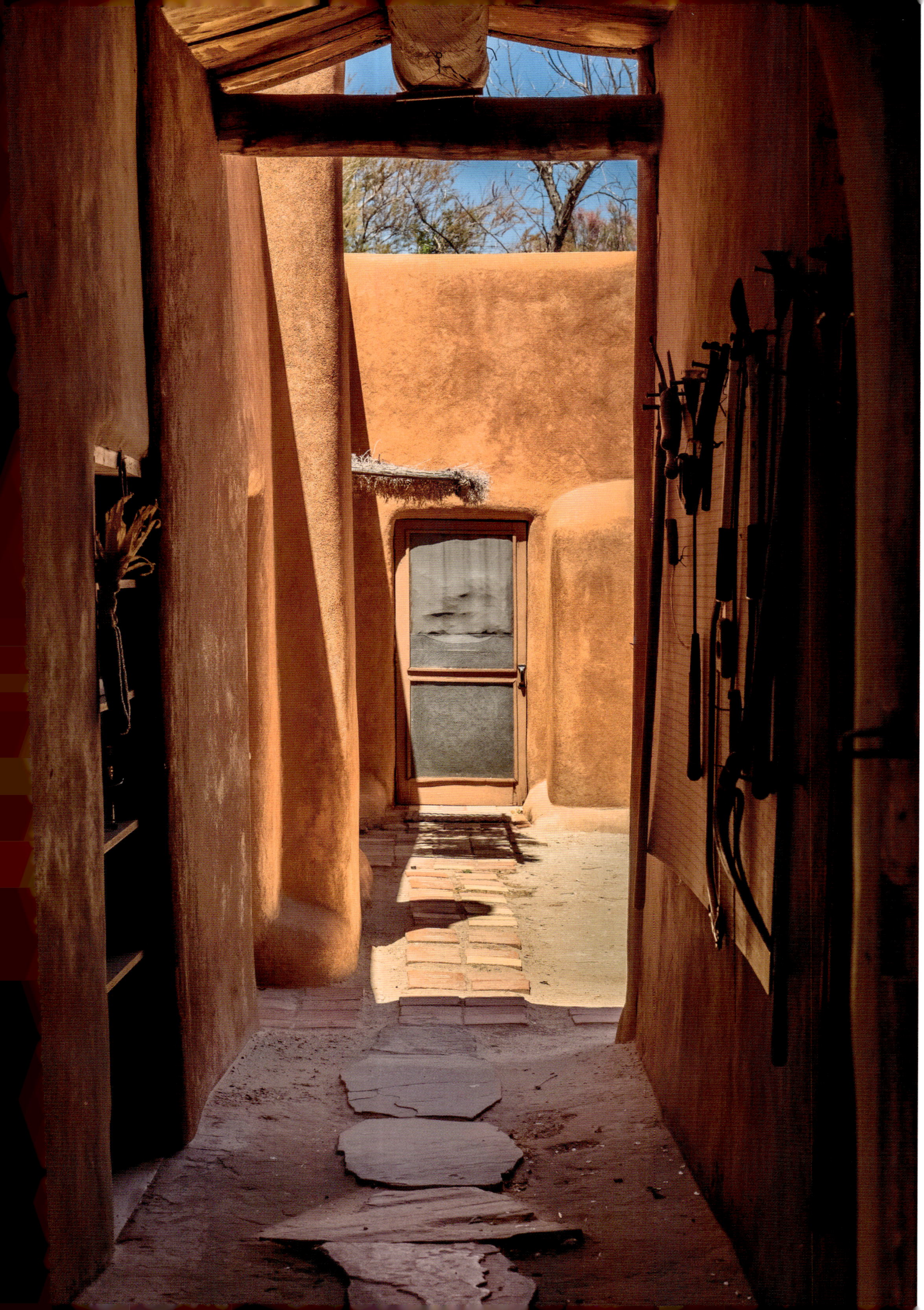

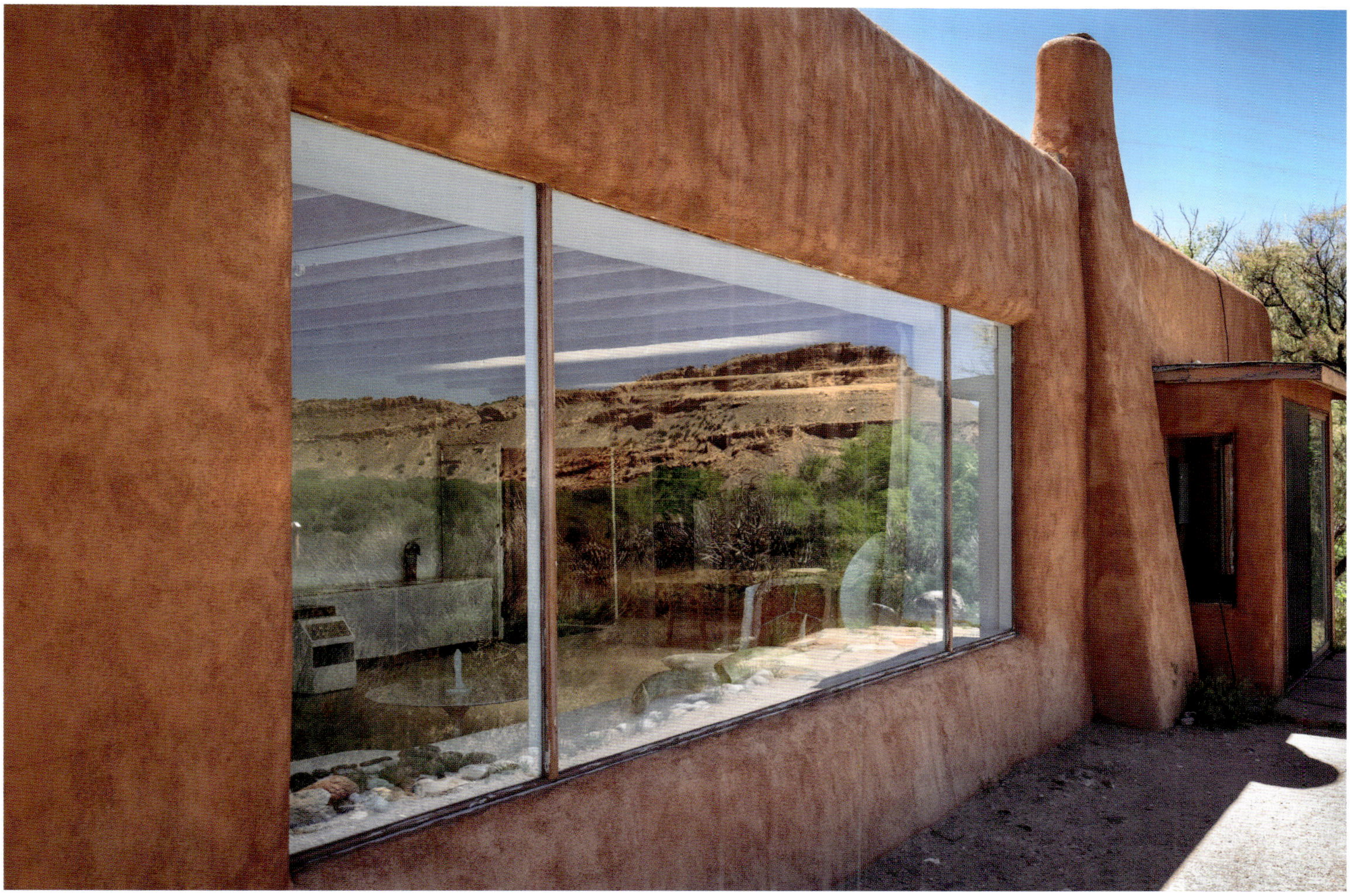

Previous page: The light and airy living room.
Above: Blending Native American and Spanish Colonial building styles, O'Keeffe's house is mainly an adobe hacienda. She lived there simply, never tiring of the views from her windows – one of which can be seen here reflected in the window.
Following page: Abiquiú's 'roofless room'.

finally free, and moved permanently to New Mexico. The house in Abiquiú became her winter home and she went to the smaller Rancho de los Burros during the summer months.

O'Keeffe grew food for her guests in the fertile garden of the house in Abiquiú. A blend of Native American and Spanish Colonial building styles and regional architectural traditions, the oldest rooms of the house were probably built in 1744; the building was then expanded in the nineteenth century into an adobe hacienda, with rows of rooms organised around a common open space, or *plazuela*. The house made the most of the natural light and contained minimal but contemporary amenities and furniture. As in the house on Ghost Ranch, she filled it with her collections of rocks, wood and bones. She lived and worked there until 1984, when macular degeneration meant that she was unable to travel to and from Ghost Ranch and Abiquiú. Eventually, she moved to Santa Fe, where she died in her ninety-ninth year.

'To me it [Ghost Ranch] is the best place in the world.'

Georgia O'Keeffe

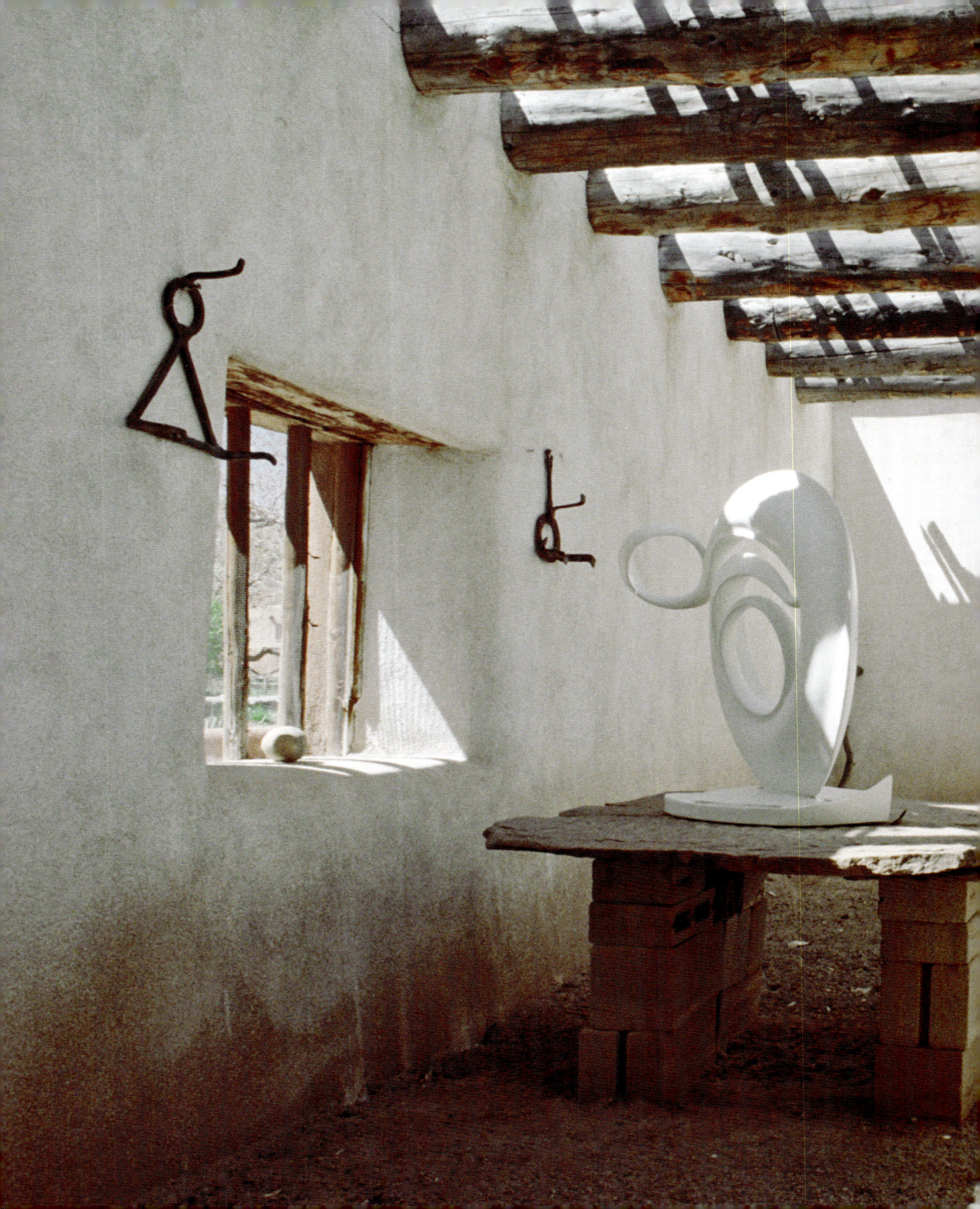

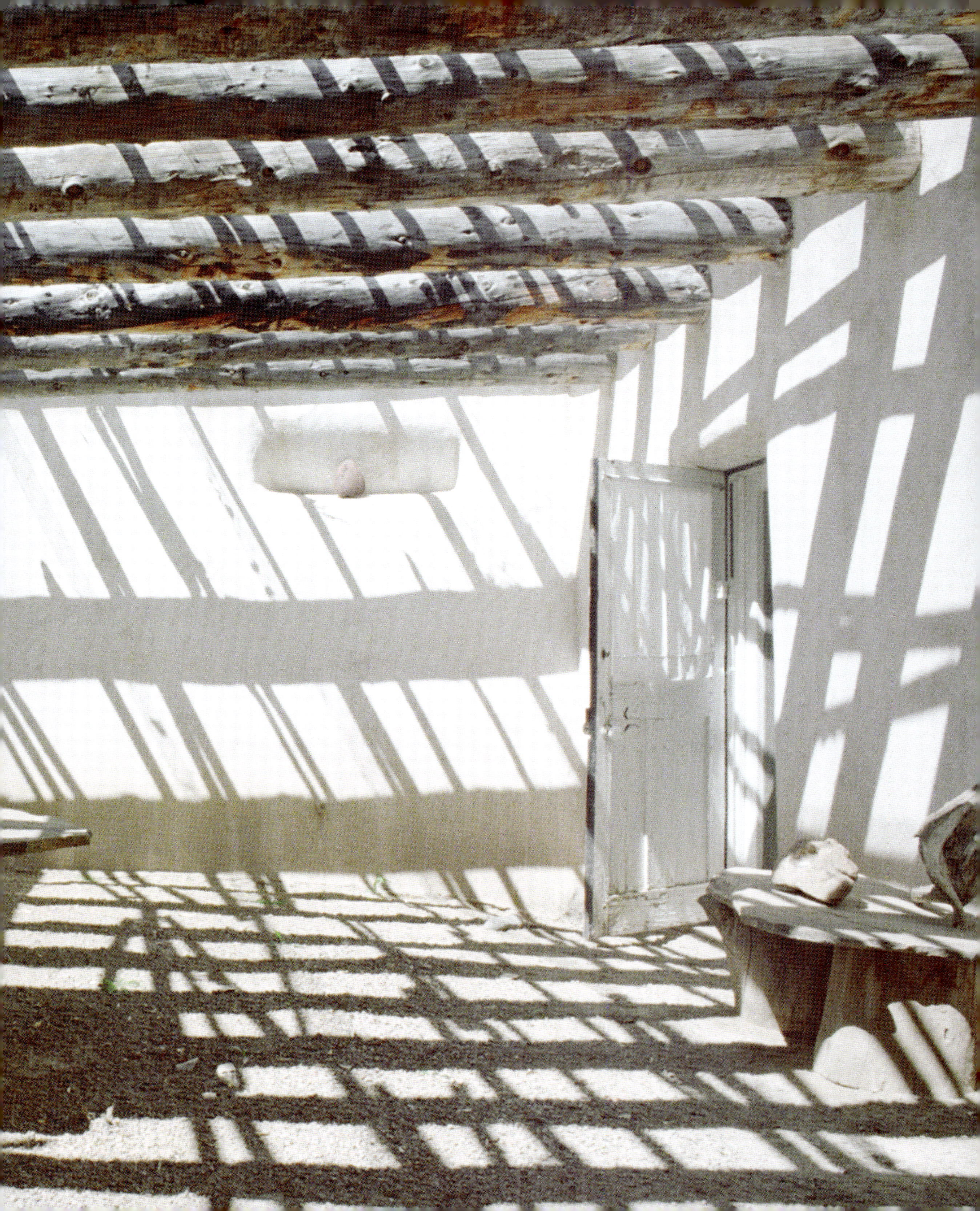

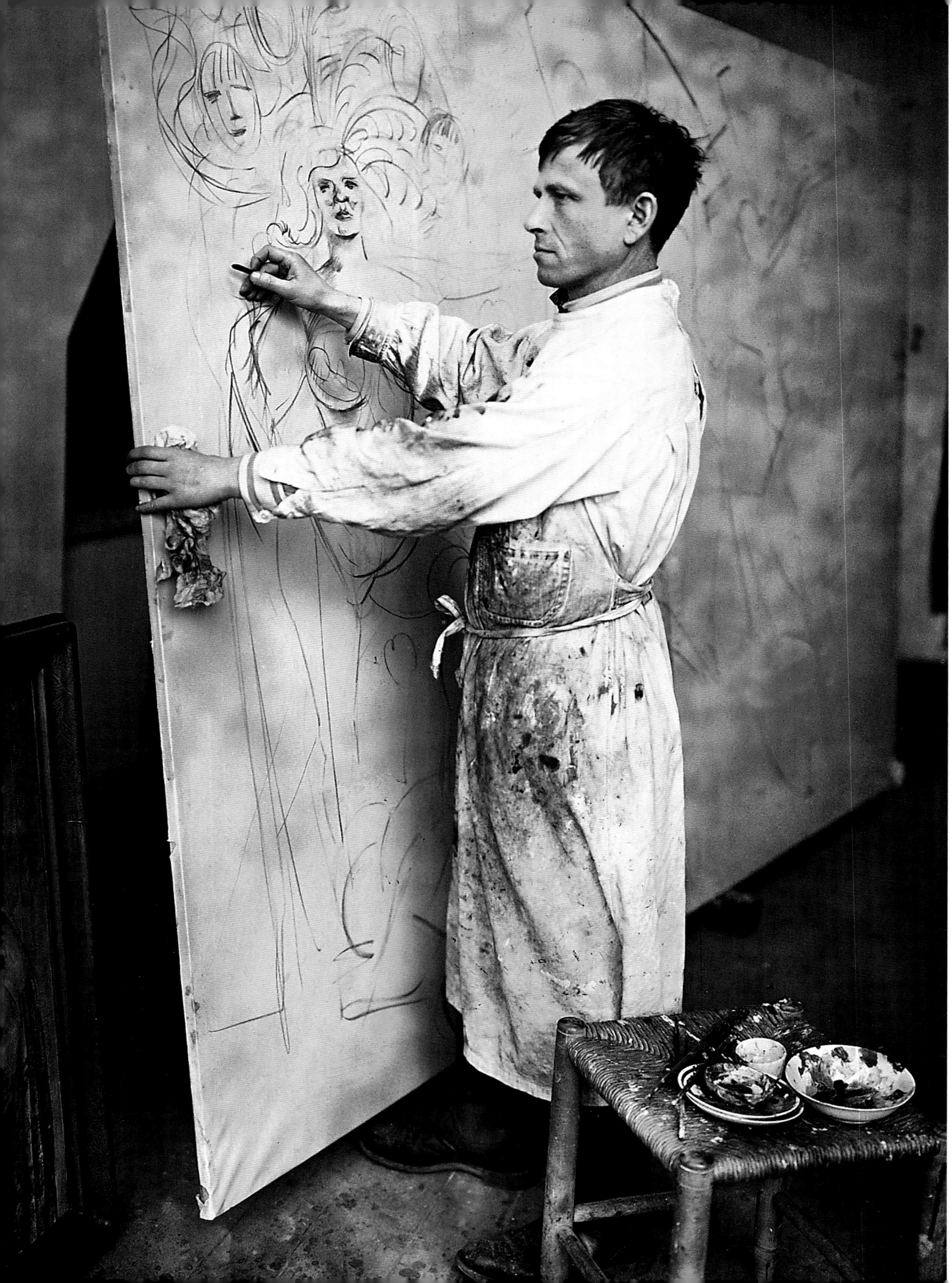

OTTO DIX

Hemmenhofen, Germany

Otto Dix (1891–1969), having moved frequently in his life, moved with his family to their new house overlooking Lake Constance, on the German–Swiss border when he was in his forties in 1936. Through his criticisms of war and his judgemental art, he had become a target for the Nazis, and in 1933, soon after they came to power, they dismissed him from his professorship at the State Academy in Dresden. They displayed several of his paintings in the Degenerate Art Museum in Munich and later destroyed them.

NAZI NEGATIVITY

Dix had been born in eastern Germany, and moved to Dresden in 1910 to study art. When World War One began in 1914, he immediately enlisted in the German army. By 1915, he was a machine gunner in the trenches at the Front in France. He earned an Iron Cross and was wounded several times. Throughout his experiences, he sketched the horrors he saw all around him. After the war, he resumed his art education at the Dresden Academy of Art, co-founded the Dresdner Sezession Gruppe and, in 1921, participated in exhibitions in Berlin and Dresden, before moving to Düsseldorf in 1922. The following year, he married Martha Koch (née Lindner). Haunted by his horrific experiences in World War One, he changed from painting landscapes and portraits, to distorted, unnerving, satirical images of crippled soldiers, nudes, prostitutes and well-known figures from Germany's intellectual circles. His canvases were disturbing and unflinching, depicting as they did scenes of sexual violence, murder and cruelty.

Throughout the 1920s, Dix participated in many of the most significant exhibitions of avant-garde art in Germany and became involved with the Neue Sachlichkeit (New Objectivity) movement, which was a development of Expressionism. Neue Sachlichkeit artists, who also included Max Beckmann and George Grosz, created unsentimental images that were highly critical of German society during the Weimar Republic. In 1926, Dix was engaged as a professor of art at the State Academy in Dresden and, in 1931, he was appointed a member of the Prussian Academy of Arts in Berlin. He showed his art in exhibitions all over Germany and at the Museum of Modern Art in New York, and was becoming well-known for his scathing observations. However, in 1933 the Nazis rose to power, and they considered his art to be depraved and his antipathy to war damaging to their cause. As a result, they began to target him. They had him sacked from his job and banned him from exhibiting in Germany. Refusing to emigrate, as the Nazis would have destroyed his paintings, he withdrew from public life and relocated with his family to the shores of Lake Constance in Baden-Württemberg.

In 1936, Dix, Martha and their three children – Nelly, Ursus and Jan – moved. Through an inheritance, Martha had bought a prime plot of land on a hill in the east part of Lake Constance, in Hemmenhofen, and there, she and Dix had a spacious house built and designed by a Dresden architect. The house took just a few months to complete, and the family soon moved in.

PEACE AND TRANQUILLITY

Set back in a serene garden surrounded by trees and with a straight path leading to the front door, the pretty house built by Dix and his wife, with its steep gable roof and large windows, is divided into three storeys. Plain and spacious, it was modern for the time, and filled with light. A wraparound balcony with fine

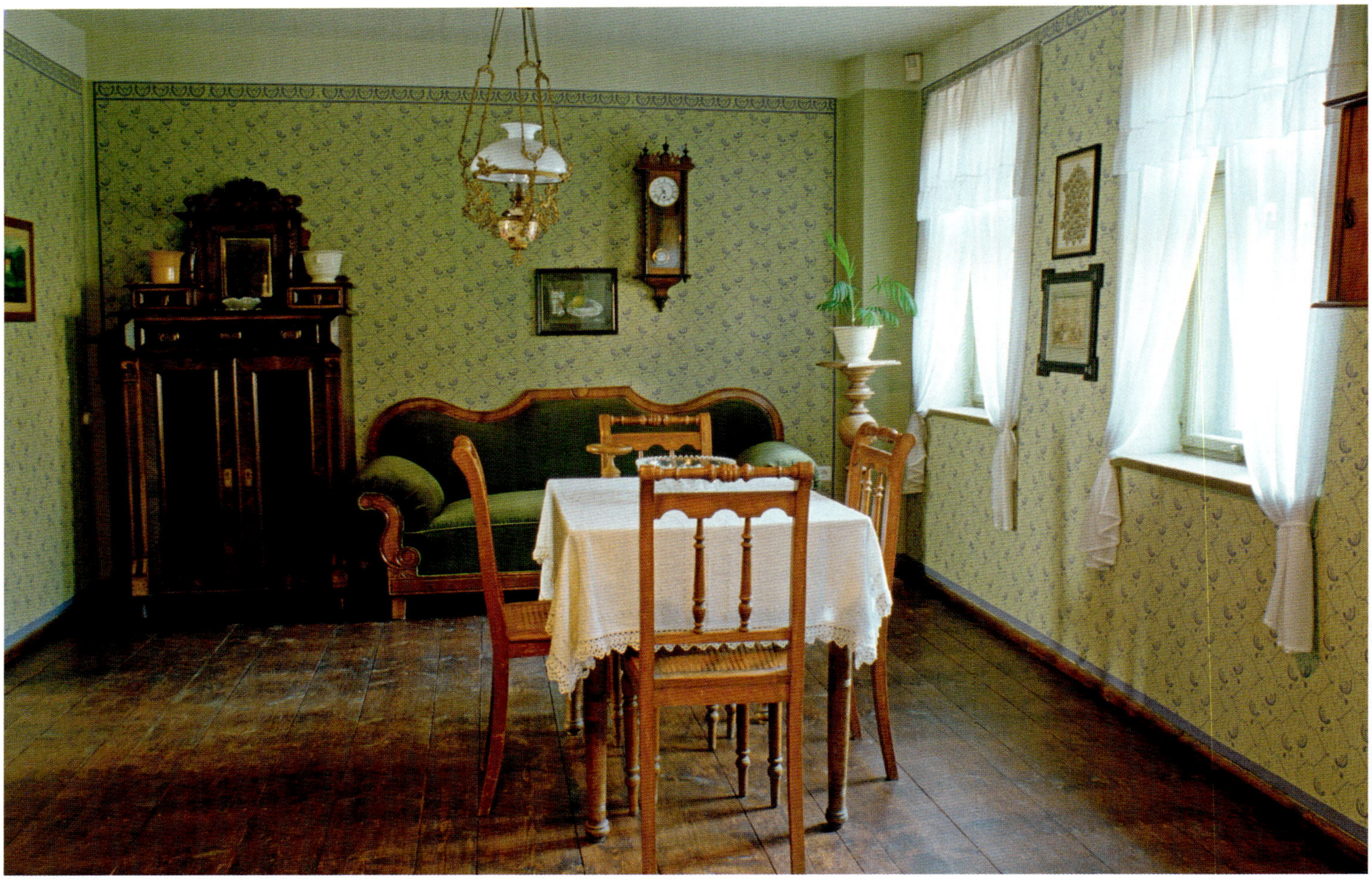

Above: The dining room of the house where Otto Dix was born, in Gera in the German state of Thuringia.
Opposite: The exterior of the house in Hemmenhofen.

metal railings hugs the back and sides of the building, from where the vast Lake Constance can be seen. Several windows around the house also give extensive views over the lake, and wooden benches surrounded by flowers and a path beneath the balcony afforded peaceful additional vistas across the water and beyond. In the 1960s, Dix and some friends painted several murals on the walls of the cellar, which the family used as a library, and elsewhere around the house Dix displayed several of his bold works, including his 1925 *Portrait of the Dancer Anita Berber*, 1927–28 triptych *Großstadt* (*Metropolis*) and 1934 painting *The Triumph of Death*. On the ground floor was the kitchen, painted in turquoise blue and cream, the yellow dining room, the living room and the music room, where Martha frequently played the piano for family and friends. They also had a gramophone, which was played a lot – Dix and Martha were extremely sociable. Their parties were legendary and guests frequently stayed there.

A wide set of wooden stairs leads to the first floor, where Martha relaxed in her salon and Dix worked in his studio on the east side of the house. The studio was fairly large, and generally kept tidy – for a studio. Dix kept his easel in the middle of the wooden floor, where light poured through an enormous double-glazed window that kept out winter chills and the winds that whipped around the lake. The children often played in the studio while he worked, but if they became too loud, Dix threw them out. While living there, Dix altered his style quite dramatically, painting landscapes and 'softer' subjects. Generally, he spent the mornings in the studio, and the afternoons painting outside. During the mid-1930s, he travelled to Switzerland several times and participated in several exhibitions there.

The Nazi government forced all artists in the Reich to join the Reich Chamber of Fine Arts, and two years before moving into the house, Dix was forced to do so and paint only innocuous

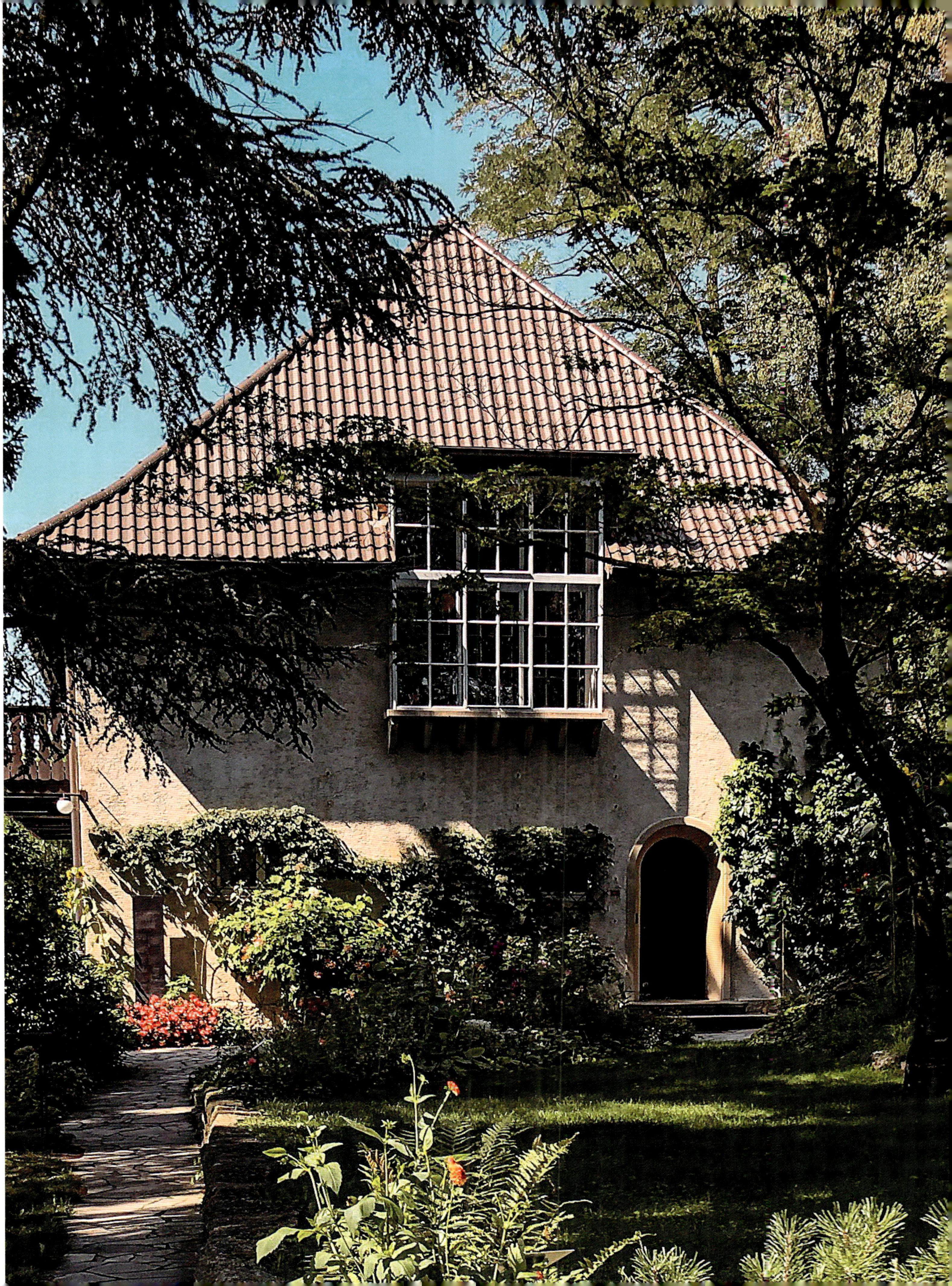

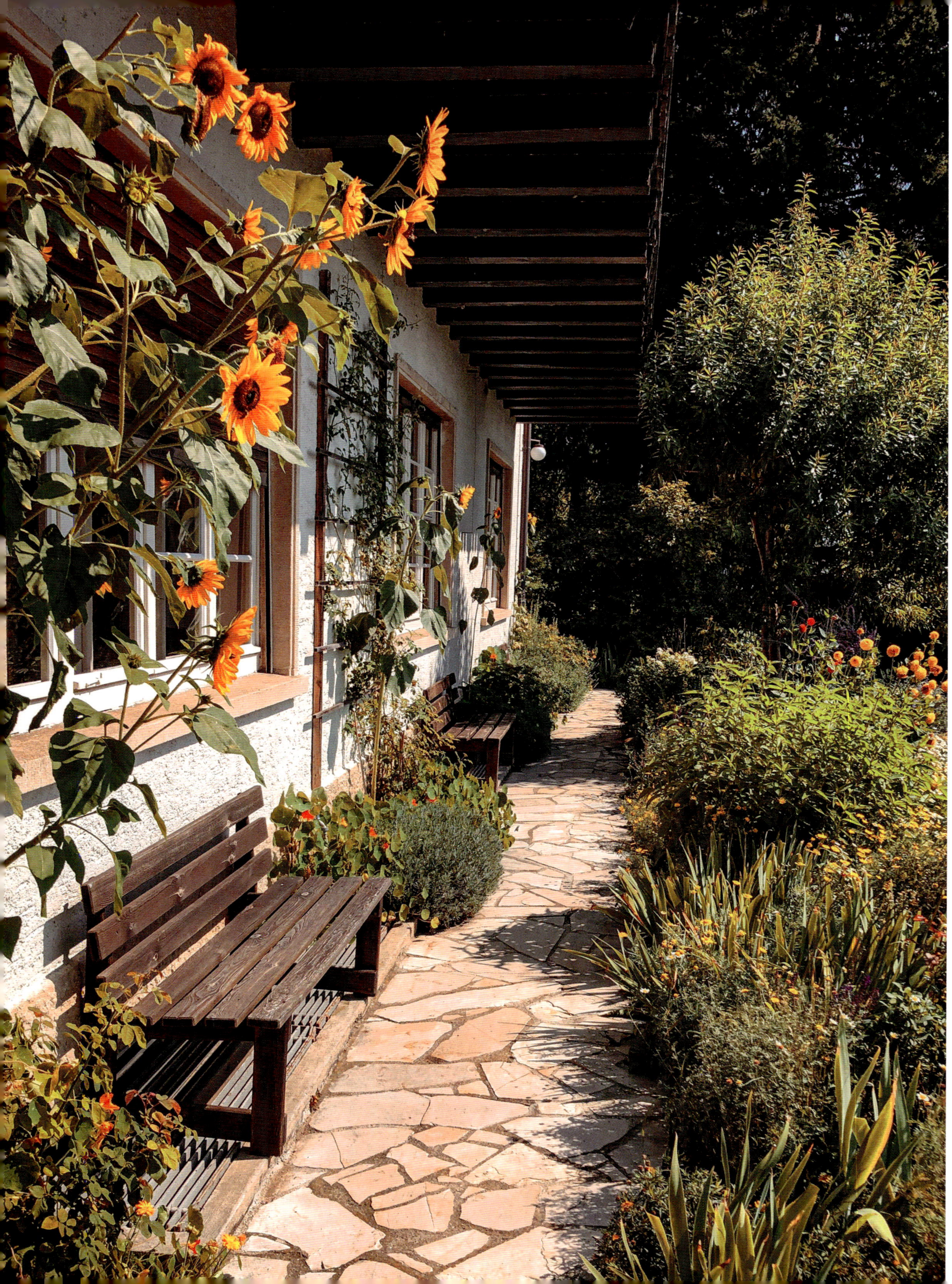

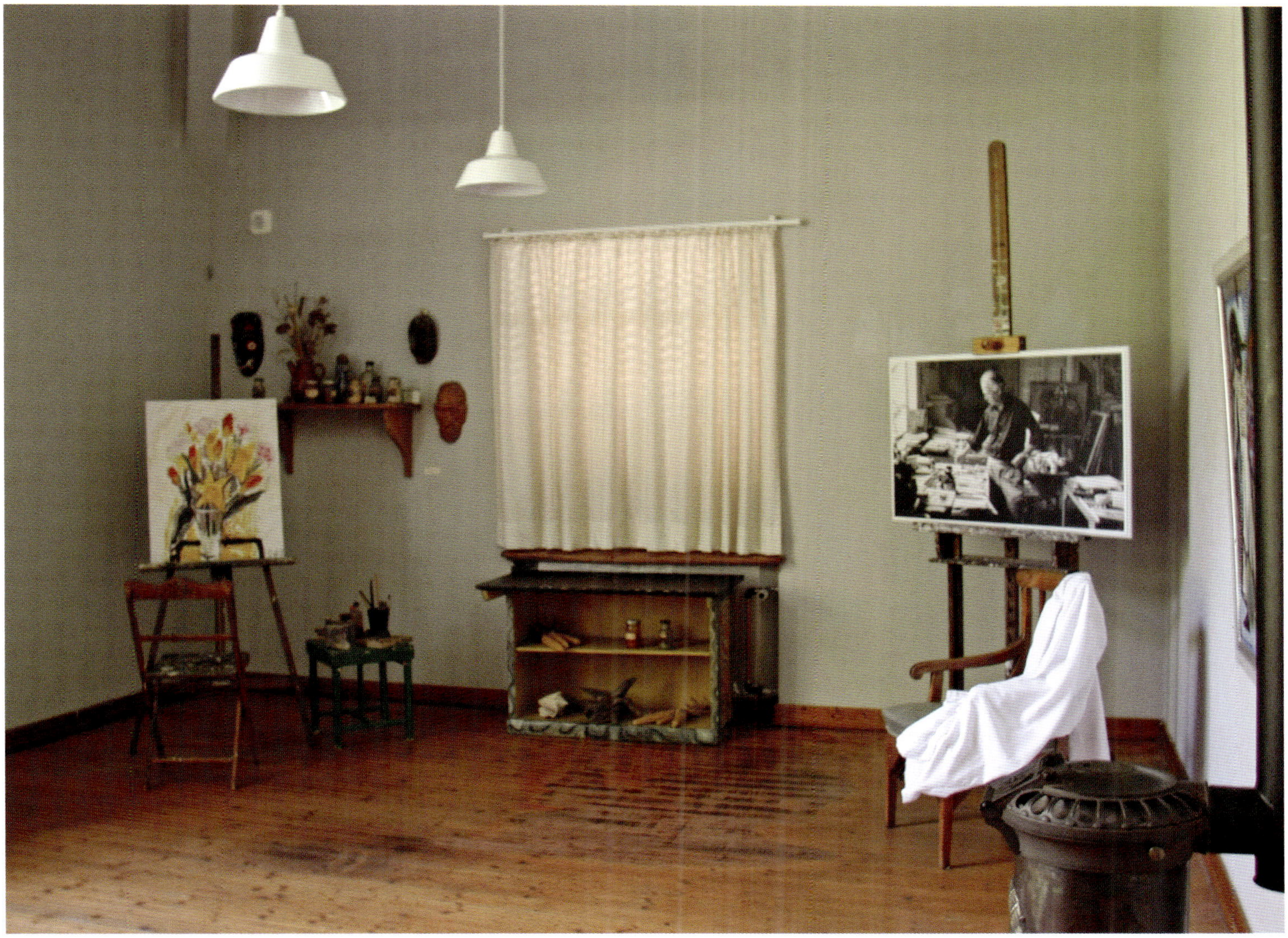

Above: Dix's house and studio have now been turned into a museum.
Opposite: Wooden benches surrounded by flowers offer peaceful vistas across the water and beyond.

landscapes. Although he mainly adhered to this, he still painted occasional allegorical paintings criticising Nazi ideals. In 1939, he was arrested on charges of plotting to kill Hitler, but these were soon dropped and he was released. Towards the end of World War Two, he was conscripted into the Volkssturm, a national militia comprising males between the ages of sixteen and sixty years old, established by the Nazis in an attempt to overcome their enemies' military strength. While part of this, Dix was captured by French troops and held in a French prisoner of war camp until 1946.

In 1955, after the death of their daughter Nelly, Dix and Martha took their granddaughter Bettina to live with them. He continued to work until his death in 1969, including on the house itself. Although he loved the peace and scenery surrounding his home, it did not make him happy.

'A beautiful paradise. Beautiful enough to make you puke. I'm standing in front of the landscape like a cow.'

Otto Dix

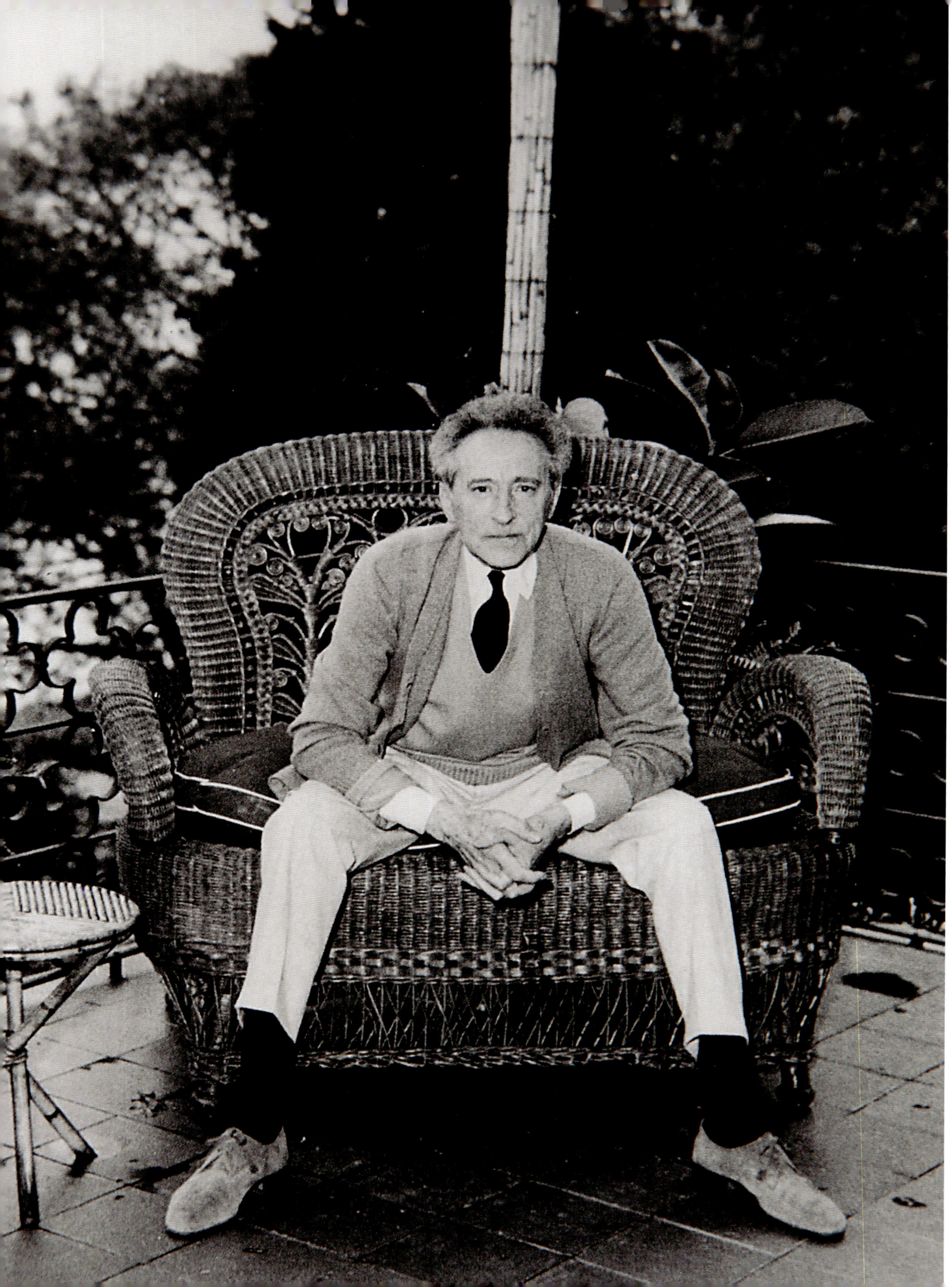

JEAN COCTEAU

Milly-la-Forêt, France

In 1947, the poet, filmmaker, designer and artist Jean Cocteau (1889–1963) bought a private mansion with the actor Jean Marais at the height of their fame, following the success of their 1946 film *La Belle et La Bête* (Beauty and the Beast). For the rest of his life, Cocteau divided his time between Paris and this house in Normandy, which became his sanctuary from the hectic pace of the city.

Exceptionally creative, Jean Cocteau worked across many artistic disciplines, including writing, painting, drawing, theatre and film. He became extremely influential to the Dada and Surrealist movements, and well known for his novels, stage plays and films. Yet, though he worked in many different mediums, he described himself as a poet. Although never connected with the Surrealist group, his work explores dreams and the unconscious.

Cocteau was born in Maisons-Laffitte, a town in northern France, near Paris, the youngest child in a fairly affluent family. His father, a lawyer and amateur painter, retired early and taught Cocteau to draw and paint at a young age, encouraging his artistic and creative abilities. When Cocteau was nine years old, however, his father committed suicide. From that time, he became exceptionally close to his mother, but they never spoke of his father's death. After a difficult time at school and then private lessons at home, when he was eighteen, he went to Italy with his mother. In Venice, he had a brief affair with a young man who shot himself an hour after Cocteau left him on the steps of Santa Maria della Salute. A few months later, he published his first volume of poems.

MOVING AROUND

On his return to France, Cocteau moved into a flat in the Hôtel Biron, a Rococo building in Paris where other tenants included sculptor Auguste Rodin and American dancer Isadora Duncan. While living there, he had relationships with both men and women. In 1910, he moved back to his mother's apartment in the rue d'Anjou, in Paris. Cocteau founded a journal, *Scheherazade*, which introduced him to contributors including the artists Pierre Bonnard and Marie Laurencin. At the time, his closest friends were the novelist Marcel Proust, and writer and poet Anna de Noailles. After seeing the Russian ballet dancer Vaslav Nijinsky perform in Paris in May 1909 at the Chatelet theatre, Cocteau liaised with Sergei Diaghilev and wrote a libretto for *The Blue God* for the Ballets Russes, but it was a critical and popular failure.

In 1914, at the start of World War One, Cocteau enlisted, but was exempted from military service due to a weak constitution. Instead, he collected milk from farms to give to troops departing to fight. Next, he joined a Red Cross ambulance crew. In 1915, he was sent to the Front as an engineer, and he later wrote about his experiences in his 1923 novel *Thomas the Imposter*. After the war, he became interested in Cubism and began pursuing Picasso with gifts. Initially, Picasso ignored him, but eventually they became friends and colleagues, working together on sets for *Parade*, a ballet for the Ballets Russes – choreographed by Léonide Massine, with music by Erik Satie, a one-act scenario by Cocteau, and costumes and sets by Picasso.

Over the next two decades, Cocteau became addicted to opium, and in 1928, he entered a clinic in an effort to cure himself of his addiction, but he was unsuccessful. By then, he felt that he was failing as a poet, and began writing more for theatre and film. In 1932, he met the Russian Princess Natalia Pavlovna Paley and they embarked on an opium-fuelled affair that ended when she returned to her husband.

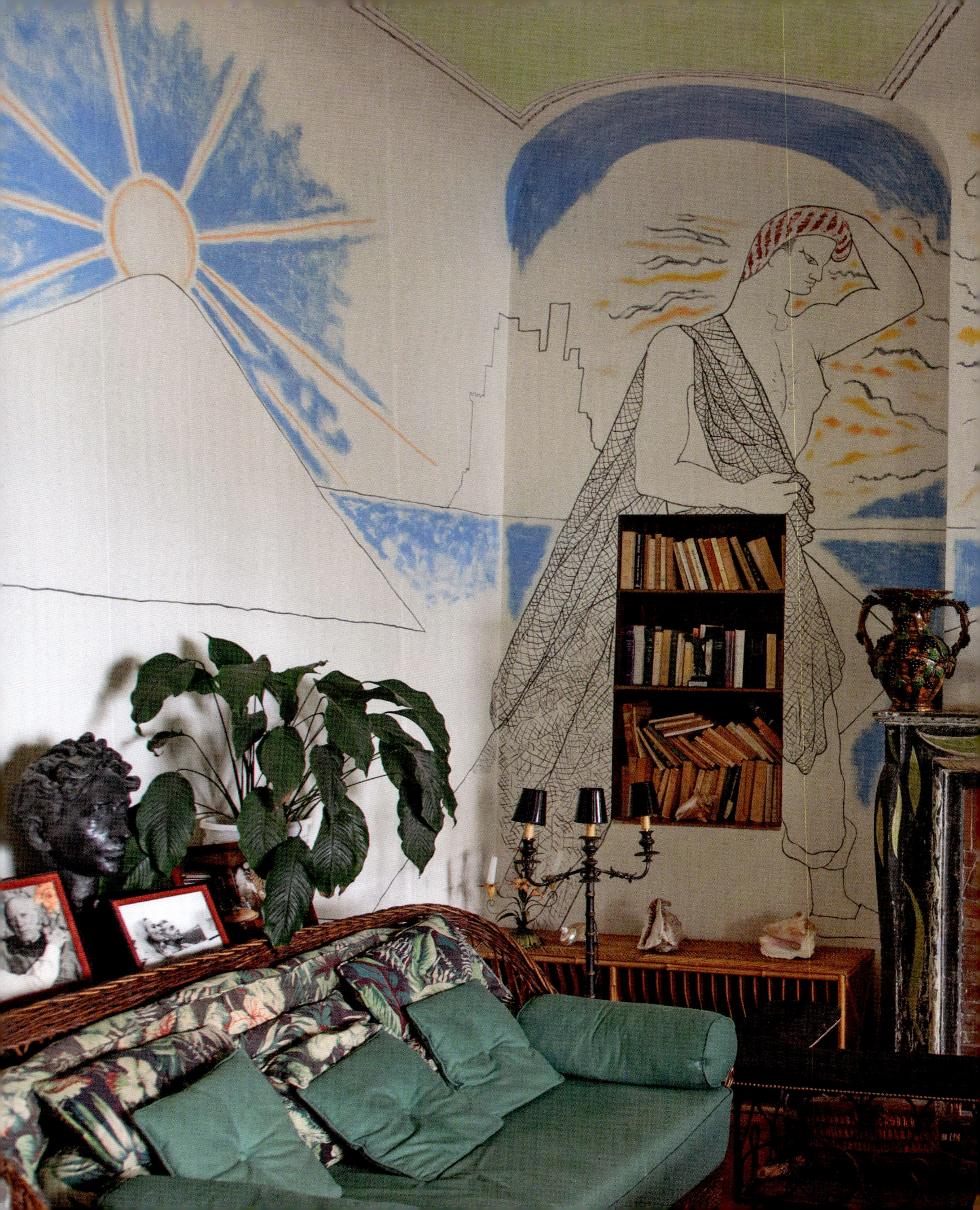

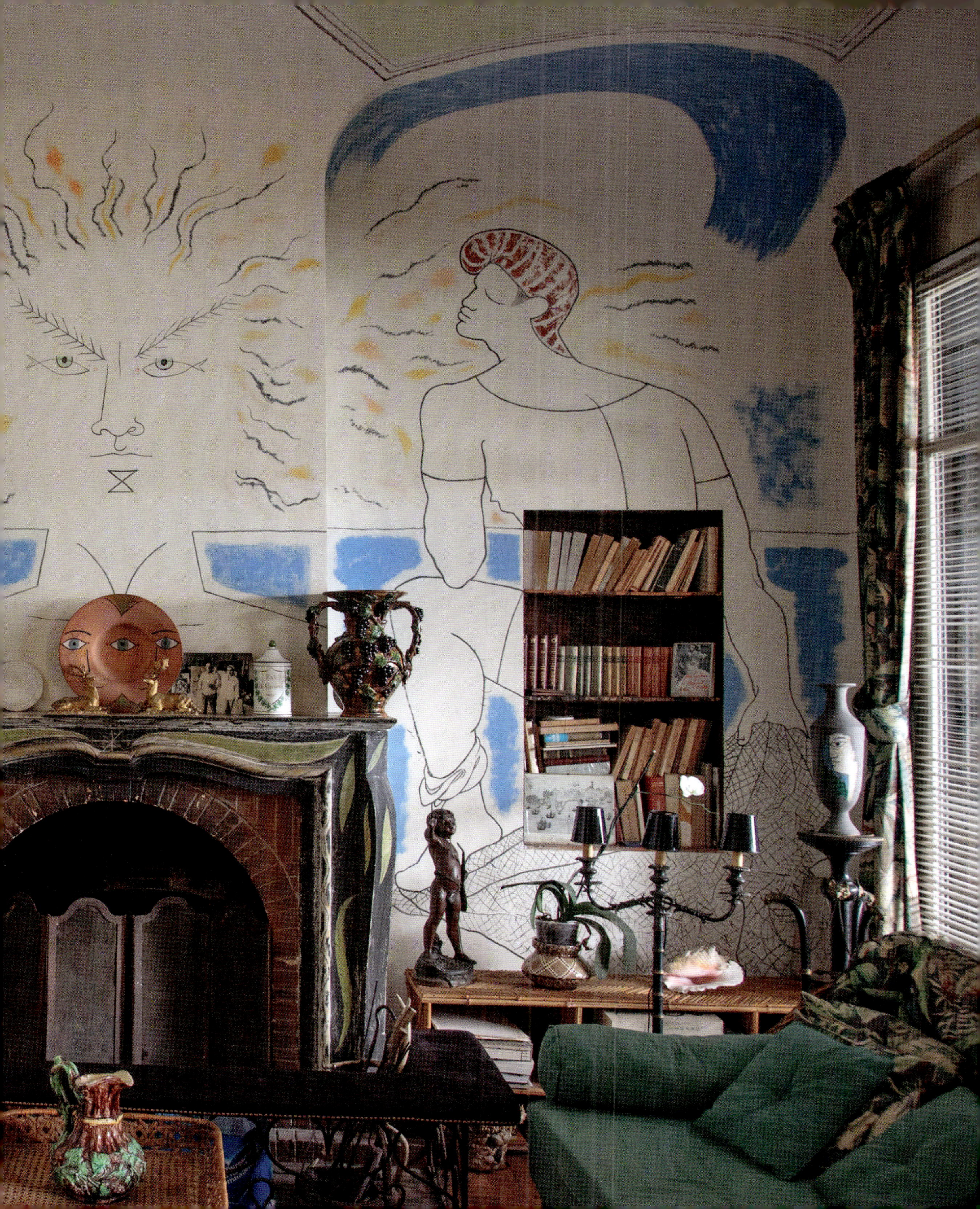

In 1937, he met Jean Marais, who became a close friend and occasional lover. Five years later, when Marais was away fighting, Cocteau became friends with Arno Breker, a German architect and sculptor who made public works in Nazi Germany, was made official state sculptor by Adolf Hitler and was exempted from military service. Cocteau wrote an article celebrating Breker's work and Breker temporarily persuaded him to support the Nazi Party. Both instigated outrage among the Parisian artistic community.

> 'I love cats because I enjoy my home; and little by little, they become its visible soul.'
>
> *Jean Cocteau*

ECLECTIC INTERIOR

About 50 kilometres (31 miles) south of Paris in the village of Milly-la-Forêt, near the forest of Fontainebleau, Cocteau's sixteenth-century house was built during the reign of Henry IV of France. Originally part of the thirteenth-century Château de la Bonde, the grounds contain a moat and a ruined tower. Around the house are also gardens and a small wooded park. The twelve-roomed house was originally built as a clerical residence, and in 1947, when his fame and fortune had been greatly increased by the enormous success of his film *Beauty and The Beast*, Cocteau and Marais bought the house, garden and part of the woods, and they used it as a retreat from Cocteau's primary residence in Paris. At first, they stayed there occasionally, and then later, Cocteau entered into a relationship with the actor and artist Édouard Dermit. After that, he and Dermit stayed in the house for longer periods. Cocteau created many of his later works there.

When Cocteau and Marais first saw the modest house in 1947, almost hidden down a pathway, they loved it instantly. It was in a peaceful and secluded setting, away from the bustle of Paris, where Cocteau believed he could work. Using the advice of his friend, antiques dealer and international interior designer Madeleine Castaing, he chose the décor for all rooms in the house, including the living room and bedrooms, exploring mythology and affinities with the Baroque style he loved. By combining his ideas and Castaing's expertise, he created some diverse schemes that included leopard tapestries, sphinxes, mermaids and carousel horses.

Perhaps the most important room in the house, Cocteau's study was on the first floor. Every day, he sat there at his writing table in a nineteenth-century Gothic Revival-style chair, facing the window. He adorned the walls with photographs, drawings and other souvenirs, including a bust of Lord Byron, a signed photograph of Orson Welles as Othello, a photograph of Picasso, a drawing of Charles Baudelaire by Manet, and a photomontage of Jean-Paul Sartre and Pope Pius XI. On the mantelpiece he displayed small works of antique Roman sculpture.

He was exceptionally popular with friends and lovers from all backgrounds, including writers, actors, artists, filmmakers, musicians, members of the nobility and more. They socialised in Paris, abroad and at his house in Milly. Summer soirées were often spent in the garden, contained by the moat of the Château de la Bonde. Abundant with plants, flowers bloomed and fruit grew during almost every month. Cocteau also loved animals, especially cats, and he filled his home with many feline companions.

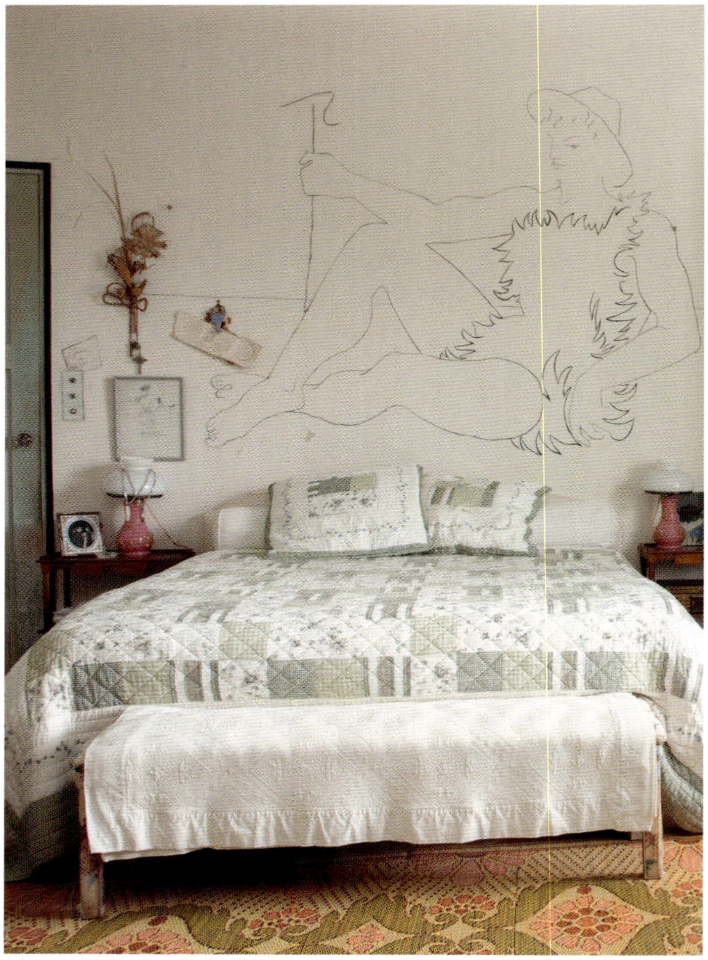

Above: Milly was described by Cocteau as his 'refuge' from the bustle of the city. 'Here I find the memories of the ancient countryside I dreamed of in Paris – just as later, in Paris, I dreamed of taking flight', he wrote.

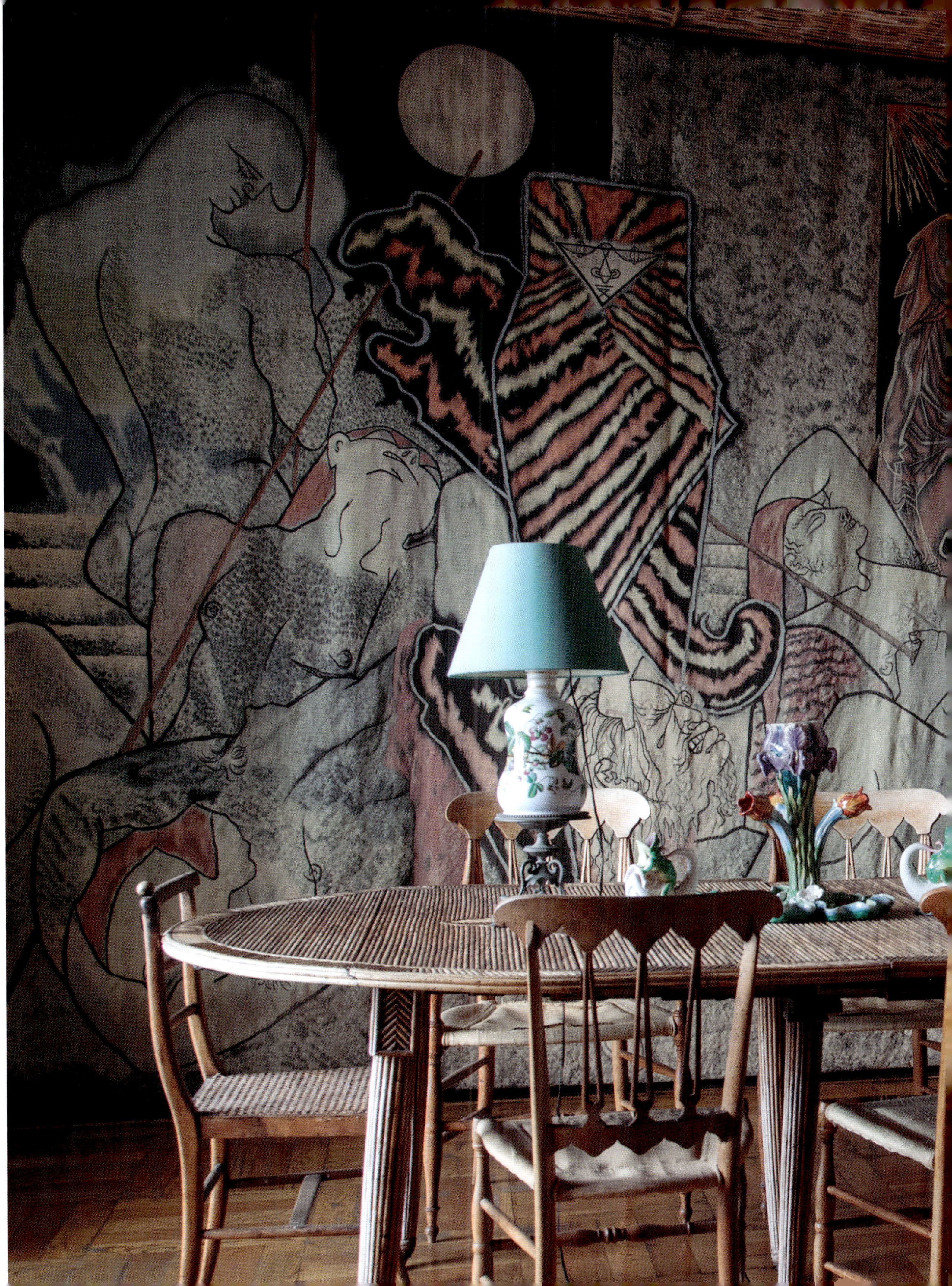

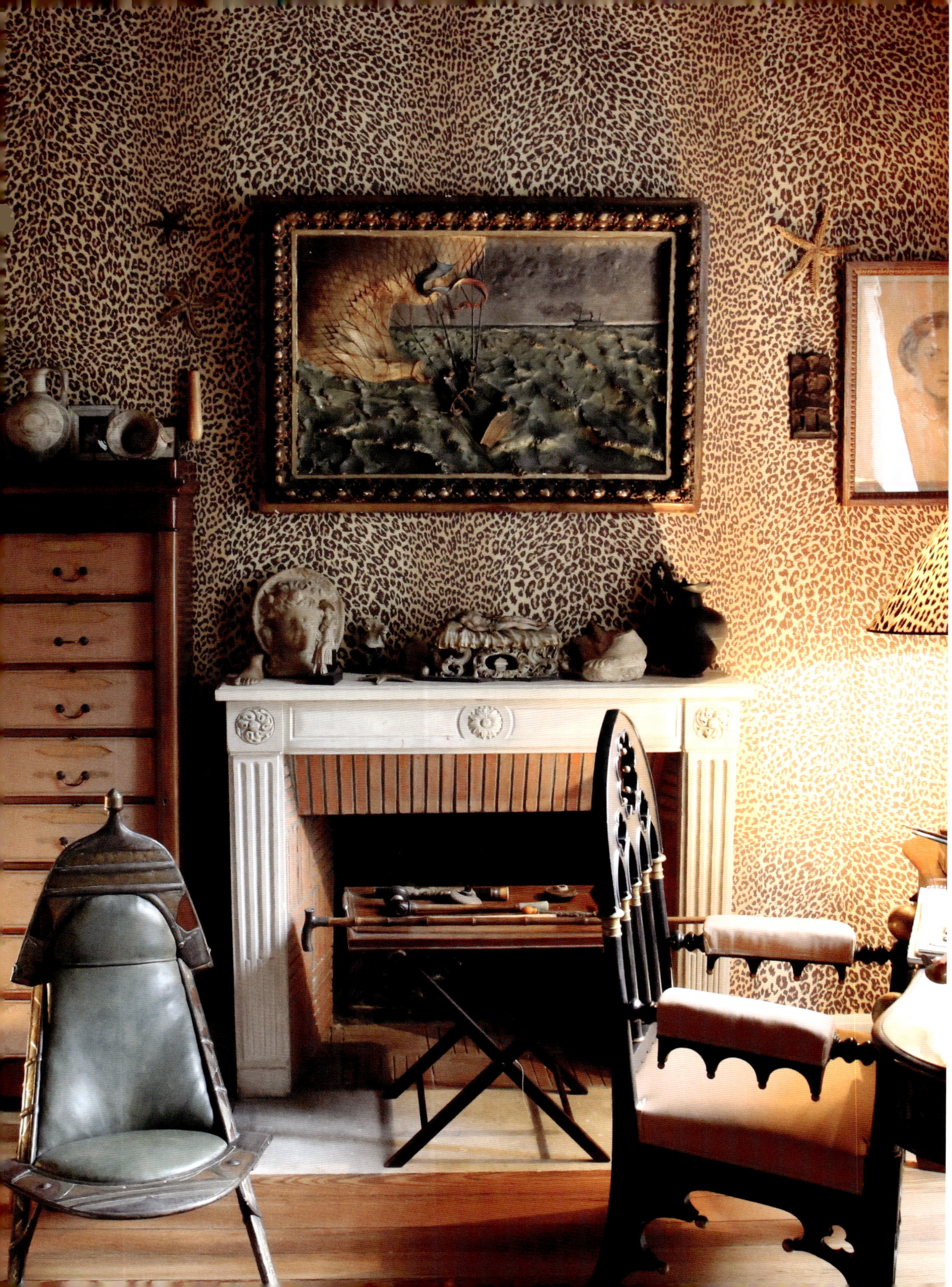

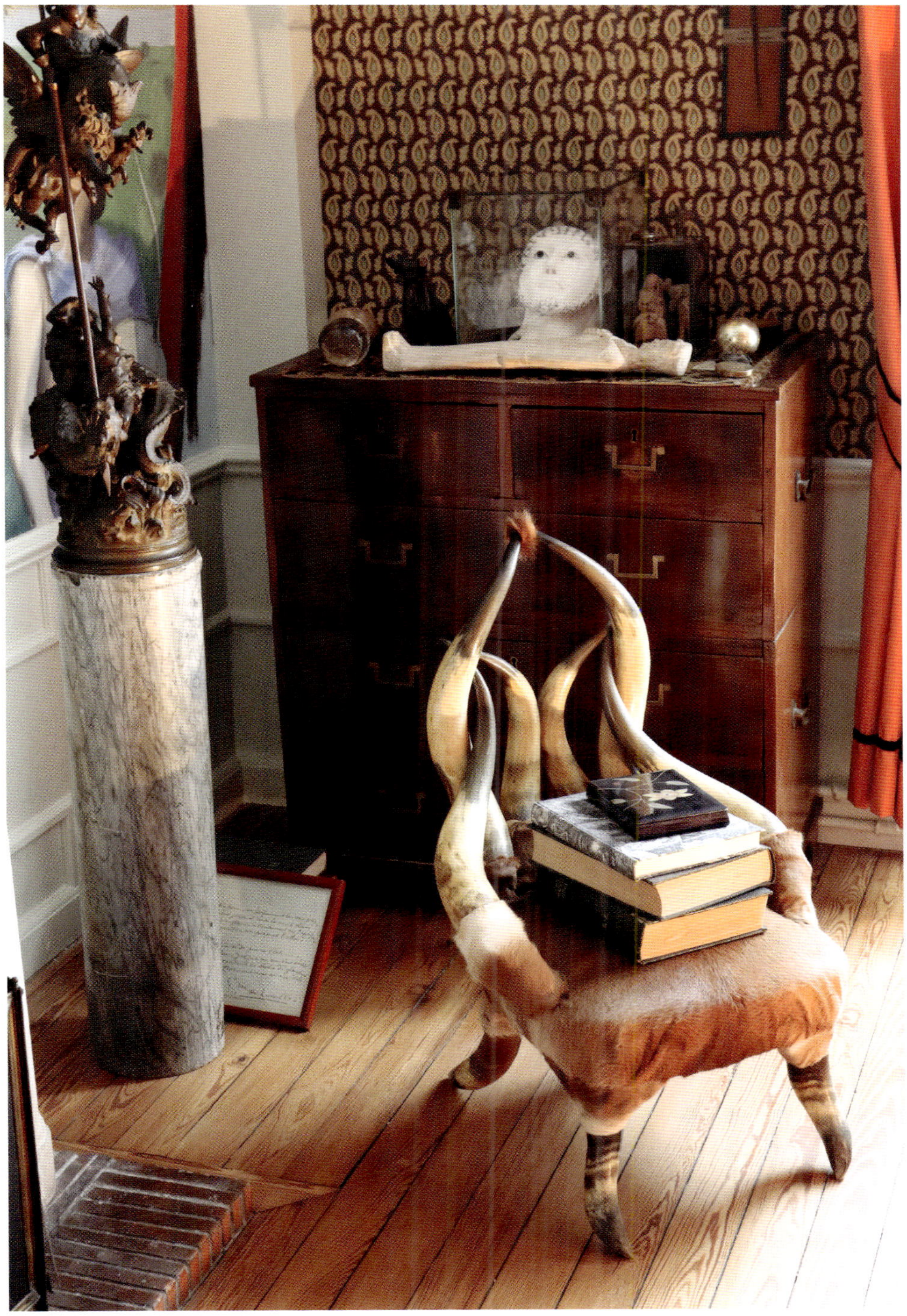

Above and opposite: Every item of furniture was chosen for its pleasing qualities. Set against the patterned wallpapers, Cocteau's furniture and ornaments amalgamate into a richly eclectic environment.

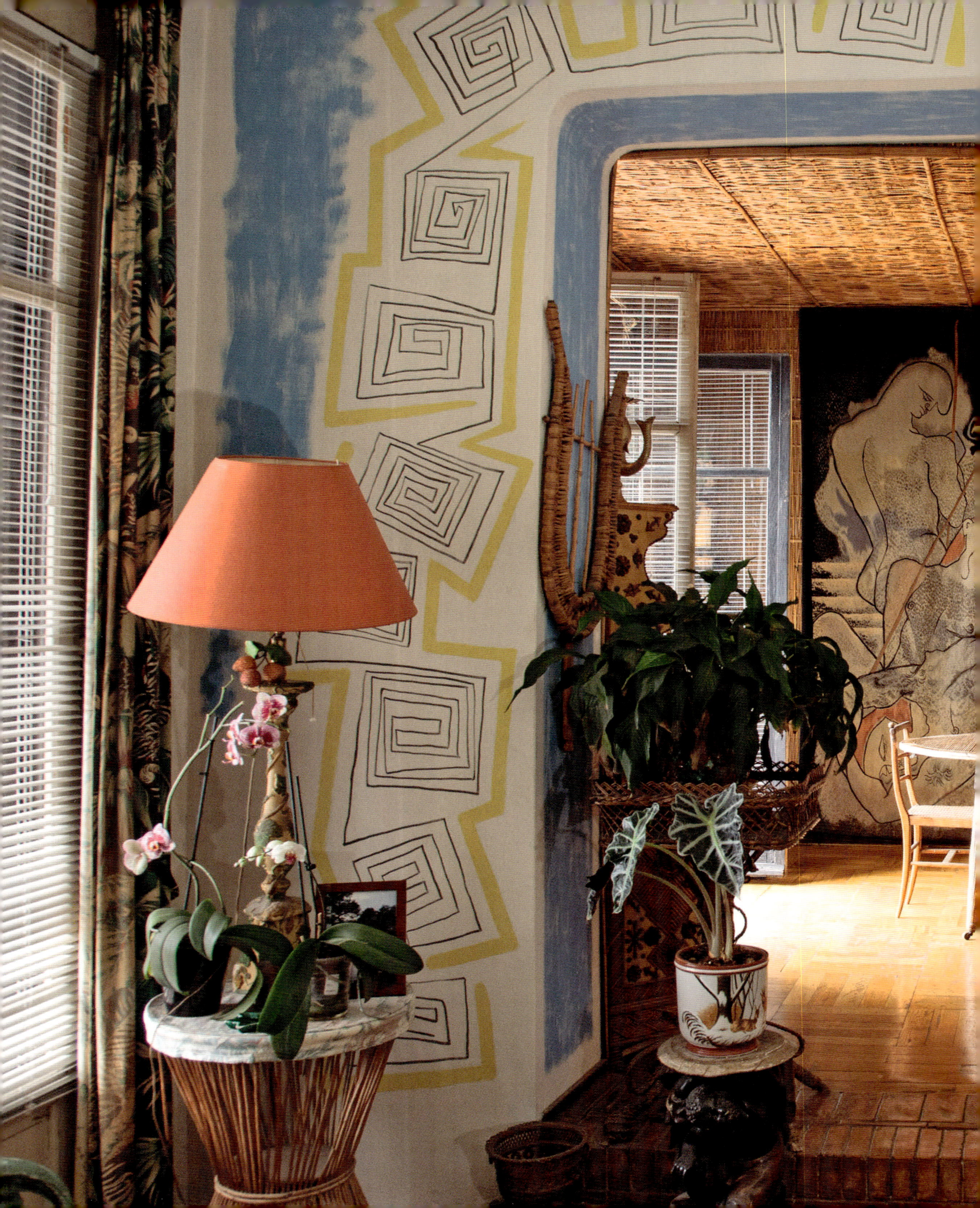

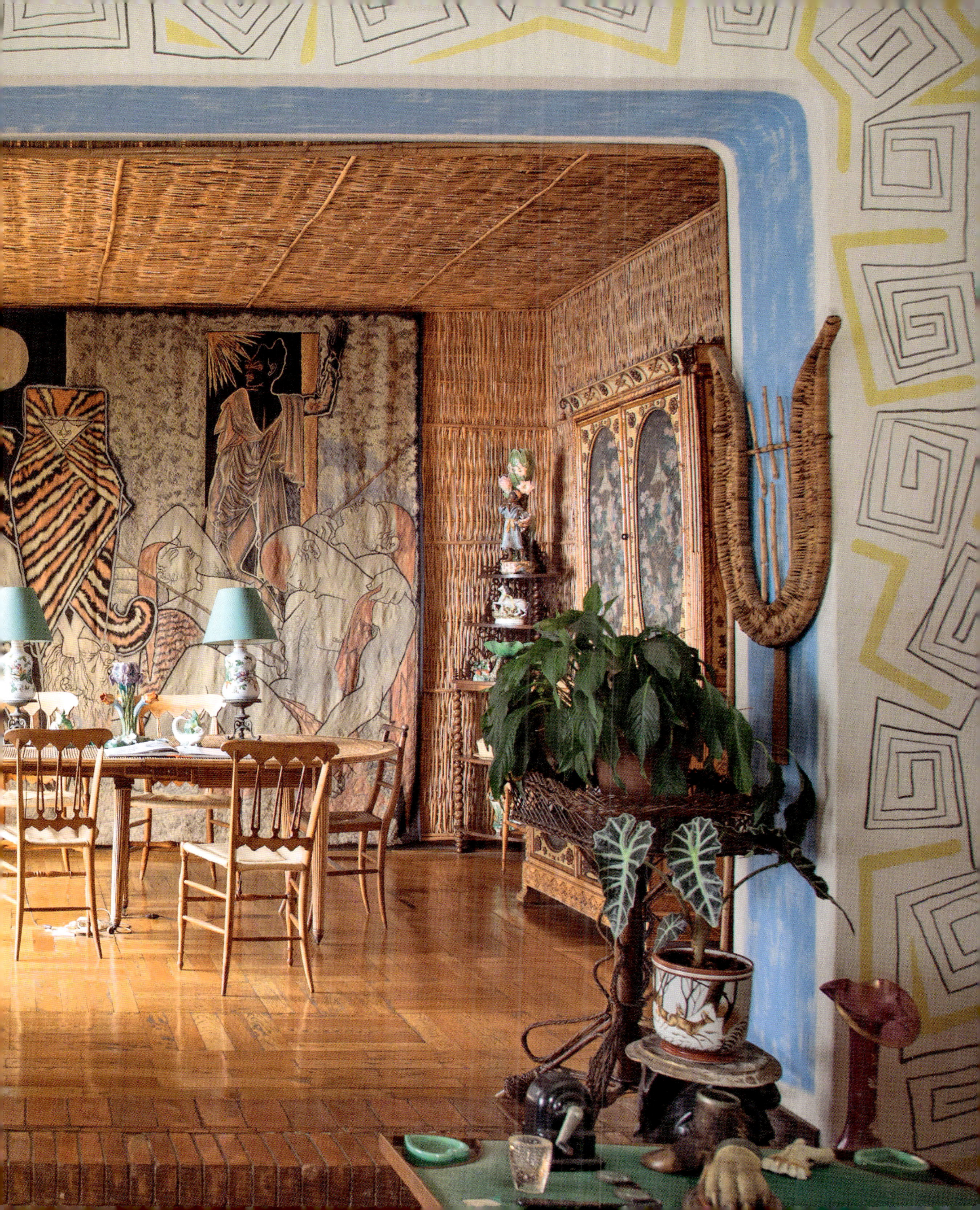

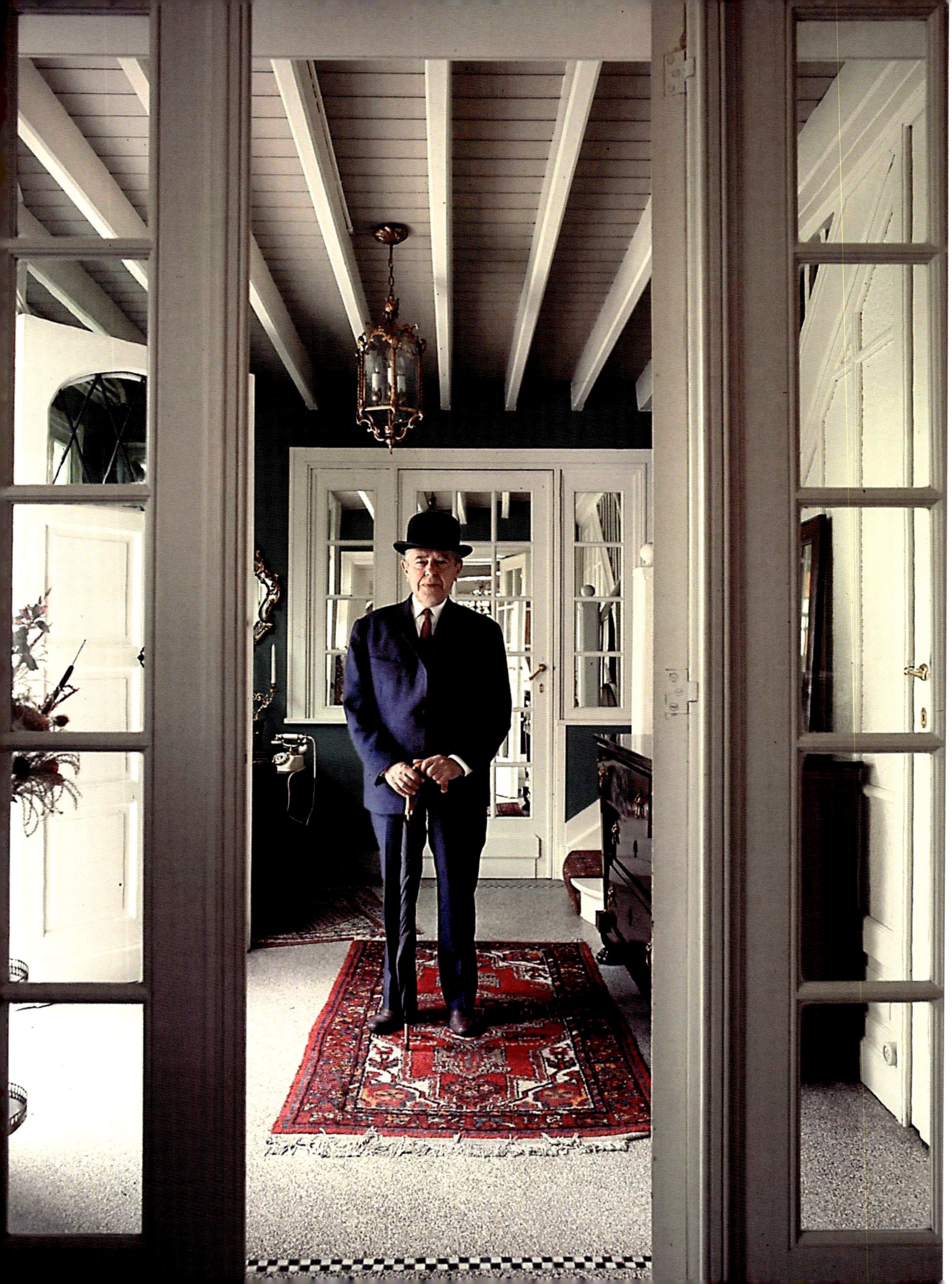

RENÉ MAGRITTE

Brussels, Belgium

For most of his life, the Belgian Surrealist artist René Magritte (1898–1967) and his wife Georgette lived in a house in Brussels at Esseghemstraat, 135. The couple rented the ground floor apartment of the narrow four-storey terraced house that was entered via a door at street level.

Possibly the most plagiarised Surrealist, René Magritte became well known for creating mysterious and thought-provoking images, usually using ordinary objects in unexpected situations that challenge viewers' preconceived perceptions of reality. His art influenced many other artists and movements, including Pop and Conceptual art.

Magritte became a successful Surrealist painter after many years working as a commercial artist, during which he produced advertising and book designs. Living in quiet anonymity in his unassuming apartment, he painted men in bowler hats that can be interpreted as self-portraits. While most other artists experimented with changing styles and techniques, Magritte continued his impassive, illustrative style throughout his career. Fascinated by the interactions of text and images, he explored both rational and illogical ideas in his imagery.

THE SURREALIST MOVEMENT

The eldest of three boys, Magritte was born into a fairly comfortable family, but when he was thirteen, his mother, who had suffered with depression for years, committed suicide. Three years later, Magritte entered the Académie des Beaux-Arts in Brussels to study painting. In 1921, he undertook his mandatory military service and the following year, he married his childhood sweetheart, Georgette Berger. He also began working as a draughtsman in a wallpaper factory and then became a designer, producing posters and other publicity material. In about 1925 he saw the work of Giorgio de Chirico and began to work in a more Surrealist style, but after his first solo exhibition in Brussels in 1927 was scorned by critics, he moved to Paris where he became friends with André Breton and involved with the Surrealist group there. Remaining in Paris for three years, he became a leading member of the movement, and began to experiment with the use of words and language in his paintings. In 1929, he exhibited in Paris with Salvador Dalí, Jean Arp, de Chirico, Ernst, Miró, Picasso, Francis Picabia and Yves Tanguy.

By 1930, he returned to Brussels to take up work in commercial advertising once again. He and Georgette moved into their new home: a flat on the outskirts of Brussels with a small back garden. He worked in the kitchen – the warmest room in the house – or the dining room. Then in 1933, he had a purpose-built studio erected in the back garden. By the late 1930s, international collectors, including the British poet Edward James, began buying Magritte's work, giving him greater financial independence. In 1937, James hosted him for three weeks at his home in London, where Magritte painted several works for him. While there, Magritte wrote: 'London is a revelation. Of course, I'm only just beginning to discover it. But until now, everything is perfect.'

In 1936, Magritte had begun an affair with a young performance artist. He arranged for one of his friends to entertain and distract his wife, which resulted in an affair between Georgette and his friend. In 1940, he and Georgette reconciled. By then, he was able to give up most of his commercial work, but World War Two broke out. He wrote: 'The sense of chaos, of panic, which Surrealism hoped to foster so that everything might be called into question was achieved much more successfully by those idiots the Nazis… Against widespread pessimism, I now propose a search for joy

> 'We are surrounded by curtains. We only perceive the world behind a curtain of semblance. At the same time, an object needs to be covered in order to be recognised at all.'
>
> *René Magritte*

and pleasure.' In 1946, he separated from Breton and signed a manifesto called *Surrealism in Full Sunlight*. He tried a new style that was not popular, and by the end of the 1950s, he returned to his characteristic style and subjects. By the end of his life, he was renowned, admired and extremely successful.

BRUSSELS

For twenty-four years, between 1930 and 1954, Magritte and Georgette rented the ground floor at rue Esseghem/Esseghemstraat, 135 in Jette, Brussels. The house had been built in 1925 and they moved in after their three-year stay in a Paris suburb. When they first arrived, there was no bathroom, so Magritte had one installed. They lived fairly frugally for most of the time. Magritte decorated the apartment in colours that complemented his work. So, for instance, the walls of the living room and kitchen were blue and light green, which matched the background of many of his paintings. The rug-covered parquet floor was dyed in the tradition of many old Belgian families. Magritte produced over 800 paintings in their apartment, often using elements and items from the home, including the fireplace, some of the furniture, the windows, staircase and façade. The couple had no children, but usually had a pet dog. He entertained his friends; fellow artists and the Brussels group of Surrealists met there regularly to discuss ideas and aesthetics. It became the Belgian Surrealists' headquarters.

In 1954, with Magritte's reputation increasing, he and Georgette moved to a larger apartment in Lambermont Avenue, in Schaerbeek, a different municipality of Brussels, which they believed was a better reflection of their social standing.

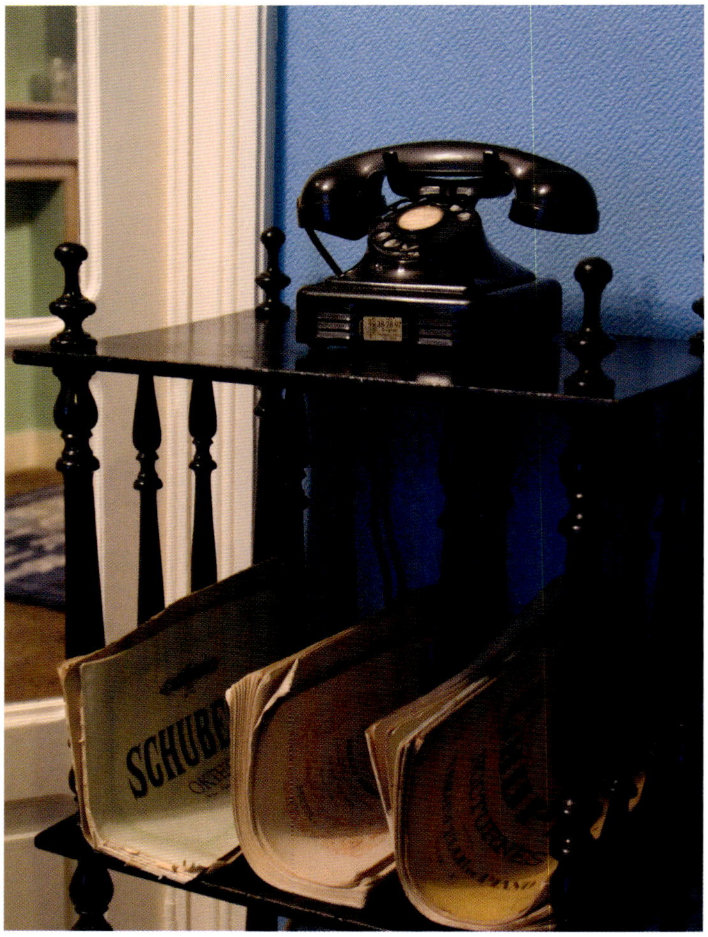

Above and following page: The walls of Magritte's living room were cobalt blue, one of the colours he regularly used in his paintings.

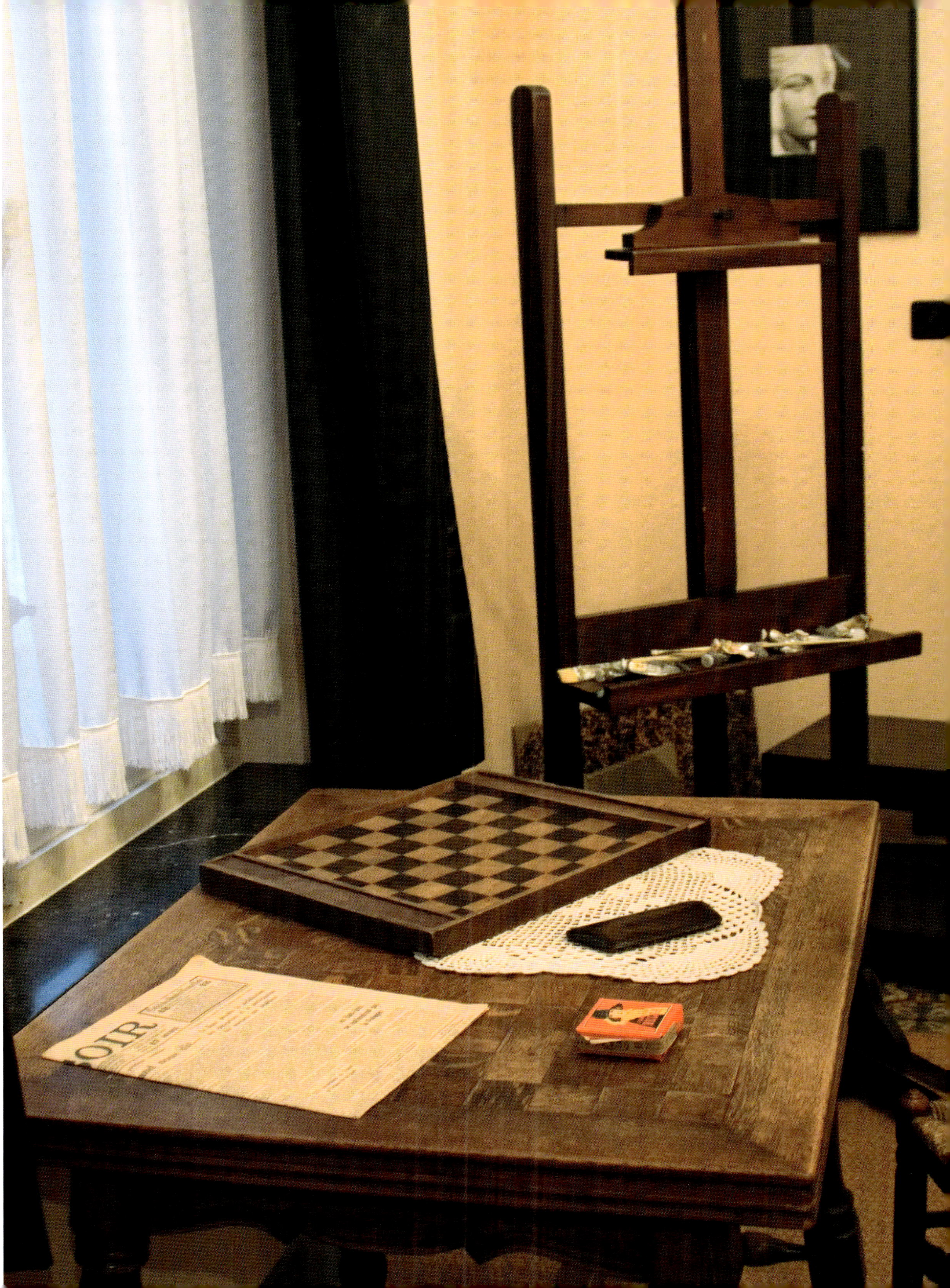

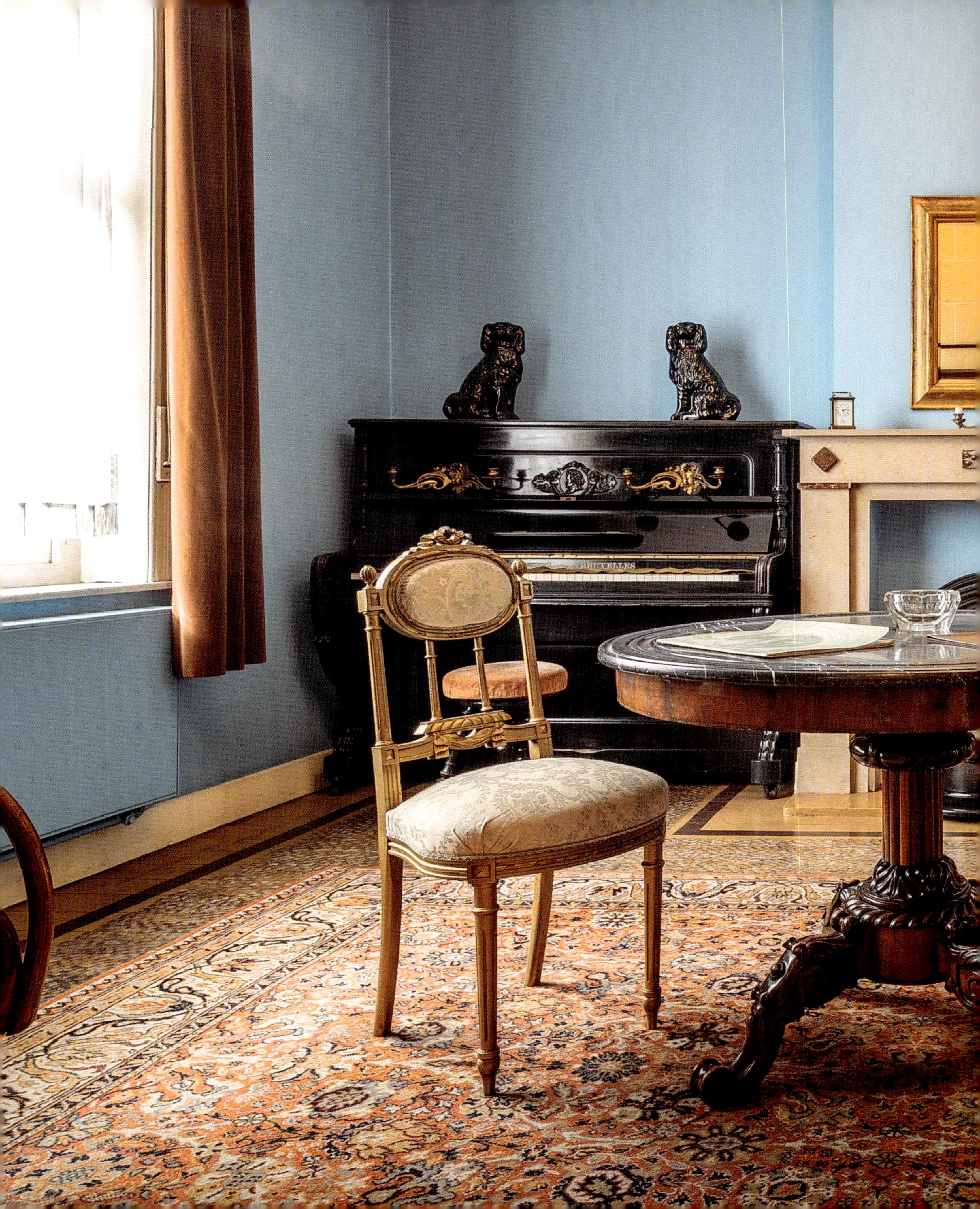

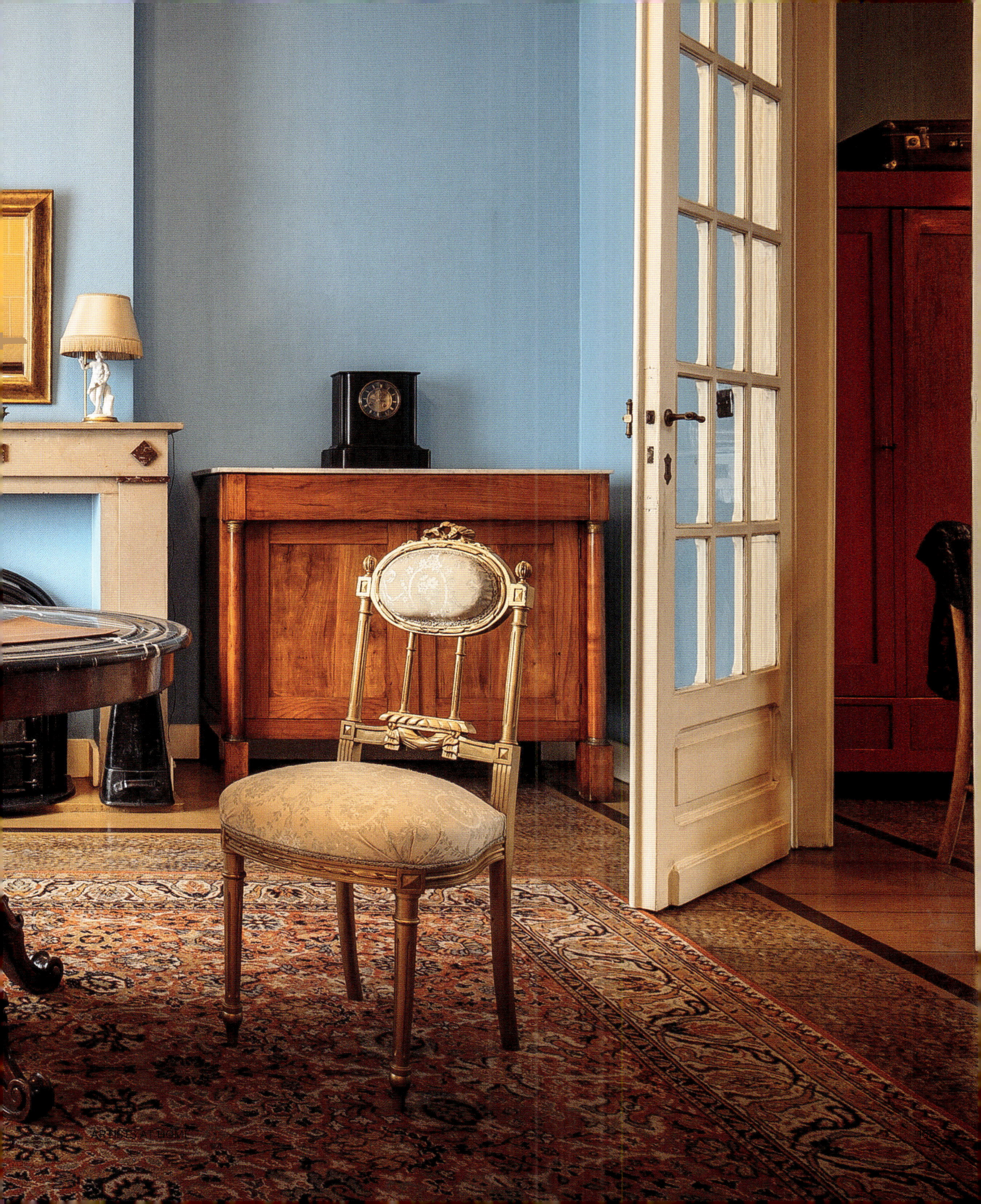

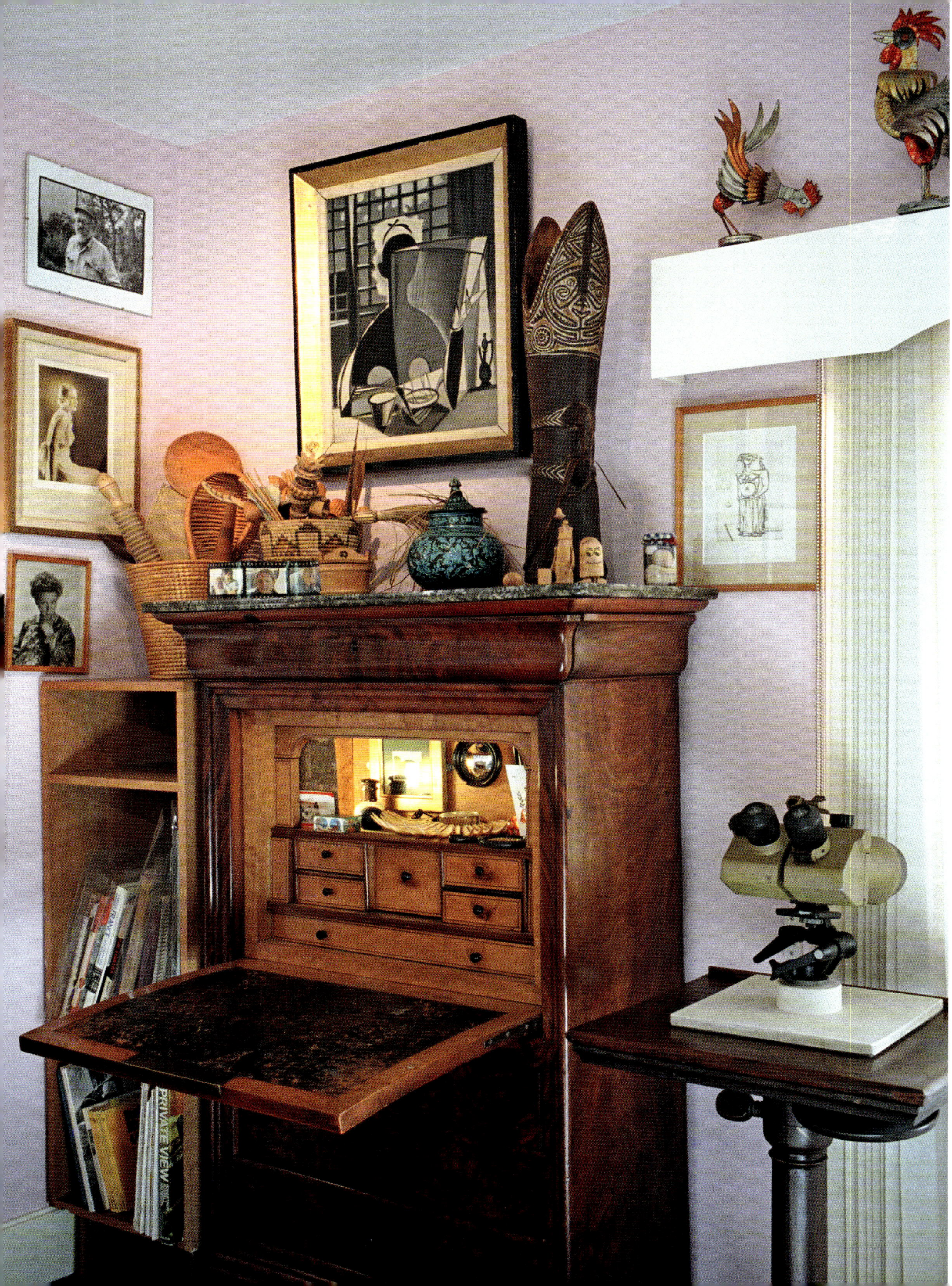
PRIVATE VIEW

LEE MILLER AND ROLAND PENROSE

East Sussex, UK

An American fashion model who became a photographer and an English Quaker who became a Surrealist painter and art collector, Lee Miller (1907–77) and Roland Penrose (1900–84) influenced modern art with their vision, inspired each other, and established their home in Chiddingly, East Sussex in 1949, where they collected contemporary art and welcomed many avant-garde artists of the day.

MILLER AND PENROSE

During her childhood in New York, Lee Miller's father taught her photography. Her early years had been happy until she was seven years old, when she was raped by a family friend and contracted gonorrhoea. At that time, the disease could only be treated with invasive, painful and humiliating procedures. Traumatised, she struggled at school, and later suffered with depression and alcohol abuse. At nineteen, she left home, began modelling and enrolled in the Art Students League in Manhattan, where she studied drawing and painting. That winter, she became a model for *Vogue* magazine, but she soon left New York City for Paris.

In the French capital she became the student, muse and lover of American artist Man Ray. She lived with him for three years, while he taught her photography, and together, they developed the process of 'solarisation', a technique that reverses the negative and positive parts of a photograph. While living in Paris, Miller mixed with the avant-garde of the art and literary world, including the poet and joint founder of the Surrealist movement Paul Éluard, Max Ernst, Picasso, Joan Miró and Jean Cocteau. In 1932, she left Man Ray and returned to America.

Back in New York, Miller resumed her modelling career and also established a photographic studio with her younger brother. She produced Surrealist-style photography and images for *Vogue* and advertising. She married, but then met the British Surrealist artist Roland Penrose, with whom she fell in love. They travelled together, visiting prominent artists around Europe, and then she left her husband and moved to London with Penrose. There, she photographed the city during and after the Blitz, in 1940–41. In 1943, she was made an accredited war correspondent for *Vogue* magazine and she photographed troops, the Liberation of Paris, the battle of Saint-Malo, field hospitals in Normandy, and the liberation of both Dachau and Buchenwald concentration camps in 1945. Her images were among the first photographic examples of the Holocaust.

Struggling with depression and what is now recognised as post-traumatic stress disorder, Miller married Penrose in 1947, after World War Two, when she was forty, and gave birth to their son, Antony. The following year, they bought Farleys House in the south of England, and lived there for the rest of their lives. While hosting their friends, who included prominent writers and artists from both sides of the English Channel, Miller would often create her 'Surrealist'-style dishes, such as 'Goldfish' – baked cod covered in a carrot, onion and butter garnish – and 'Persian Carpet' of sliced

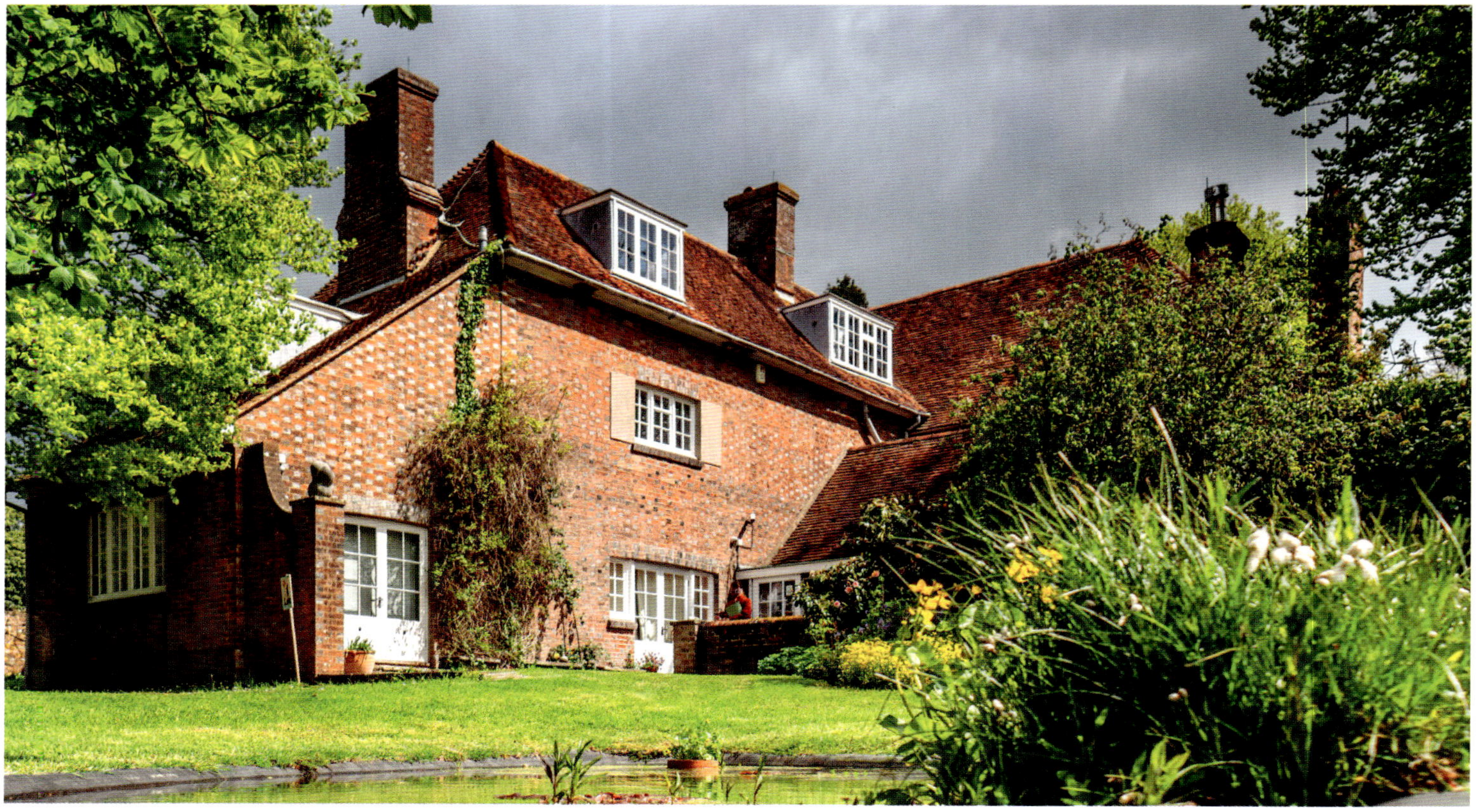

Above: For 35 years, Lee Miller and Roland Penrose lived in their red brick home Farleys in the Sussex countryside, filling it with their contemporary art collection and entertaining their friends, who were some of the key figures of 20th century art.

oranges, orange blossom water, crème de cassis and grenadine, decorated with candied violets.

Sir Roland Penrose CBE was an English artist, historian and poet. Well-educated, he grew up in a strict Quaker household in Watford, Hertfordshire. In August 1918, as a conscientious objector to World War One, he joined the Friends' Ambulance Unit and served with the British Red Cross in Italy. After studying architecture at Queens' College Cambridge, he moved to France, where he studied painting with the Cubist André Lhote and Fauvist Othon Friesz. In 1925, he married his first wife, but they separated in 1934 and divorced three years later. Penrose became good friends with Picasso and Ernst, in particular; he established the British Surrealist group in 1936, and became a major promoter and collector of modern art. In 1937, he met Miller, and they began a romantic relationship and travelled together around Europe. She took photographs and later they collaborated on a poem.

As a Quaker, Penrose was a pacifist, but during World War Two, he volunteered as an air raid warden, then taught the painting of military camouflage, and later he became a captain in the Royal Engineers. He was also involved in the Artists' Refugee Committee, which found artists safe passage to England from Nazi-occupied countries. In 1946, after the war, he reopened the London Gallery and established the Institute of Contemporary Arts (ICA). In 1960, he was awarded the CBE and, in 1966, he was knighted for his services to the visual arts.

FARLEYS HOUSE

Hidden away in the leafy Sussex countryside, in a hamlet with a good rail link to London called Muddles Green, the Penroses found Farley Farm: a Georgian farmhouse with a Queen Anne-style façade surrounded by land and outbuildings. They bought it, along with some surrounding farmland, cottages, barns, a pigsty and a cow byre. From their extensive grounds, they could see the giant prehistoric figure, known as the Long Man of Wilmington, cut into the turf on the South Downs. They retained their flat in London and, for the first few years, their son Antony remained at Farley Farm with the nanny, while Miller and Penrose lived in London during the week, returning on Friday evenings with their car laden with furniture and artworks. Guests would often accompany or join them, including Ernst, Miró, Man Ray, Leonora Carrington and Dorothea

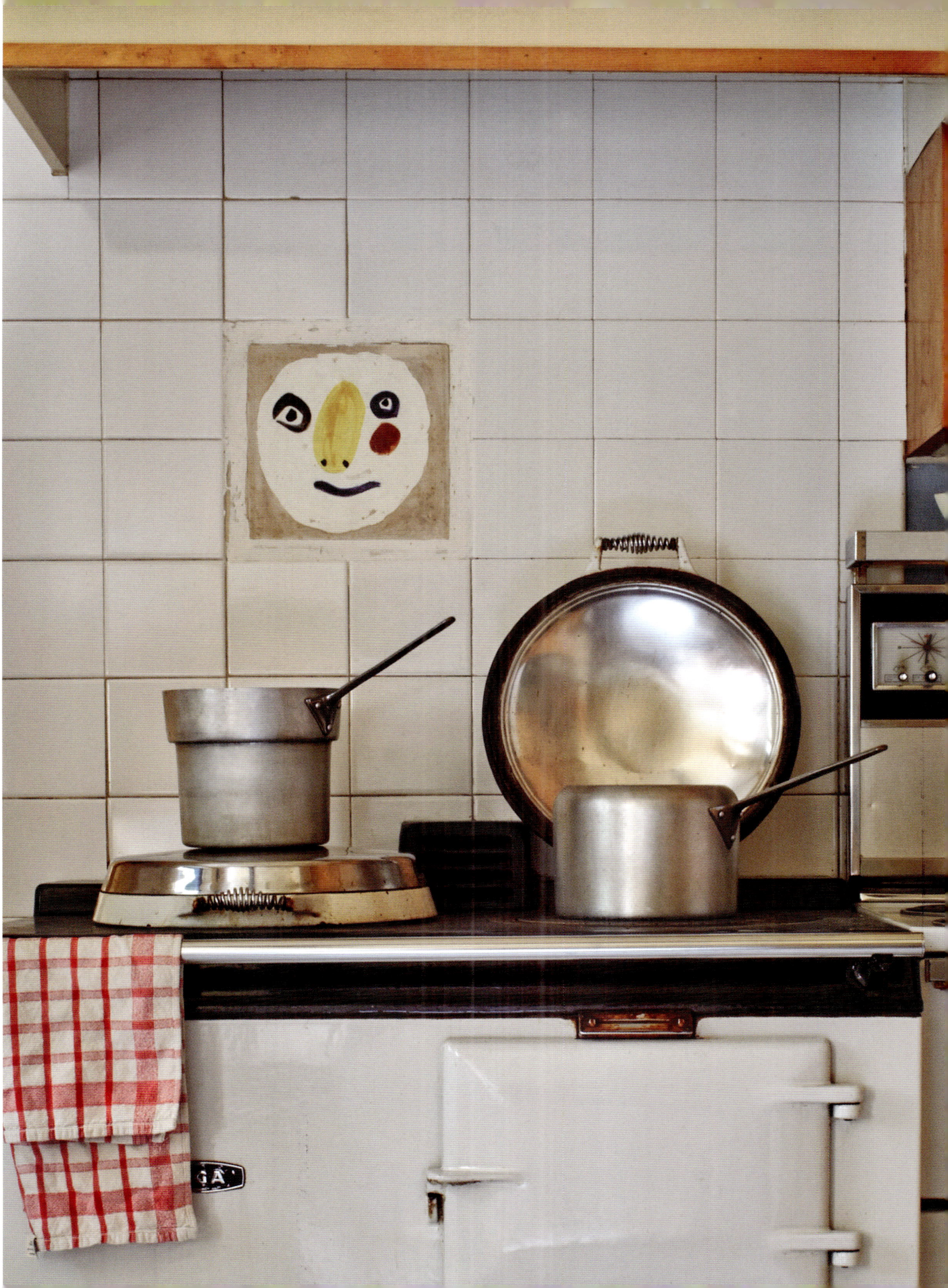

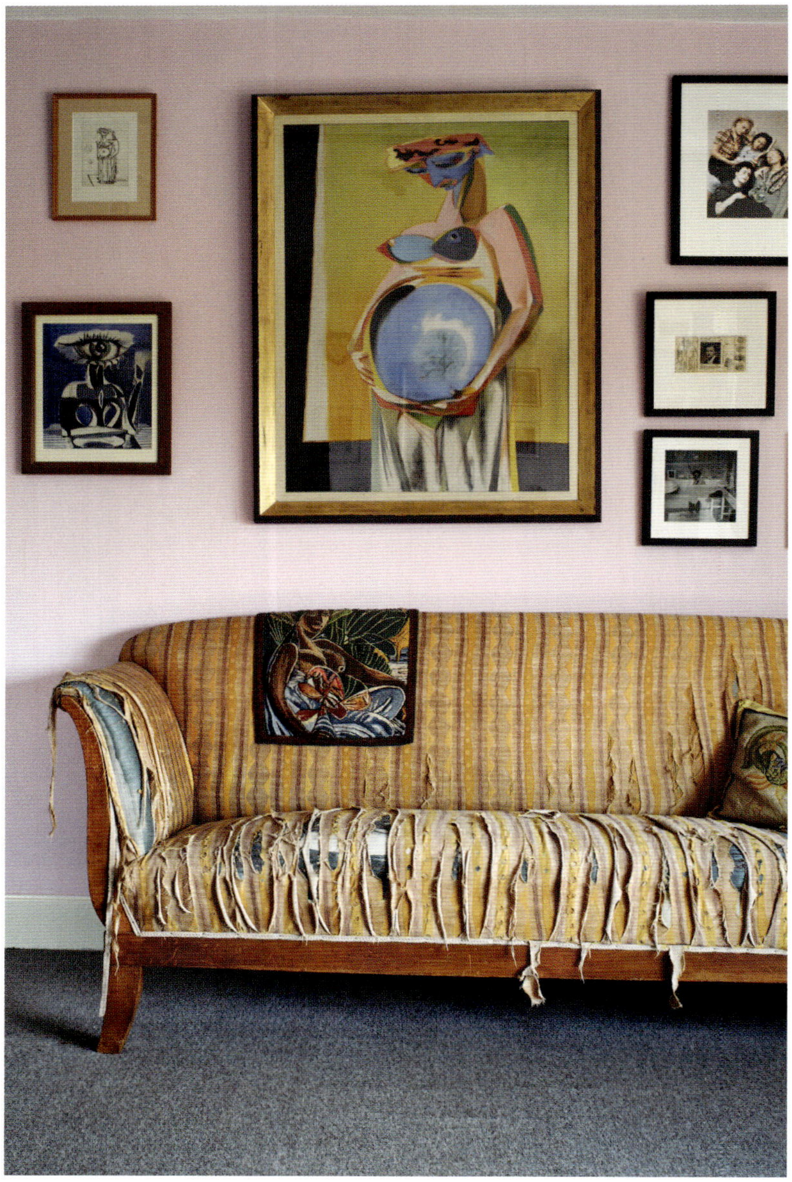

Above: *First View*, painted in 1947 by Penrose,
hangs above the sofa in the pale pink-walled living room.
Opposite: Detail of the fireplace in the dining room at Farleys House.

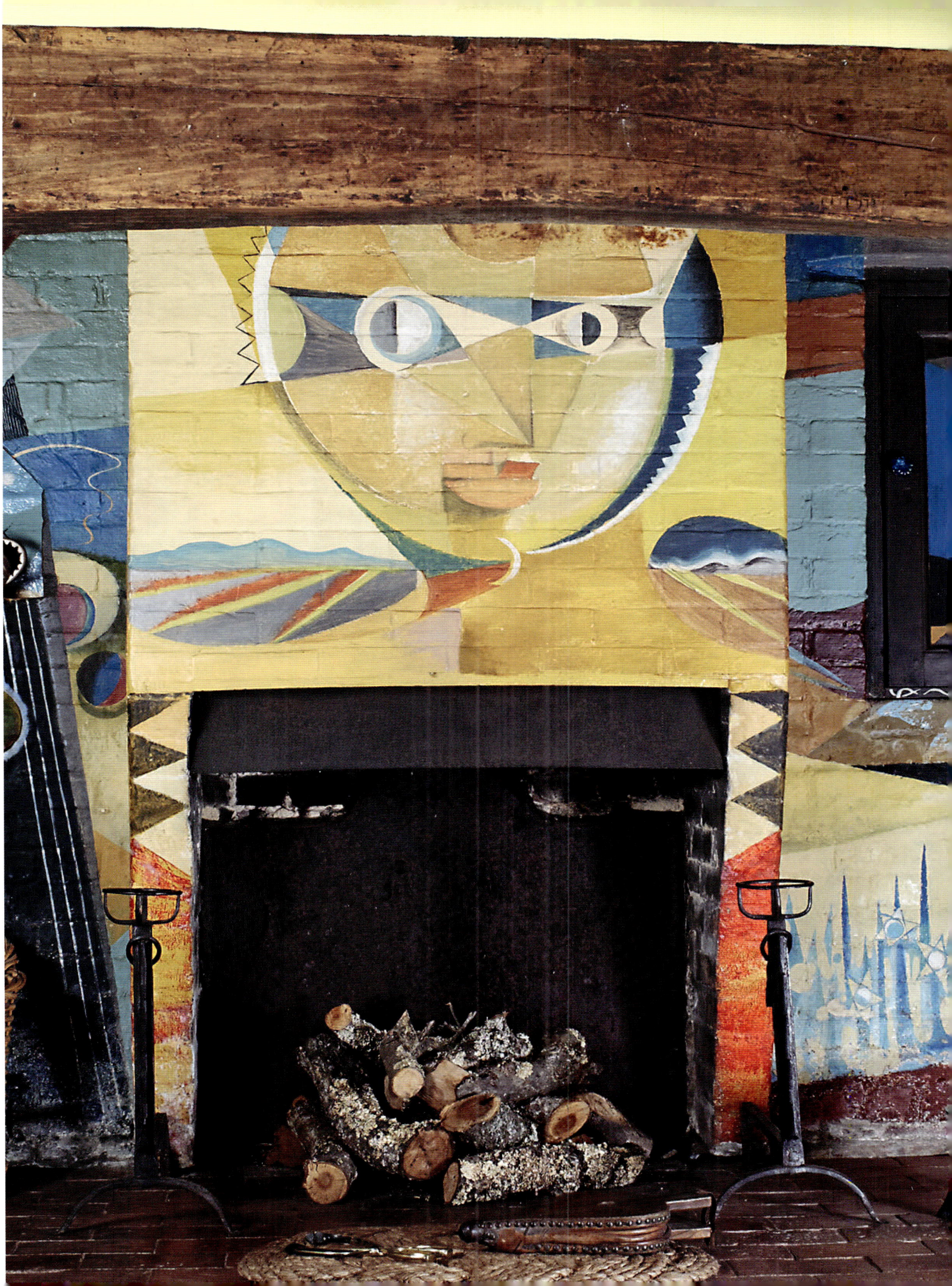

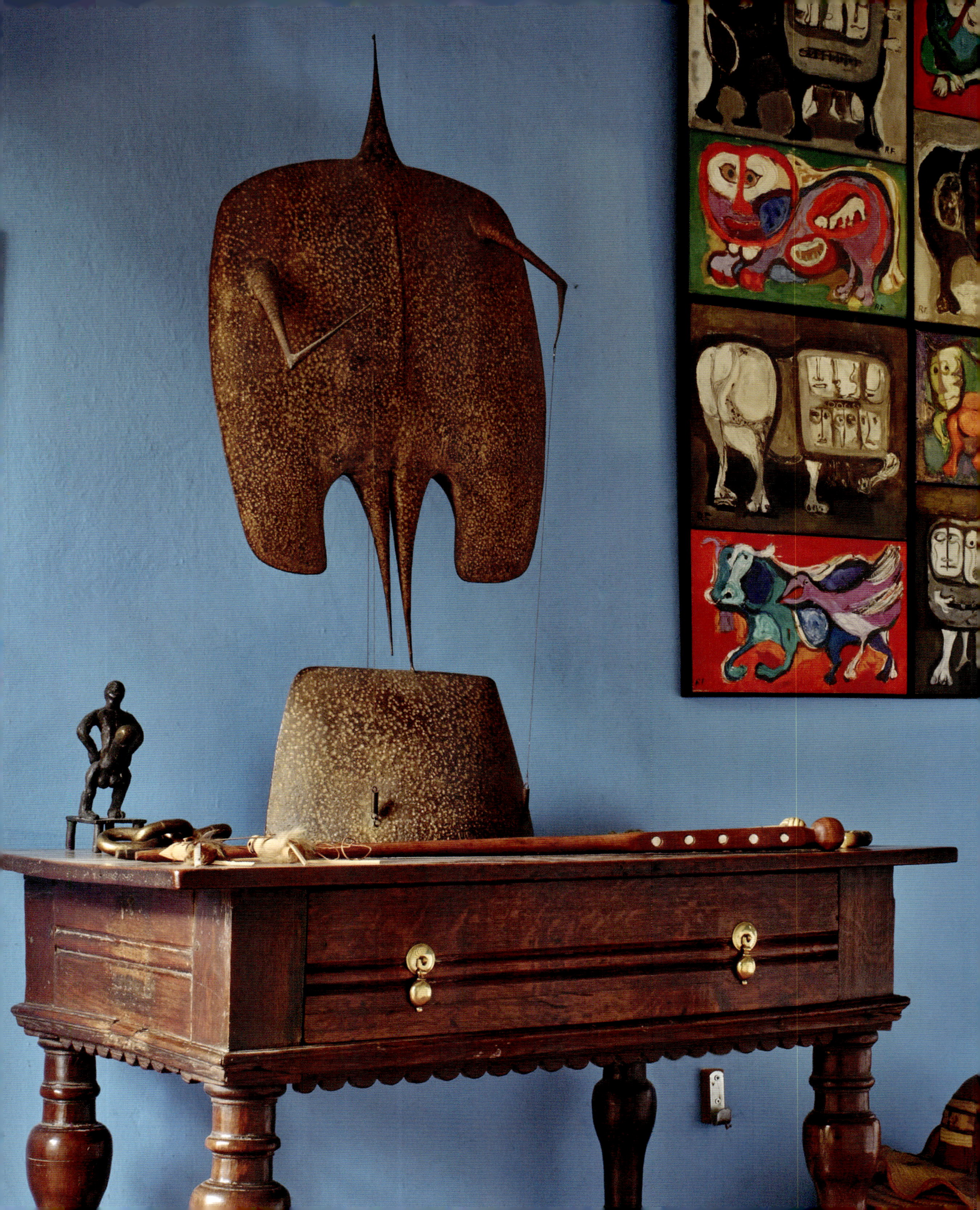

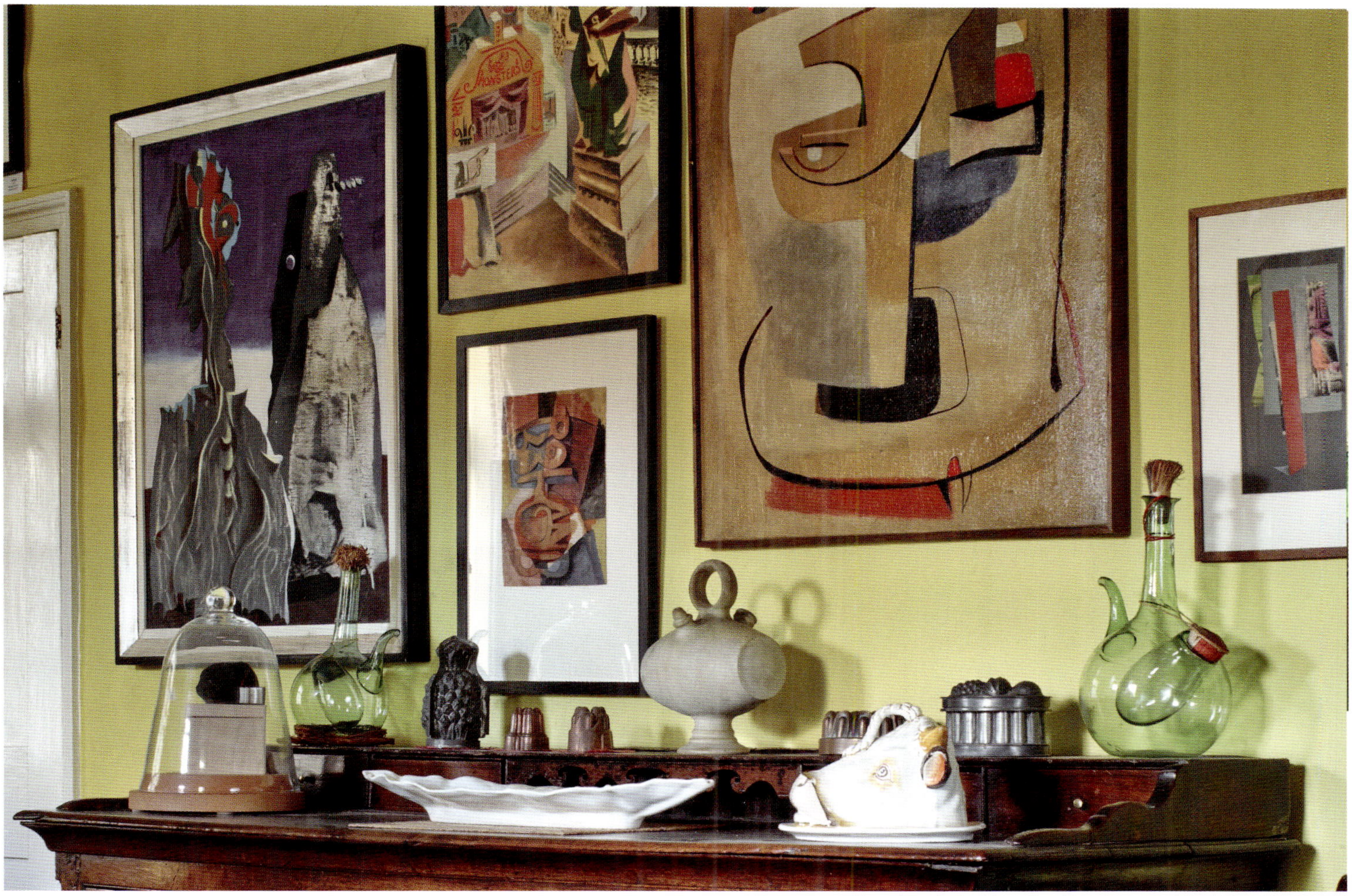

Above: Set against their vibrantly coloured background walls, Miller and Penrose decorated their home with their own art and the art of their friends.
Opposite: Detail of the hallway table, featuring a sculpture by Philippe Hiquily.

Tanning, Eileen Agar, Kenneth Armitage, Richard Hamilton and Picasso, who stayed in 1950 and filled the visitors' book with lively drawings. Meanwhile, the house was being renovated, repaired and reshaped. It became a regular meeting place for some of the major figures of twentieth-century art and literature, and Miller and Penrose decorated it with both their own art and their extensive collection of their friends' artworks, and eventually, sculptures made by their son. Antony also transformed one of the barns into a gallery for rising and local artists to exhibit, and he created a sculpture garden in the grounds.

Inside the house, rooms were an asymmetrical assortment of different periods and styles, connected by long passageways. Directly around the house was a garden and an orchard, and the Penroses converted some of the outbuildings into studios and a darkroom. The interiors of the house were fitted with large, comfortable furniture and painted in vibrant colours. Miller's study was turquoise; the sitting room was pink, with intense pink window-seat cushions; and the dining room was brilliant yellow, with a mural depicting the Long Man of Wilmington amid stars and planets, painted by Penrose. Miller cultivated a successful vegetable garden and, using her home-grown produce, she experimented with dishes from around the world. She began writing and compiling a cookery book, but never completed it.

Around the house, valuable and precious items were nestled among objects that most people would have thrown away. Tables, sideboards and cupboards were strewn with ornaments, photographs, and other odds and ends from junk shops or made by friends, such as ceramics by Picasso and a chess set by Man Ray, and 'found objects', such as shells, a chimpanzee skull, a cast of a molehill and a mummified rat.

In the late 1970s, Miller died at Farleys. In 1980, Penrose had a minor stroke, then another in 1984, which severely incapacitated him, meaning he could no longer write, and he spent his final months at Farleys creating postcard collages.

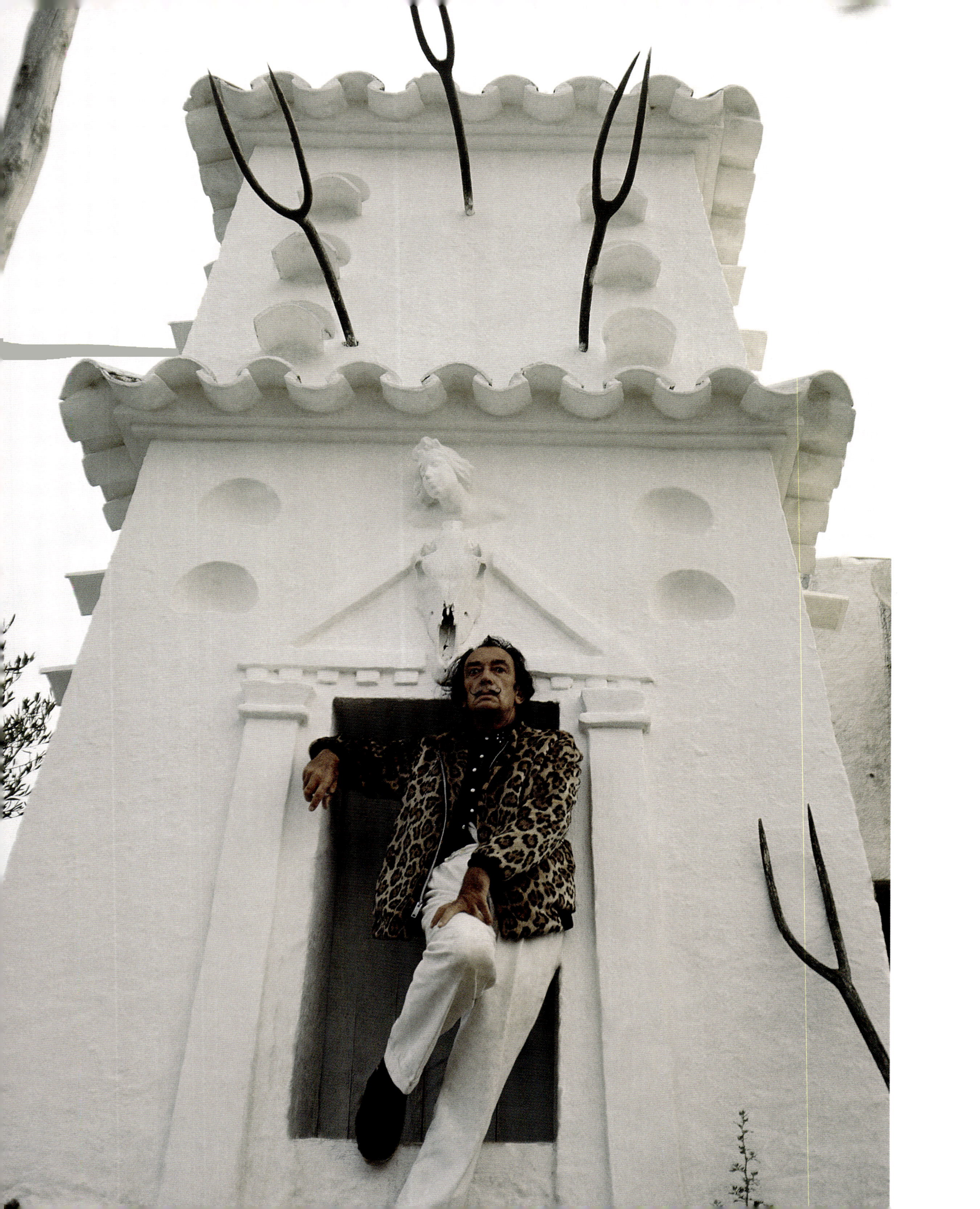

SALVADOR DALÍ

Portlligat, Spain

In 1930, Salvador Dalí (1904–89) set up home in a small fisherman's hut in the village of Portlligat, on the Costa Brava, in the municipality of Cadaqués, Spain, drawn to it by the surrounding landscape, the light and the isolation of the location. Over forty years, he bought more huts around it, and built his own grand villa out of them.

Throughout the course of his long career, Dalí created paintings, sculpture, prints, fashion, advertising and films – on the latter, he collaborated with Luis Buñuel and Alfred Hitchcock. Renowned for his flamboyant personality, provocative and blatant self-promotion, and technical skill as an artist, Dalí illustrated his dreams and hallucinations, including themes of eroticism, death and decay. Exploiting autobiographical material and childhood memories, he created his own overt symbolism, alluding to preoccupations such as sexual obsessions, religion, nostalgia, myth and time.

OUTRAGEOUS AND CONFRONTATIONAL

Early in the twentieth century, in Figueres, a small town outside Barcelona, Dalí was born to a prosperous middle-class family, soon after his elder brother (also named Salvador) had died at just under two years old. Dalí was often told that he was the reincarnation of his dead brother, which probably intensified his difficult behaviour as he grew up. His parents encouraged his interest in art, and he took his first drawing lessons from the age of ten. In his late teens, after the premature death of his mother, he enrolled at the Madrid School of Fine Arts, where he began to express his eccentric, flamboyant and provocative personality. He grew his hair long and dressed in the style of English aesthetes from the nineteenth century, including knee-length britches. Outspoken and confident, he drew attention to himself, and he mixed with some of the foremost artistic and intellectual figures of the period. In 1926, however, he was expelled from art school during his final examination before graduating, for insulting one of his professors, and after several months, he went to Paris, where he visited Picasso and became inspired by Cubism and Futurism. He also began studying the psychoanalytic concepts of Sigmund Freud and the art of Giorgio de Chirico, and consequently began painting images that explored the subconscious mind, aiming to convey strange realities and alter perceptions of viewers.

In 1929 Dalí produced a short film with Buñuel: *Un Chien Andalou* (*An Andalusian Dog*) explored uncomfortable preoccupations using sexual and political imagery that caused great scandal among the public and critics. The following year, the Surrealists sent the poet – and one of the founders of the Surrealist movement – Paul Éluard and his wife Gala, along with René and Georgette Magritte, to visit Dalí. Soon after, Dalí moved to Paris and joined the Surrealists, and he and Gala began an affair, which eventually resulted in her divorce from Éluard. Gala became Dalí's lifelong companion, muse and business manager, and later his wife.

Dalí described his method of painting as his 'Paranoic-Critical Method', in which he suppressed his conscious mind, creating a self-induced paranoid state and allowing intuition to guide his work. He said that his resulting paintings using this method were 'hand-painted dream photographs', evolving out of what he witnessed while hallucinating. His work became popular and his success grew, but his father disapproved of his unconventional approach to art and his relationship with a married woman who was ten years older. When Dalí was quoted by a Barcelona newspaper in 1929 as saying: 'Sometimes, I spit for fun on my mother's portrait,' Dalí senior had enough and expelled his son from the family home.

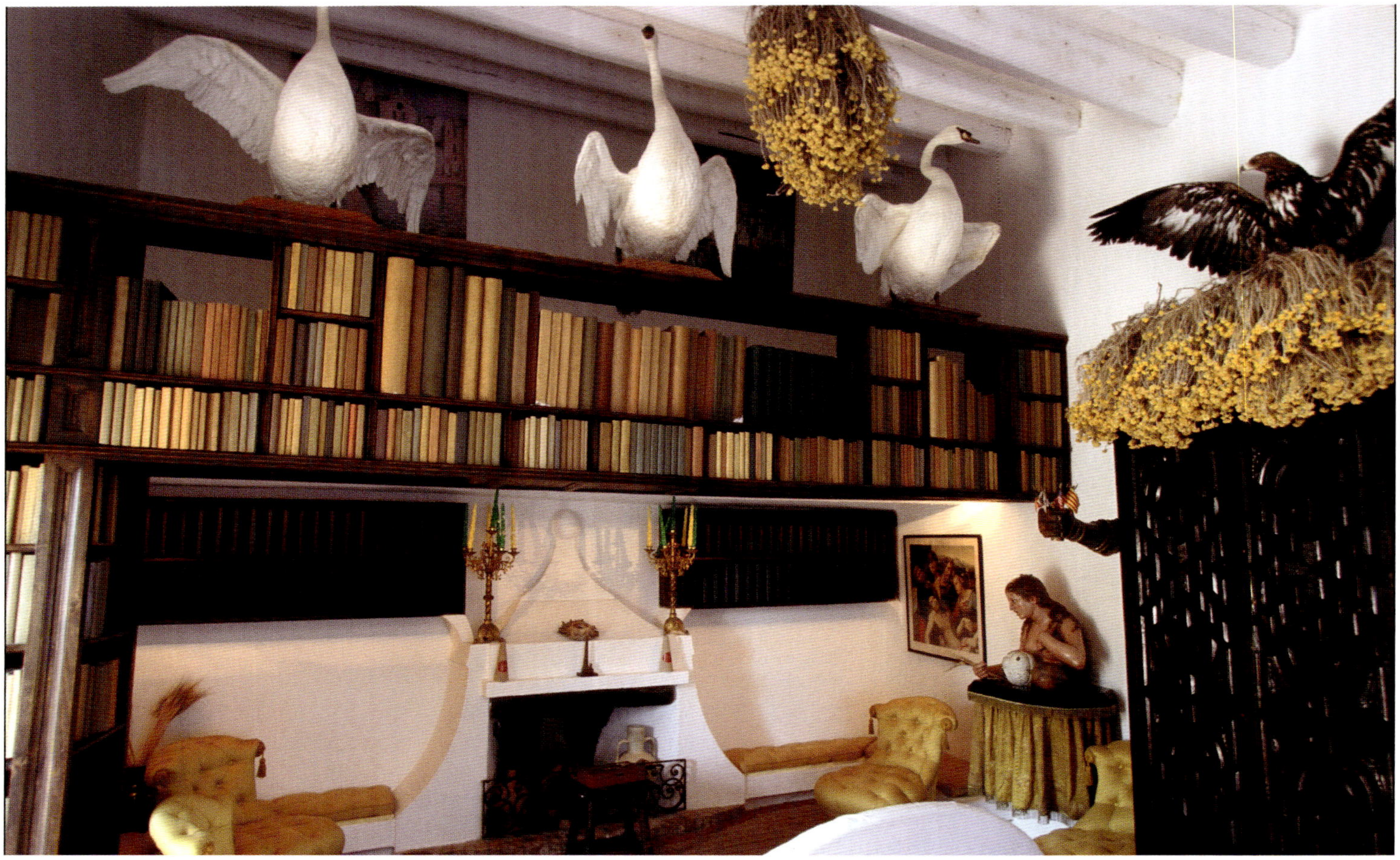

Above: The library at Portlligat.
Opposite: Alabaster egg-shaped sculpture balanced on the roof of Dalí's house.

BUILDING HIS HOME

With nowhere to go, Dalí and Gala rented a small fisherman's hut in a bay at Portlligat, then bought it from its owner Lídia Noguer. It had been where Noguer's sons kept their fishing gear, and the roof was in poor condition. Dalí soon also bought a second hut close by, intending to create a proper home out of them, as he explained in his autobiography: 'Our little house was to consist of a room of about four square metres that was to serve as a dining room, bedroom, studio and an entrance hall. You go up some steps and as you land, three doors open out, taking you to a shower, a toilet and a kitchen of very tight dimensions that you can hardly squeeze in. I wanted it all good and small – the smaller the more womblike'.

Ultimately, however, the home became far more ambitious. In 1932, Dalí refurbished both huts, and they eventually became the entrance, dining room, workshop, bedroom, bathroom and annex of his grand villa. In 1934, after living together for five years, he and Gala married in a civil ceremony and later, in 1958, in a Catholic ceremony in the Pyrenean hamlet of Montrejic. In the year he and Gala first married, Dalí was banished from the Surrealist group because of his views opposing those of the other members on communism, Fascism and General Franco. Responding to his ejection, Dalí declared, 'I myself am Surrealism'.

Dalí reflected that Portlligat was a perfect place to work: peaceful, solitary and with breathtaking views. Only other fishing huts surrounded his home. Gala organised the décor and furniture. As there was no electricity, they brought gas lamps from Paris, and had their belongings delivered by donkey. They lived there throughout the summer months, and in hotels in New York and Paris during the winter. In 1935, Dalí employed a local builder, Emili Puignau, to follow his own designs and expand the property. However, with the outbreak of the Spanish Civil War in 1936, Dalí and Gala moved to the United States and did not return to Portlligat for twelve years. When they did, they bought another hut, and in

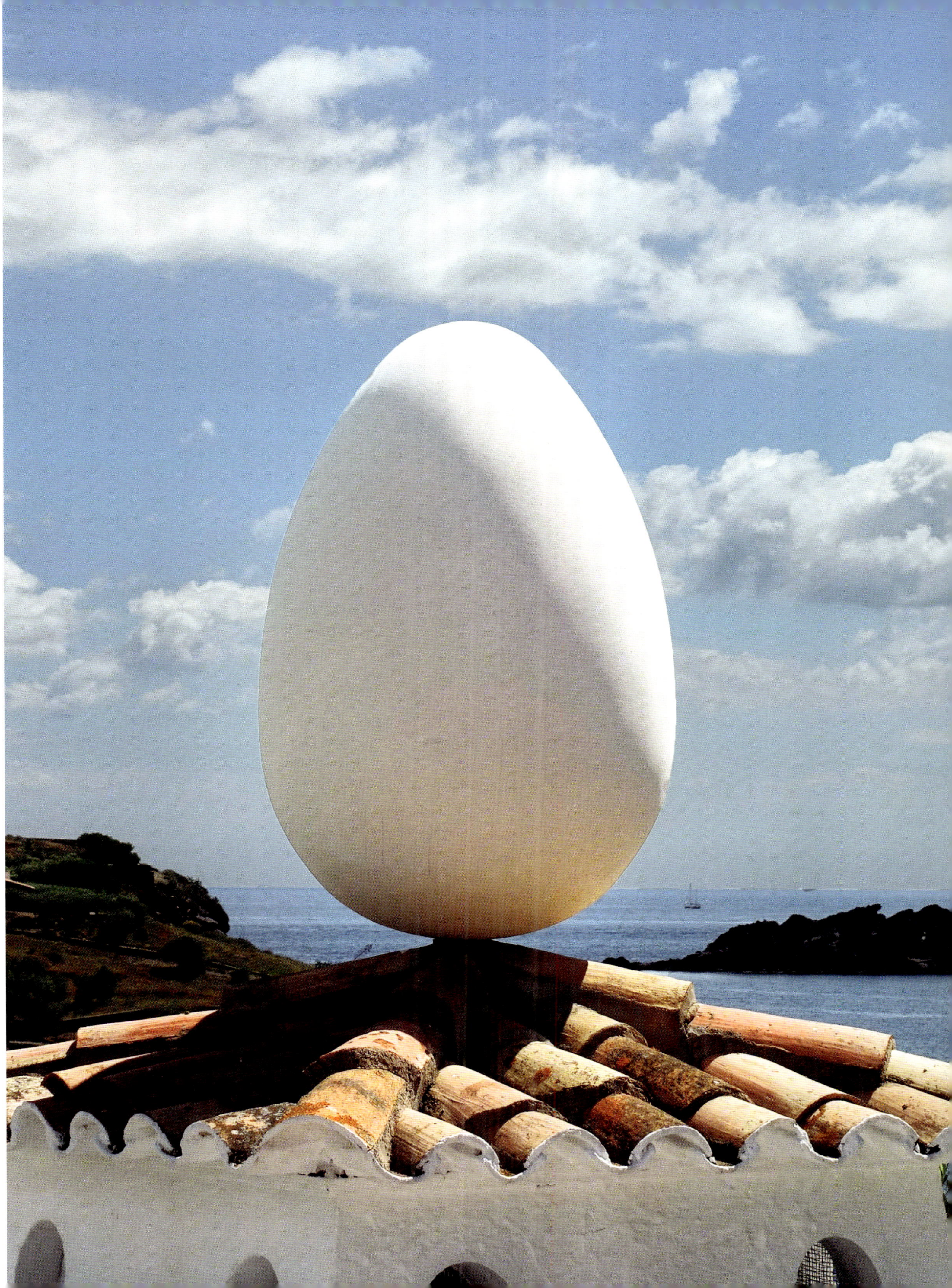

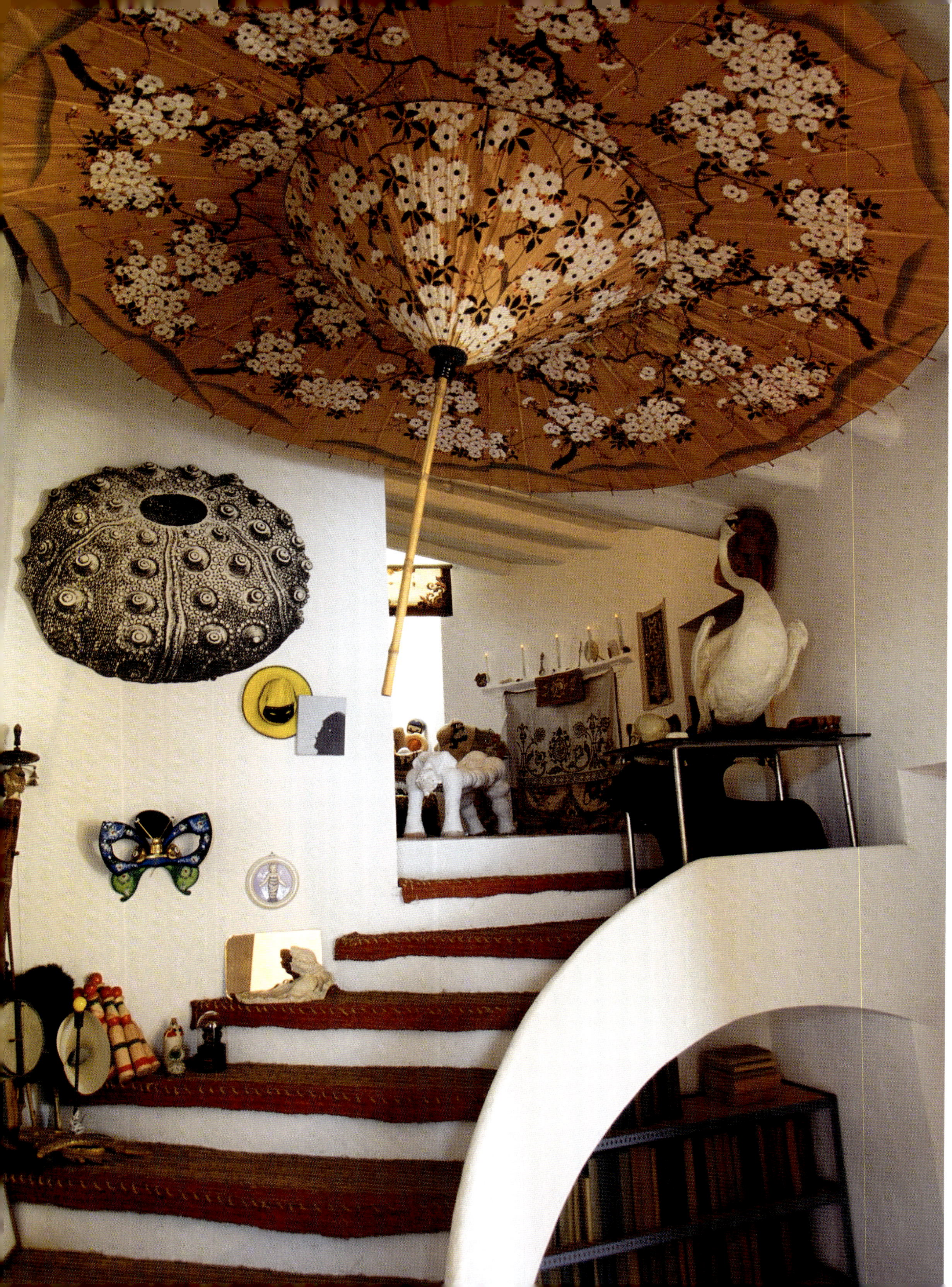

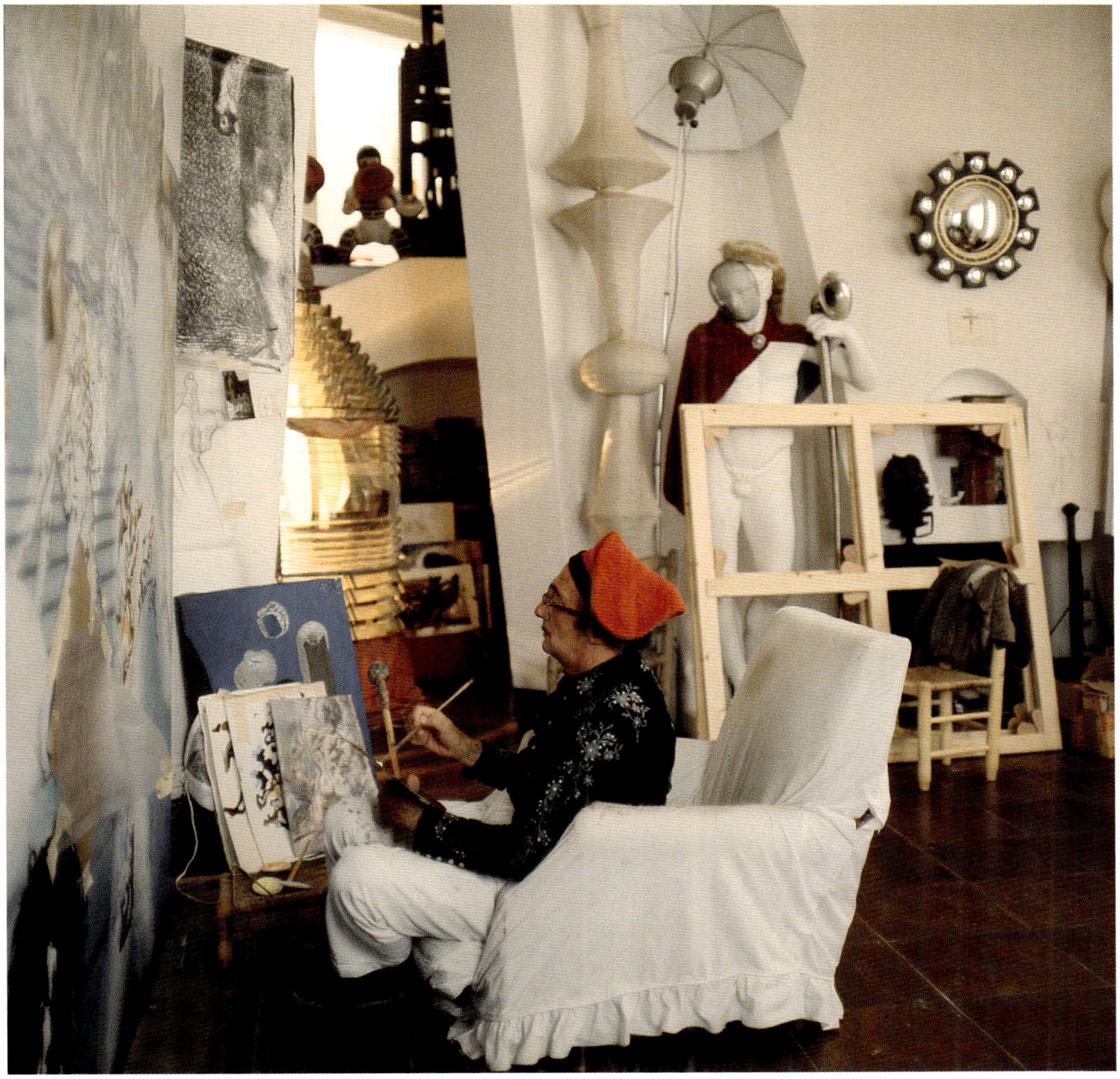

Above and opposite: Dalí's house in Portlligat was originally a small fisherman's house but he transformed it into a large villa, where he lived and worked.

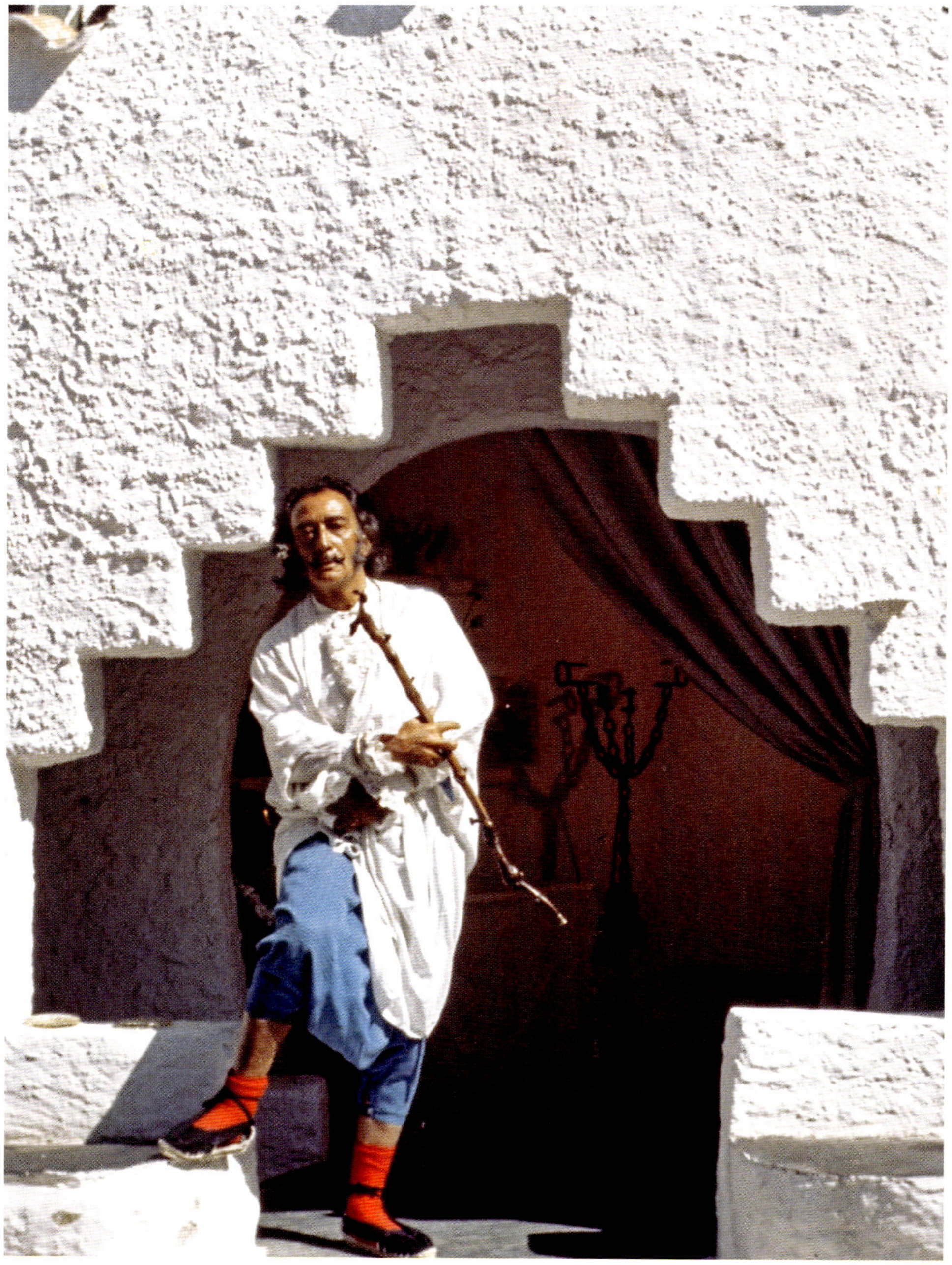

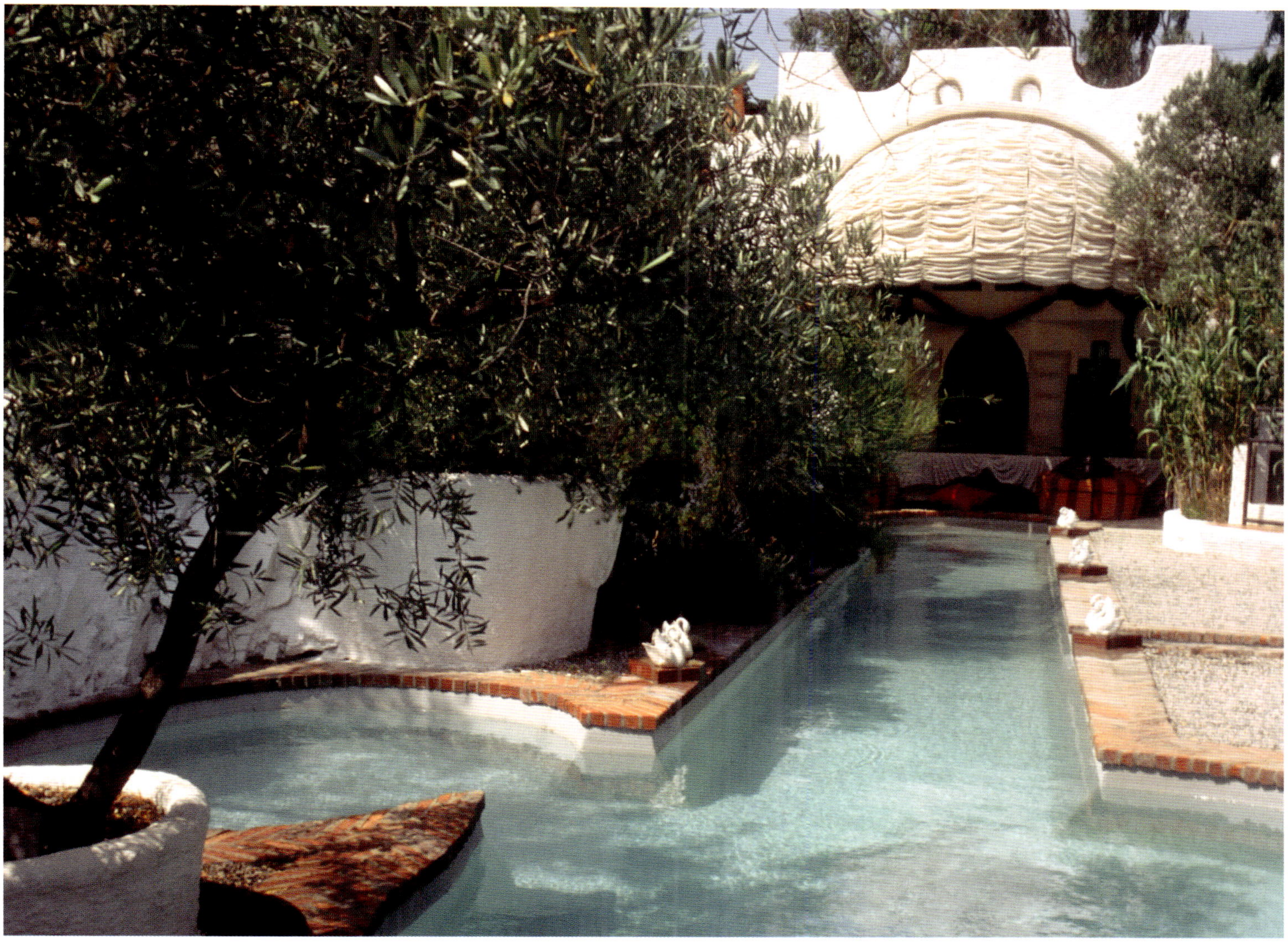

Above: As the house grew, Dalí added a pool to his quirkily-designed home in Cadaqués.

1949, it was converted into the library and living room. A further three huts were soon added, and rooms – including the kitchen, a new studio, bedrooms, a tower and a semi-spherical room – were added. The house continued to grow and, ultimately, was built over forty years. Dalí reflected that it was 'like a real biological structure... Each new pulse in our life had its own new cell, its room. The resulting form is the current labyrinthine structure which... spreads out around in a succession of spaces linked by narrow corridors, slight level changes and blind passageways'.

With a step-like structure, echoed by outside steps, all whitewashed, the building includes a new studio, a dovecote and a swimming pool that was completed in the summer of 1971. All the rooms have windows of different shapes and proportions, from where different aspects of Portlligat bay can be viewed. Dalí lived there until 1982, when his beloved Gala died. He then moved into the castle he had given her in Púbol, where she was buried.

'There is a geological peacefulness [to Portlligat]: it is a unique planetary case.'

Salvador Dalí

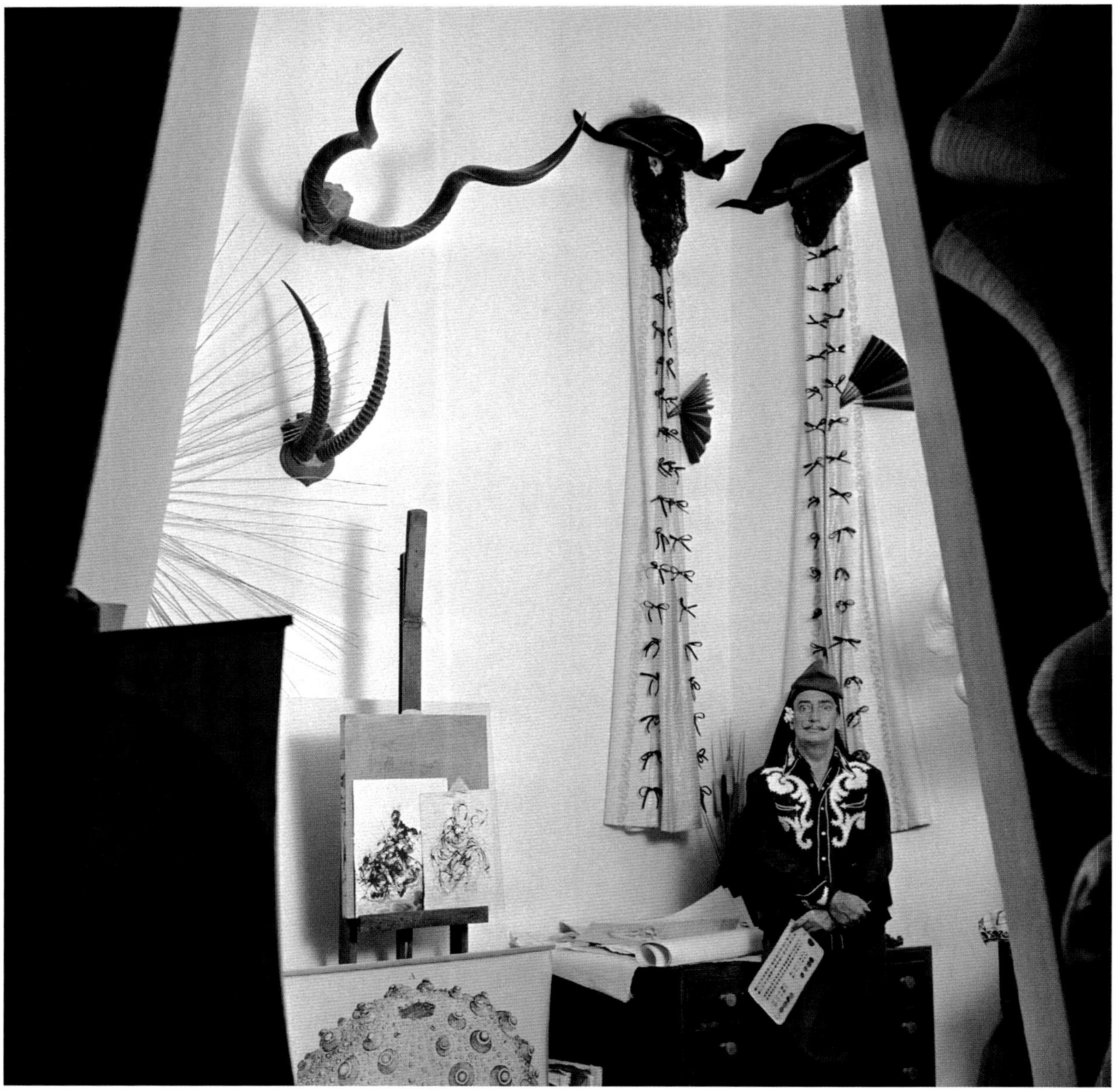

Above: Salvador Dalí at home.
Opposite: Dalí with Gala, his lifelong companion and muse.

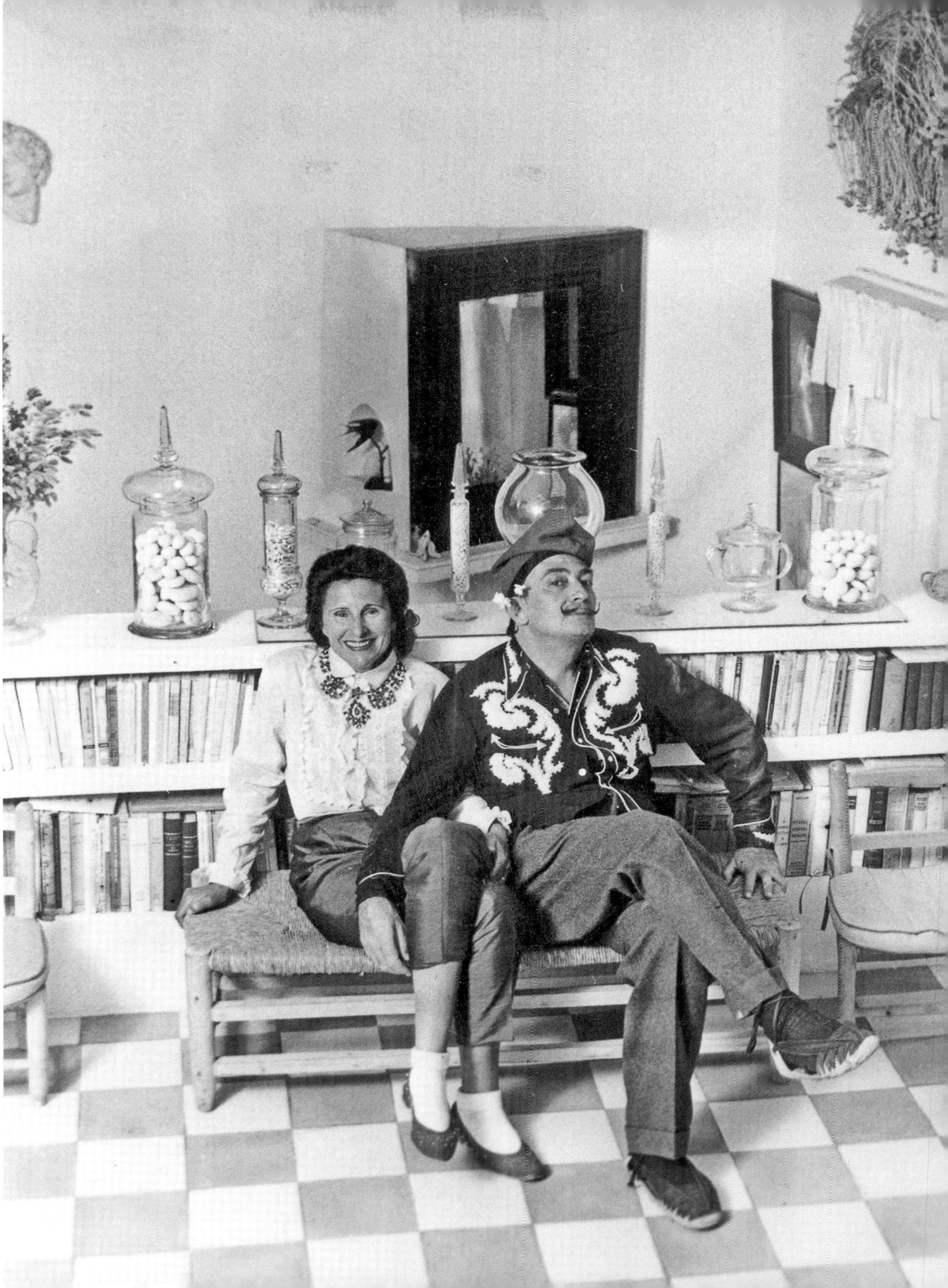

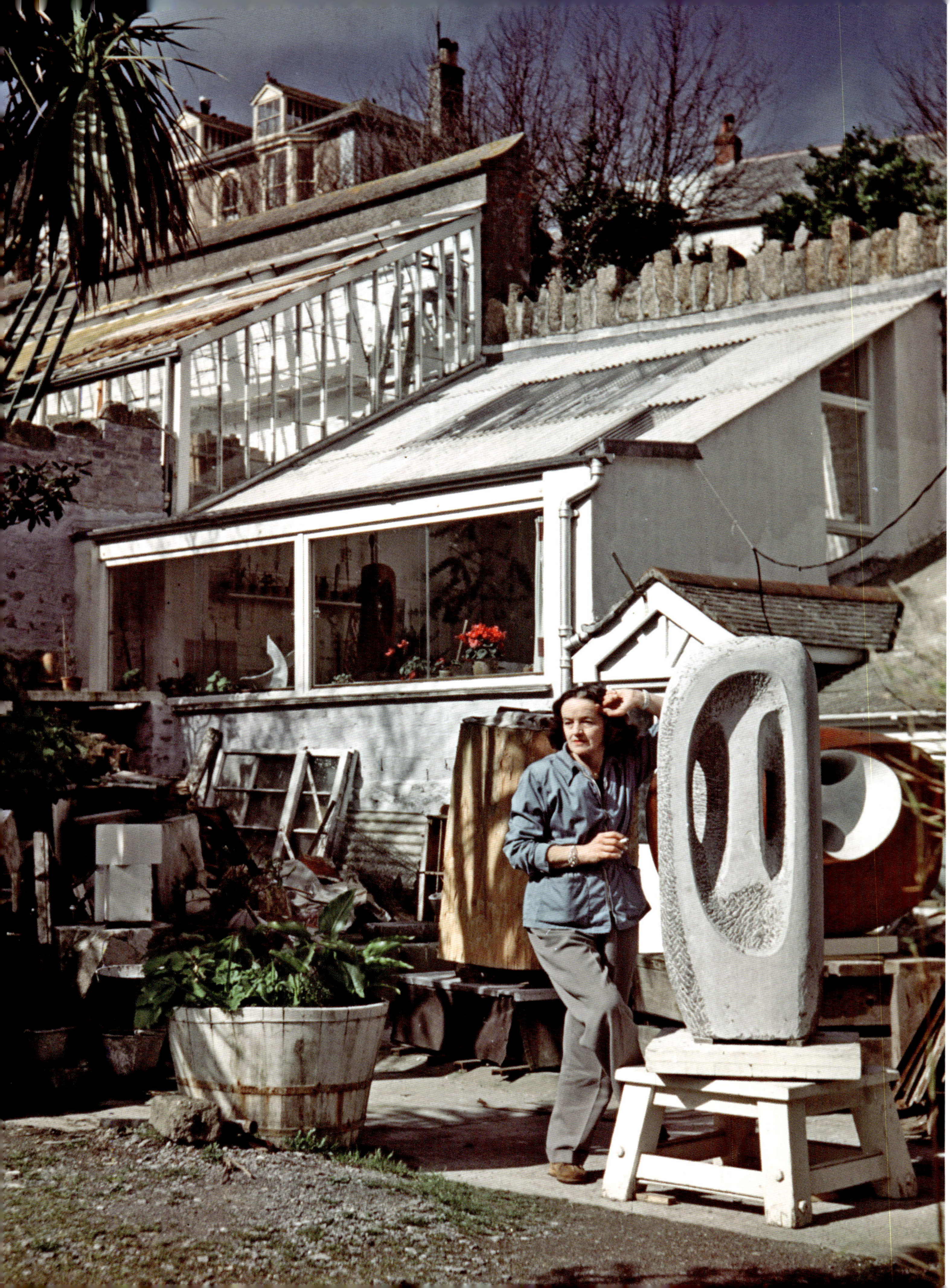

BARBARA HEPWORTH

St Ives, Cornwall, UK

Distinctive for her world recognition as a sculptor at a time when female artists were rare, Barbara Hepworth (1903–75) helped to change the direction of three-dimensional art with her innovative ideas. In 1949, she created a studio and sculpture garden in St Ives, Cornwall, where she lived and worked for the rest of her life.

Born in Wakefield, in Yorkshire, Barbara Hepworth grew up in West Riding where, she said, 'the hills were sculptures; the roads defined the form'. After attending Wakefield Girls' High School, she studied sculpture at Leeds School of Art and then the Royal College of Art in London – both with fellow student Henry Moore, with whom she established a lifelong friendship and rivalry.

After learning to carve marble in Italy, Hepworth met and married sculptor John Skeaping. They lived in London and had their son Paul in 1929. Two years later, Hepworth created her first work of pierced sculpture and also began an affair with another sculptor, Ben Nicholson who, like her, was married. She and Skeaping divorced and later, in 1938, she married Nicholson. They travelled to Paris together several times, and visited the studios of Picasso, Constantin Brâncuşi and Jean Arp. In 1934, she gave birth to triplets: Rachel, Sarah and Simon. She raised all her children while managing to continue to work as an artist. 'A woman artist,' she said, 'is not deprived by cooking and having children, nor by nursing children with measles (even in triplicate) – one is in fact nourished by this rich life, provided one always does some work each day; even a single half hour, so that the images grow in one's mind.'

A SENSE OF COMMUNITY

In 1939, just before the outbreak of World War Two, Hepworth and Nicholson were invited by the art critic Adrian Stokes to stay in St Ives, in the south-west of England. They decided that Cornwall would be a safer option with a young family than London and stayed there until the war was over, first with Stokes and then in a small rented cottage nearby, which was cramped and difficult. Hepworth did not enjoy the experience. However, the small seaside town and Cornish countryside inspired her – as much as West Riding had done when she was growing up. She began creating more natural forms that reflected the landscape around her. After the war, she chose not to return to London, and in 1949, she bought a house and studio: Trewyn Studio on Barnoon Hill, in St Ives. For Hepworth, it was an ideal environment. She wrote to a friend the day after she bought the property at a public auction: 'It will be a joy to carve in such a perfect place, both serene and secluded – the courtyard and garden protected by tall trees and roof tops, so that I can work out of doors for most of the year.'

The 'barbaric and magical countryside' of West Penwith, as she described it, with its rocky coastline and prehistoric history, affected Hepworth hugely. For a start, she found many similarities between the Yorkshire landscape of her childhood and the Cornish land. She loved the sense of community there, too: friends visited, as well as fellow artists, writers and musicians, and the townspeople welcomed them all. In June 1953, she co-founded the St Ives Festival with her friends, the composers Michael Tippett and Priaulx Rainier. Celebrating two Elizabethan ages on the accession of Queen Elizabeth II, the Festival included music, drama and the visual arts. In 1954, Hepworth helped to form the St Ives Trust, which aimed to protect the town in various ways. After her son Paul was killed in 1953 in a plane crash while serving with the Royal Air Force in Thailand, she created *Madonna and Child* (1954) for the local church. She also gave her *Ascending Form (Gloria)* (1958) to Longstone Cemetery, *Dual Form* (1965) to the Guildhall,

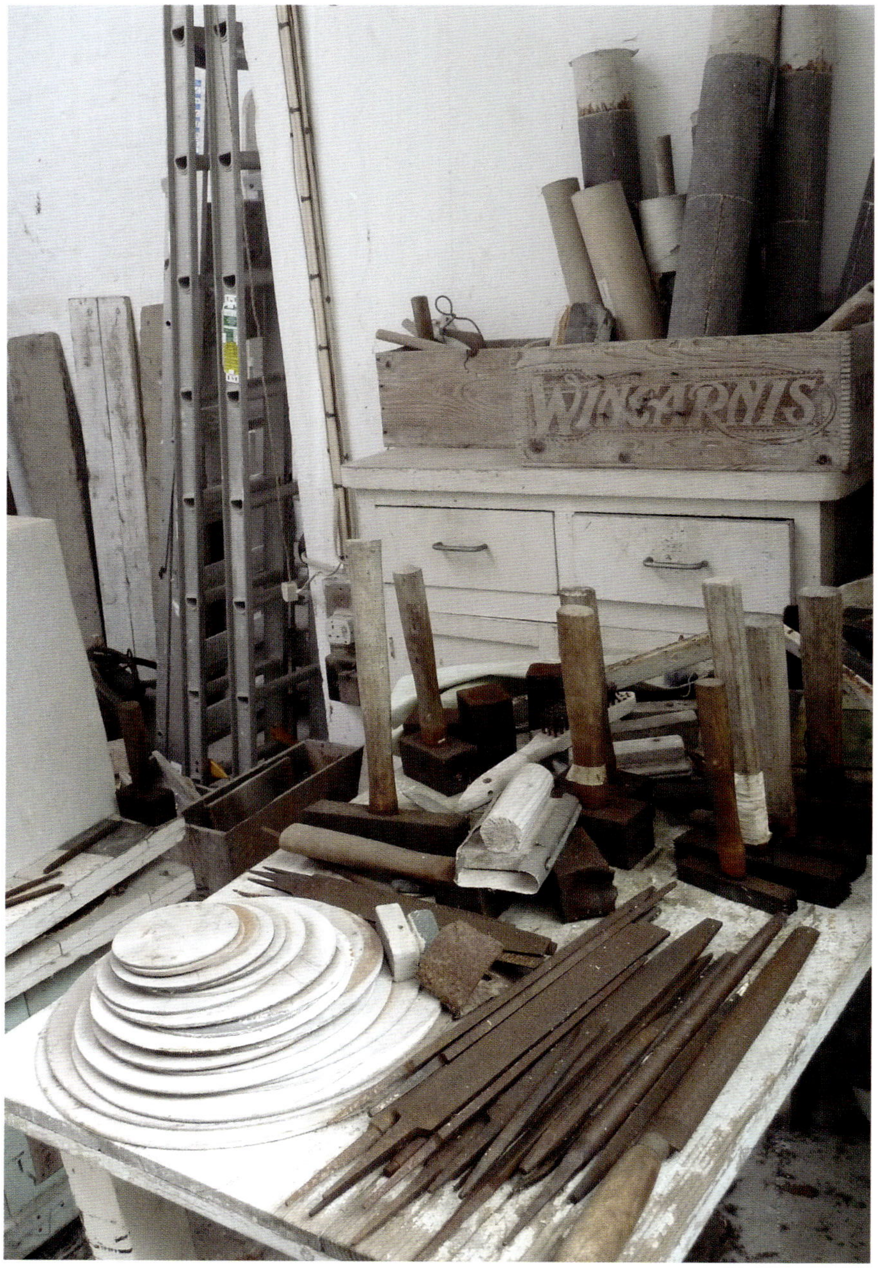

Above and opposite: Part of Barbara Hepworth's studio in Cornwall.

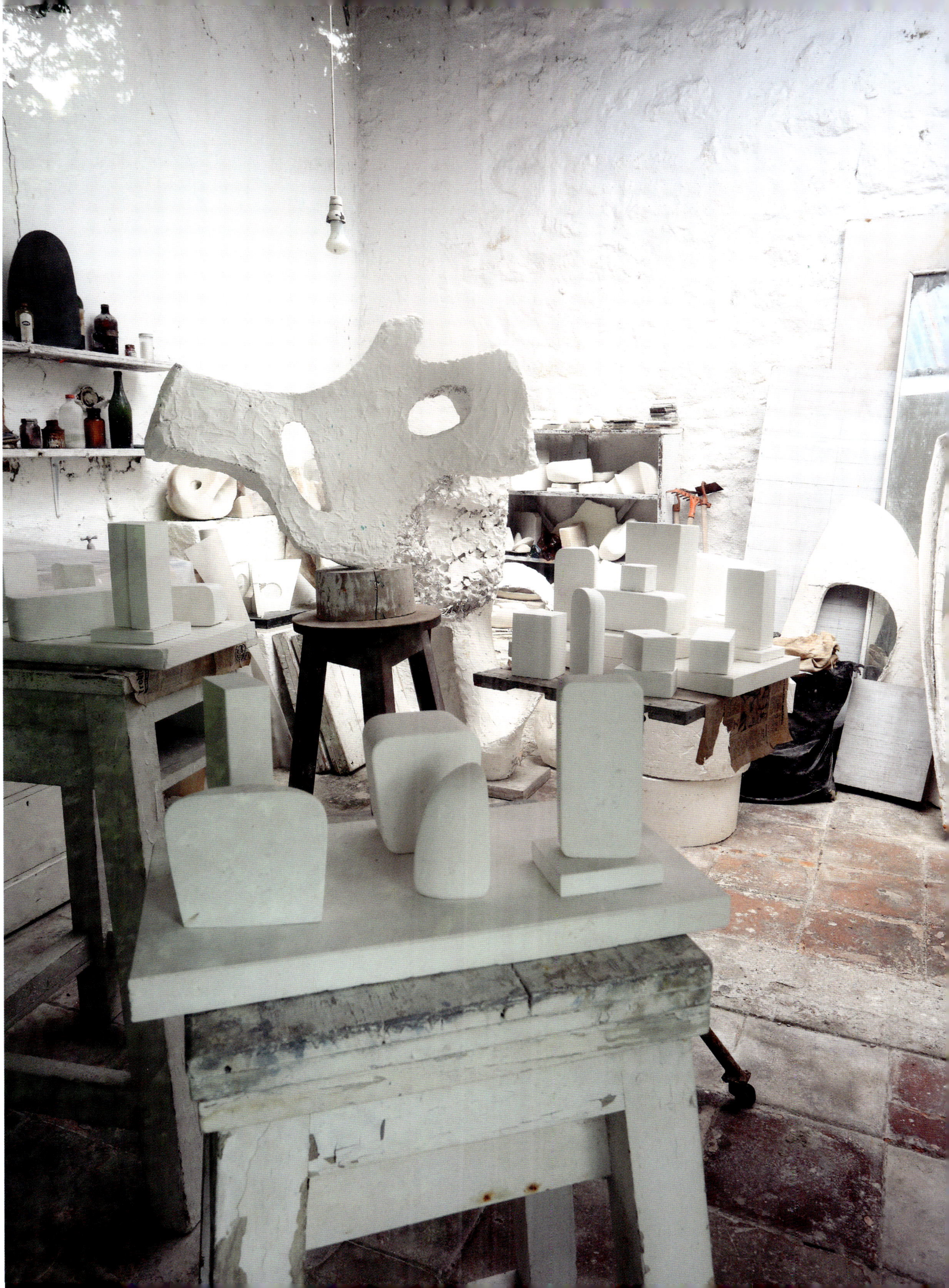

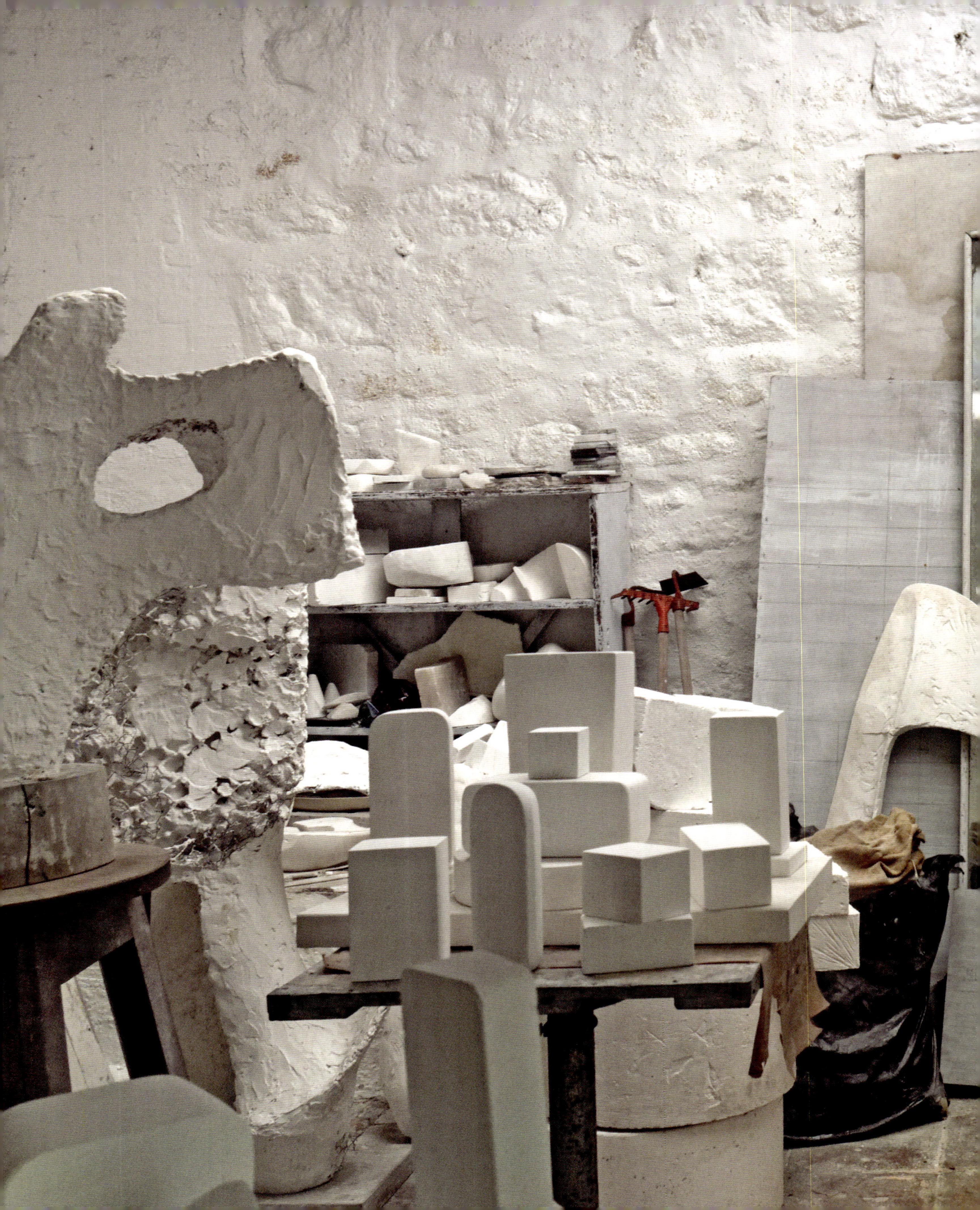

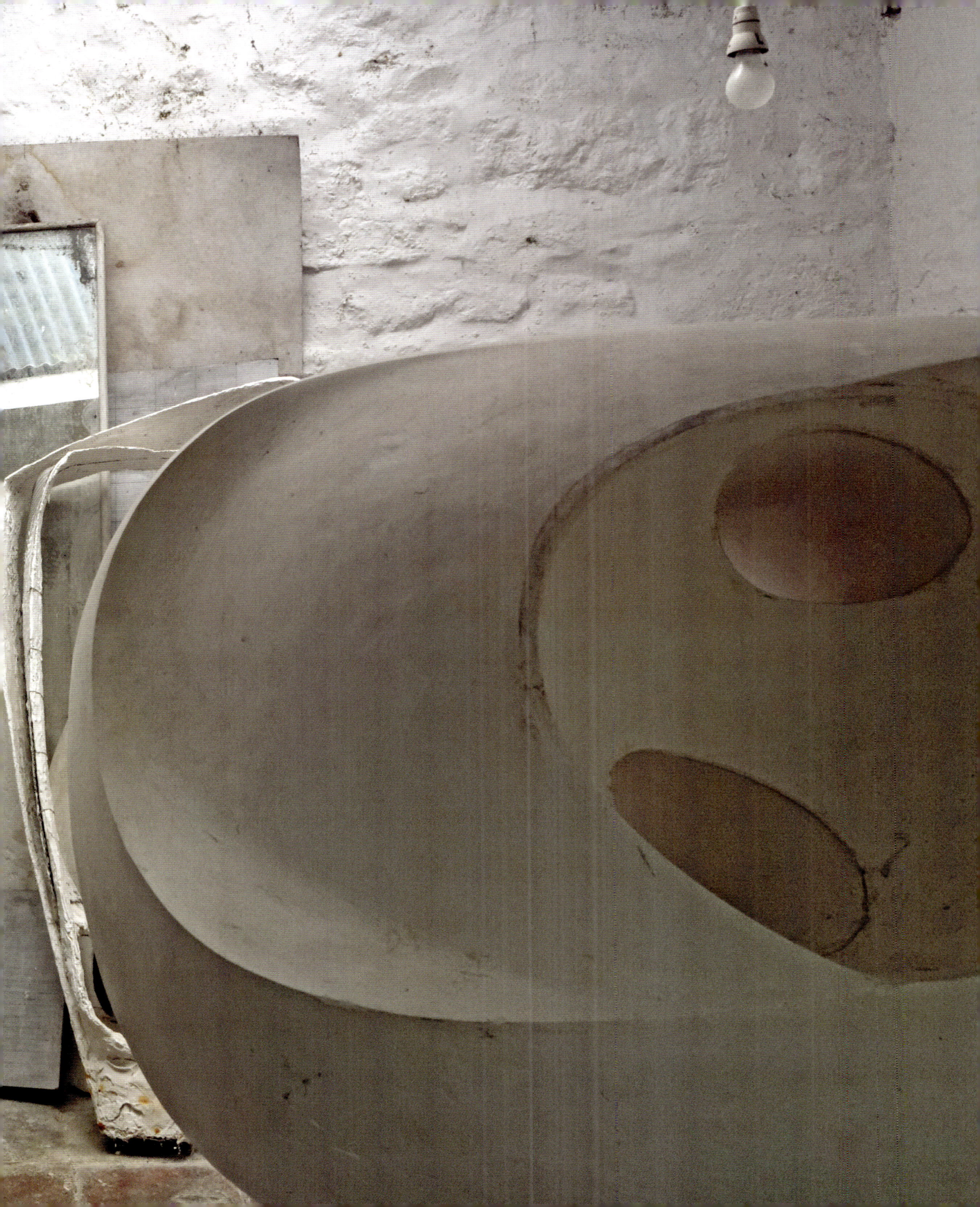

and *Conversation with Magic Stones* (1973) to the Penwith Gallery. She was a founder-member of the Penwith Society and remained deeply involved with it for nearly three decades.

In 1968, Hepworth was granted the Freedom of the Borough of St Ives in recognition of her international contribution as a sculptor. In her acceptance speech, she spoke of it being her 'spiritual home'. In her 1971 book, *A Pictorial Autobiography*, she wrote: 'Surrounded by beaches, the town is bathed in a pristine light and the sea, a flat diminishing plane, held within itself the capacity to radiate an infinite number of blues, greys, greens and even pinks of strange hues.'

TREWYN STUDIO

Hepworth lived and worked in Trewyn Studio for twenty-six years. It was a small, two-storey, stone-built, high-walled house on a steep, narrow street in St Ives. When she first bought the building in 1949, she used the downstairs as storage and there was a ladder to reach the upper floor, which she used as a woodworking studio. After separating from Nicholson in 1950, she moved into the building to live there: she converted the downstairs to a kitchen-dining area with a bathroom, installed a staircase, and still used the upstairs room as a woodworking studio, but then also had a bed put up there and some other home comforts. She divorced Nicholson in 1951; Paul was an adult and the teenage triplets were at a boarding school, so she did not need to accommodate them all as well. She used the room upstairs and a large shed and greenhouse in the garden for her work. From the garden, she had wonderful views of the beach and sea.

Her sculptural ideas were complex and diverse, and mostly explored nature and responded to her surroundings in St Ives. Particularly sensitive to the physical characteristics and properties of her materials, she used a wide range of these and allowed them to dictate the outcomes of her work. Her explorations of 'absence', as much as 'presence', in her sculptures was unique, showing how she considered relationships between her work and her environment, as she said: 'All my sculpture comes out of the landscape.'

> 'I have gained very great inspiration from the Cornish land- and seascape.'
>
> *Barbara Hepworth*

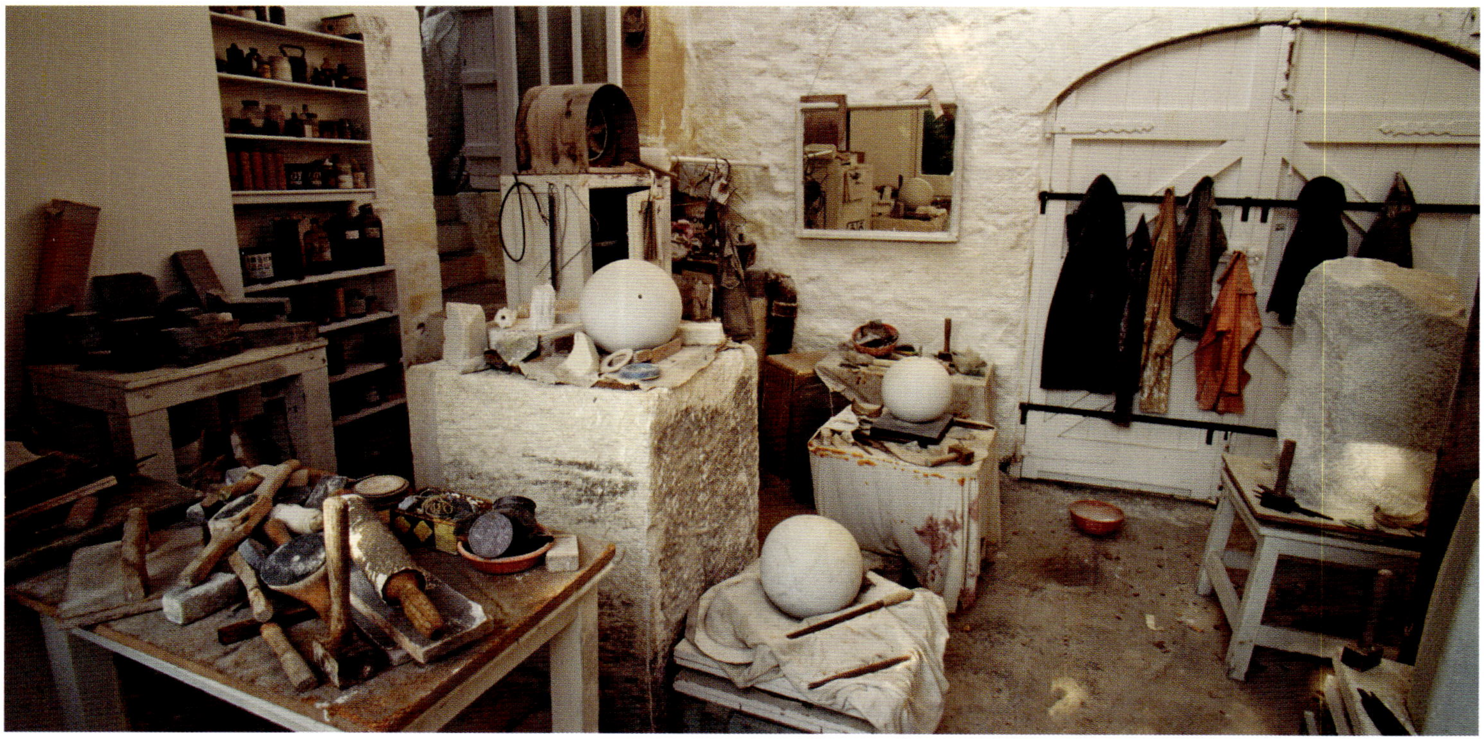

Above and opposite: Different areas of Hepworth's working studio.

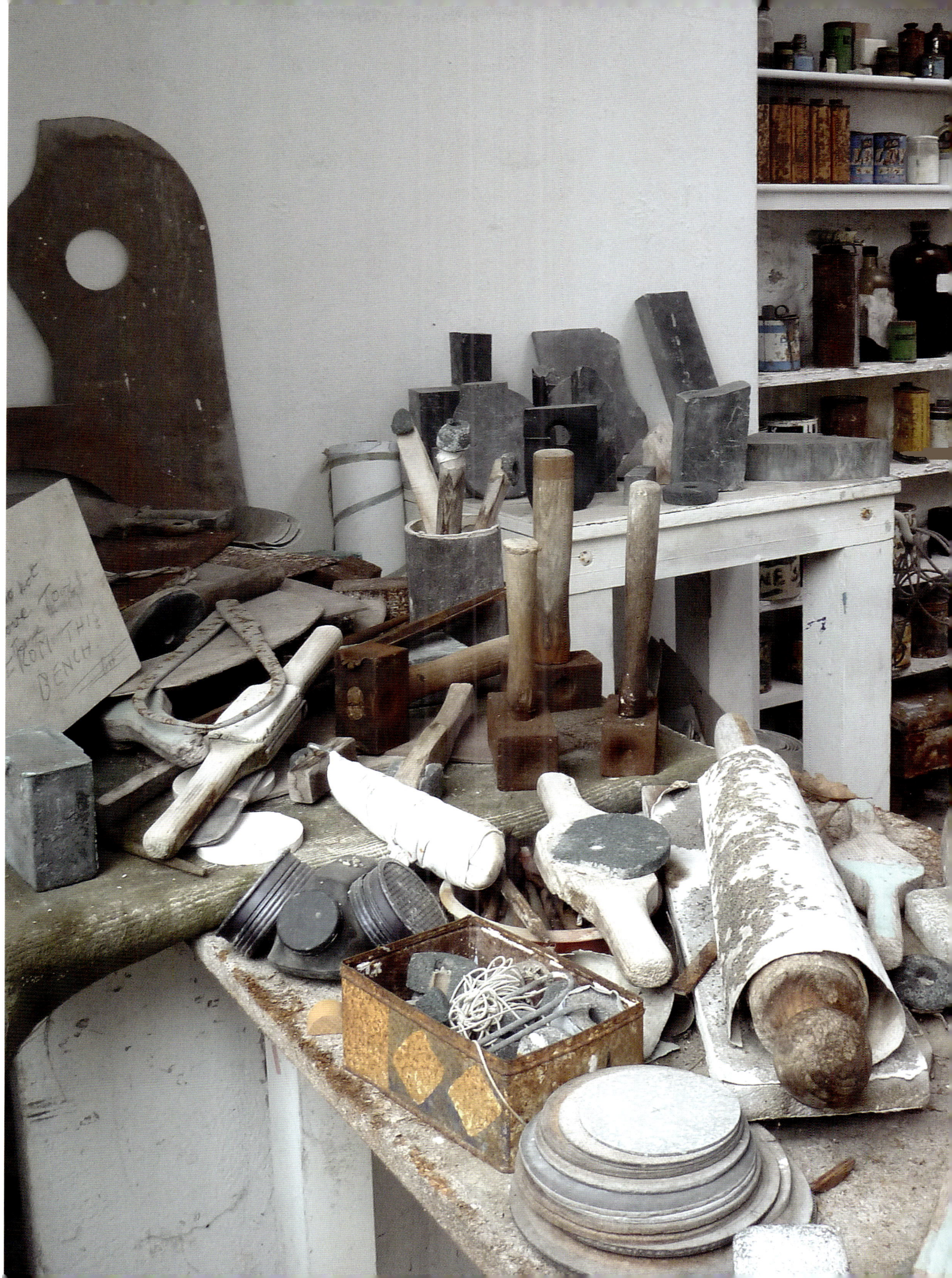
BENCH

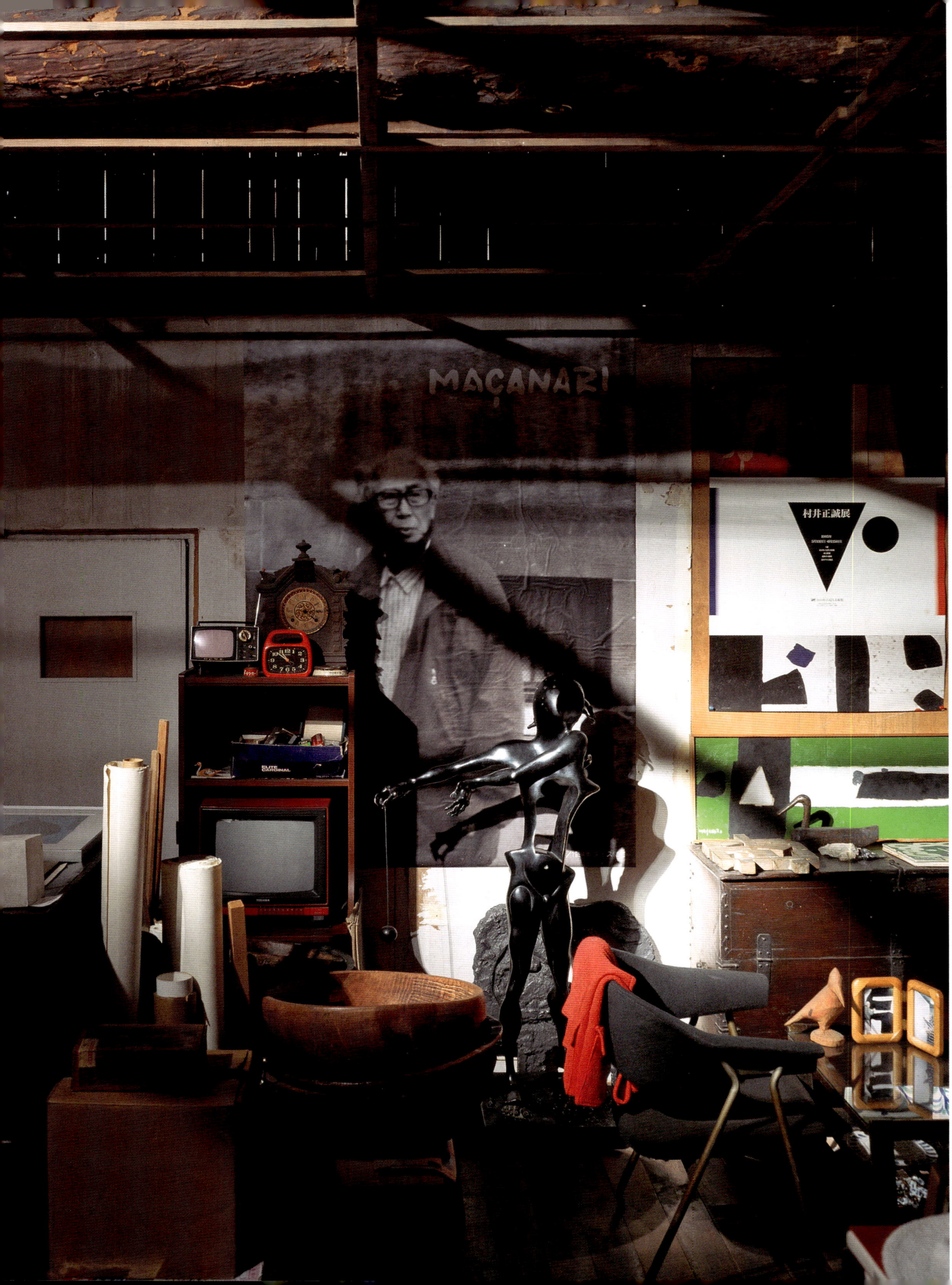
MAÇANARI
村井正誠展
ELITE CARDINAL

MASANARI MURAI

Tokyo, Japan

One of the pioneers of Japanese abstract art, Masanari Murai (1905–99) also called himself Murai Maçanari, after living and working in France for five years. In later life, he lived and worked in Setagaya City, in Tokyo, in a wooden studio, where he produced paintings and prints.

Murai was born in Ogaki City, in the Gifu prefecture in central Japan, and grew up in Shingû City, in southern Japan. As a young man, he studied painting at the Bunka Gakuin college in Tokyo, where he was taught by the artists Arishima Ikuma and Ishii Hakutei. After he graduated, intending to develop his skills as a landscape painter, he travelled to Europe, where he became fascinated by both Renaissance art and more modern movements, such as De Stijl and Suprematism. For most of the four years he spent in Europe, he stayed in France, and while there, he exhibited at the annual Salon des Indépendants. The influence of abstract art was strong, and he began simplifying his natural-looking landscapes and using bolder colours.

ABSTRACT ART

In 1932, Murai returned to Japan from Europe, where he developed his ideas and style even more. He became one of the foremost abstract artists in Japan and was particularly proactive in promoting abstract art by staging exhibitions and educating art students. In Tokyo, along with Kaoru Yamaguchi, Rokurō Yabashi, Saburo Hasegawa, Ei-Q and Yozo Hamaguchi, he founded the New Age Painting Exhibitions that were held on a monthly basis. In 1937, he helped form the Free Artists' Society which also promoted abstract painting and avant-garde art. Eventually, he left the association in 1950 and formed the Modan Âto Kyôkai (Modern Art Association), again with Yamaguchi and Yabashi. Three years after that – with Onchi Kōshirō, Japan's leading creative print artist – Murai became a founding member of the Nihon Abusutorakuto Âto Kurabu (Japan Abstract Art Club).

Leading up to and during World War Two, abstract art was seen to come from Western art and lost popularity, but after the late 1940s, it gradually became accepted once again. By then, Murai had started teaching at the Bunka Gakuin, and also producing prints as a way of making his art more accessible and to be able to give his work to his many pupils. His printmaking methods included woodblock, lithography and silkscreen, which worked well with his style of abstract paintings. Following Japanese tradition, he did the basic carving or other preparation for his prints, but professional artisans did the rest of the work to produce them. After around 1960, he worked with a limited, somewhat monochrome, palette and his abstractions became simpler and often larger than they had been earlier in his career. He also produced some stained glass and ceramics. One of the main concepts he explored was the question of what was 'inside faces'. He used certain colours to represent personality attributes, as well as particular shapes to symbolise feelings and individual characteristics and idiosyncrasies. For instance, a square with a vertical line could indicate a sense of stability or constancy, while tilted and angular shapes might suggest imbalance. However, none of these symbols was fixed; Murai believed that viewers should make up their own minds and be flexible when looking at his work.

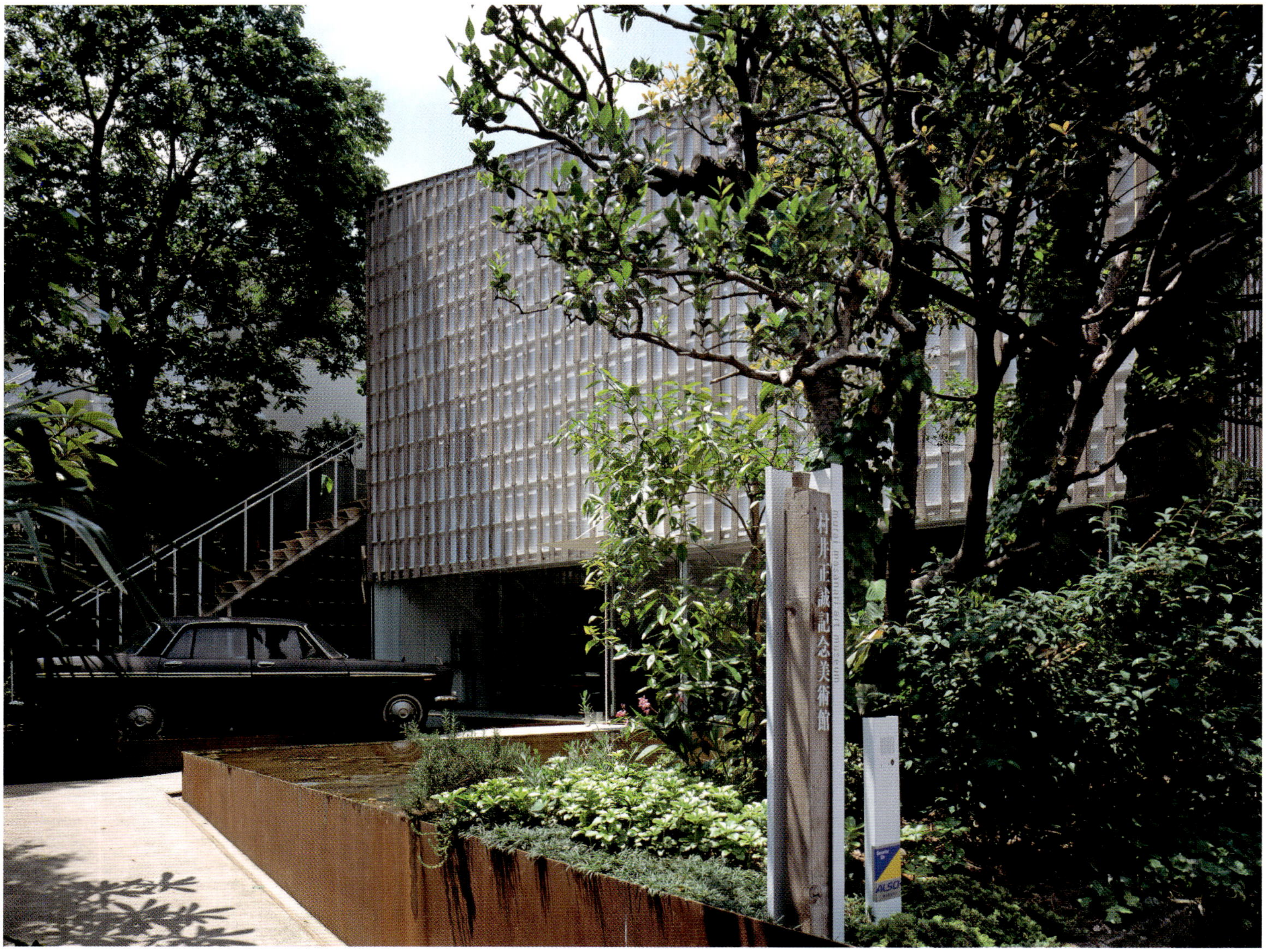

Above: Outside the Masanari Murai Memorial Museum of Art, designed by architect Kengo Kuma, using parts of Murai's original art studio. His Toyota car is still parked there.

THE MUSEUM

Over his career, Murai was extremely successful and he received many awards, including first prize at the Fifth Modern Japanese Art Exhibition and the Education Minister's Prize at the Third International Biennial Exhibition of Prints, both in 1962. In 1970, he received the Wakayama Prefecture Award of Culture; in 1997, the Chunichi Cultural Prize and Setagaya City Culture Contribution Special Award; and in 1998, the Tsune Nakamura Award. While he was still working, several retrospectives of his work were held at various important institutions, including the Museum of Modern Art in Kamakura in 1973 and 1995, the Museum of Modern Art in Wakayama in 1979, and the Setagaya Art Museum in 1993.

Murai lived until he was ninety-three, and he worked for most of those years. For much of his adult life, he lived in Tokyo and his last studio was a wooden house in Setagaya City, in the south-west of the capital. After his death, the studio was preserved, still filled with his artworks and personal belongings. On 29 March 2005, on the 100th anniversary of his birth, the Masanari Murai Memorial Museum of Art was opened, designed by the architect Kengo Kuma. With a modest budget, instead of creating a completely new building, Kuma made sure that parts of Murai's studio work in

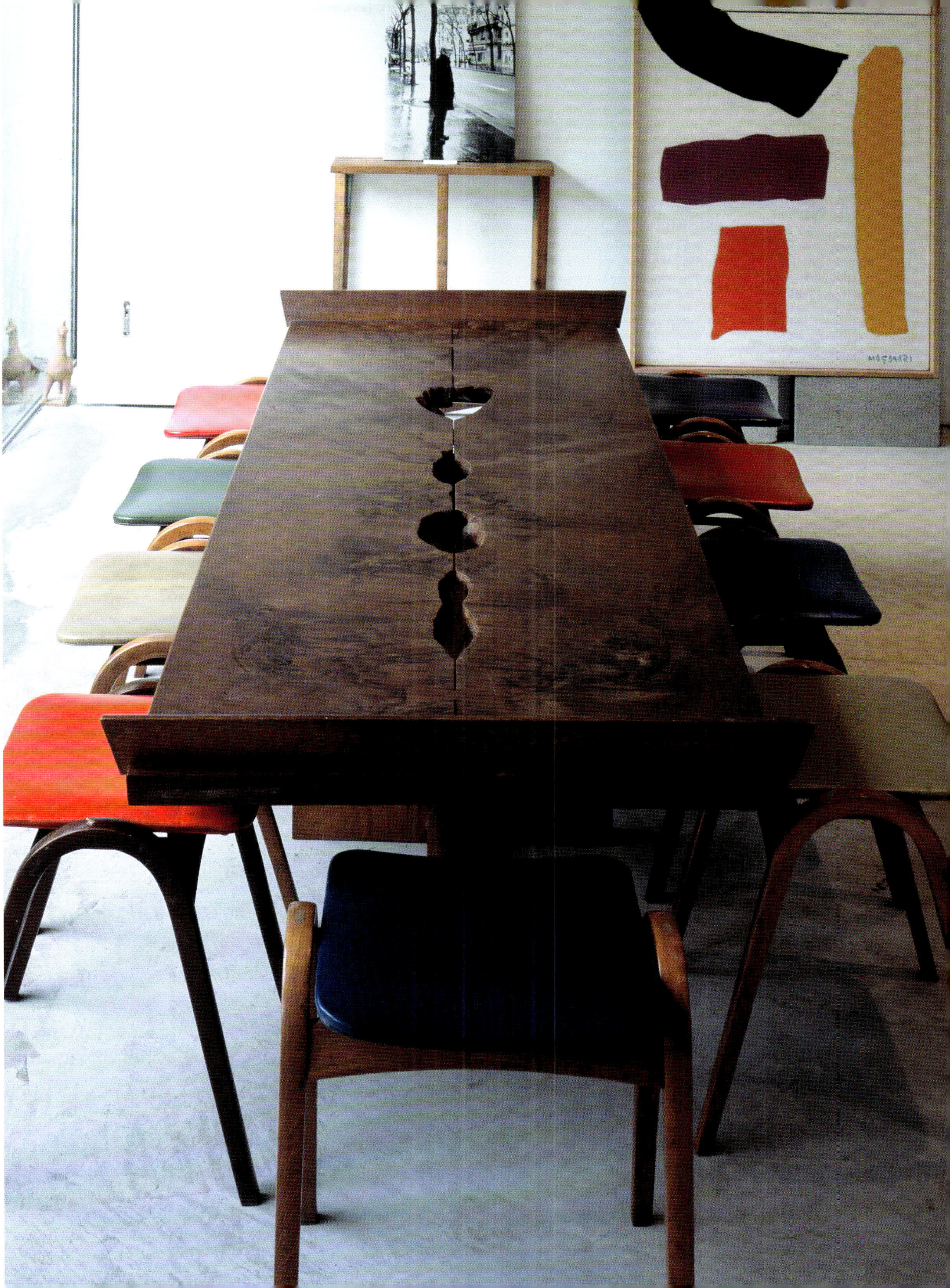

symbiosis with the new spaces. The museum was built to embrace and preserve the old timber building, while providing something more modern for the time, a space for exhibitions to be held. A mezzanine floor was built over the wooden studio and some aspects of the old wooden house have been used elsewhere in the building. For instance, wood from the old façade and inner roof has been reused to form vertical louvres on the exterior. In other areas, unusual materials were used, such as a metal mesh wall. Most of the other walls are white, which makes them sympathetic to the display of Murai's bold abstract art. Overall, the atmosphere within the building is tranquil, just as it would have been when Murai was working there. Outside, Murai's old Toyota car stands proudly surrounded by water, and within the museum are many of his artworks and possessions. It is almost as if he has just popped out.

'The spectator can follow his own imagination.'

Masanari Murai

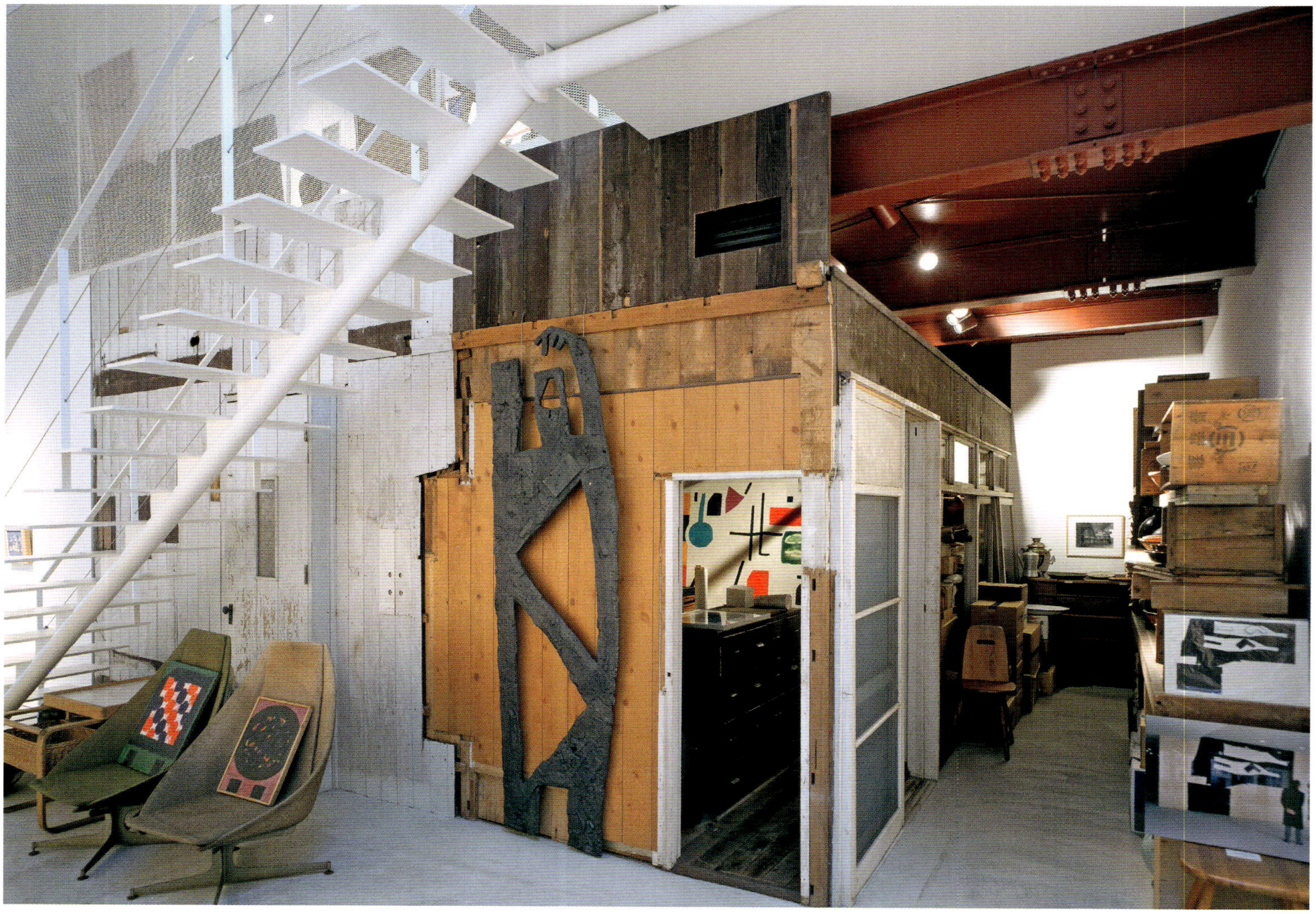

Above and opposite: Inside the building, everything has been placed as if Murai has just popped out. The atmosphere remains peaceful and filled with his artworks and possessions.

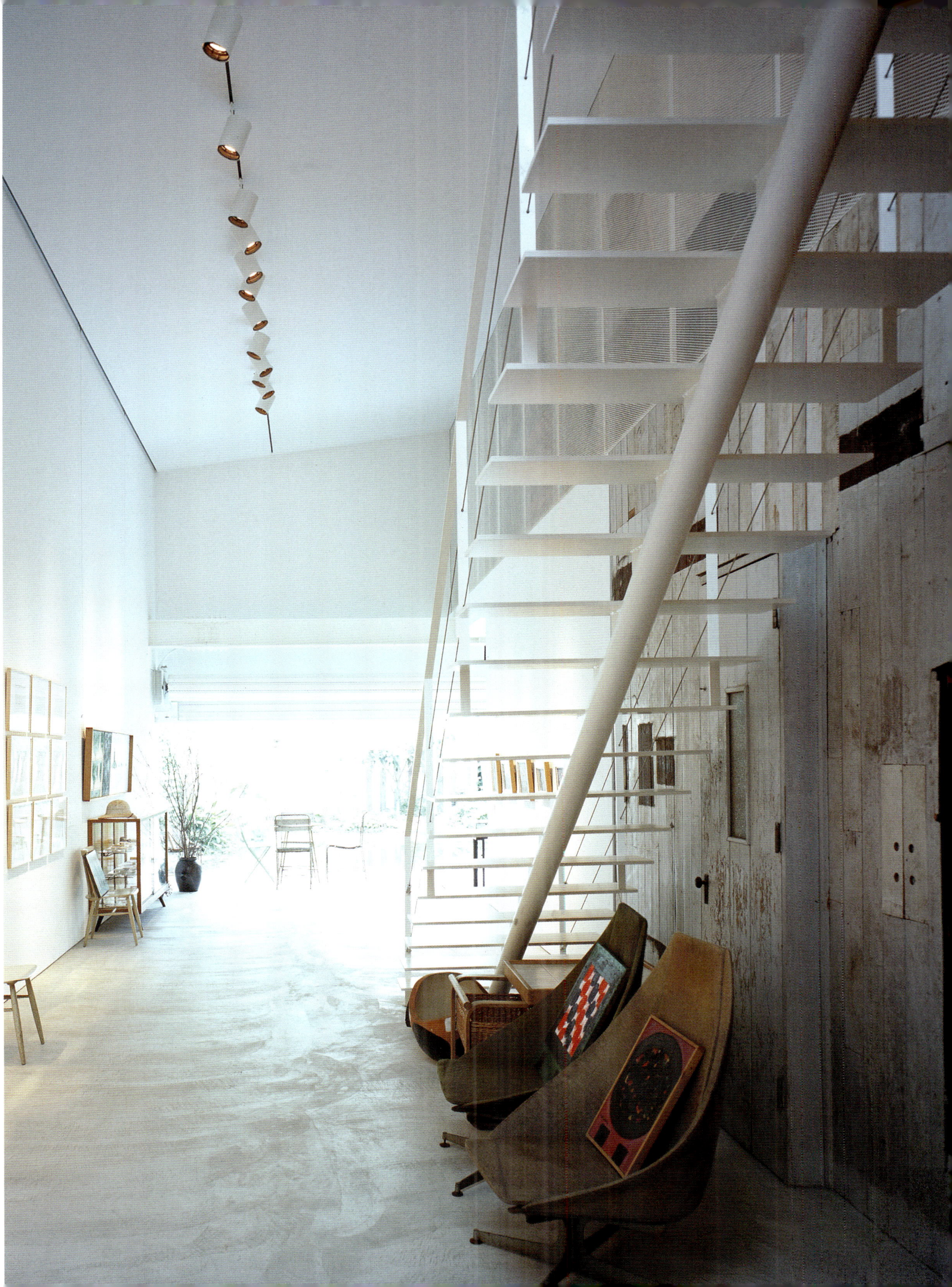

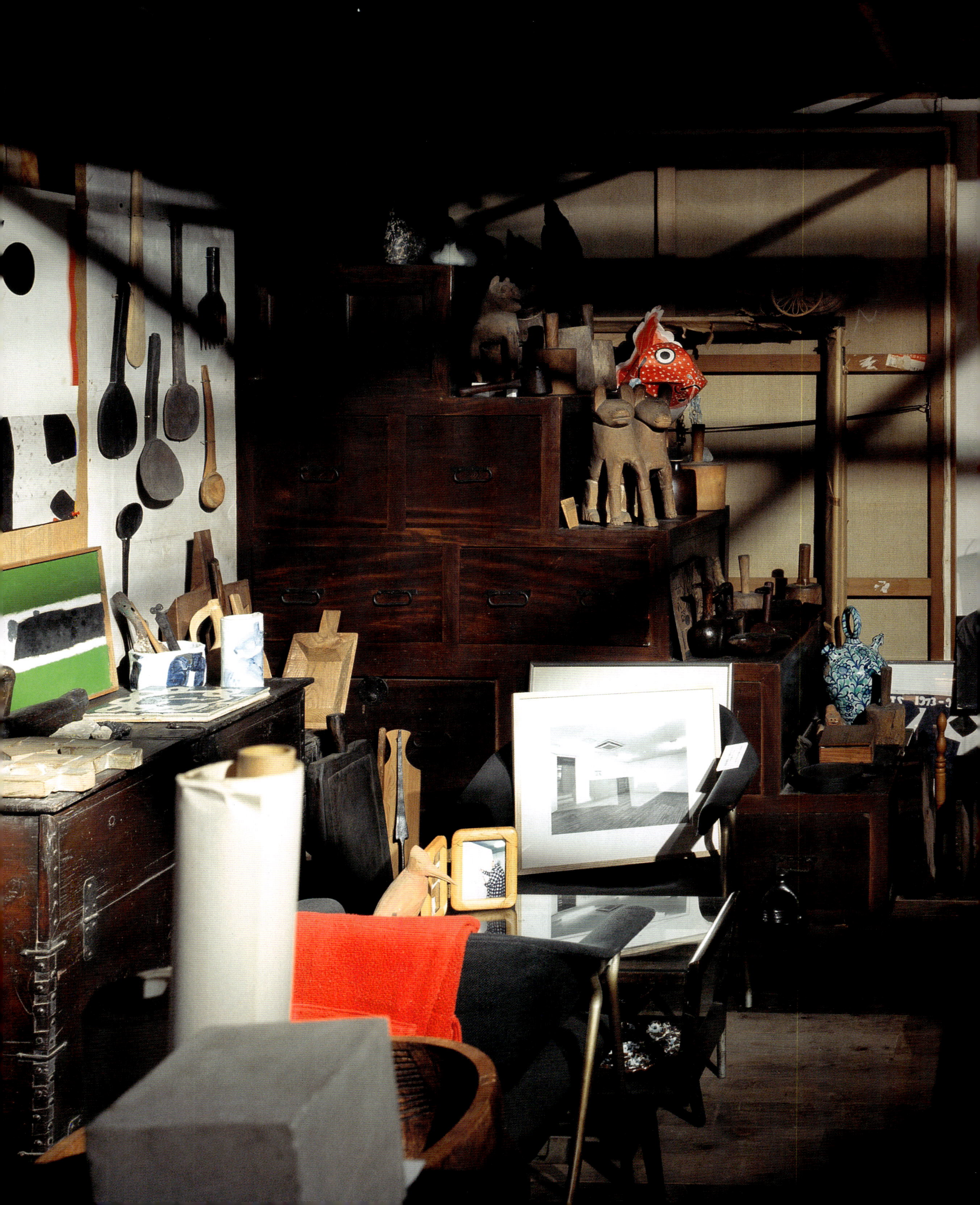

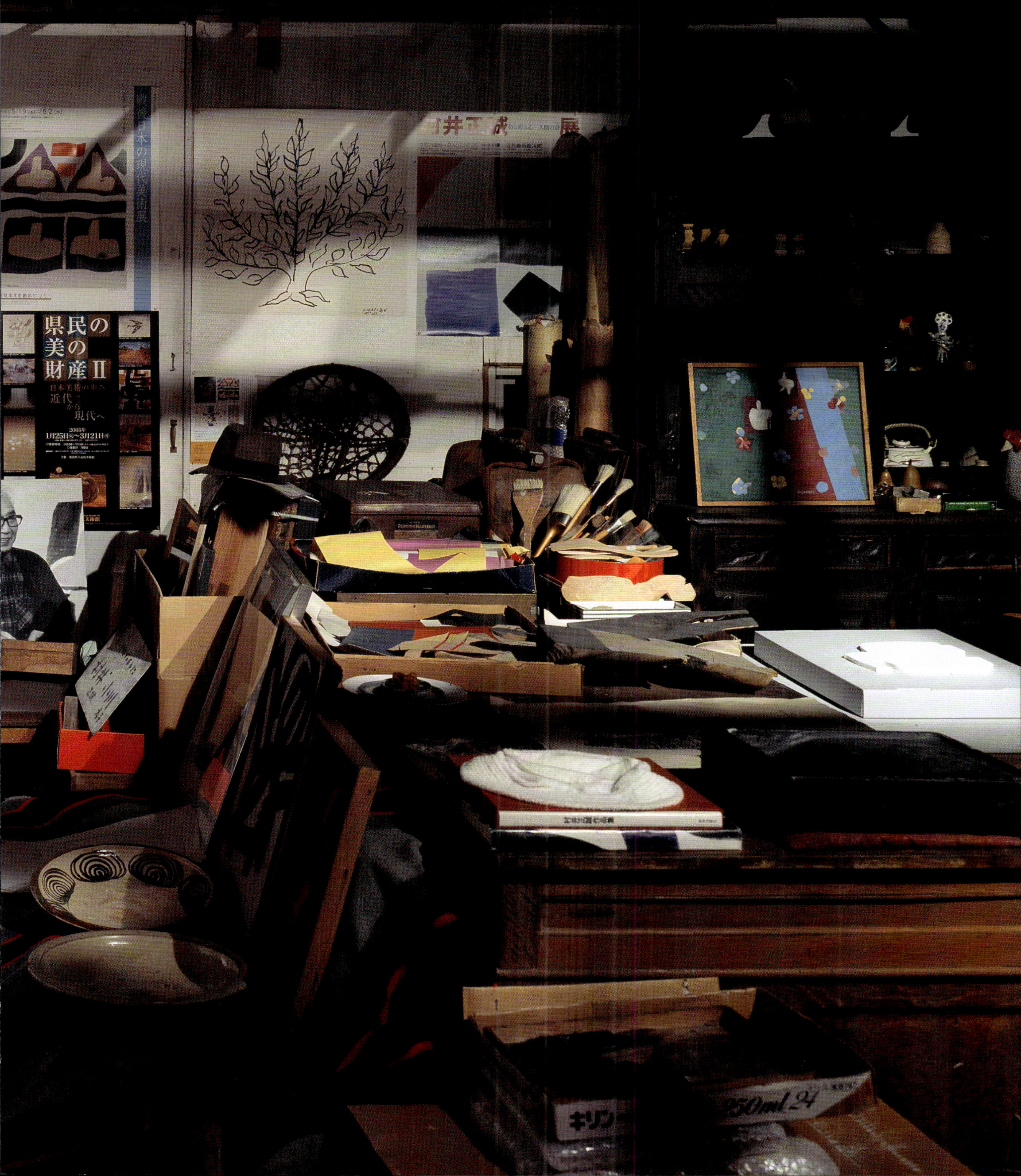
戦後日本の現代美術展
県民の
美の
財産Ⅱ
日本美術の歩み
近代から
現代へ
2005年
展
キリン
250ml 24

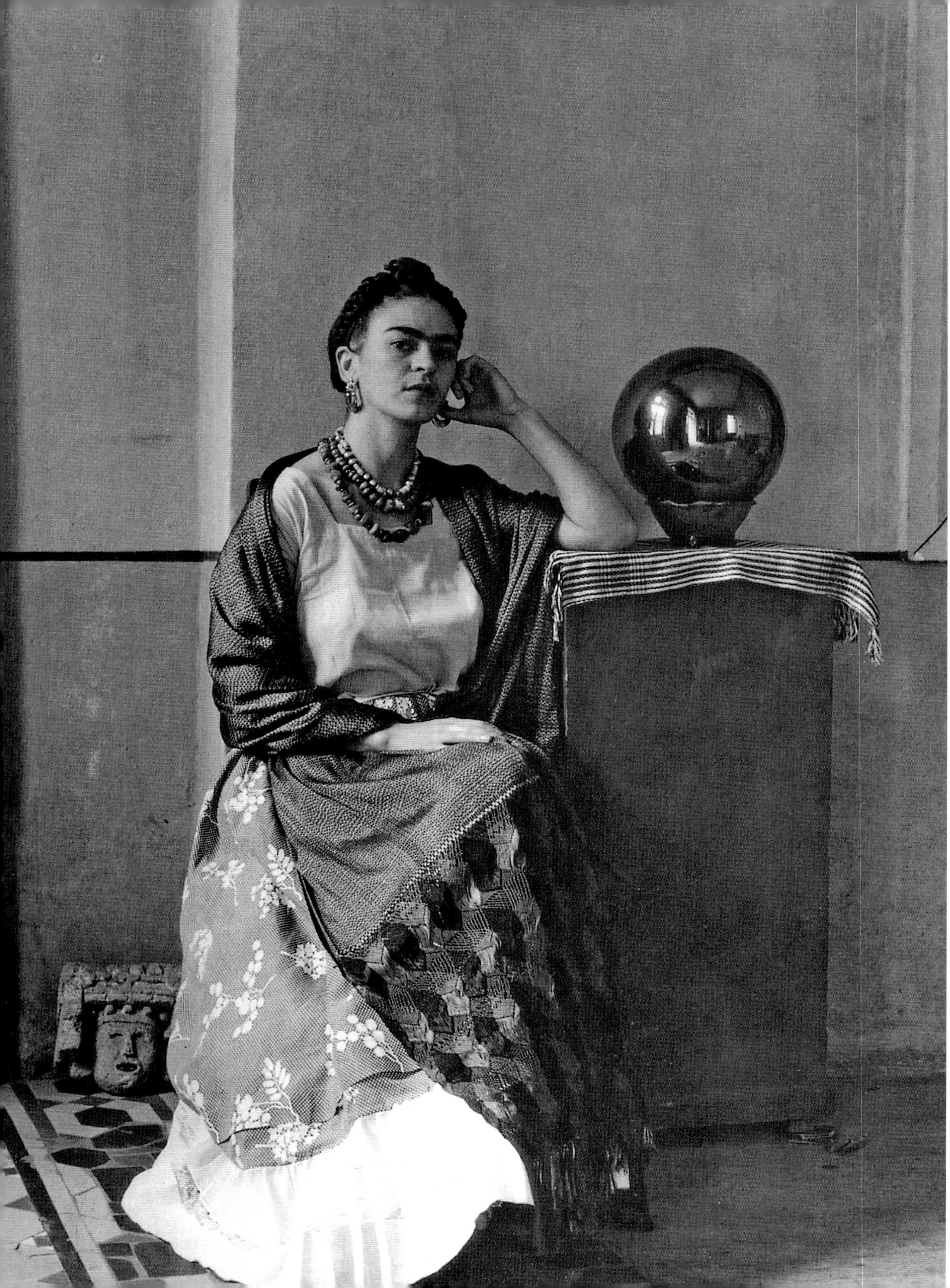

FRIDA KAHLO

Coyoacán, Mexico

Meaning 'place of coyotes', Coyoacán in Mexico City retains much of its original sixteenth-century layout, with narrow streets, cobbled lanes, verdant plazas and vibrant markets. Frida Kahlo (1907–54) grew up in a house on a quiet residential street there. She loved it so much that she never really left it.

Frida Kahlo's house was called La Casa Azul (The Blue House) after its cobalt-blue walls. Built originally in 1904, it was commissioned by Frida's German father Wilhelm (Guillermo in Spanish), who had moved to Mexico at a young age. Her mother, Matilde Calderon y Gonzalez, was of mixed Spanish and indigenous ancestry. She raised Frida and her three sisters in a strictly religious household. At the age of six, Frida contracted polio and spent the long recovery period at home. The illness left one leg shorter than the other, causing her to walk with a limp for the rest of her life. As she grew up, her photographer father introduced her to the writings of European philosophers, and she became fascinated by literature and politics. She was also one of the first girls admitted to the National Preparatory School, where she studied medicine, botany and the social sciences, intending to become a doctor. Then one day in September 1925, when she was eighteen and travelling home on the school bus, she was involved in a near-fatal accident. A tram collided with her bus, and she suffered multiple fractures – including a crushed pelvis and three displaced vertebrae – and an iron handrail impaled her womb. She spent a month in hospital, and almost two years confined to her bed at home in casts and orthopaedic devices. Over the rest of her life, she endured pain and multiple hospital stays and operations.

While convalescing at La Casa Azul, Frida's parents made her a special easel, gave her a set of paints and fixed a mirror above her head so that she could paint self-portraits from her bed. Abandoning her plans of becoming a doctor, she joined the Mexican Communist Party (PCM), and became close friends with the photojournalist Tina Modotti and Cuban revolutionary Julio Antonio Mella. They introduced her to an influential member of the PCM and one of Mexico's most famous artists, Diego Rivera. Although he was twenty-one years older than Frida, an atheist and a known womaniser, the pair married in 1929. Her disapproving mother described the union as being between an elephant and a dove. For the first three years of their marriage, the couple travelled in Mexico and the United States, as Rivera completed mural commissions. For her own art, Frida began drawing inspiration from Mexican folk culture, and painted mostly small self-portraits, amalgamating elements from pre-Columbian and early Christian art, with a flat-looking, colourful style. She also began wearing traditional Mexican Tehuana costumes, with flowered headdresses and long skirts to cover her wasted leg.

REBUILDING

While Frida travelled with Rivera, she suffered two miscarriages and her mother died. Soon after their return to Mexico, in 1934, Rivera paid off her father's debts, incurred through Guillermo's loss of work during the Mexican Revolution in 1910 and Frida's many medical expenses. He also paid off the family mortgage on La Casa Azul, and he and Frida moved in, starting renovations soon after. Frida and Rivera lived together in La Casa Azul from 1934 to 1939 – for some of that time with Frida's younger sister Cristina and her two children, Isolda and Antonio. Cristina had moved out of La Casa Azul in 1928 when she married, but returned with her children after her husband left her.

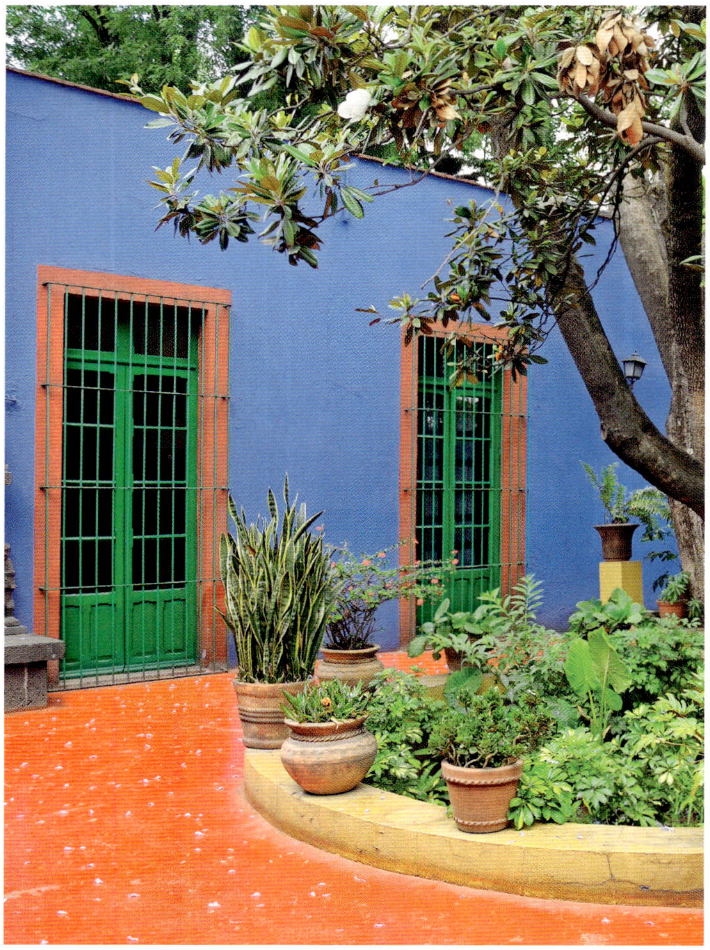

Above: Along with the cobalt blue walls,
La Casa Azul features orange and bright green details.

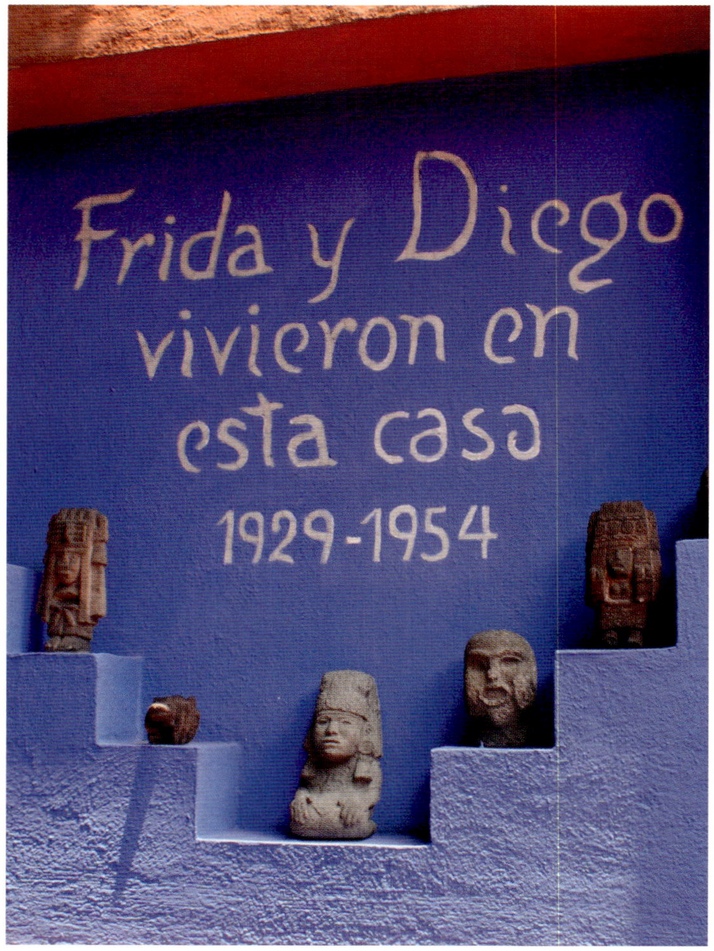

Above: A sign on the vibrant blue walls of La Casa Azul,
stating that Frida anc Diego lived there from 1929–1954.

However, Frida and Rivera's marriage was not a happy one; his frequent infidelities damaged her fragile health further. She also plunged into affairs with men and women, underwent two abortions and an appendectomy, and had two gangrenous toes amputated. After Rivera and Cristina had an affair, Frida divorced him and lived alone in La Casa Azul, until they remarried the following year.

When it was built, the two-storey La Casa Azul was originally created in a French style. It had three sides enclosing a courtyard and was fairly small, so Rivera had a fourth side added to enclose the courtyard entirely. This was built with local volcanic rock and had ceramic vases set into it. A terraced roof was also built, decorated with marine shells and mirrors. In 1946, Frida's studio and bedroom were moved to the new part of the house. Other rooms included further bedrooms, a large kitchen, a dining room and an entrance hall – or patio – decorated with mosaics. Everywhere is brightly coloured and adorned with Mexican art. A stone wall divides the courtyard, which also features a fountain, a stepped pyramid, a reflection pool, and a room for Frida and Rivera's archaeological collection; they were fascinated by Mesoamerican objects.

The couple frequently entertained their many friends, who included prominent cultural figures, intellectuals and artists from Mexico and beyond, such as André Breton, Tina Modotti, Edward Weston, José Clemente Orozco, Isamu Noguchi and Leon Trotsky. In 1936, Rivera convinced the Mexican President to offer Trotsky – an exiled Russian politician – asylum in Mexico, and in January 1937, Trotsky and his wife arrived. For once, Rivera, not Frida, was sick, so she met them at the port, with a troop of armed guards. La Casa Azul had been prepared for them to stay, with guards, barricades, covered windows and alarm systems. Trotsky's wife later recalled her impressions of the place: 'A blue house, a patio filled with plants, airy rooms, collections of Pre-Columbian art, paintings from all over: we were on a new planet, in Rivera's house.' While she and Trotsky lived there – until April 1939 – he and Frida conducted an affair.

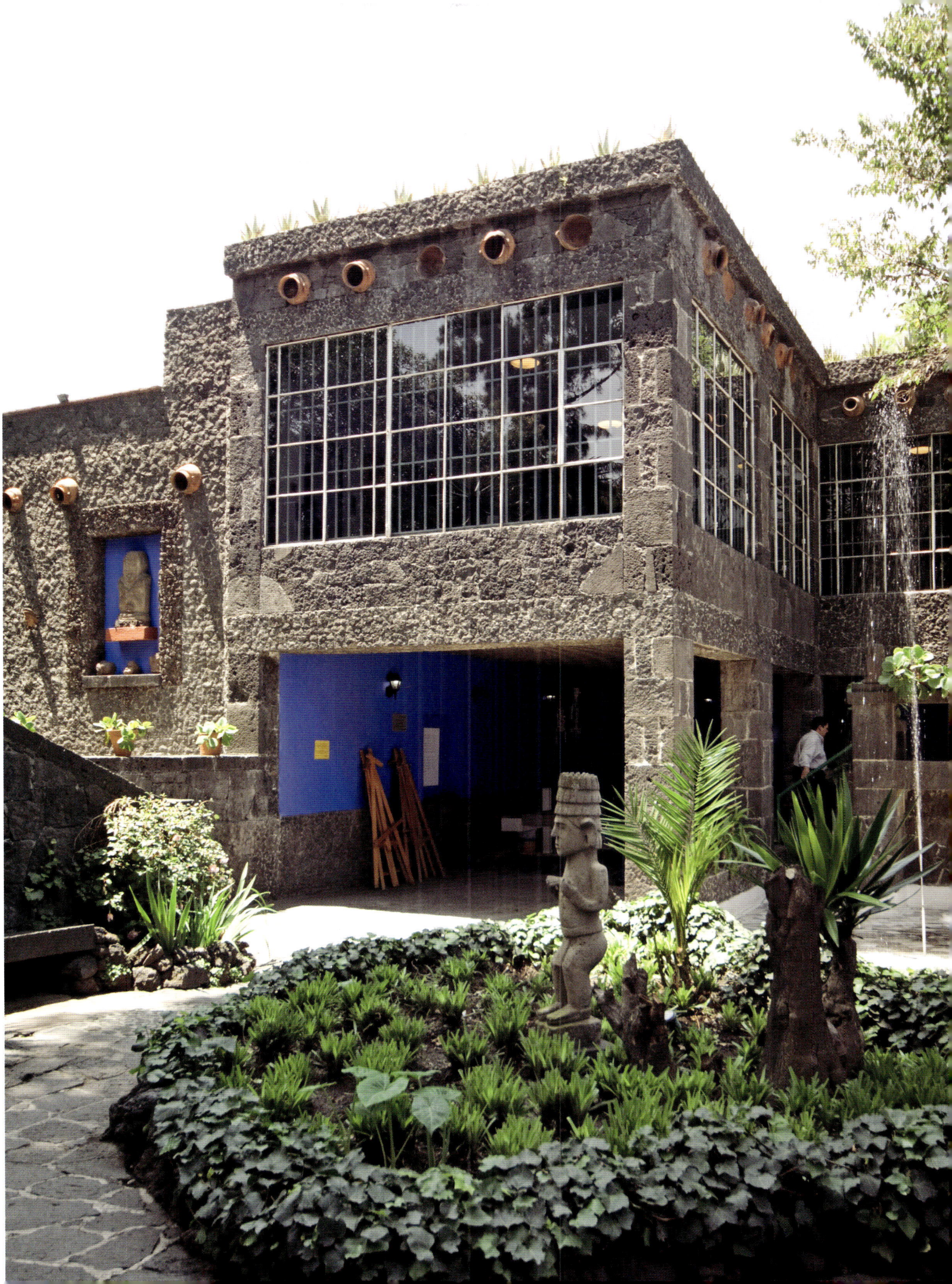

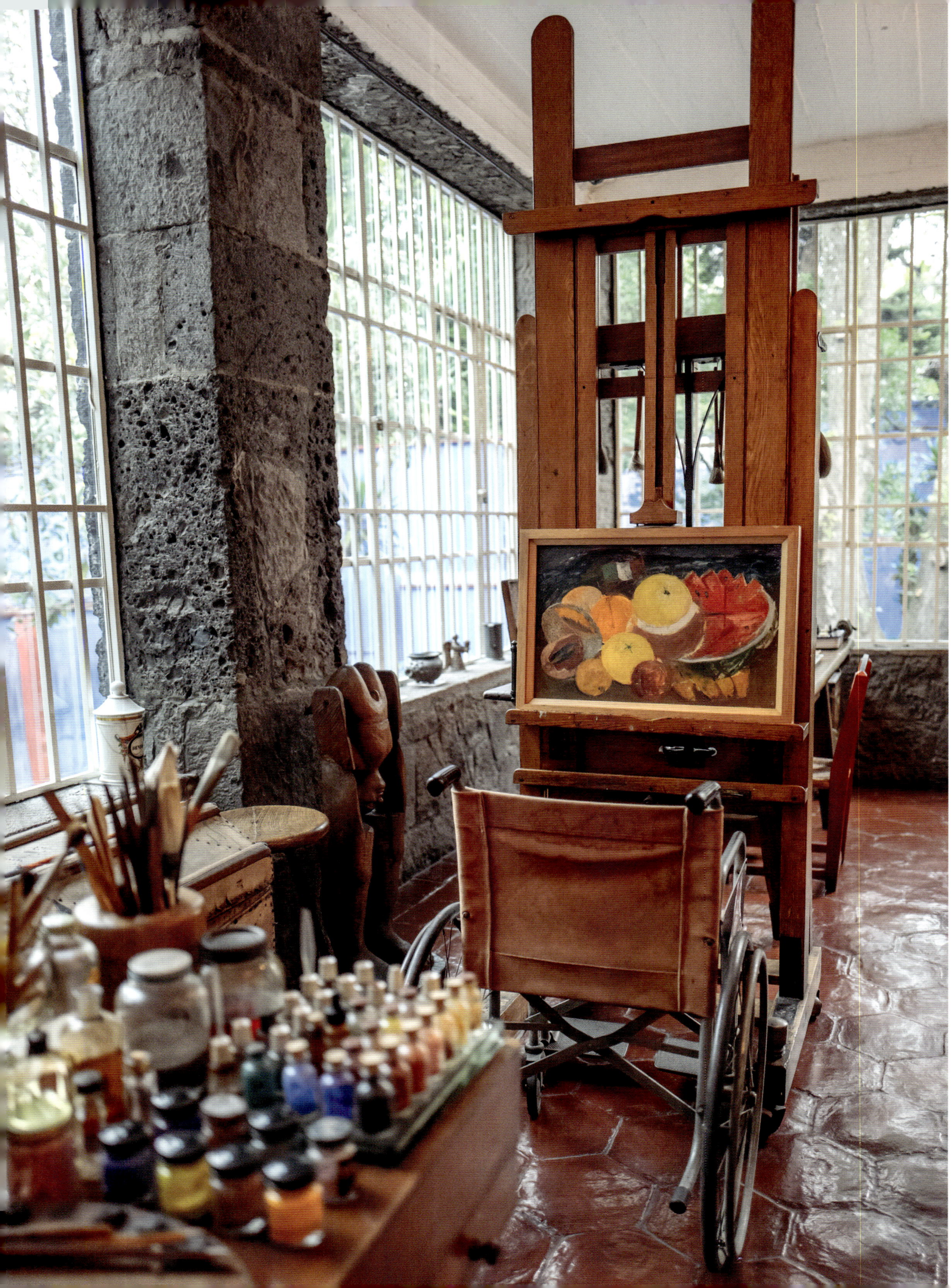

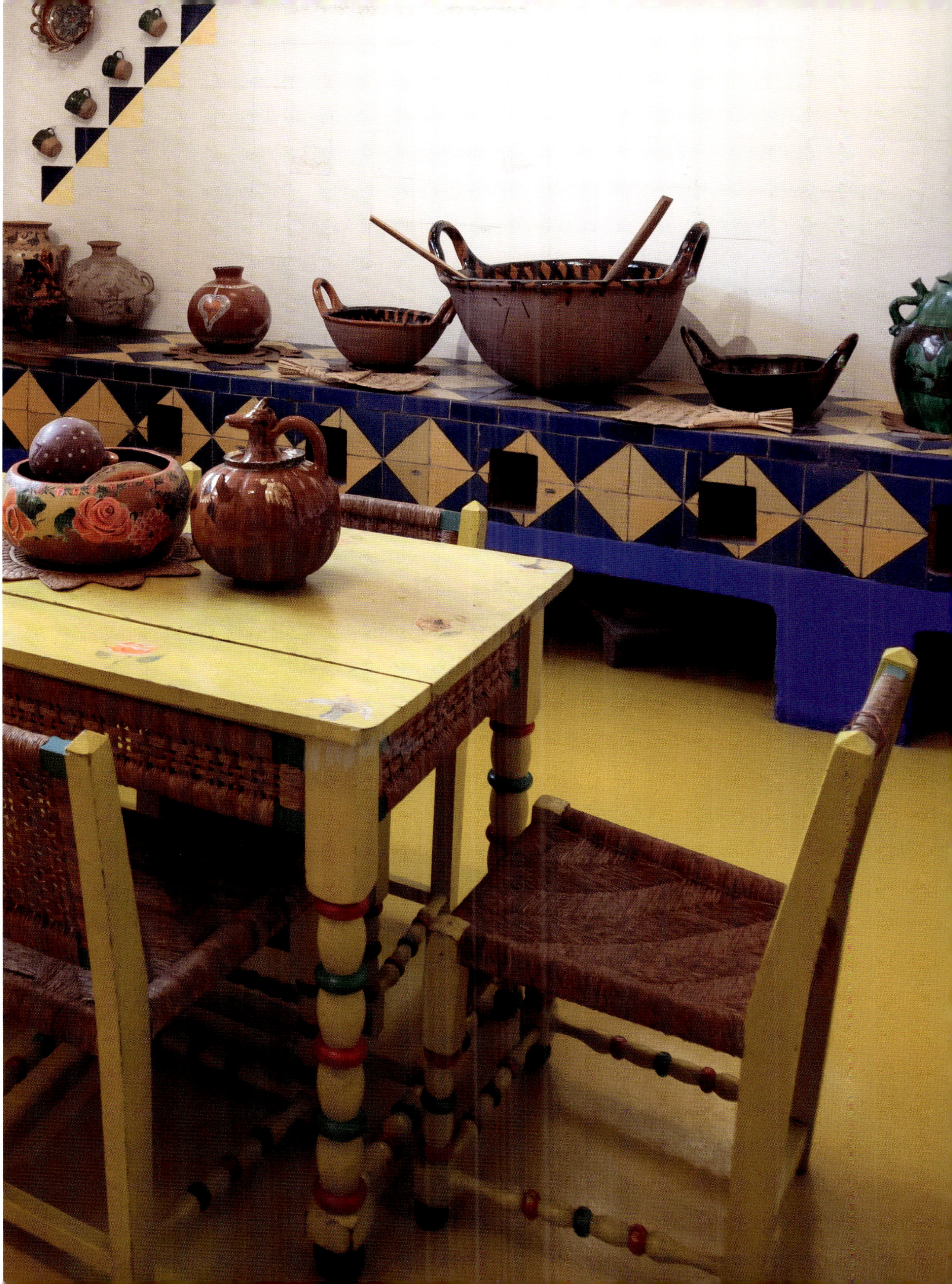

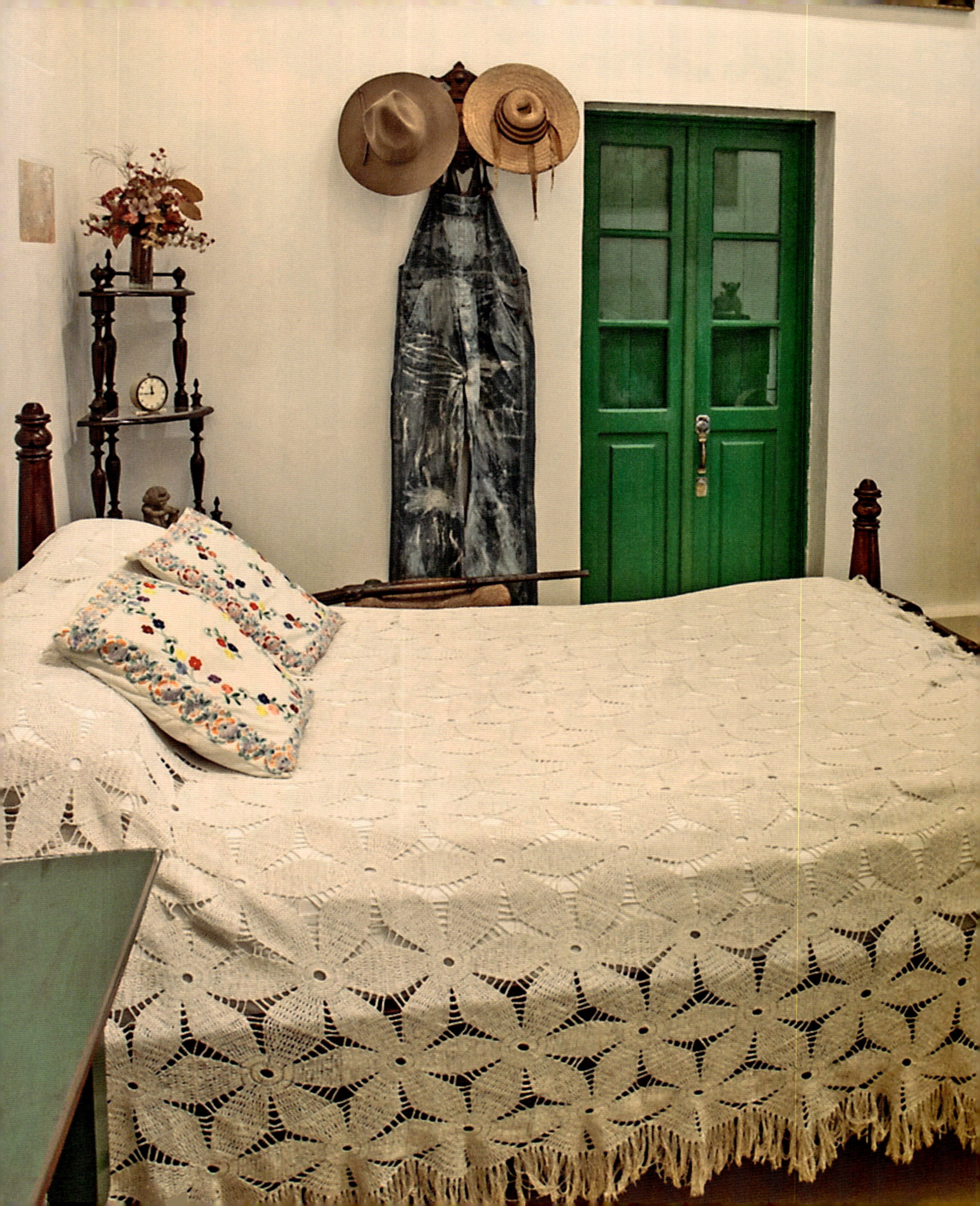

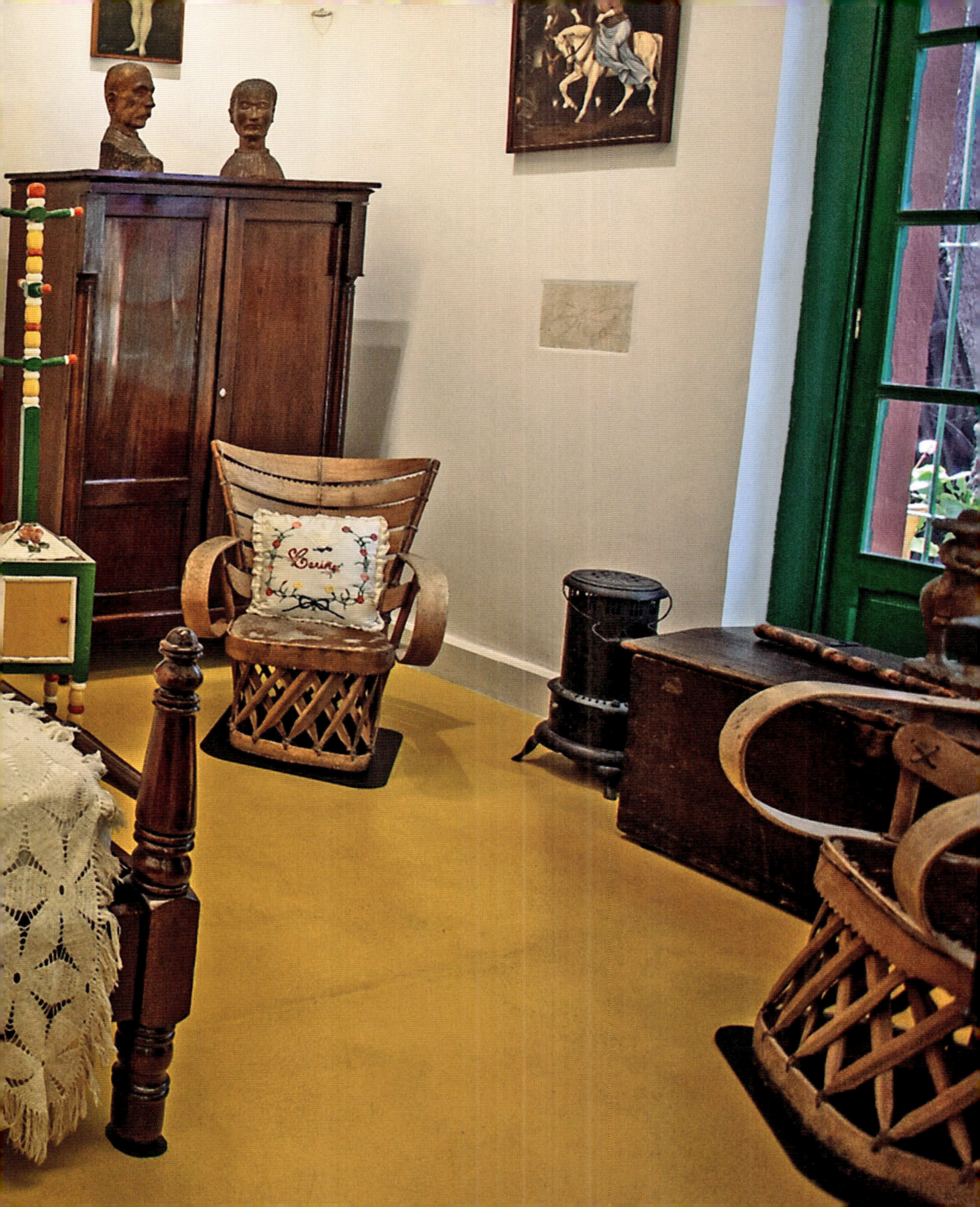

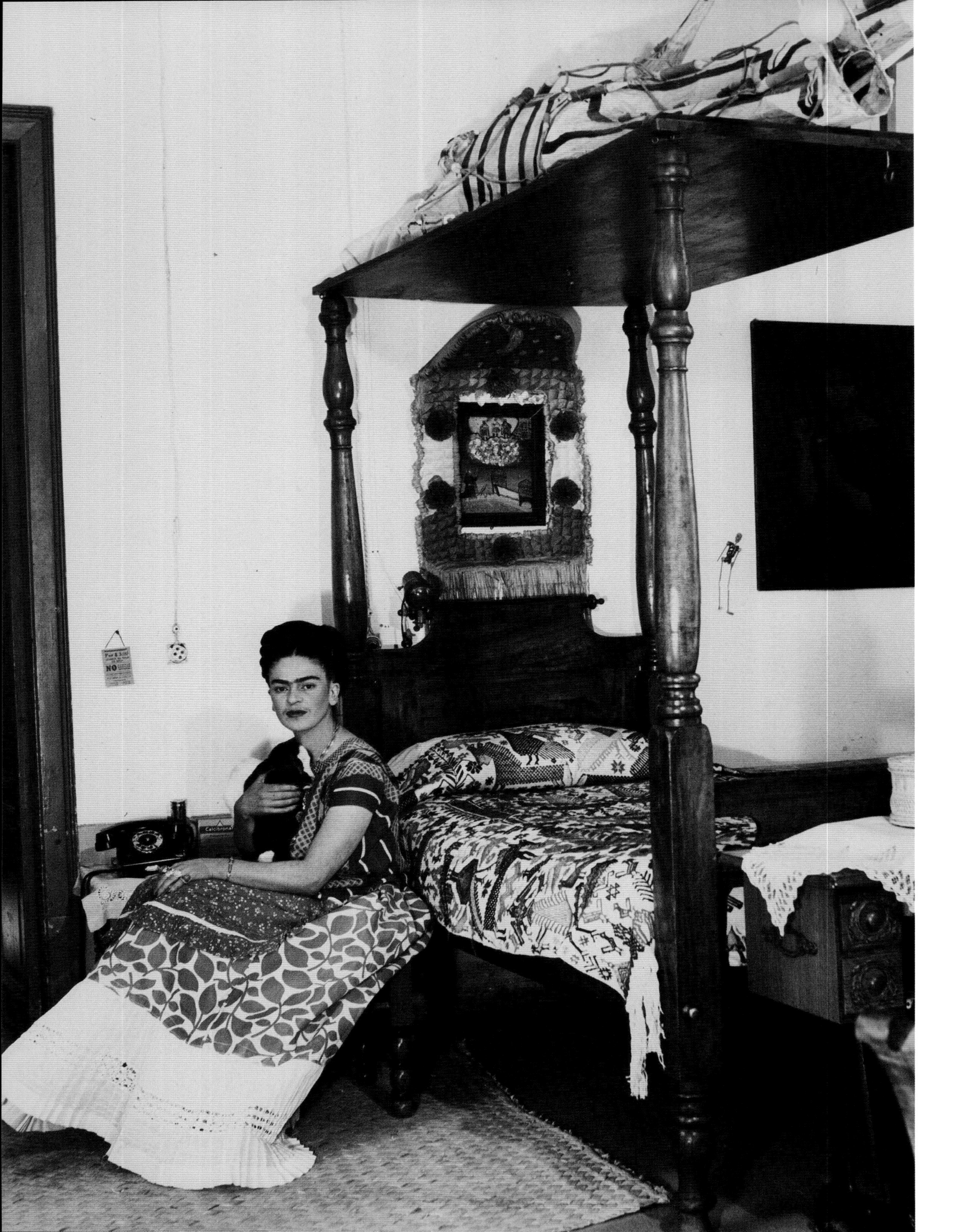

ANIMALS AND TEACHING

Frida kept many animals as pets. These included Mexican Xoloitzcuintli (hairless) dogs, spider monkeys, cats, a deer, an eagle, parakeets, macaws, hens and sparrows. All lived freely in the house or courtyard, and she often included them in her paintings. Her monkeys included Fulang Chang, a gift from Rivera, and Caimito de Guayabal; her deer was Granizo; her favourite dog was Mr Xoloti; her eagle was Gertrudis Caca Blanca; and Bonito was her Amazon parrot who performed tricks at the table for guests.

In 1943, Frida became an instructor for the Escuela de Pintura y Escultura de La Esmeralda (school of painting and sculpture), but her poor health meant that she mainly gave classes at her home. Two years later, she was once again confined to bed. She could no longer sit or stand for long and, in June 1945, she travelled to New York for a difficult operation on her back. Ultimately, the operation was a failure, and in 1950 she underwent further surgery on her spine that caused an infection and resulted in further operations. When not in hospital, she was mostly confined to La Casa Azul, using a wheelchair and crutches. In August 1953, her right leg was amputated at the knee due to gangrene. She became severely depressed, and her dependency on painkillers escalated. When Rivera began yet another affair, she attempted suicide. In February 1954, she wrote in her diary, 'They amputated my leg six months ago ... I keep on wanting to kill myself. Diego is what keeps me from it, through my vain idea that he would miss me... But never in my life have I suffered more. I will wait a while...' For the next few months, she was bedridden with bronchopneumonia and, in July, she died at home at the age of forty-seven.

> 'Nothing is absolute. Everything changes, everything moves, everything revolves...'
>
> *Frida Kahlo*

Below: Frida's bed, where she spent the last painful weeks of her life.
Opposite: Frida Kahlo in her bedroom.

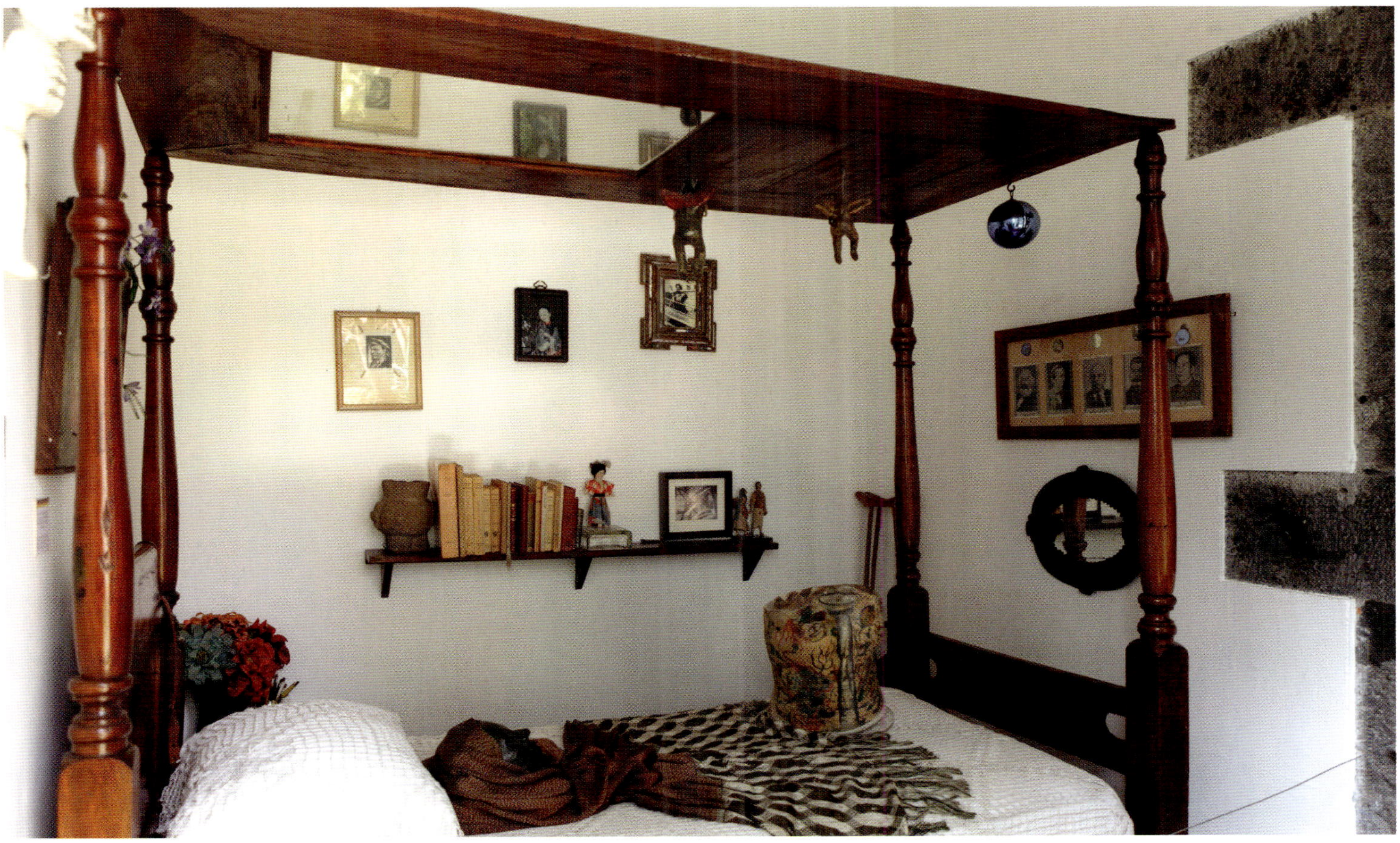

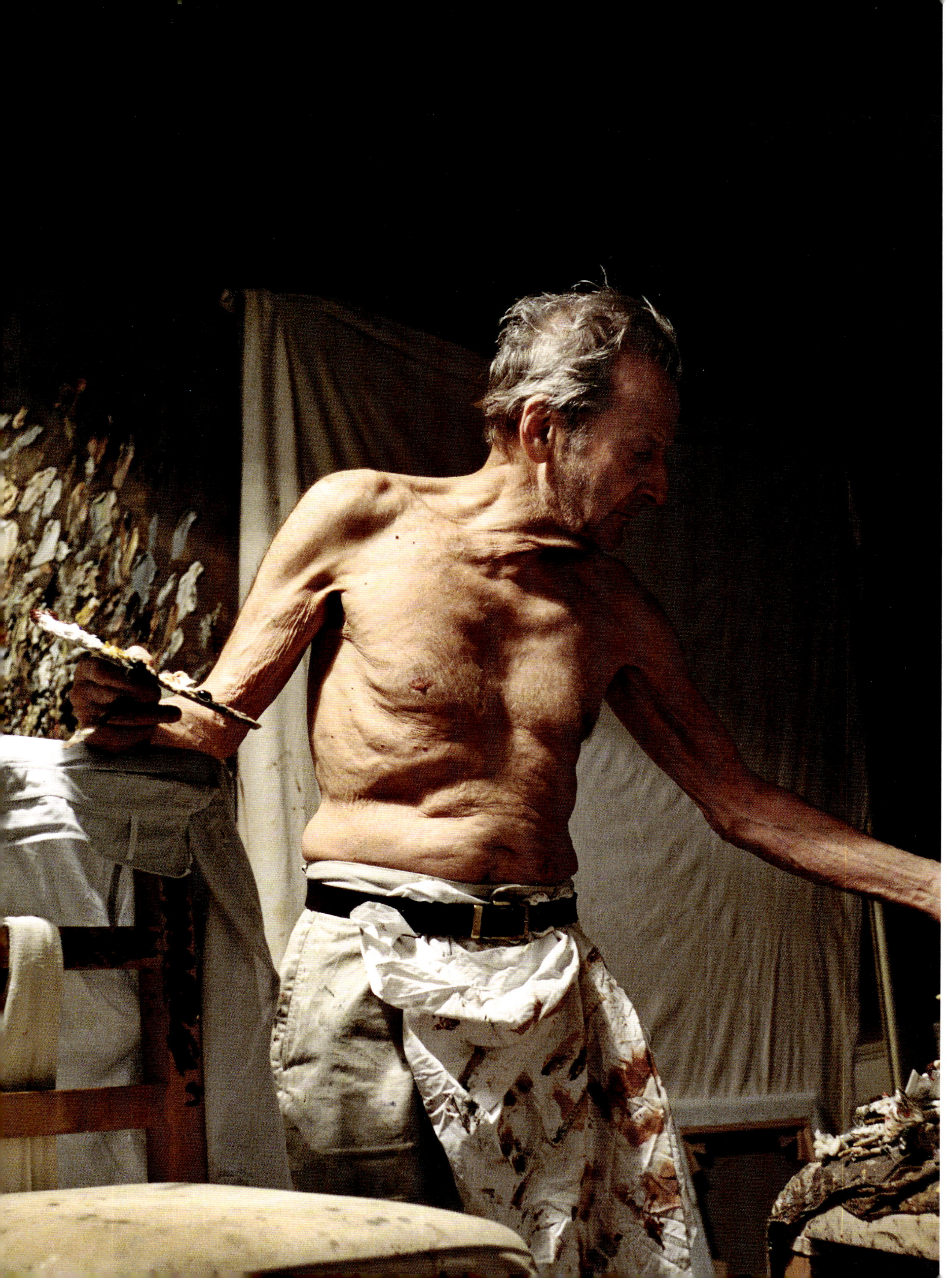

LUCIAN FREUD

London, UK

A Georgian terraced house in Kensington, London, built in 1736–37 on three storeys, plus a basement and an attic within the mansard roof, became both home and workplace for the artist Lucian Freud (1922–2011) for approximately forty years, from the 1970s to 2011.

Lucian Freud was born into a middle-class Jewish family. His father was an architect, his mother studied art history and his grandfather was the renowned psychoanalyst Sigmund Freud. When he was ten, Freud and his family escaped the Nazis and left Berlin for London, where they settled in the area called Swiss Cottage. Five years later, a drawing he had made when he was eight years old was selected for a show of art by children at a London gallery. Soon after this, Freud enrolled in the East Anglian School of Painting and Drawing in Essex, where he remained for two years. In 1941, he spent three months in the Merchant Navy, and then he continued his studies at Goldsmiths College in London. In 1945, he met the man who became both his greatest friend and rival, Francis Bacon, and soon after, in Paris, he also befriended Picasso and Alberto Giacometti. Back in London, he started teaching at the Slade School of Art, and he also began exhibiting in the city's galleries.

EXAMINING RELATIONSHIPS

Charming, hot-tempered and a philanderer, Freud had numerous relationships with women, as well as two wives, and he claimed to have fathered at least fourteen children. He also admitted that he was an absent father to those children. Yet, despite his misogynistic and remiss behaviour, he was popular with both men and women. During the few hours a day when he did not paint, he dined, gambled, and socialised with other artists and British aristocrats. He often drew attention to himself by carrying his pet hawk on his shoulder.

A figurative painter at a time when most other artists were abstract, Freud came to be categorised as belonging to the School of London painters. This was a loose group of figurative painters based principally in London during the late twentieth century, who contrasted with the more abstract movements that were dominant at the time. Freud painted mainly portraits and his early style was smooth, precise and detailed, but after he changed from using soft sable to stiff hogs' hair brushes, he began applying paint with greater vivacity, impasto, broader strokes and heavy layers. He also began painting more nudes, and none of his paintings, nor his later etchings, flattered his sitters. He insisted that each model posed for him for many hours, even when he was painting the background. His method involved first drawing in charcoal on his canvas, and he often started each painting with the head of his subject, then worked on the body, later returning to the head and background. Each finished painting took months of intense observation and work.

In later life, his work became exceptionally popular – he was shortlisted for the prestigious Turner Prize in 1989 – and it sold for huge sums of money. For example, in 2008, his 1995 painting *Benefits Supervisor Resting* was sold by Christie's in New York for $33.6 million, setting a world record auction price for a living artist.

An intensely private person, Freud mainly painted his friends and family, wives and mistresses, and himself, often set in unsettling spaces, seeming to examine relationships between the artist and model.

KENSINGTON CHURCH STREET

To the west of central London, Kensington and Chelsea is a leafy borough that historically has been home to many artists and

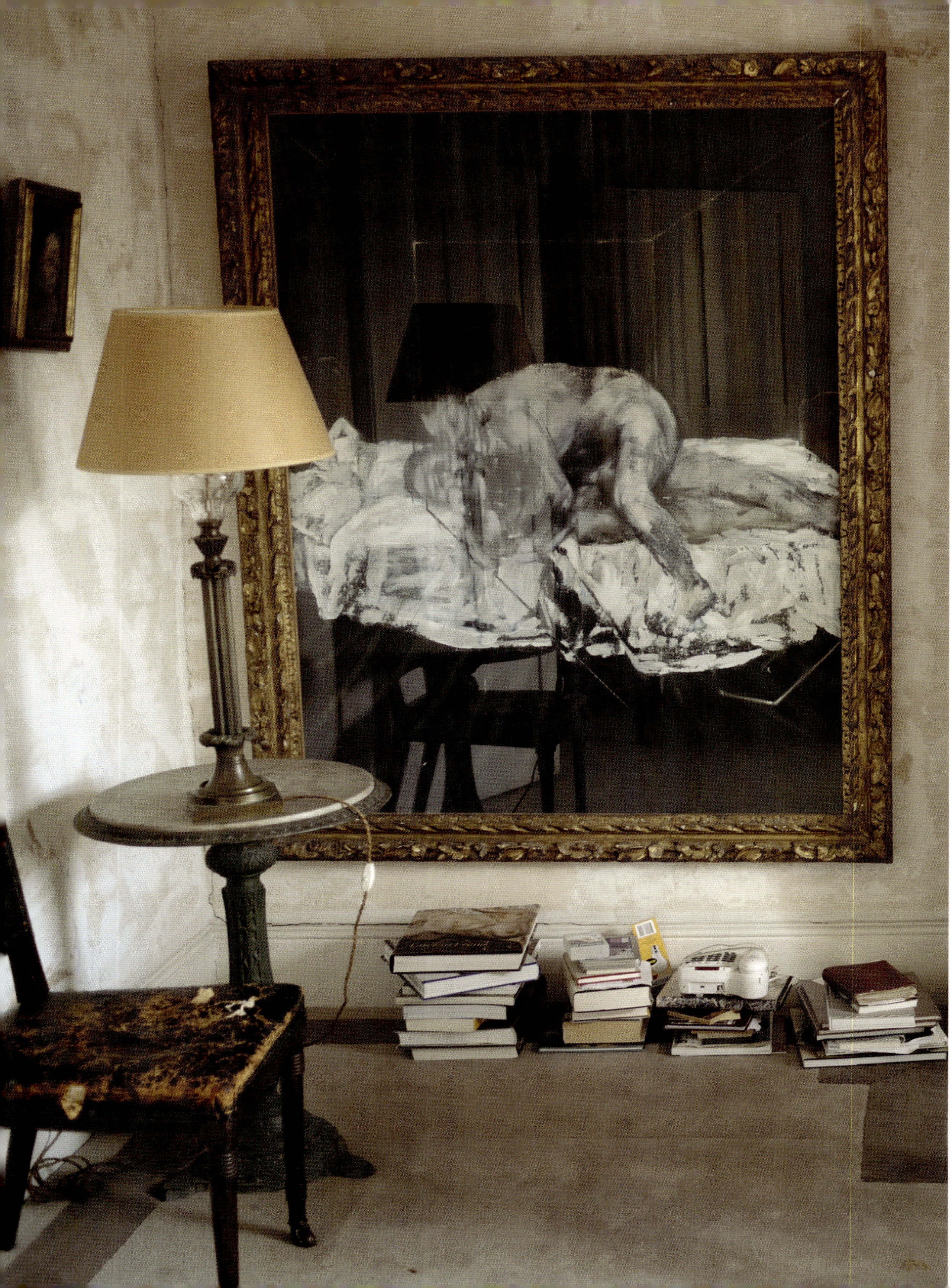

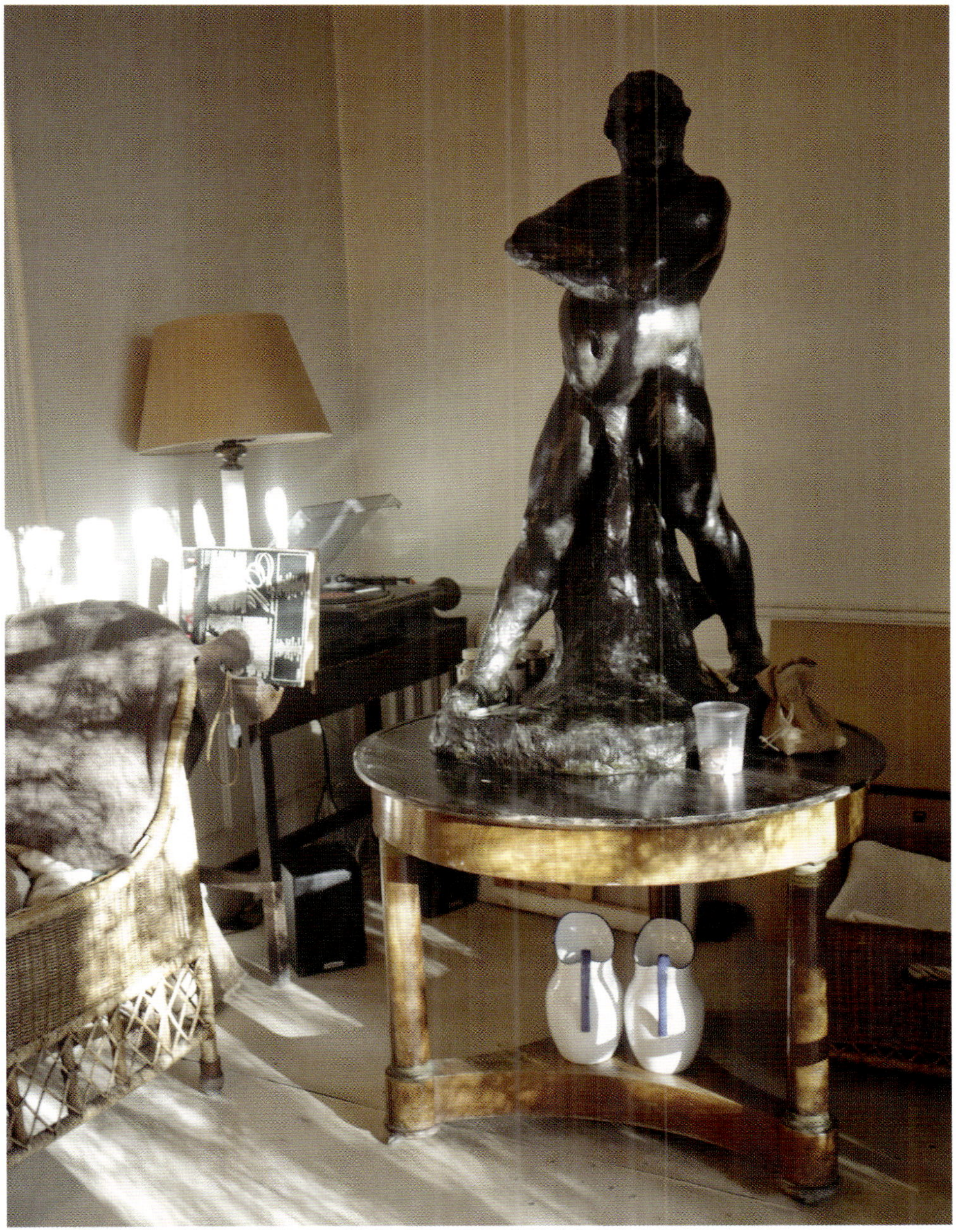

Above: Interior of Lucian Freud's studio with Rodin's bronze *Naked Balzac*.
Opposite: Interior of Lucian Freud's studio with Francis Bacon's *Two Figures*.

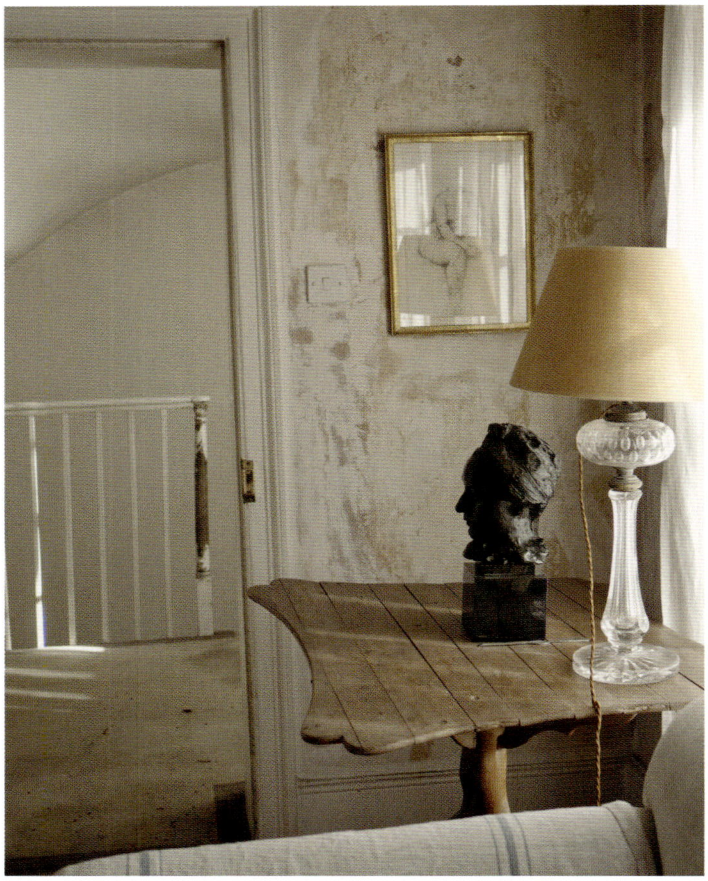

Above: The elegance of some areas of Freud's Kensington home contrasts with the messiness of how he worked (see opposite).

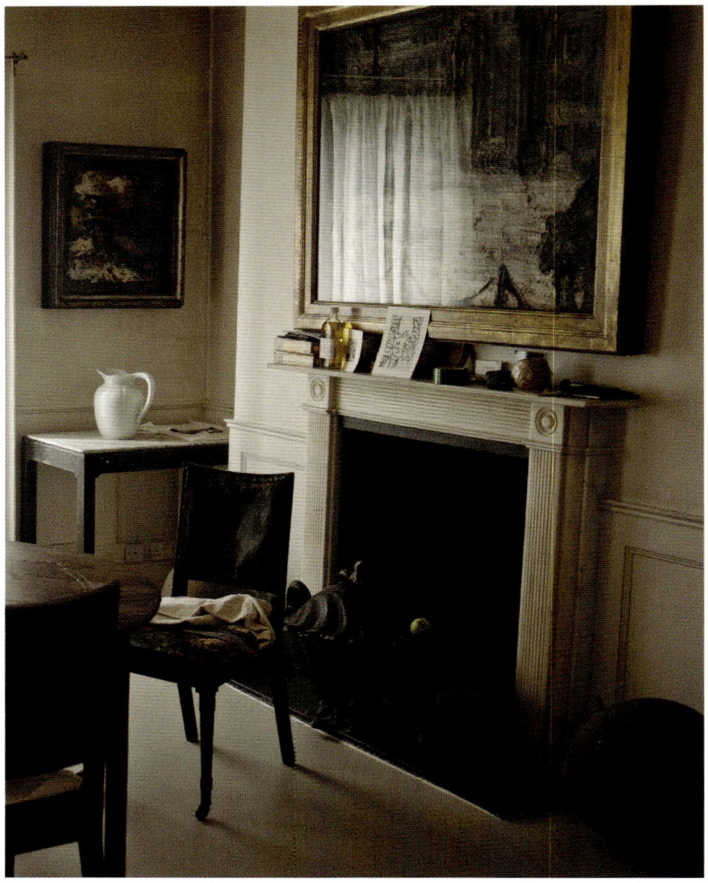

Above: A refined fireplace surrounded by art everywhere – by Freud's friends and other artists he admired.

musicians. Named after Kensington's original church of St Mary Abbots, Kensington Church Street runs north to south from Notting Hill Gate to Kensington High Street, and it was there that Freud lived for almost four decades.

His house and studio were in a tall brown-brick-fronted building that was refitted almost a century after it was constructed, in 1820–30, and probably also in the later nineteenth century, but Freud liked the house as soon as he saw it, as many of its original features remained. These included large sash windows, mouldings adorning the ceilings, roundel fireplaces, candelabras and wide panelled doors. Freud changed little. He stripped back the walls to reveal their original lime plaster, and he turned the garden into an additional studio accessed by a wooden deck, surrounded by bamboo and bay trees.

His main studio extended over two areas on the first floor. He used one for painting under natural light and the other for painting with artificial light. There he kept many props, easels, brushes, paints and rags. He painted the walls brown umber and kept them bare, although he used them to write reminders to himself, and often smeared them and the door frames with paint scrapings. His assistant, David Dawson, recalls: 'Lucian was very particular about his props. He'd scour second-hand shops for just the right piece, but once he tired of them, they'd live out their retirement in the drawing-room.'

In later life, he slept with his dog, a pile of books by his bed – including art books and novels by Balzac and Proust – and a garden spade, in case of intruders. He decorated the walls of the house with works of art, including paintings by his friends, Bacon and Frank Auerbach, and also works by John Constable, Jean-Baptiste-Camille Corot and Rodin. Antique furniture and objects were carefully chosen, and curiously timeless. He chose flowers for the house that appealed to his neutral palette, most often white blooms, including narcissus and stocks. The windows were hung with pleated voile curtains that admitted light but prevented him being overlooked by passers-by.

Each morning, he and Dawson would breakfast and lunch in Clarke's, a restaurant a few doors down from the house, owned by chef Sally Clarke, who sat for several portraits. In the afternoon, after a morning's work, Freud would usually have a nap, then begin working again from around 6pm, and from then he worked into the early hours of the morning.

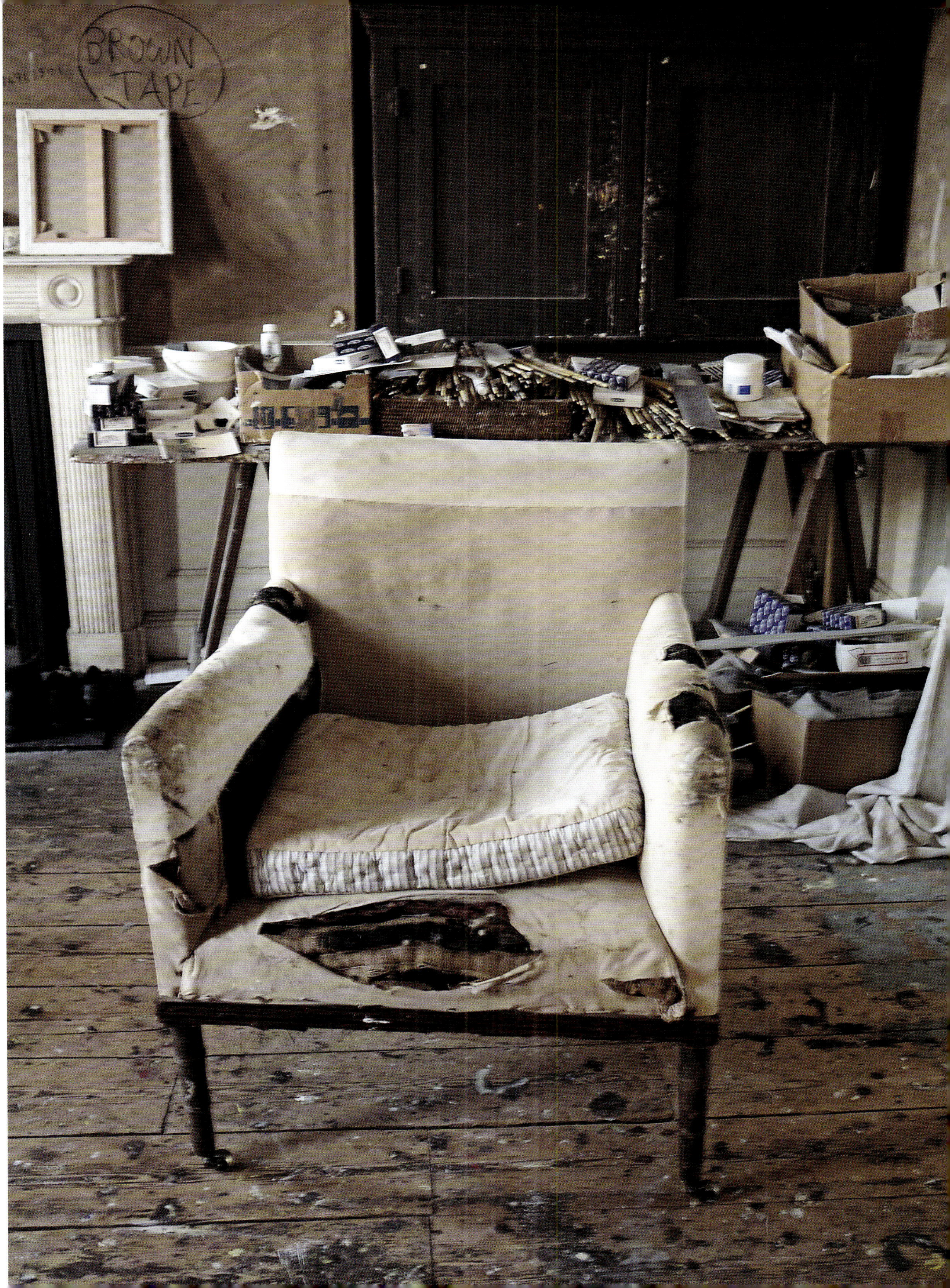
BROWN
TAPE

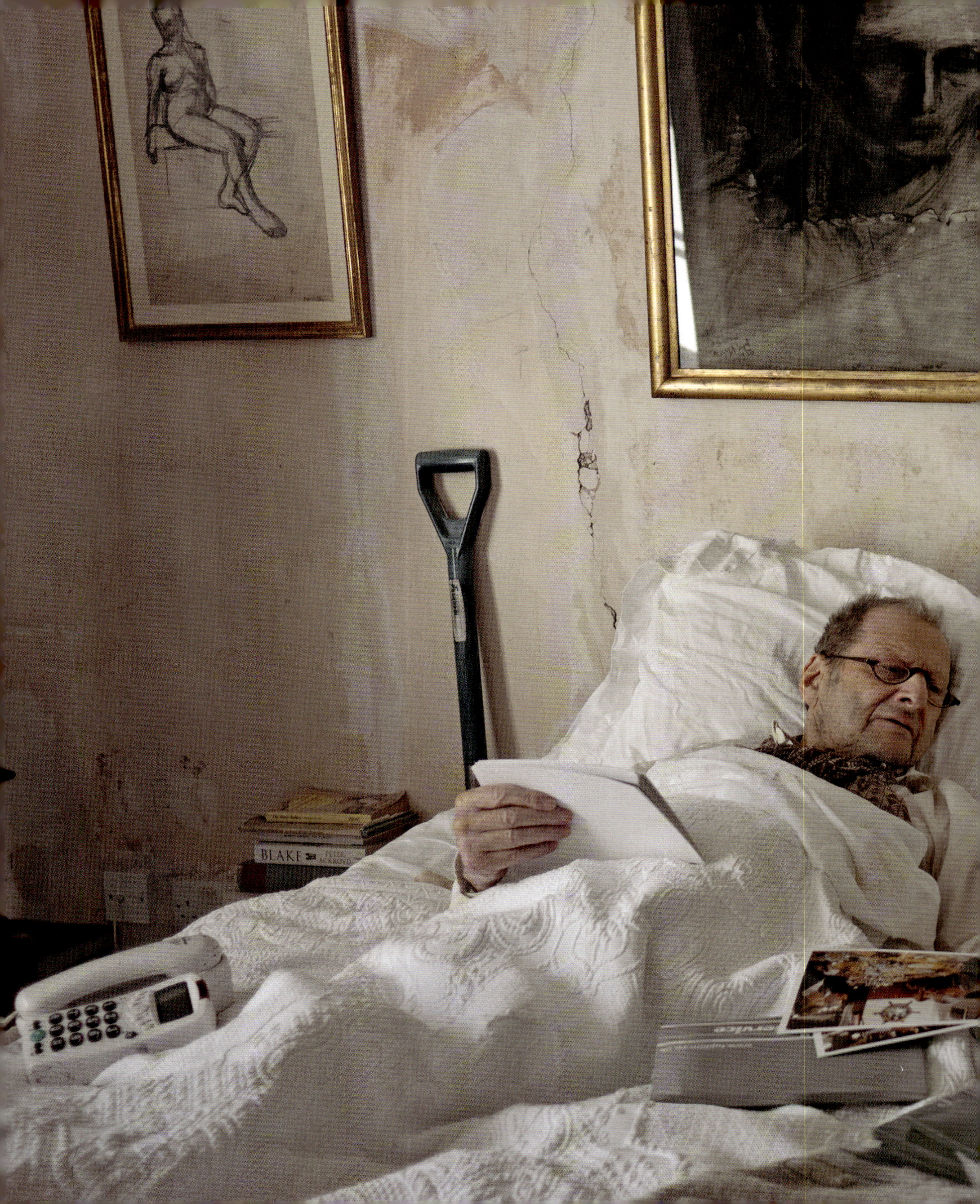
BLAKE
PETER ACKROYD

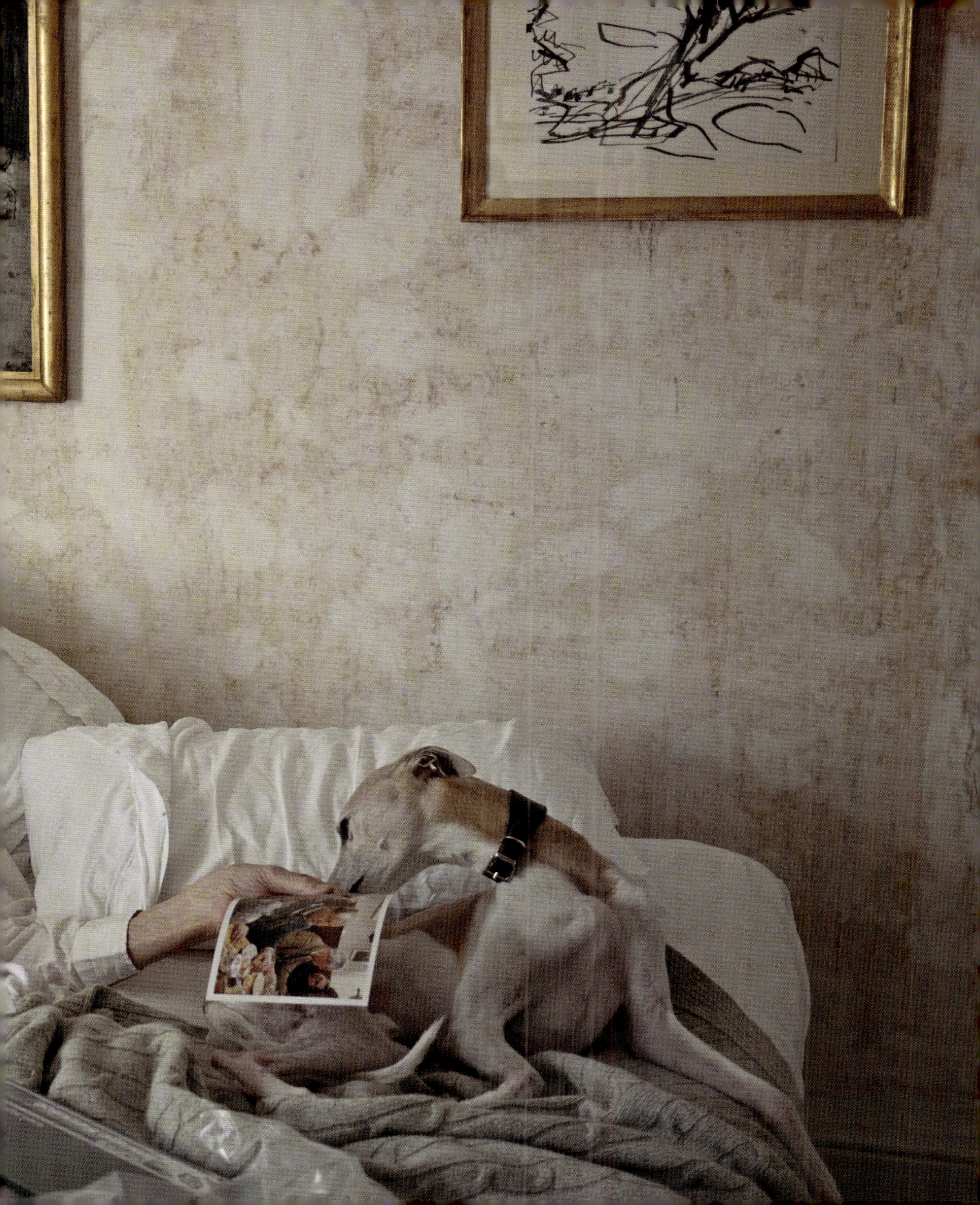

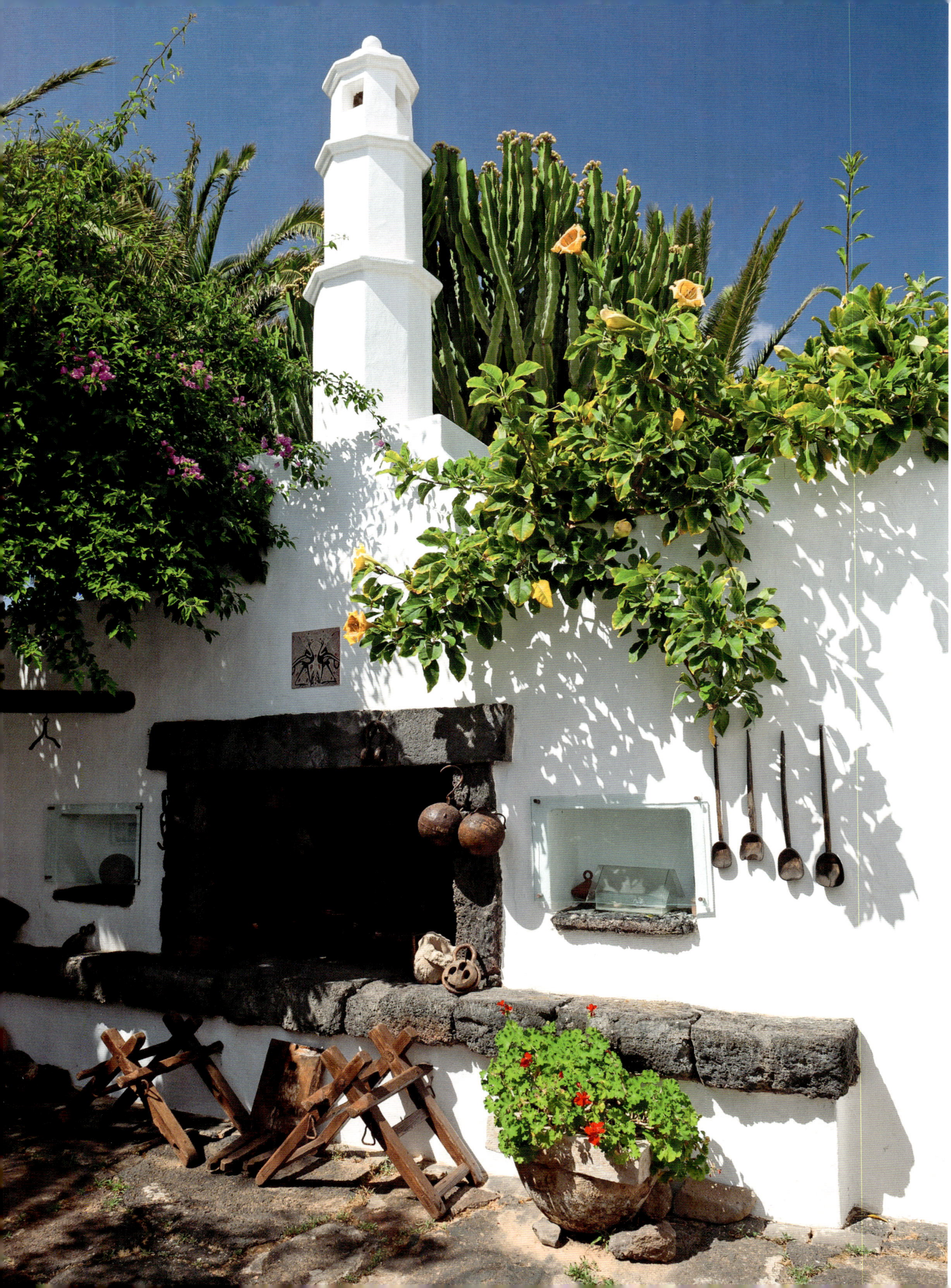

CÉSAR MANRIQUE

Haría, Lanzarote

In 1986, artist, sculptor, architect and environmentalist César Manrique (1919–92) built a mainly subterranean house in a palm grove in the village of Haría, on his native Lanzarote. He lived and worked there until his death.

Situated in a valley of the same name, Haría is the greenest part of Lanzarote, one of the Canary Islands. Because of its lush vegetation, Haría is often called the Valley of 1,000 Palms. It was formed by the eruption of three volcanoes between 1730 and 1736: La Atalaya, Los Helechos and La Corona. By the time Manrique designed and built his home there, he had spent years working as an artist and environmental activist, particularly focusing on protecting his beloved Lanzarote.

ART, ARCHITECTURE AND NATURE

A few minutes before his twin sister, Manrique was born in Arrecife, on Lanzarote, not long after World War One had ended. As the Canary Islands are part of Spain, in 1936 at the age of seventeen he was involved with the Spanish Civil War. After that, he studied architecture at the University of La Laguna on Tenerife, but he left within two years. With no formal artistic education, he began painting and exhibiting in Arrecife and in Las Palmas on Gran Canaria, and soon after World War Two ended, when he was twenty-six, he received a scholarship for the Real Academia de Bellas Artes de San Fernando (the Royal Academy of Fine Arts of San Fernando) in Madrid.

Manrique spent three years studying art there, gaining a degree in both painting and teaching art. He exhibited his work all over Spain. Then in 1964, invited by the governor of New York Nelson Rockefeller, who had bought some of his work, he moved to New York City for two years. When he returned to Lanzarote, tourism was beginning to increase and, aiming to ensure that any negative impact of the leisure industry would be minimal, Manrique worked closely with Lanzarote's council. As the president of the council Pepín Ramírez was also a family friend, Manrique successfully lobbied for legislation to be passed on the island to ban high-rise hotels, apartments and advertising hoardings, and for electricity pylons to be submerged away from sight. He also actively encouraged sustainable tourist developments and, through his tireless campaigning, he had a major influence on the planning regulations on Lanzarote. Largely because of him, the island remains picturesque, with many traditional features. At his insistence, all new houses had to be simple, low and whitewashed, with woodwork painted brown or green. Closer to the coast, doors and windows were painted blue.

In addition to his campaigning for Lanzarote, Manrique designed several buildings and other architectural projects there, always seeking to convey harmony between nature and humanity. In 1968, commissioned by the council, he created Jameos del Agua, an art and cultural centre that incorporates huge tunnels and bubbles of volcanic rock. *Jameos* are caves or lava bubbles that open to the sky, caused by previous volcanic eruptions. At the centre of Jameos del Agua is a natural auditorium, a museum, a science hub and a restaurant with a terrace beside a garden of palm trees surrounding an artificial lake. Next, Manrique designed Mirador del Río: a restaurant camouflaged on the Risco de Famara – a huge cliff that hugs the western coast of Lanzarote. Almost 500 metres (1,640 feet) above sea level, with several terraces and huge windows, it gives diners a panoramic view of El Río, a narrow stretch of sea separating Lanzarote from La Graciosa and the group of islets that are part of the Chinijo Islands

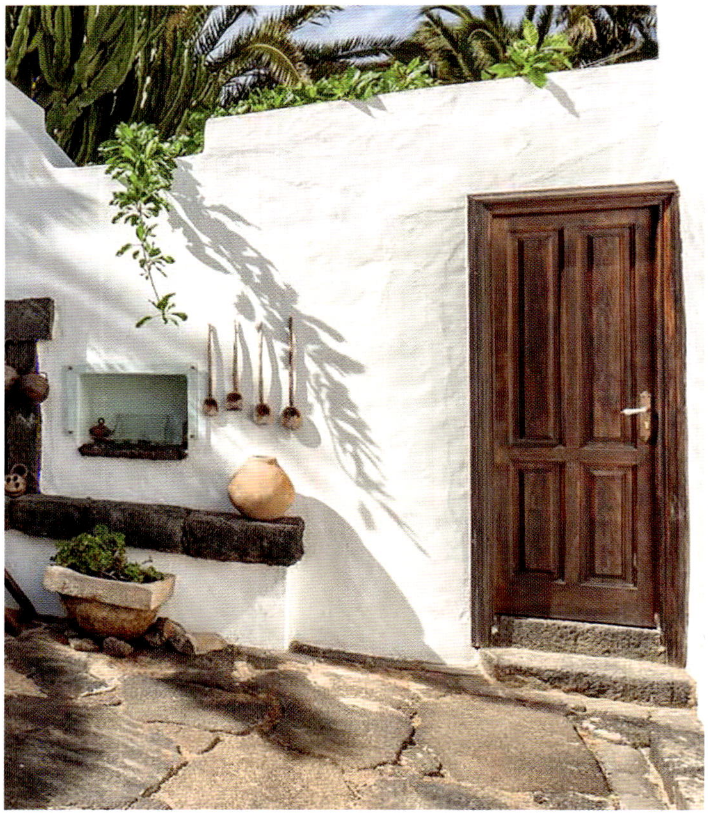

Above: The entrance to Manrique's home in Lanzarote, the site of several volcanic eruptions.

National Park. The building was dug out of the cliff and covered with volcanic rock to appear inconspicuous and part of the natural surroundings.

Also in the 1970s, Manrique designed a cactus garden in the village of Guatiza. Not built until 1989 and officially inaugurated two years later, the Jardín de Cactus is a botanical garden comprising 7,000 plants, including over 1,000 cacti species from around the world. Close by the entrance is a huge metal cactus sculpture and, inside, the garden itself is a grand circular space, with winding paths between all the plants. Built with hand-carved basalt stones laid out on terraces, it resembles a Roman amphitheatre, with a small pond and shop in the centre.

INTERNATIONAL FAME

In 1974, Manrique collaborated with the Spanish architect Fernando Higueras on a book called *Architecture Unpublished*. In 1978, he was awarded the 'Weltpreis für Ökologie und Tourismus' (World Prize for Ecology and Tourism awarded by Germany). In 1990, he created a BMW Art Car with the German designer and artist Walter Maurer, which made him well-known beyond Lanzarote.

While Manrique was working on the majority of his architectural designs during the 1970s, he also planned a special home for himself. Adhering to his aesthetic principle of 'art-nature/nature-art', he wanted his home to be integrated into the surroundings. He bought a large area of disused farmland with a derelict farmhouse in the village of Haría. As the site of several volcanic eruptions, the land features five *jameos* and a palm grove. In 1986, he began building his home there, using aspects of the old farmhouse and also the *jameos* to create a predominantly subterranean building. Combining traditional architecture with modern functional elements, including wide staircases, picture windows and airy hallways, the building, named Taro de Tahiche, is filled with light. As he said: 'To be absolutely free to create without fear or formula heartens the soul and opens a path to the joy of living.' The house is approached by a formal courtyard of lush and simple plantings of cacti and succulents in varying shades of green, with wide, winding paths, a pool with a fountain, and a large mural on one wall. Made from broken ceramic tiles in a few bold colours, it depicts several bulls in a style reminiscent of the work of Picasso, who was one of Manrique's close friends. The walls of the old farmhouse that are on show above ground are whitewashed, and anywhere that is painted is whitewashed with black outlines. Nowhere is more than two storeys high.

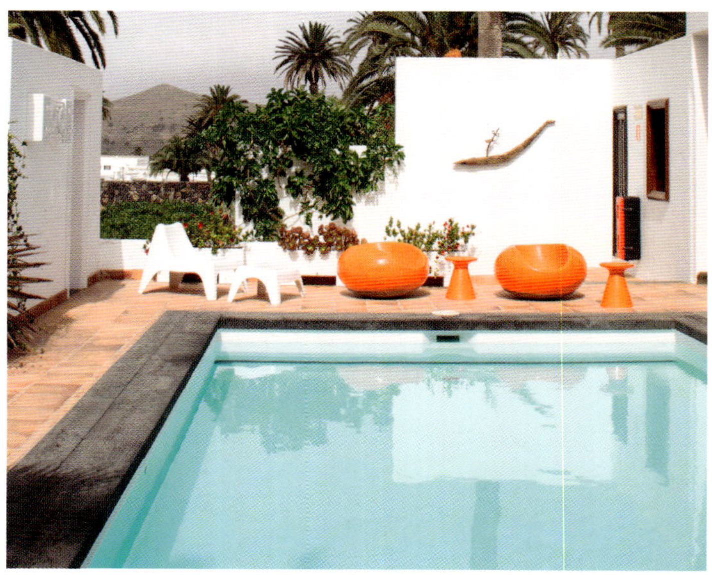

Opposite: Using aspects of the previous farmhouse, Manrique made much of his modern subterranean home that is nonetheless filled with light.

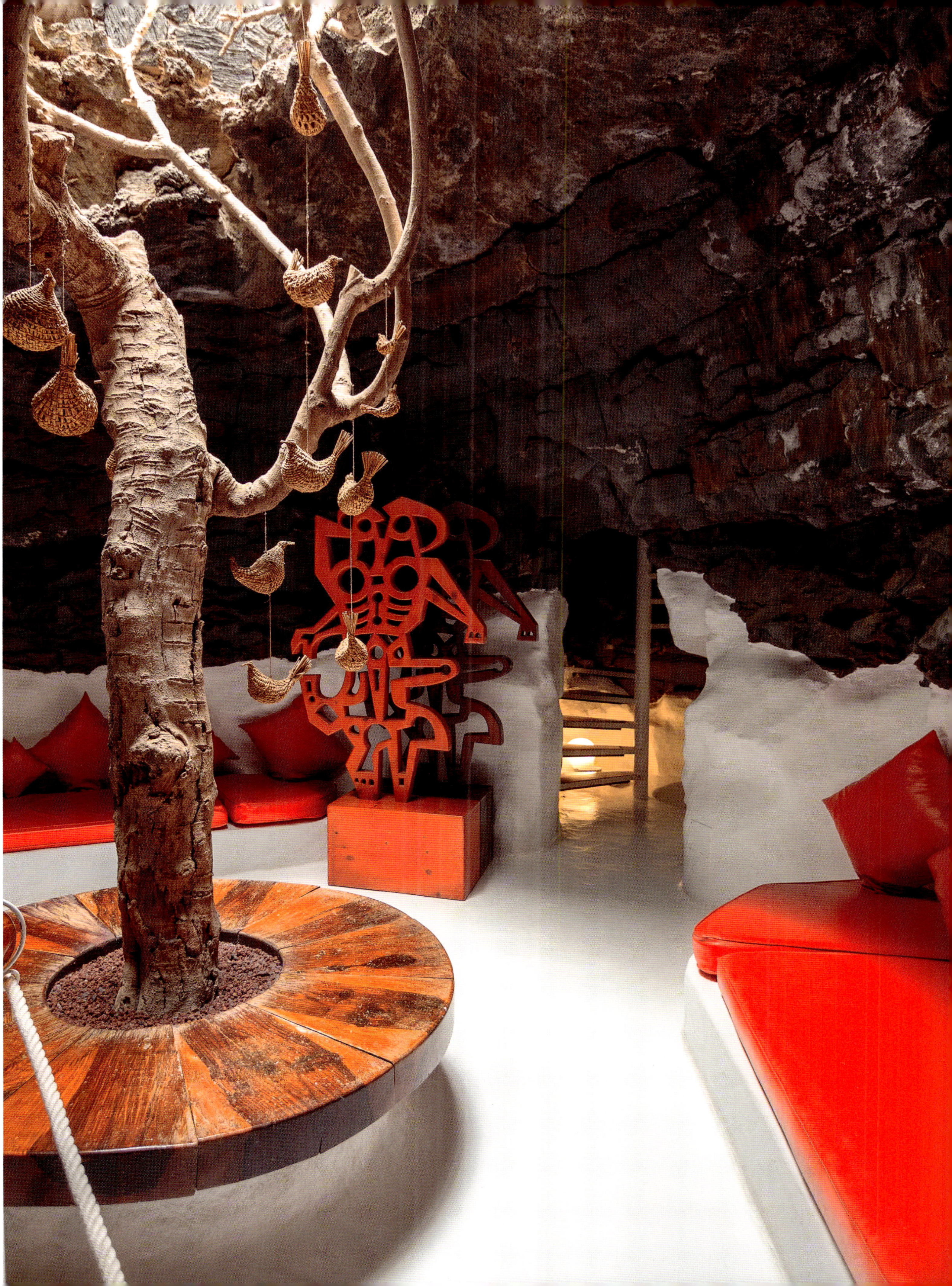

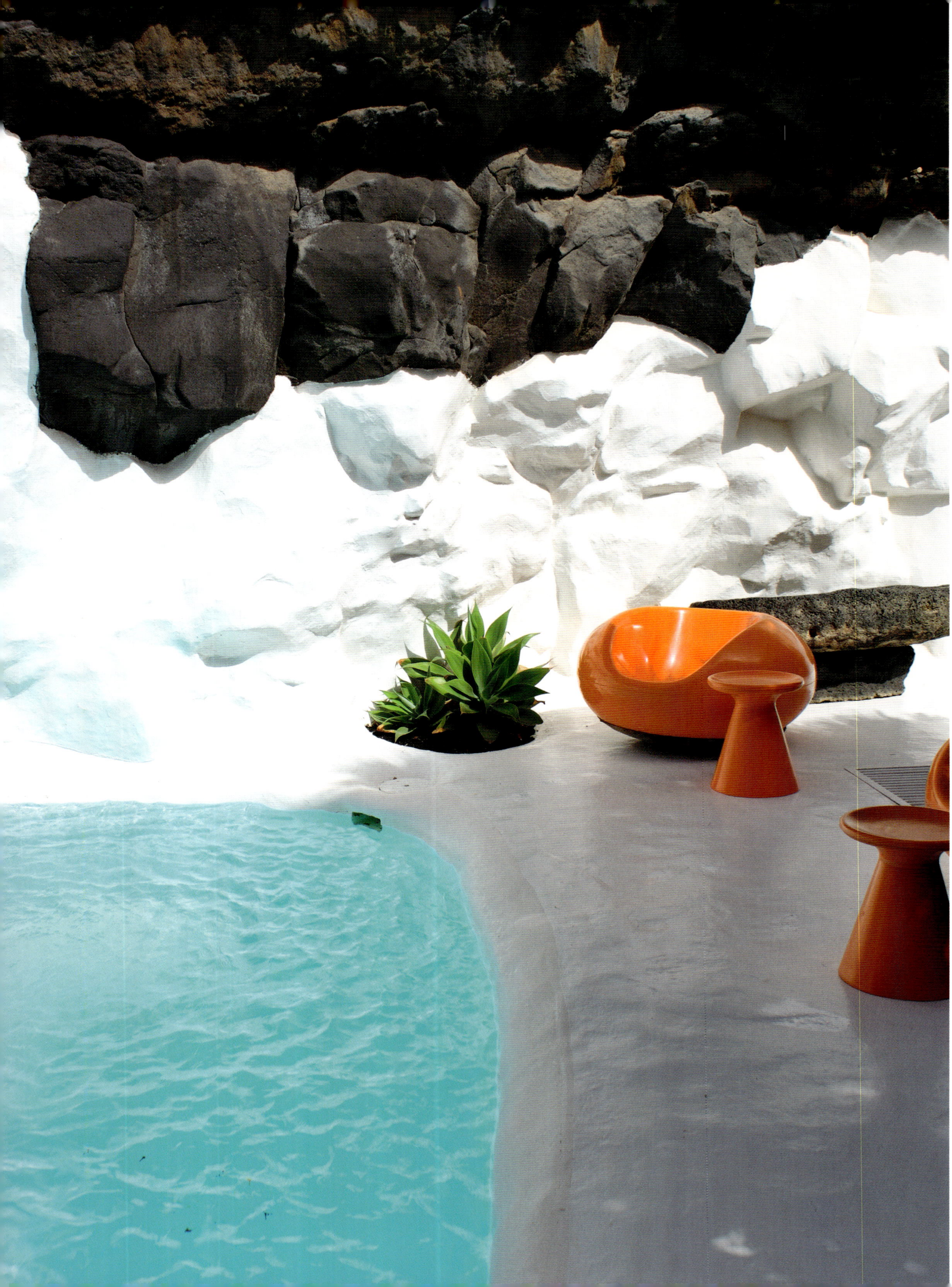

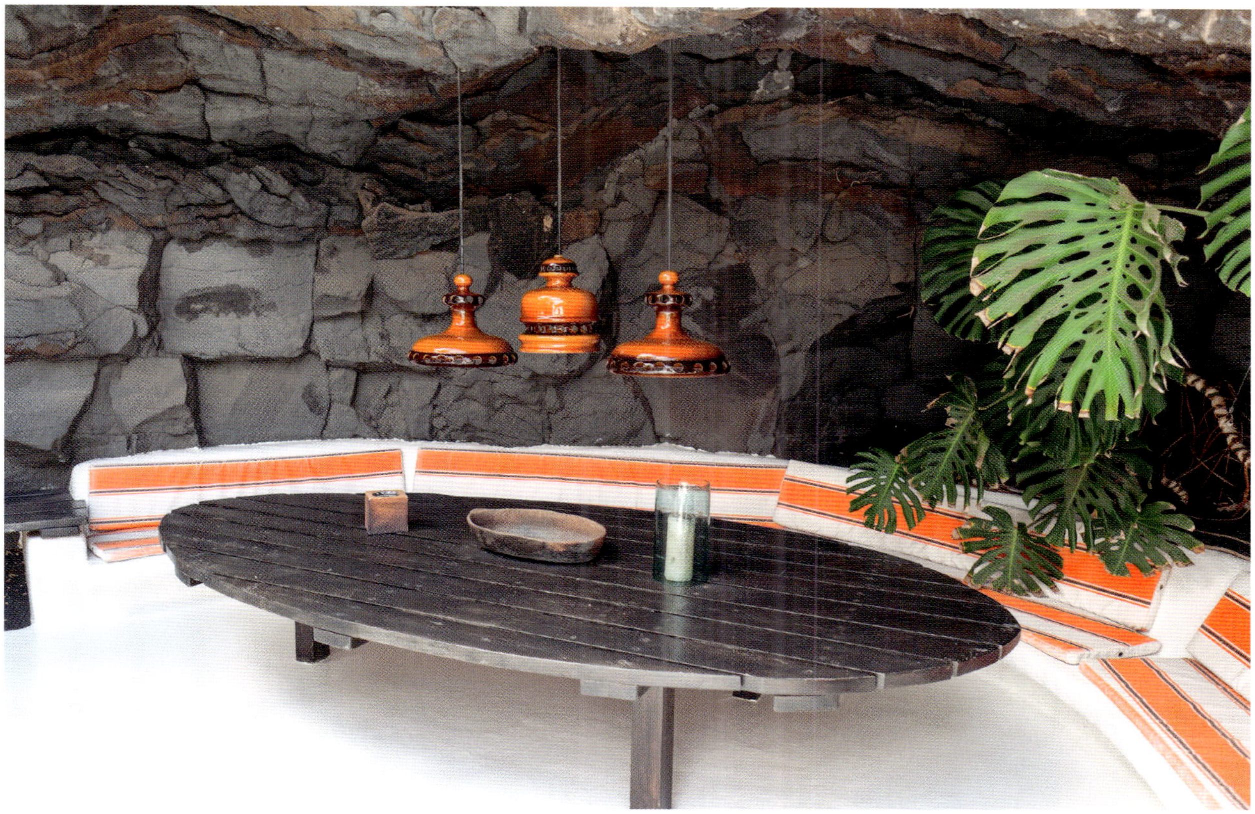

Above: Every aspect of Manrique's home has been built sympathetically within the natural rock formations.

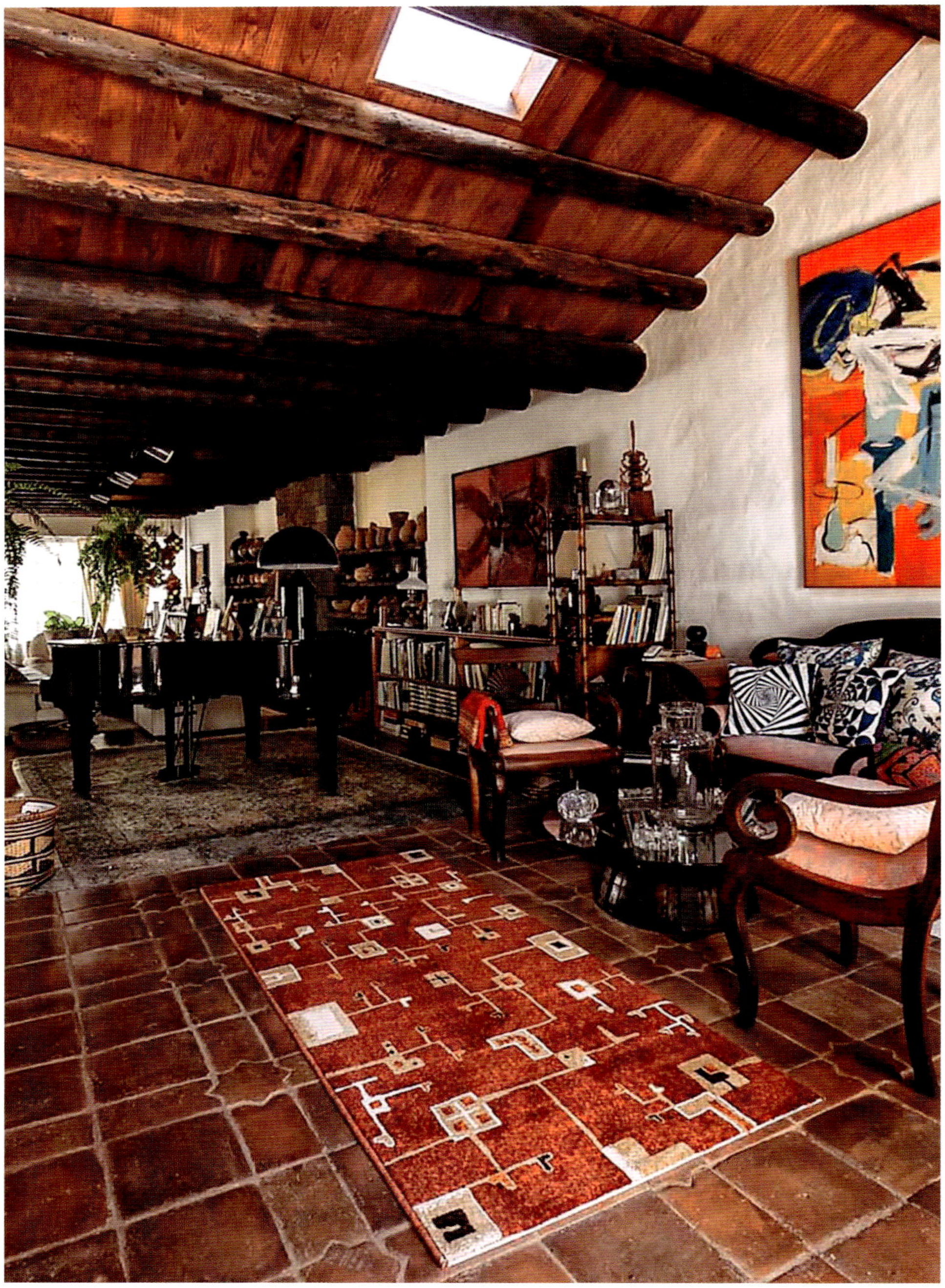

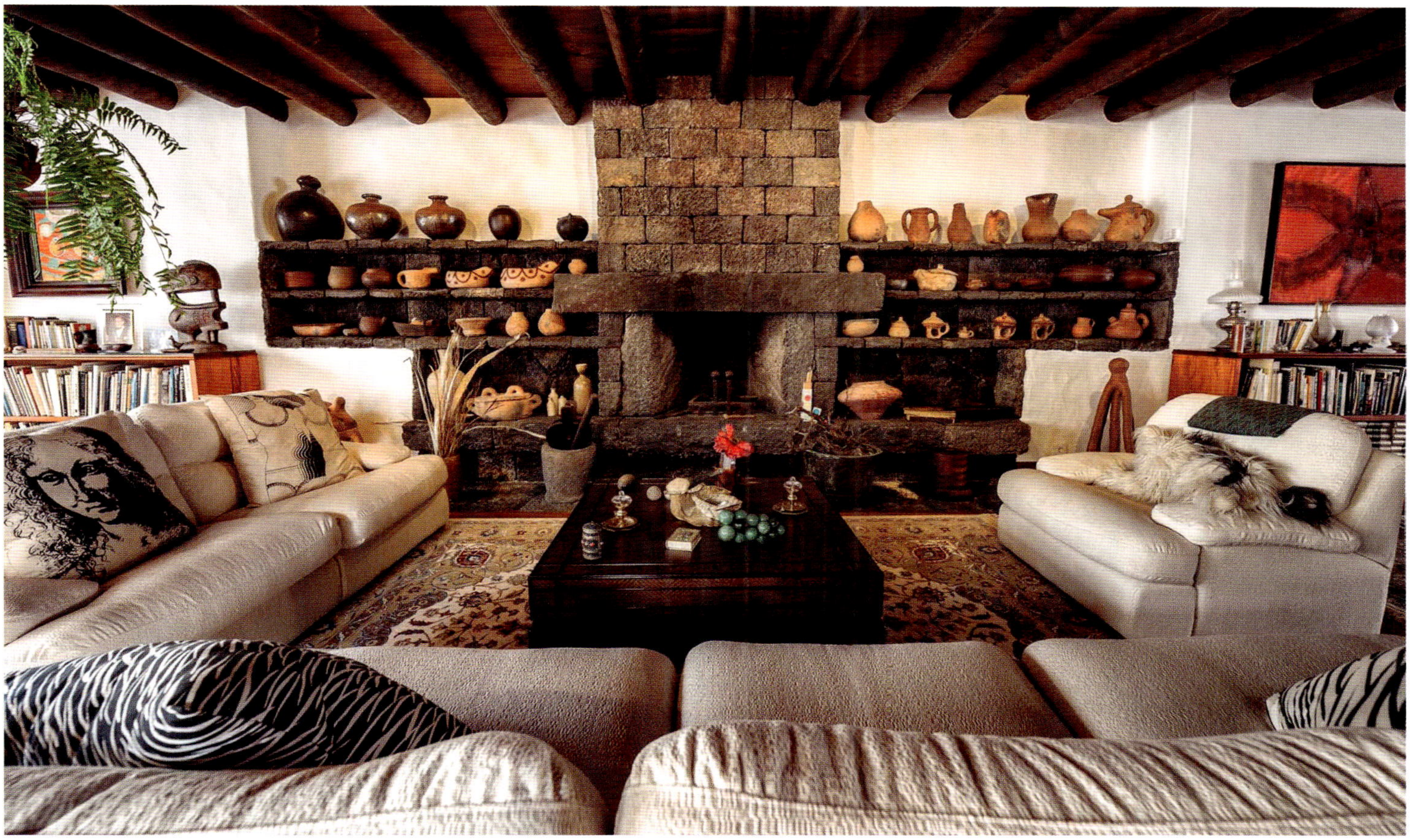

Above and opposite: Featuring a piano and a stone fireplace, the lounge has a low beamed ceiling.

Using the five natural *jameos*, most of the home is made of volcanic rock and sprawls beneath ground level, connected by narrow passageways bored into the lava, with glass-domed roofs. The central cave includes a relaxation area with a swimming pool, a barbecue and a small dance floor. Other caves include a living room, a bathroom and Manrique's bedroom. Above ground are a kitchen and a guest room, plus Manrique's studio, and everywhere are plants that convey his belief in the need to balance the man-made world with nature. For example, palm and fig trees grow from the lower rooms through holes in the lava roofs, and a sunken garden is situated between two of the *jameos*. The whitewashed building of his studio is flooded with natural light from the large windows, overlooking his 'back garden' of the lava field that descended from Mount Maneje during its eruption in the 1730s. He worked there every day, painting his abstract works and planning a series of kinetic sculptures that he called *Wind Toys*, inspired by the wooden windmills that once dominated the rural landscape, and his principal belief of the synergy between humans and nature. He lived as naturally as possible, never drinking alcohol, not smoking and not allowing others to smoke next to him. He usually went to bed early and rose at dawn. For the creation of his projects for Lanzarote, including Jameos del Agua and the Jardín de Cactus, he took no payment. Sadly, he was killed in a tragic car accident close to his home in Arrecife in 1992.

'For me, Lanzarote is the most beautiful place in the world.'

César Manrique

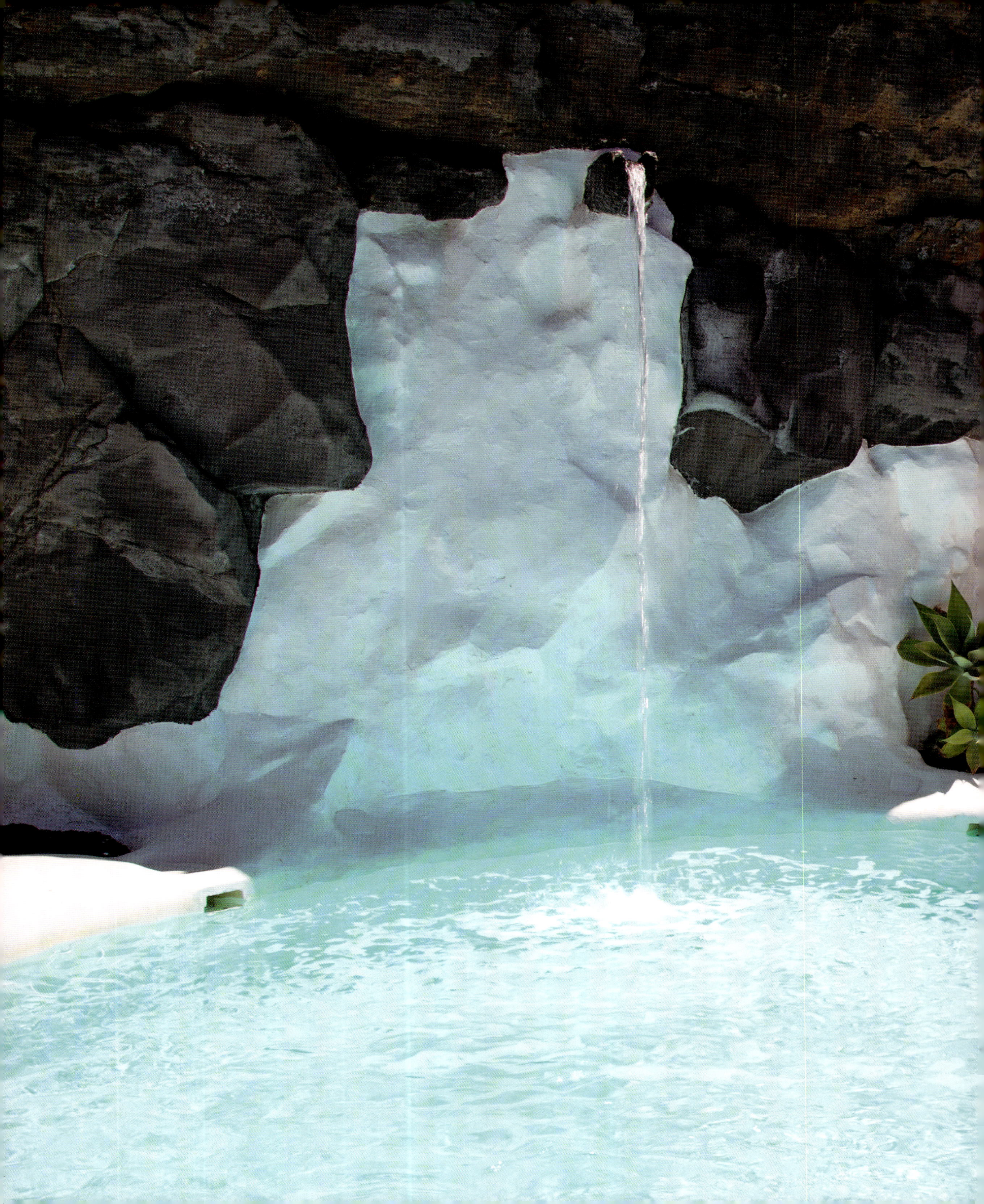

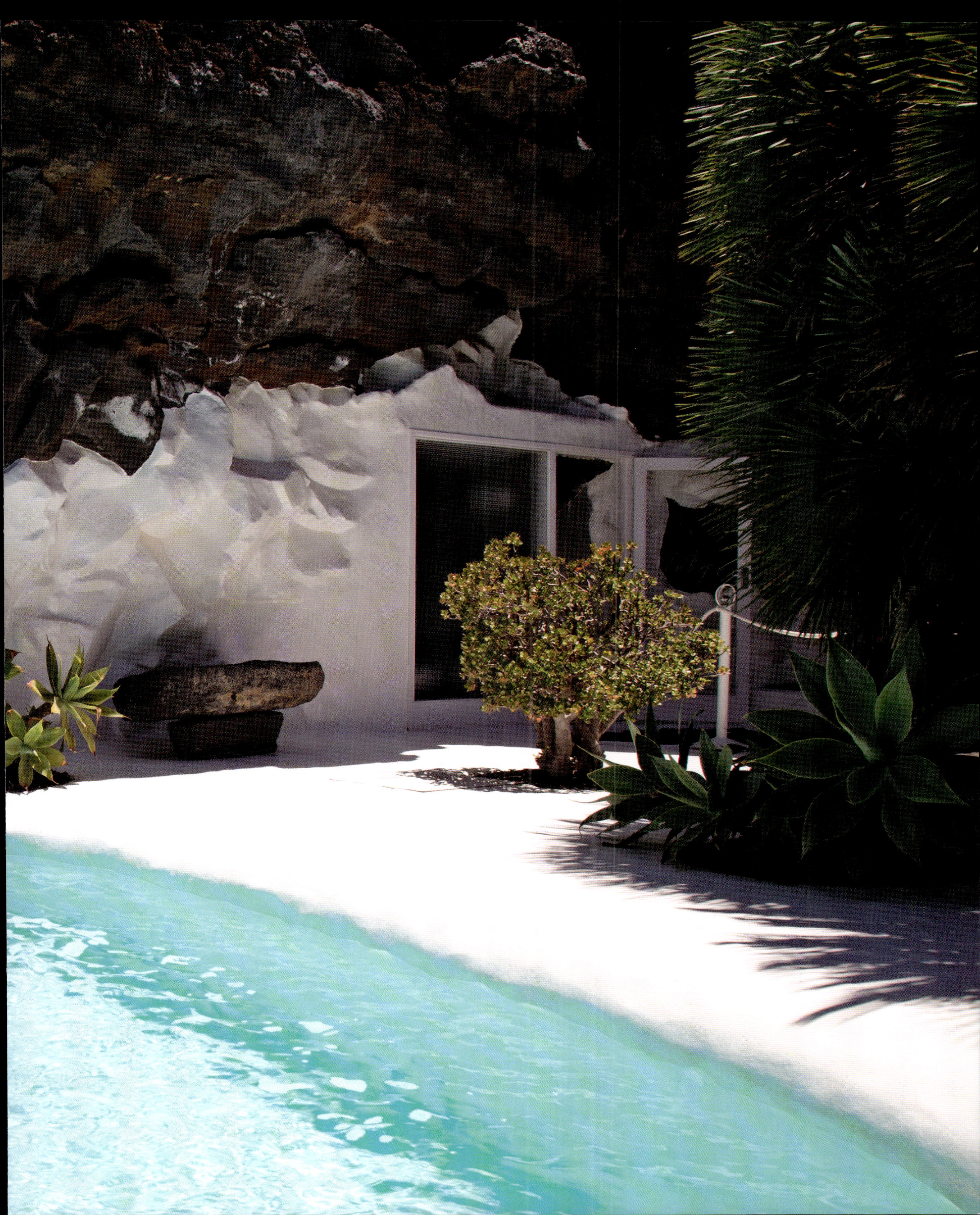

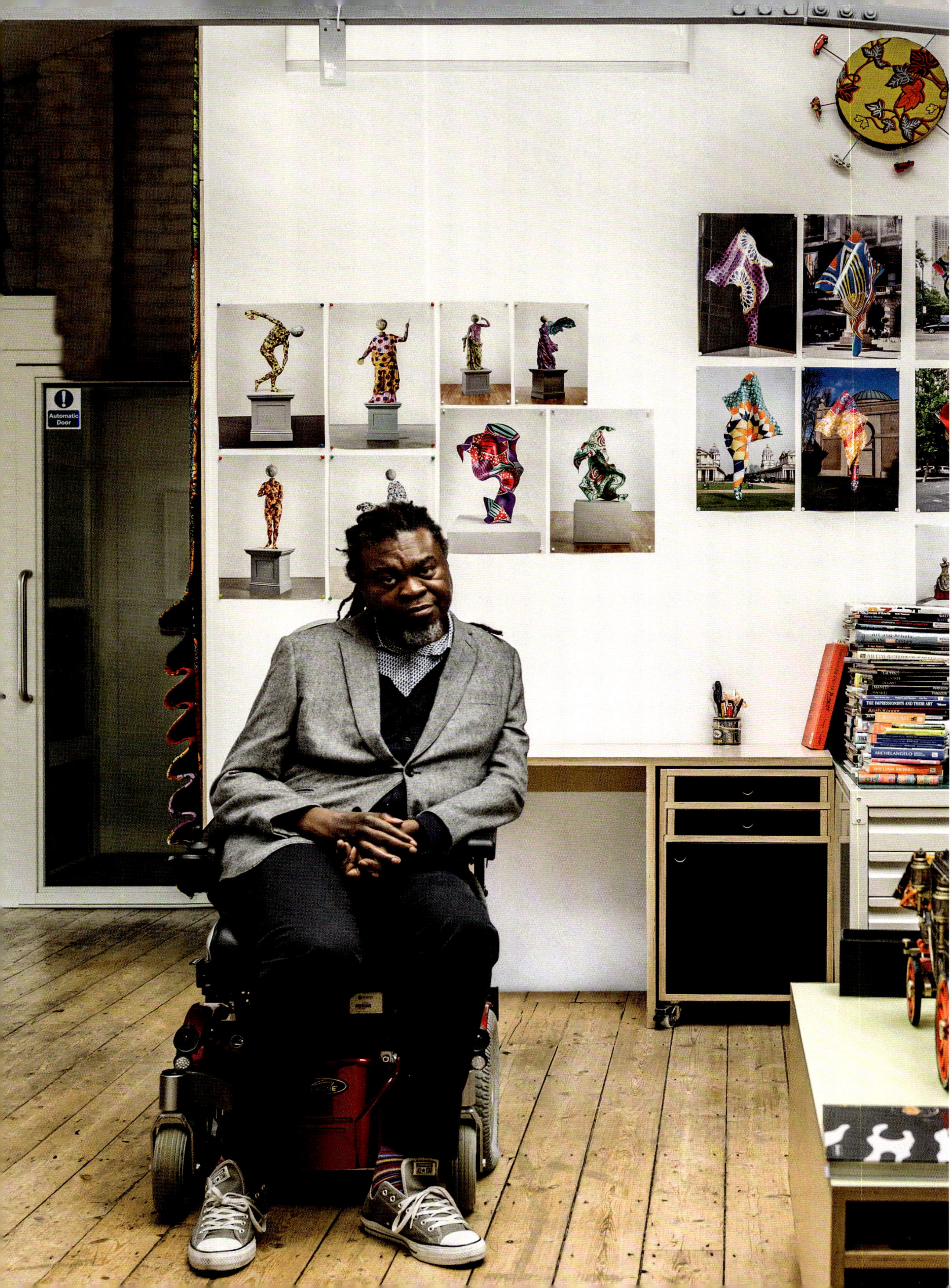
Automatic Door
Art and Artists
MANET
THE IMPRESSIONISTS AND THEIR ART
Anish Kapoor
MICHELANGELO
WILLIAM MORRIS

YINKA SHONIBARE

London, UK

One of the Young British Artists of the 1990s, Yinka Shonibare (b.1962) was shortlisted for the prestigious Turner Prize in 2004. Currently, he lives and works in East London; an area that was deprived and downtrodden when he first moved in, but has now been gentrified. He has another studio in Peckham, south-east London – a place he calls 'the dirty studio', as he uses it for his messiest work.

In 2016, Shonibare reflected: 'I'm interested in where people come from. I can't be defined without the British-colonial experience of my birth and background. I don't exist without it.'

'A MULTIPLICITY OF IDENTITIES'

Born in Britain to Nigerian parents, Shonibare moved with his family to Lagos in Nigeria when he was three years old. His father, Olatunji, was a corporate lawyer, and his mother Laide looked after Yinka and his three siblings. He was taught by Irish nuns, and although he is no longer attached to any religion, he says: 'Catholicism stays with you – the concept, if not the reality, of guilt and shame.' When he was fourteen, Shonibare travelled with his family to Rome, where he visited the Sistine Chapel and drew the Coliseum. The trip had a huge impact on him. Growing up, he travelled back and forth between London and Lagos, and at seventeen, he returned to Britain more permanently to take A Levels. He then enrolled at Wimbledon College of Art for the art foundation course, but within three weeks of starting, he contracted the rare illness of transverse myelitis and was in a coma for a fortnight. His spinal cord was permanently affected, and he was paralysed from the neck down.

Eventually, Shonibare gained some movement on one side and returned to art school, firstly studying at Byam Shaw School of Art (now Central Saint Martins) and then at Goldsmiths, both in London. Initially, he worked as a development officer for an organisation that makes art accessible to disabled people, but he also began working as an artist; this was a time when exhibitions were often held in disused warehouses, and it was at this time that the businessman and art patron Charles Saatchi bought his early work. In 1997, he came to prominence after his art was included in the Royal Academy's controversial exhibition *Sensation*. Then followed several eminent commissions, an MBE (Most Excellent Order of the British Empire) in 2004, an Honorary Doctorate (Fine Artist) of the Royal College of Art in 2010, election as Royal Academician in 2013, and in 2019 a CBE (Commander of the Most Excellent Order of the British Empire). Just as he physically travels between continents, so his work expresses overlaps and the interweaving of cultures and eras. 'Ideas about a multiplicity of identities, global travel, trade, and migration have always interested me,' he says. 'My works are about ambivalence and nuance.'

Because of his disability, Shonibare now uses a wheelchair and works with the help of studio assistants. 'I was determined that the scope of my creativity should not be restricted purely by my physicality. It would be like an architect choosing to build only what could be physically built by hand.' Often borrowing art historical references from artists such as William Hogarth, Thomas Gainsborough and Jean-Honoré Fragonard, he works with sculpture, printmaking, installation and video, and also uses patterned batik fabrics that similarly draw on other references. These materials are inspired by prints designed in Indonesia, which was a Dutch colony until 1949. The prints are made in the Netherlands and have been used in West Africa since the nineteenth century, so they are now perceived by many as being traditionally West African. As well as their vibrant colours and

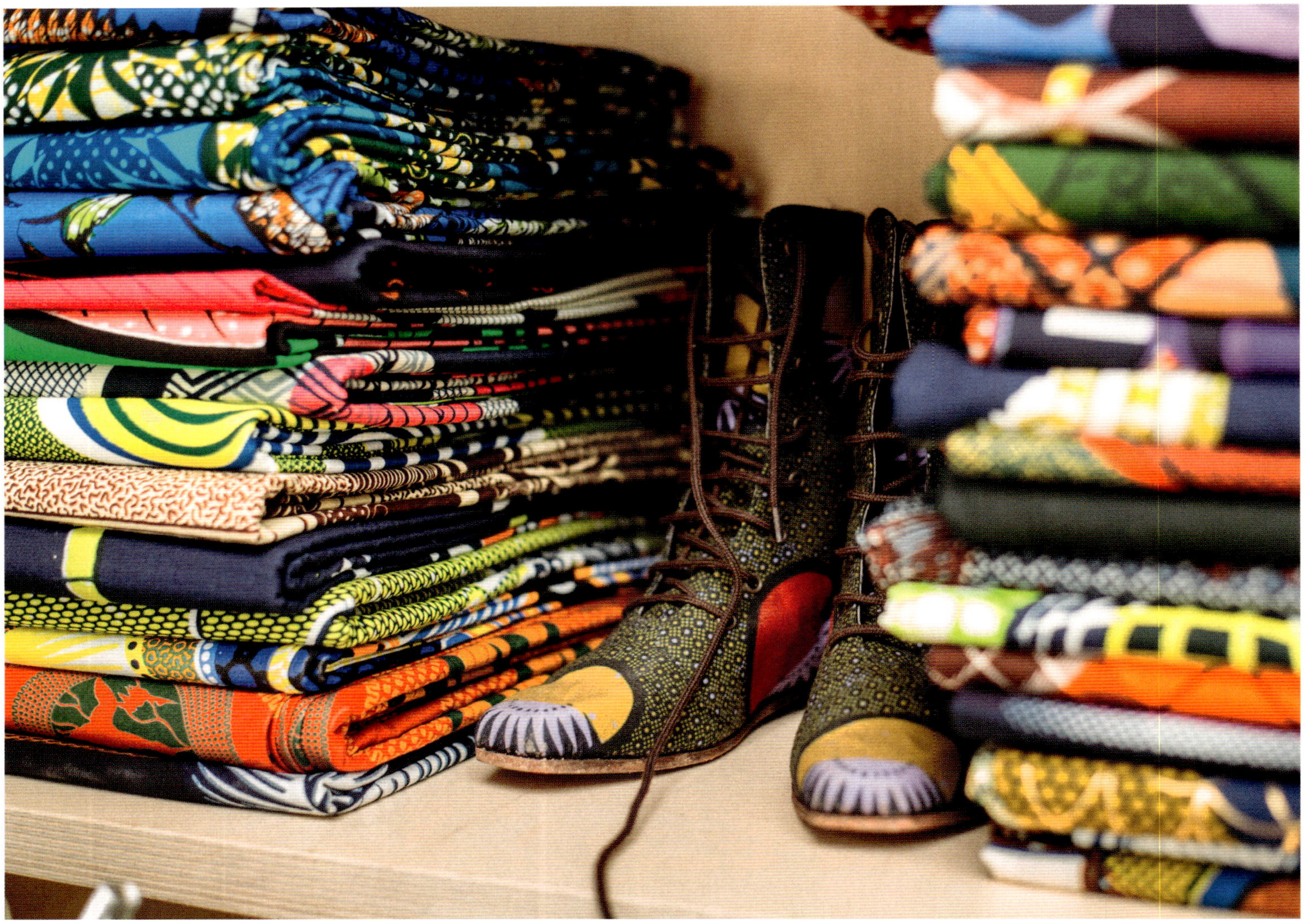

Above: Some of the patterned batik fabrics that Shonibare often uses, inspired by prints designed in Indonesia that have been used in West Africa since the 19th century.

patterns, the fabric suggests themes of cultural identity, post-colonialism and globalisation.

A SPACE FOR IDEAS

In 2008, Shonibare bought his studio on Regent's Canal in Hackney, East London. Previously, the building had been a carpet warehouse and he described the area at the time as being 'distinctly rough at the edges and slightly scary'. Now it has been regenerated. No longer dirty and rundown, it buzzes with life and colour: frequented by people of all ages and backgrounds, who enjoy strolling and cycling along the canal and sitting in the new artisan cafés.

When he moved into his studio, Shonibare instructed his architect to 'renovate it so that it is still like a warehouse and feels as if nothing has been done'. He duly opened up the roof with a large skylight so light floods in. He had the partition walls pulled down, the wooden floor sandblasted, the exposed brick repointed and other walls whitewashed. The airy first-floor space is where he develops most of his projects with his small team of assistants. It is also where he hosts supper parties for friends. There, he often also entertains other artists he does not know, as he explains: 'I wanted this space to be not just for me, but for others to try things out. So I have a proposal box outside the building where artists can post their ideas. The best ones get a residency in the studio for a month... it's quite a sociable space.' This idea, called *Guest Projects*, developed when he thought about how London has become too expensive for many artists to either live or work in, so he offers part of his home and the ground floor of his studio as a free exhibition space for other artists; they can work in any art form. Correspondingly, in 2021, he opened *Guest Artists Space Foundation* in two separate sites in Nigeria. This is an artist residency programme: one in Lekki, Lagos, and the other on a 54-acre farm in the Ijebu region. Shonibare says: 'What I'm doing is a drop in the ocean, but symbolically it's important. I'm using my art as a means of social change.'

'My biggest preoccupation is with the idea of universal humanism. We all influence each other.'

Yinka Shonibare

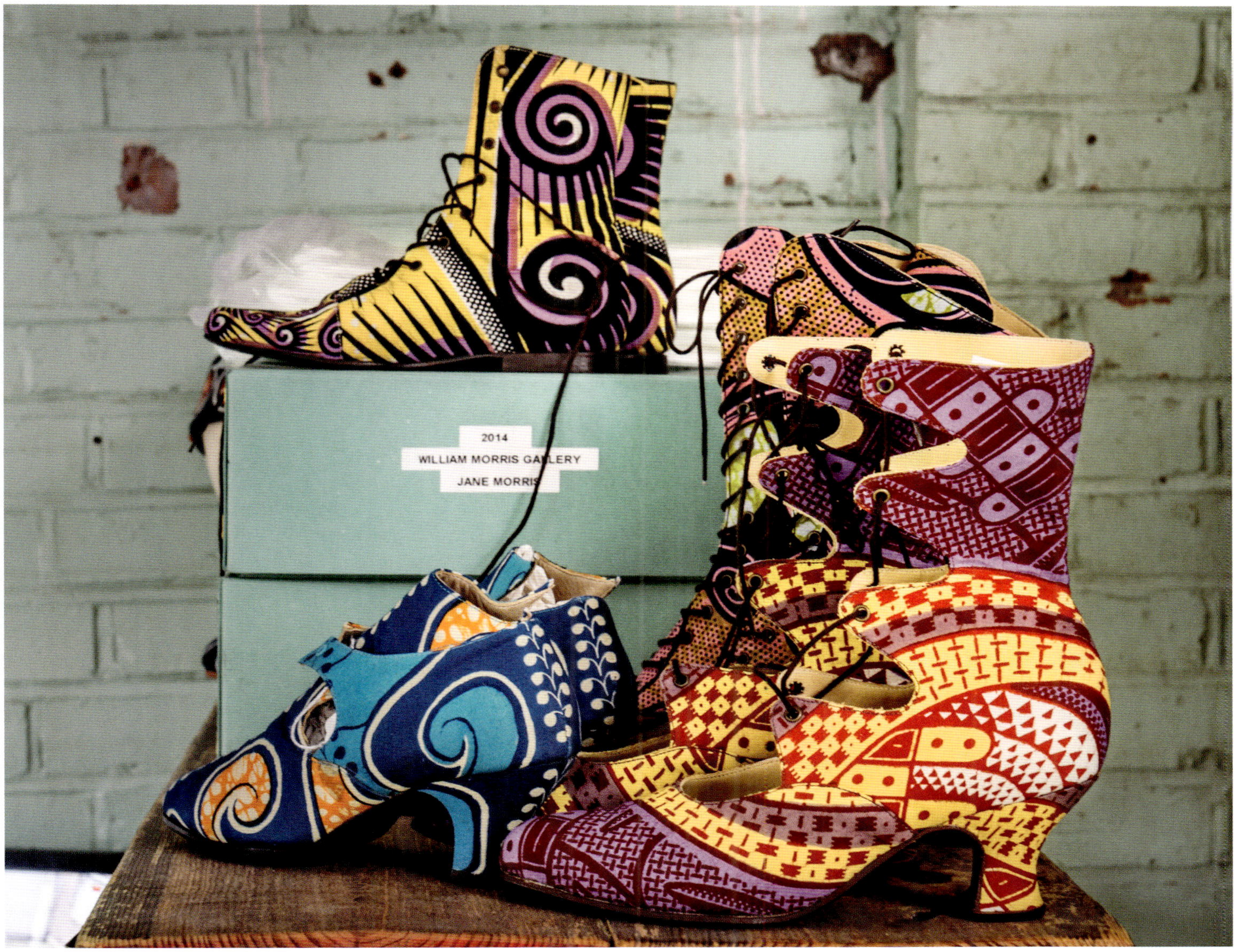

Above: More bright, bold patterns often used by Shonibare in his art, these reflect his keen interest in history.

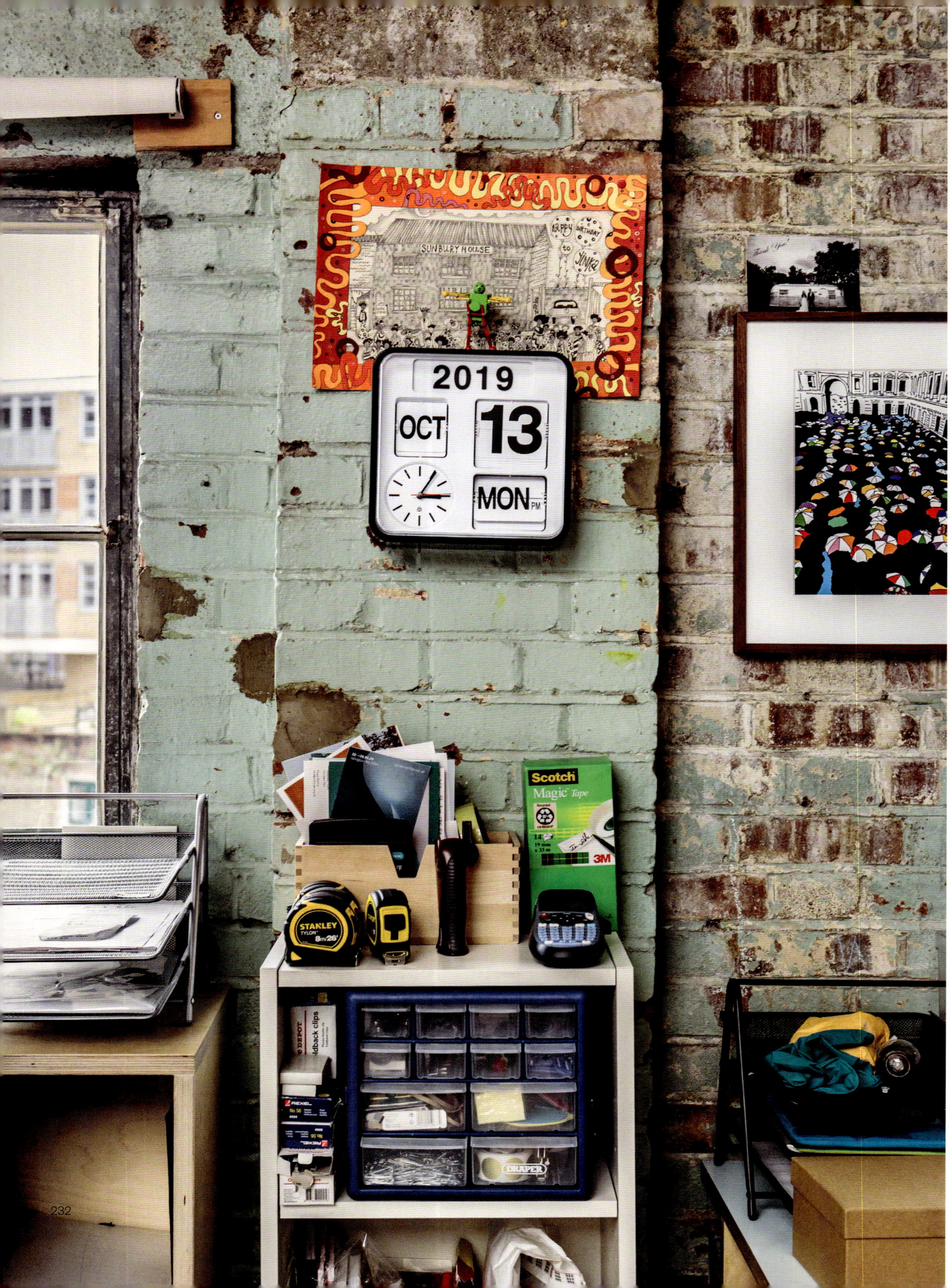
SUNBURY HOUSE
2019
OCT
13
MON
PM
Scotch
Magic Tape
3M
STANLEY
DRAPER

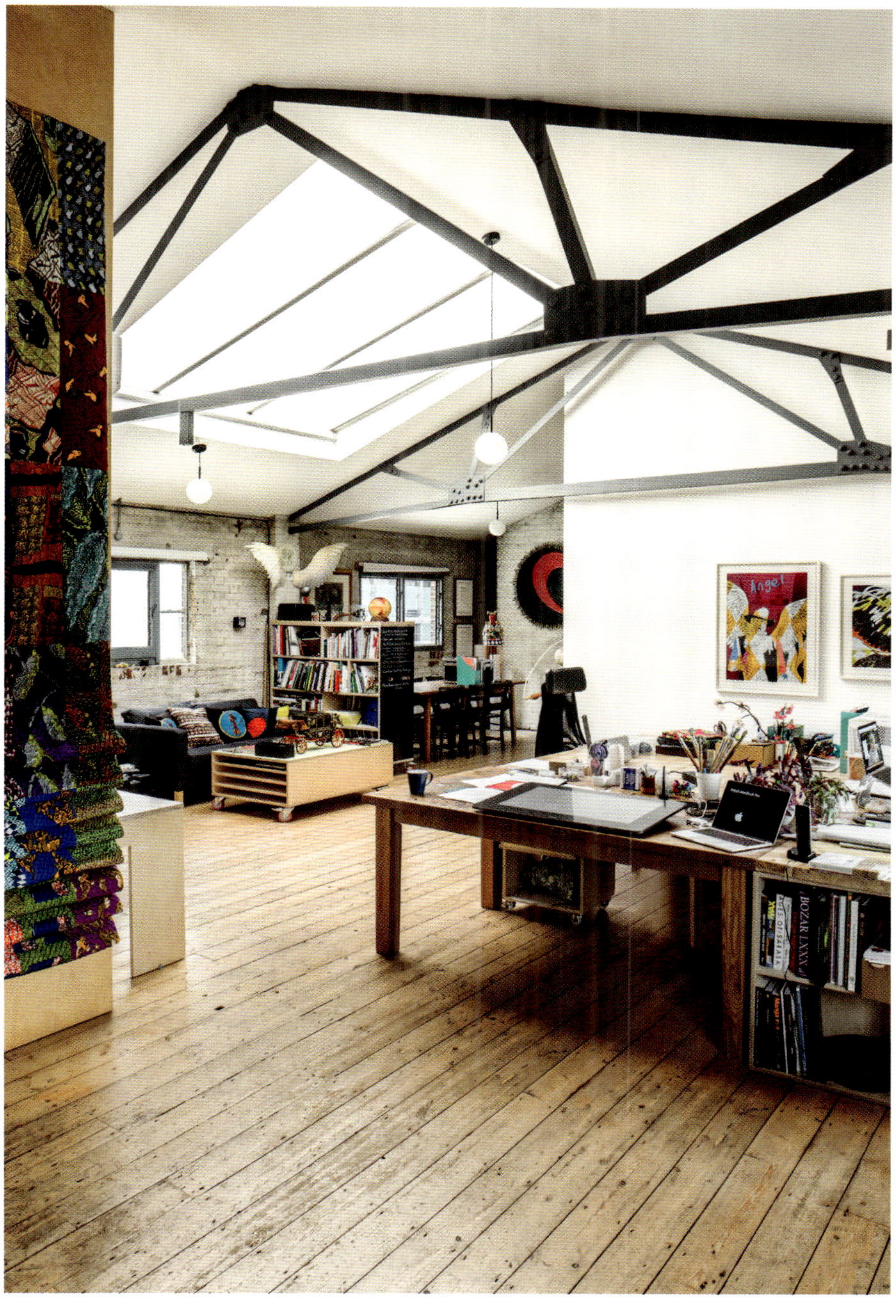

Above: The converted warehouse (now Shonibare's studio) is airy, with high ceilings and filled with natural light.

INDEX

F

G

H

I

J

K

L

M

N

O

P

R

S

T

U

V

W

Y

Z

ACKNOWLEDGEMENTS

This is my opportunity to thank the people who really made this book. Every image for each artist featured was expertly managed by the exceptionally professional, helpful, optimistic and constantly cheery Bella Skertchly, John Parton and Alice Graham. Thank you! Thank you too, to Mariana Sameiro, Daniela Nava, Joe Hallsworth, Lesley Malkin and Vanessa Bird. Making books is teamwork and you have been a brilliant team! Finally, of course, thank you to the artists included, for having such fascinating, diverse and creative homes.

PICTURE CREDITS

Arcaid Images / Alamy Stock Photo 6, 41, 104, 105, 108, 110–111; Fondation Claude Monet, the House and gardens of Claude Monet – Giverny 8, 70, 76–77, 80–81; Alain Benainous / Getty Images 9, 51b, 176, 178; horst friedrichs / Alamy Stock Photo 10, 187; Edmund Sumner-VIEW / Alamy Stock Photo 11, 192, 194, 195, 196, 197, 198–199; akg-images / Purkiss Archive 12; Ian Bottle/Alamy Live News 14, 16–17; Im_photography / Alamy Stock Photo 15, 54–55, 59, 60–61; Stephen Taylor / Alamy Stock Photo 18, 22; Sandra Foyt / Alamy Stock Photo 20–21; Philip Scalia / Alamy Stock Photo 23; Photo by Zihnioglu Kamil/Pool/ABACAPRESS.COM / Alamy Stock Photo 24, 26; Hemis / Alamy Stock Photo 27, 28, 33, 66, 67, 68–69, 87b, 88–89, 112, 115, 116, 117; Ludovic Marin / Getty Images 29; Photo © Luc Boegly/Artedia / Bridgeman Images 30, 32; John Kellerman / Alamy Stock Photo 34; Luisa Ricciarini / Bridgeman Images 35t; Universal Images Group North America LLC / Alamy Stock Photo 35b; © Leighton House / Photo © Justin Barton / Bridgeman Images 36; Sam Mellish / Getty Images 38, 40, 42–43; © Leighton House / Bridgeman Images 39; © Jean Bernard. All rights reserved 2023 / Bridgeman Images 44, 48, 51t; akg-images / Nimatallah 46–47; Photo © Ken Welsh. All rights reserved 2023 / Bridgeman Images 49; akg-images 50, 64; akg-images / Florian Monheim / Bildarchiv Monheim GmbH 52; Bildarchiv Monheim GmbH / Alamy Stock Photo 56, 82; National Trust Photographic Library/ Nadia Mackenzie / Bridgeman Images 57; The National Trust Photolibrary / Alamy Stock Photo 58; akg-images / ullstein bild 62; Photo Scala, Florence 65; akg-images / Catherine Bibollet 72, 73; Nadia Turinsky / Shutterstock 74; Frank Nowikowski / Alamy Stock Photo 75; Oleg Bakhirev / Shutterstock 78, 79; © Nick Decombel 84–85; dpa picture alliance / Alamy Stock Photo 86, 87t; © P. Maille 92t, 92b, 94–95; Hervé Lenain / Alamy Stock Photo 93; A. Dagli Orti/Scala, Florence 96; Azoor Photo Collection / Alamy Stock Photo 98; © A. Dagli Orti / © NPL – DeA Picture Library / Bridgeman Images 99; Ungvari Attila / Shutterstock 100–101; Elizabeth Whiting & Associates / Alamy Stock Photo 102; Anna Huix 106–107, 109; Patrick Kovarik / Getty Images 114; Arnold Newman Properties / Getty Images 118; Photo Austrian Archives/ Scala Florence 120, 124; Brandstaetter Images / Hulton Archive / Getty Images 121, 125; RMN-Grand Palais / Dist. Photo SCALA, Florence 122–123; akg-images / brandstaetter images / Franz Hubmann 126, 127; © Sandro Becchetti / Bridgeman Images 128; © NPL – DeA Picture Library / G. Cigolini / Bridgeman Images 130, 132, 133; © Archivio Arici. All rights reserved 2023 / Bridgeman Images 131; © Christopher Springmann – All Rights Reserved 134; Albert Knapp / Alamy Stock Photo 136, 140, 141; Jack Young – Places / Alamy Stock Photo 137; Photo Georgia O'Keeffe Museum, Santa Fe/Art Resource/Scala, Florence 138–139, 142–143; Sueddeutsche Zeitung Photo / Alamy Stock Photo 144, 160; imageBROKER / Alamy Stock Photo 146, 202l; mauritius images GmbH / Alamy Stock Photo 147, 148, 149; FORGET Patrick/SAGAPHOTO.COM / Alamy Stock Photo 150, 152–153, 154, 155, 158–159; Sylvain Grandadam / Getty Images 156, 157; Oliver Knight / Alamy Stock Photo 162, 163; Andrea Anoni, René Magritte Museum – Jette, Brussels 164–165; © Lee Miller Archives, England 2023. All rights reserved. leemiller.co.uk 166, 169, 170, 171, 172, 173; Andrew Hasson / Alamy Stock Photo 168; Daniel Frasnay / akg-images 174, 179; Arie Storm / Alamy Stock Photo 177; Gianni Ferrari / Getty Images 180; Carma Casula / Getty Images 181; Farabola / Bridgeman Images 182, 183; Paul Popper/Popperfoto / Getty Images 184; Jim Dyson / Getty Images 186, 191; Bruno Barbier / akg-images 188–189; Stephen Saks Photography / Alamy Stock Photo 190; GRANGER – Historical Picture Archive / Alamy Stock Photo 200; John Mitchell / Alamy Stock Photo 202r; akg-images / Sambraus 203; Andrew Hasson / Getty Images 204; Paul Christian Gordon / Alamy Stock Photo 205; Alexandra Lande / Shutterstock 206–207; © Detroit Institute of Arts / Bridgeman Images 208; agefotostock / Alamy Stock Photo 209; © David Dawson. All rights reserved 2023 / Bridgeman Images 210, 212, 213, 214l, 214r, 215, 216–217; Olga Gajewska / Alamy Stock Photo 218; Fundación César Manrique 220t, 224, 225; Marjolein Hameleers / Shutterstock 220b; Jef Wodniack / Shutterstock 221; Amazing Travels / Shutterstock 222; goodcat / Shutterstock 223; Marc Lechanteur / Shutterstock 226–227; Joshua Monaghan, House & Garden © Condé Nast 228, 231, 232, 233; Wig Worland / Alamy Stock Photo 230.

Quarto

First published in 2023 by Frances Lincoln,
an imprint of The Quarto Group.
One Triptych Place,
London, SE1 9SH,
United Kingdom
T (0)20 7700 9000
www.Quarto.com

EEA Representation, WTS Tax d.o.o.,
Žanova ulica 3, 4000 Kranj, Slovenia.
www.wts-tax.si

Design by Mariana Sameiro

Publisher: Philip Cooper
Commissioning Editors: Alice Graham and John Parton
Editor: Bella Skertchly
Art Director: Paileen Currie
Junior Designer: Daisy Woods
Production Controller: Rohana Yusof

A catalogue record for this book is available from the British Library.

ISBN 978-0-7112-6943-9
Ebook ISBN 978-0-7112-6945-3

10 9 8 7 6 5 4 3 2

Printed in Huizhou, Guangdong, China, TT042026

FSC www.fsc.org MIX Paper | Supporting responsible forestry FSC® C016973